EASY PIANO

POP/ROCK

ISBN 0-634-08067-9

7777 W. BLUEMOUND RD. P.O. BOX 13819 MILWAUKEE, WI 53213

Visit Hal Leonard Online at
www.halleonard.com

CONTENTS

158 Na Na Hey Hey Kiss Him Goodbye
Steam

166 One Sweet Day
Mariah Carey & Boyz II Men

161 Please Come to Boston
Dave Loggins

170 Rainy Days and Mondays
The Carpenters

174 Respect
Aretha Franklin

180 Respect Yourself
The Staple Singers

184 Rikki Don't Lose That Number
Steely Dan

177 Sheila
Tommy Roe

188 Shop Around
The Miracles

193 The Sign
Ace of Base

198 (Sittin' On) The Dock of the Bay
Otis Redding

206 Stand by Me
Ben E. King

201 Stop! In the Name of Love
The Supremes

210 The Sweetest Days
Vanessa Williams

214 Tequila
The Champs

218 Thank You
Dido

225 Top of the World
The Carpenters

230 Traces
Classics IV

233 The Tracks of My Tears
The Miracles

236 Two Hearts
Phil Collins

243 Vision of Love
Mariah Carey

250 Walk Right In
The Rooftop Singers

252 Water Runs Dry
Boyz II Men

257 What's Going On
Marvin Gaye

262 A Whiter Shade of Pale
Procol Harum

266 Why Do Fools Fall in Love
Frankie Lymon & The Teenagers

270 Winchester Cathedral
The New Vaudeville Band

274 Yesterday Once More
The Carpenters

282 You Keep Me Hangin' On
The Supremes

279 You Light Up My Life
Debby Boone

288 You Sang to Me
Marc Anthony

300 You're Still the One
Shania Twain

294 You're the Inspiration
Chicago

- I Can't Help Falling in Love -Elvis

ABC

Words and Music by
ALPHONSO MIZELL, FREDERICK PERREN,
DEKE RICHARDS and BERRY GORDY

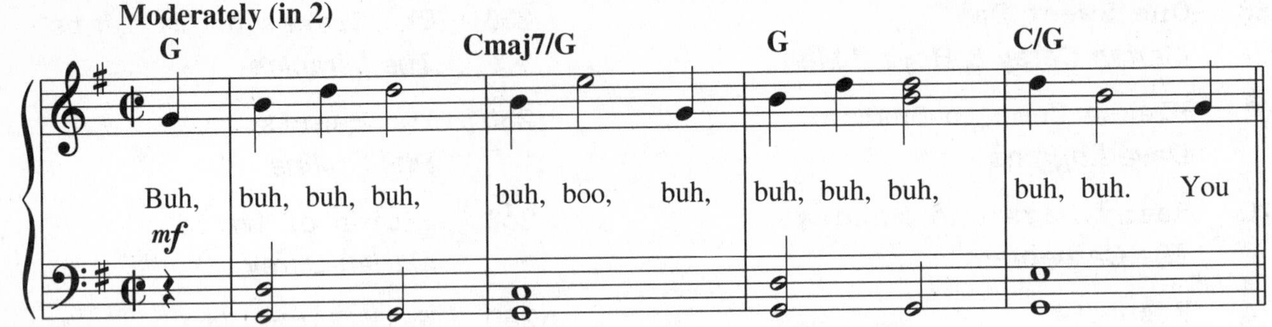

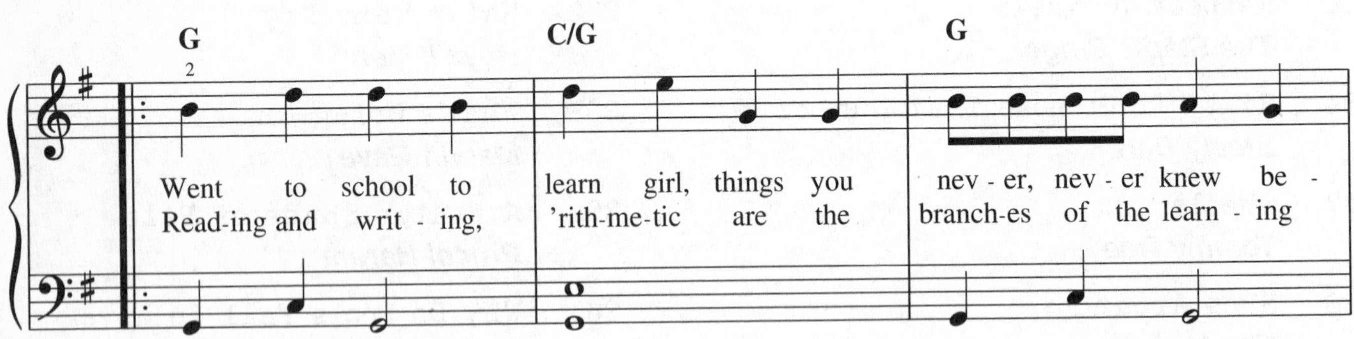

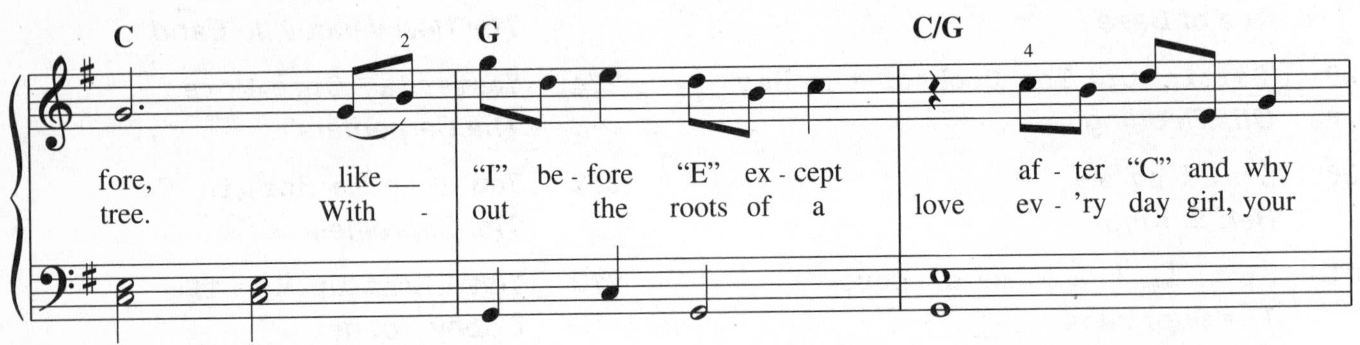

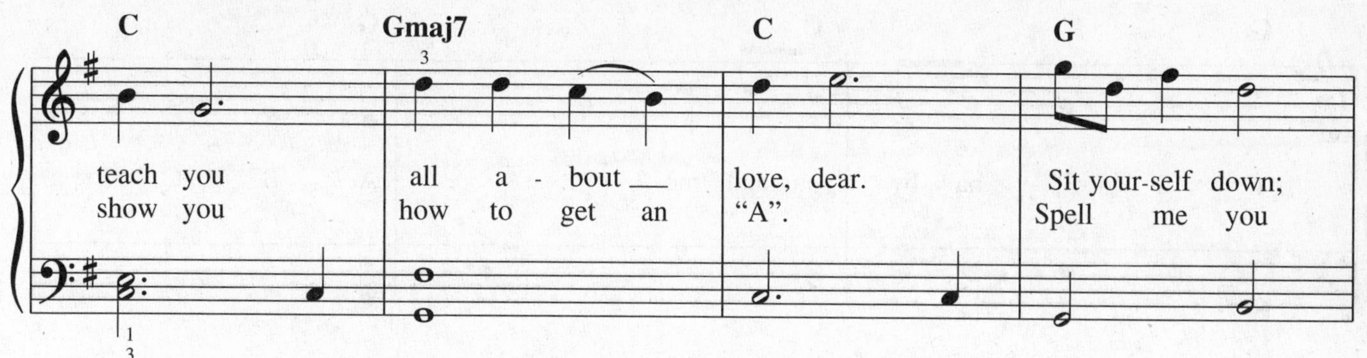
C
Gmaj7
C
G
teach you all a - bout love, dear. Sit your-self down;
show you how to get an "A". Spell me you

C
G
C
take a seat; all you got - ta do is re - peat af - ter me:
add the two, lis - ten to me ba - by, that's all you got - ta do.

G
Cmaj7
G
A B C eas - y as 1 2 3

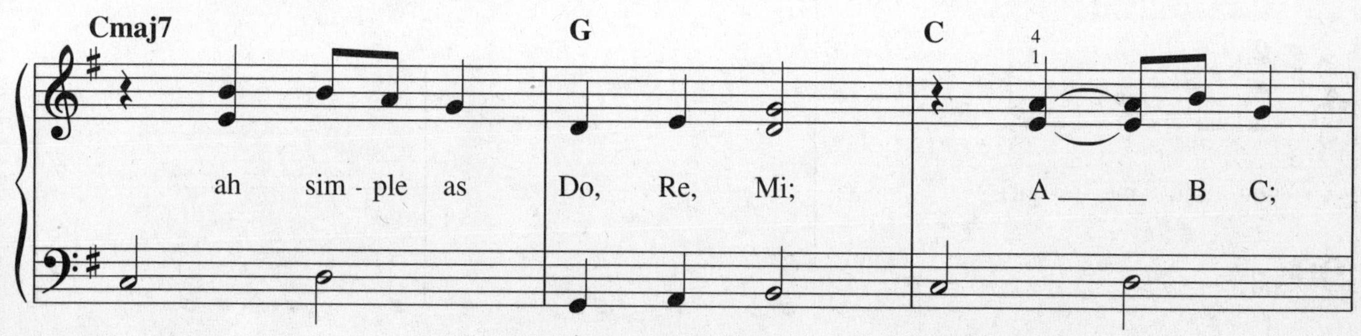
Cmaj7
G
C
ah sim - ple as Do, Re, Mi; A B C;

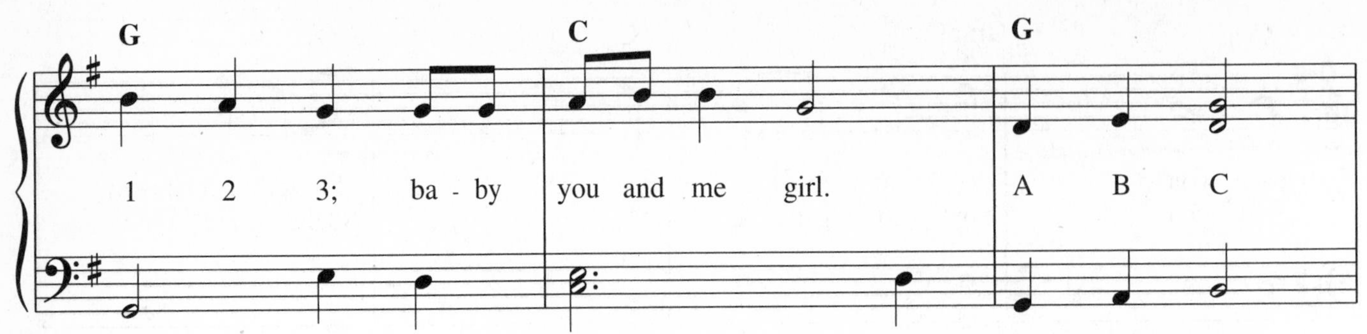
G
C
G
1 2 3; ba - by
you and me girl.
A B C

Cmaj7
G
Cmaj7
Eas - y as
1 2 3
ah sim - ple as

G
C
G
Do Re Mi;
A B C;
1 2 3; (ba - by)

C
1.
you and me girl.

C/G
G
C/G
5
Come on, let me love you just a lit - tle bit;

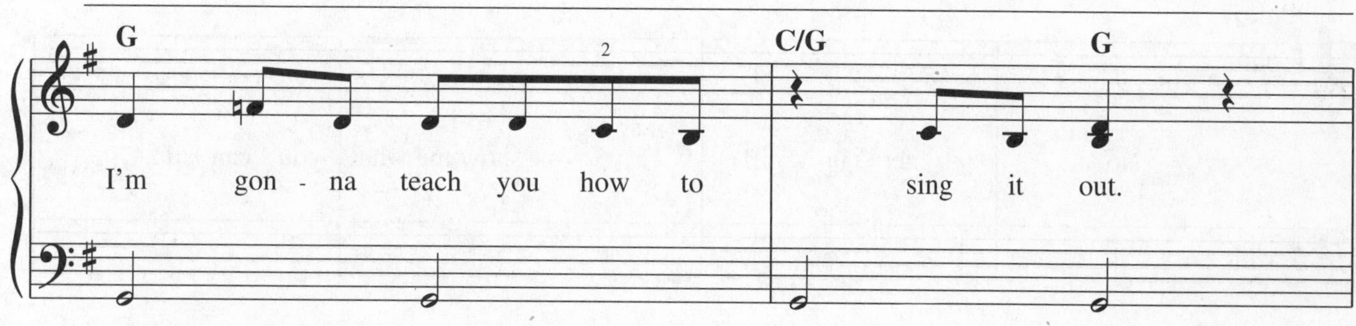
G
2
C/G
G
I'm gon - na teach you how to sing it out.

1
C/G
Com - a, com - a, come on let me show you what it's all a - bout.

2.
N.C.
Yah

3
sit down girl
I think I love you.

No
get up girl
show me what you can do.

G
C/G
3
G
1
Shake it, shake it ba - by (come on now) shake it, shake it

D.S. and Fade
C/G
G
C/G
ba - by, oo, shake it, shake it ba - by (hey.)

ADIA

Words and Music by SARAH McLACHLAN
and PIERRE MARCHAND

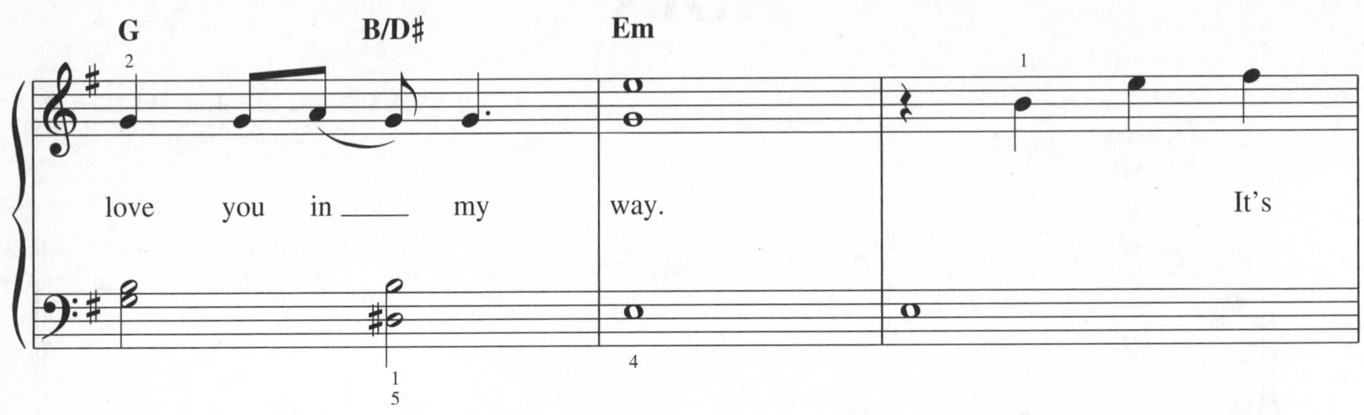
G
B/D♯
Em
love you in my way.
It's

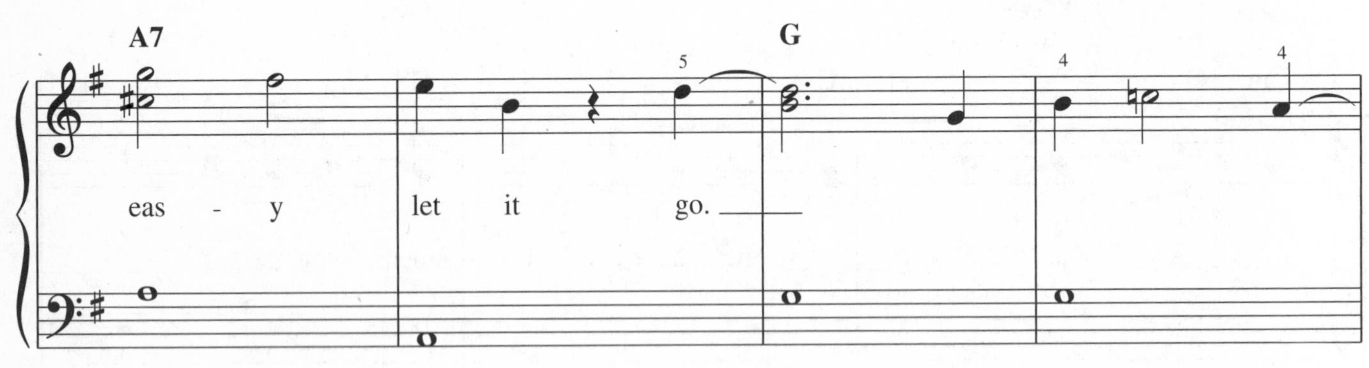
A7
G
eas - y let it go.

D
Em
A - di - a, I'm
A - di - a, I

C
G
emp - ty since you left me.
thought that we could make it.

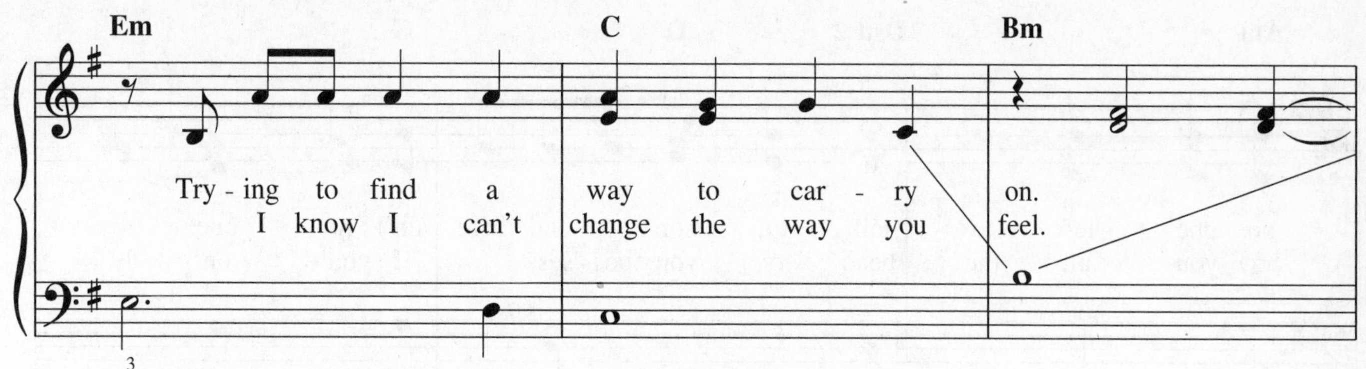
Em
C
Bm
Try - ing to find a way to car - ry on.
I know I can't change the way you feel.
3

D
G
Cmaj7
I search my - self and ev - 'ry - one to
I leave you with your mis - er - y, a

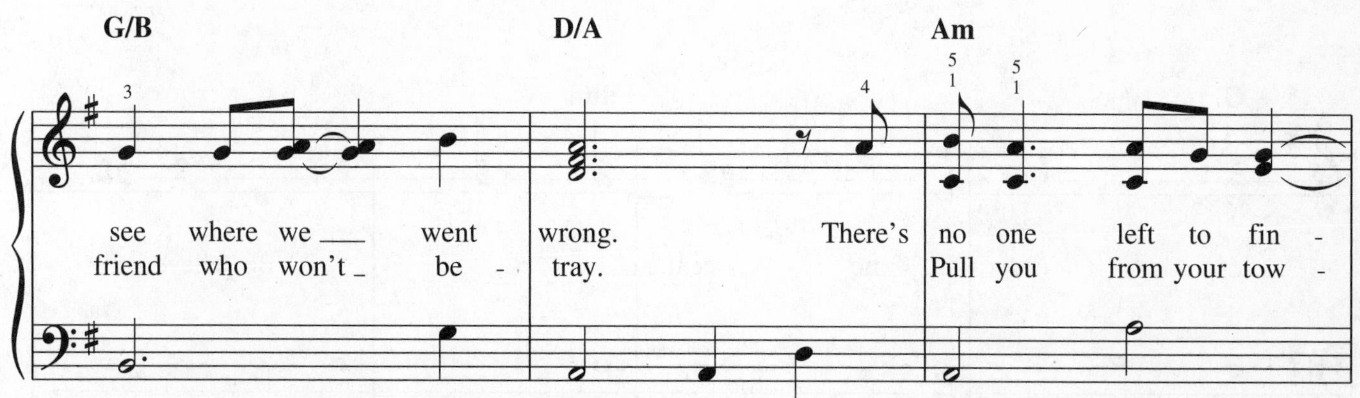
G/B
D/A
Am
see where we ___ went wrong. There's no one left to fin -
friend who won't ___ be - tray. Pull you from your tow -

D
G
C
- ger. There's no one here to blame. ______ There's
- er. I take a - way your pain. ______ I

Am
Dsus2
D
G
no one left to talk to, hon - ey, and there ain't no one to
show you all the beau - ty you pos - sess if you'd on - ly

Dm/F
C
D
buy our in - no - cence 'cause we are born
let your - self be - lieve that

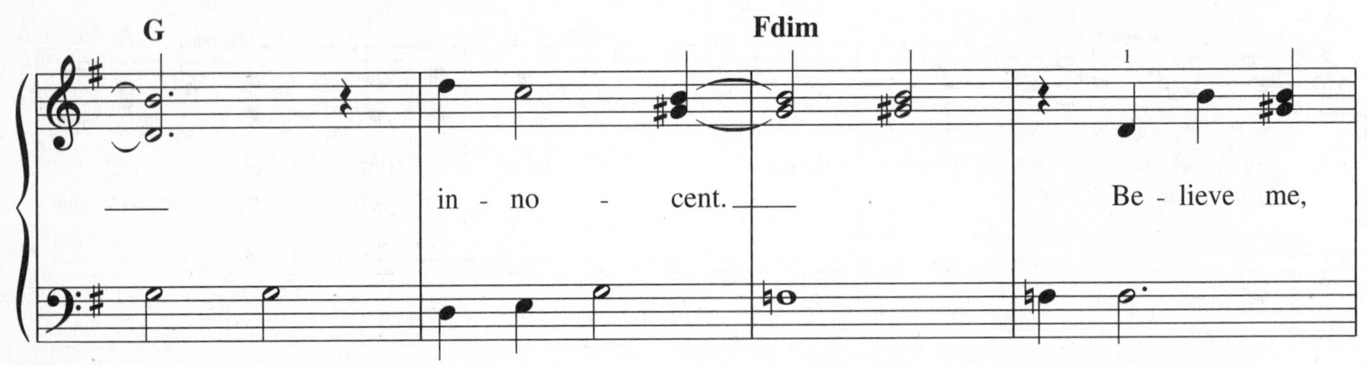
G
Fdim
in - no - cent. Be - lieve me,

C
Am
A - di - a, we are still

D
Bm
Fdim
in - no - cent.
It's eas - y,

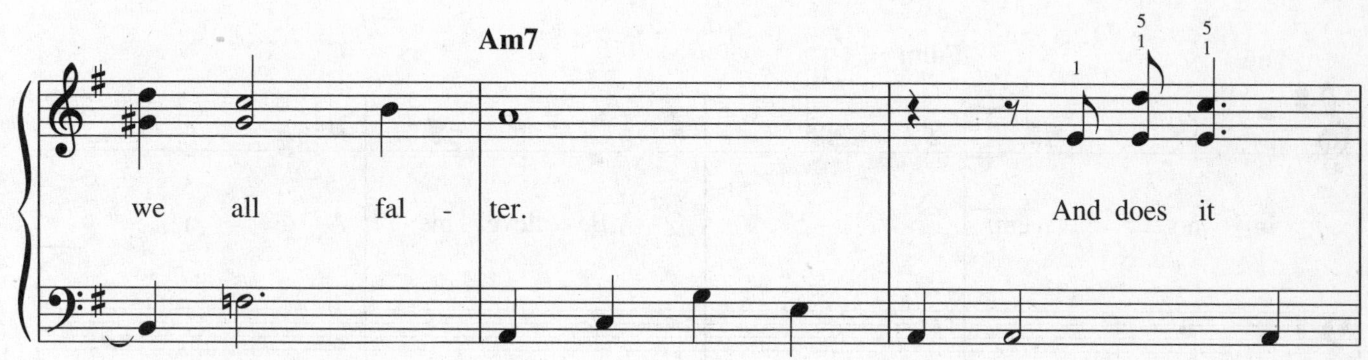
Am7
we all fal - ter.
And does it

1.
B7
mat - ter?
2.
B7
mat - ter?

N.C.
A7/C♯
G

D7
G
'Cause we are born

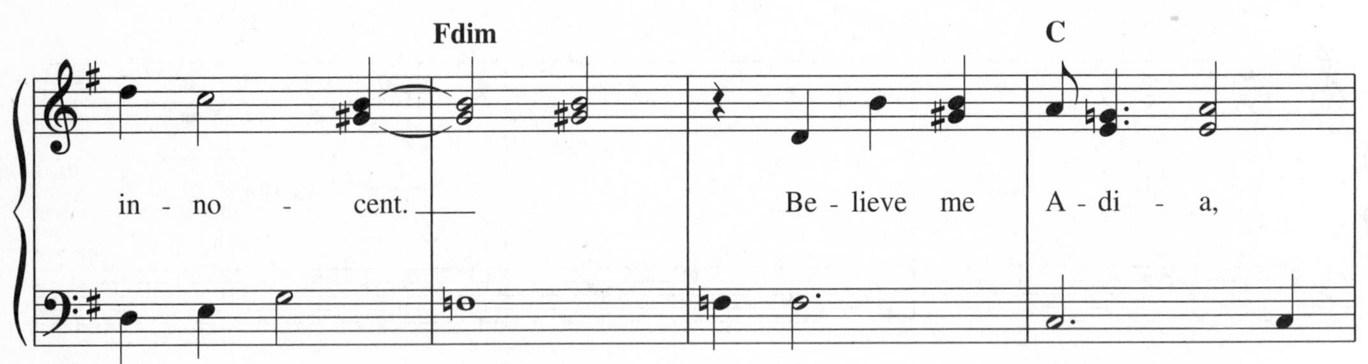
Fdim
C
in - no - cent.
Be - lieve me A - di - a,

Am
D
Bm
we are still in - no - cent.

Fdim
Am7
It's eas - y, we all fal - ter.

To Coda
D
G
Does it
mat - ter?
Be - lieve _ me,
A - di - - a,

Bm
Cmaj7
we
are
still
in - no - cent.

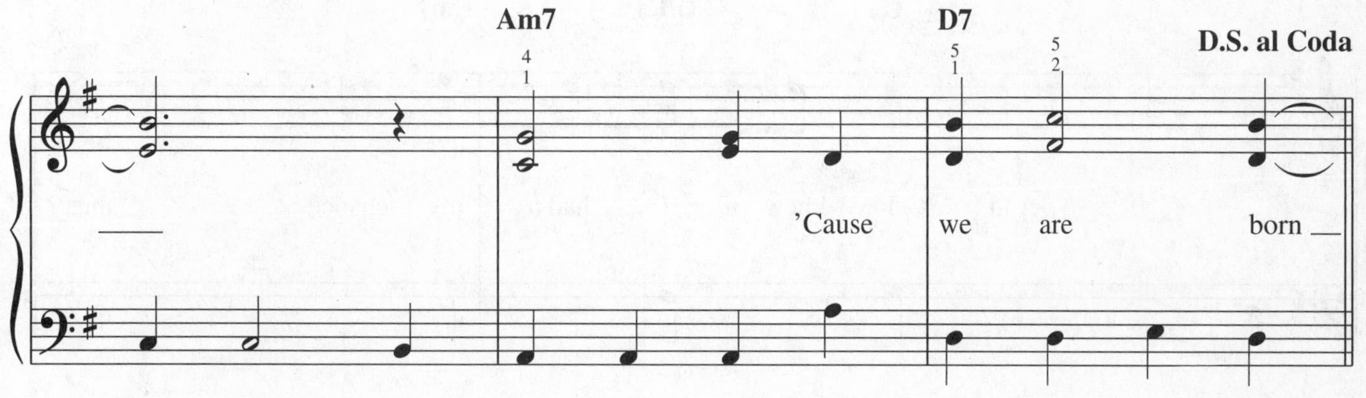
Am7
D7
D.S. al Coda
'Cause
we
are
born

CODA
D
B7
mat - ter?

AMERICAN PIE

Words and Music by
DON McLEAN

C
D
hap - py for a while.
5
1
2

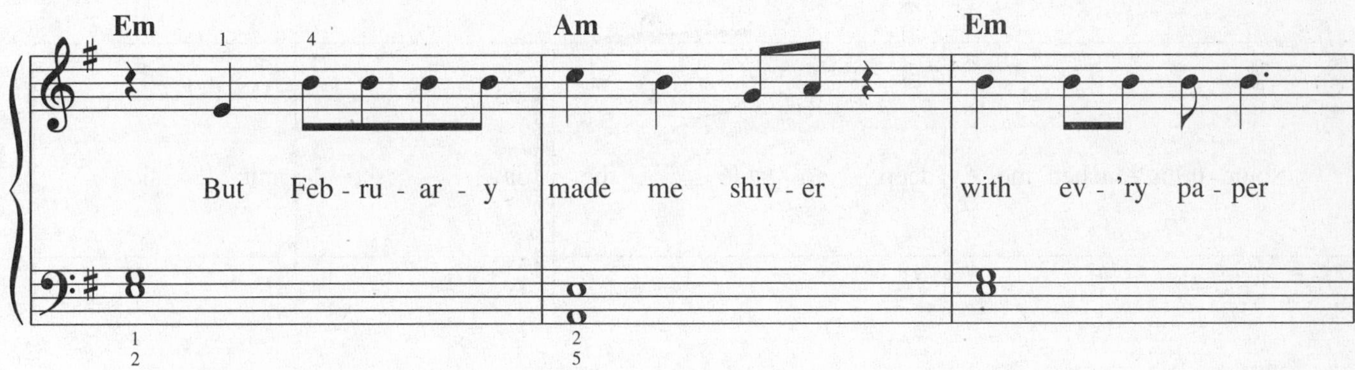
Em
Am
Em
1
4
But Feb - ru - ar - y made me shiv - er with ev - 'ry pa - per
1
2
2
5

Am
C
G/B
Am
I'd de - liv - er. Bad news on the door - step, I
3

C
D
G
D/F#
2
could - n't take one more step. I can't re - mem - ber if I
2

Em
Am7
D
cried when I read a - bout his wid-owed bride.

G
D/F#
Em
C
D7
Some-thing touched me deep in - side the day the mu - sic

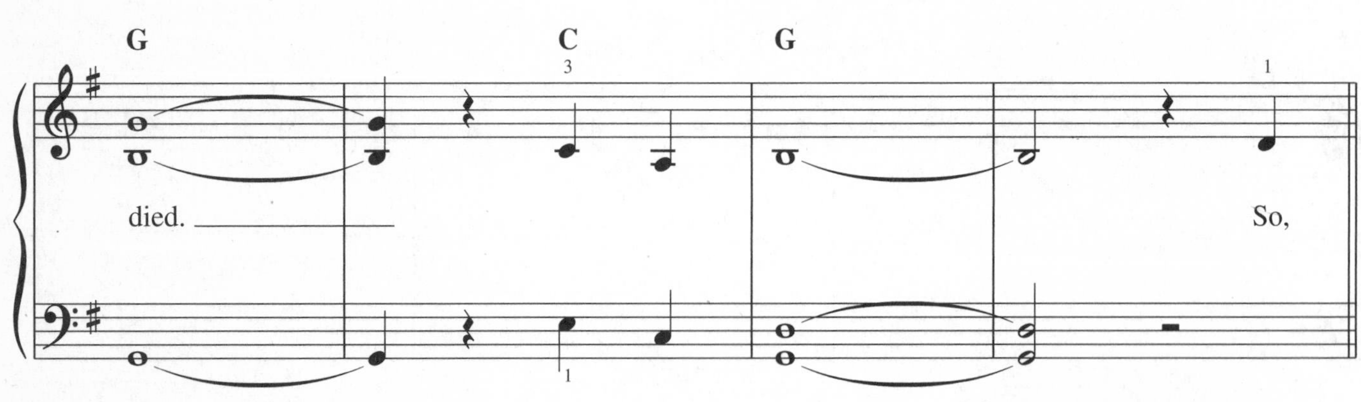
G
C
G
died.
So,

Moderately, with a beat
G
C
G
D
G
C
bye - bye, Miss A - mer - i - can Pie. Drove my Chev-y to the lev - ee but the
mf

G
D
G
C
G
D
To Coda II
lev - ee was dry. __ Them good ole boys were drink - in' whis - key and rye, __ sing - in',

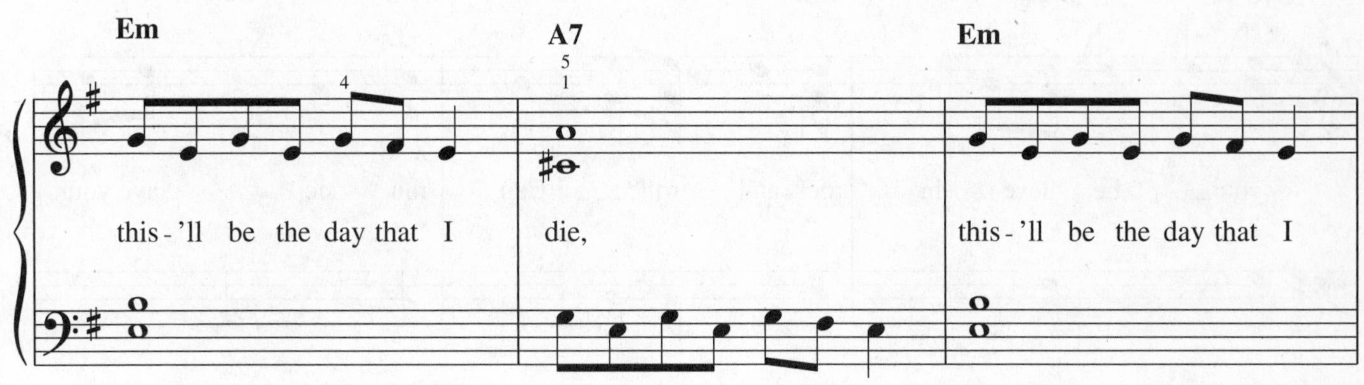
Em
A7
Em
this - 'll be the day that I die,
this - 'll be the day that I

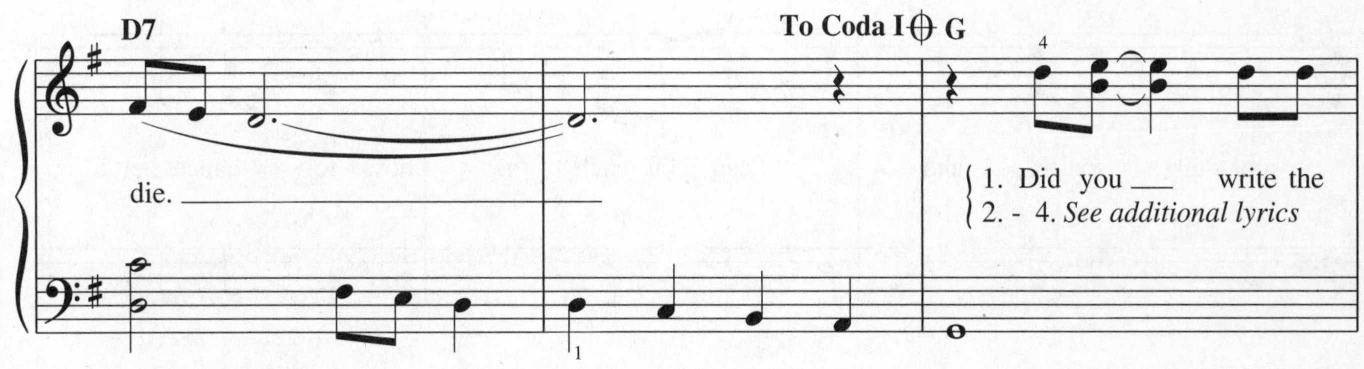
D7
To Coda I
G
die. ___
1. Did you ___ write the
2. - 4. See additional lyrics

Am
C
Am
book of love, __ and do you have faith in God a - bove __

Em
D
if the Bi - ble tells you so?
Now do

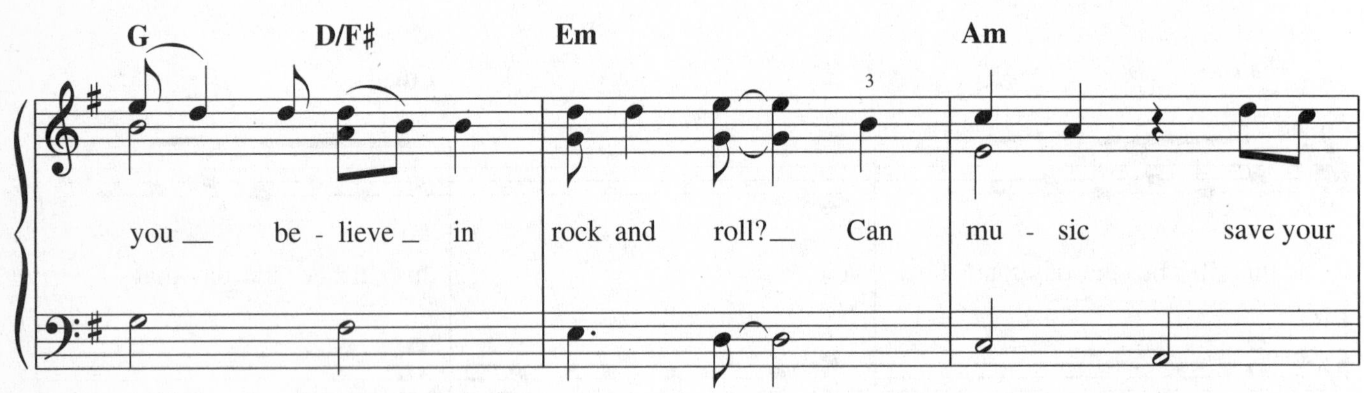
G
D/F#
Em
Am
you be - lieve in rock and roll? Can mu - sic save your

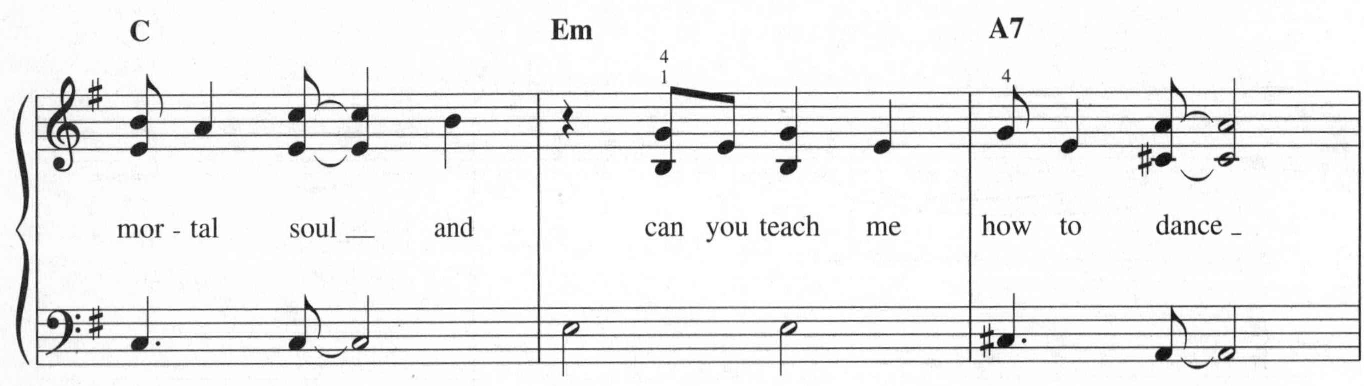
C
Em
A7
mor - tal soul and can you teach me how to dance

D
Em
real slow? Well, I know that you're in

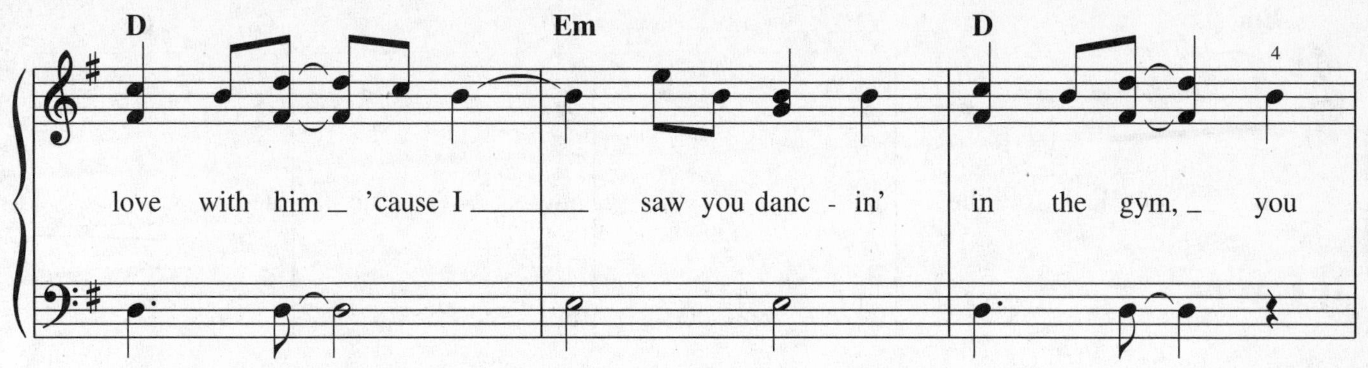
D
Em
D
love with him 'cause I saw you danc - in' in the gym, you

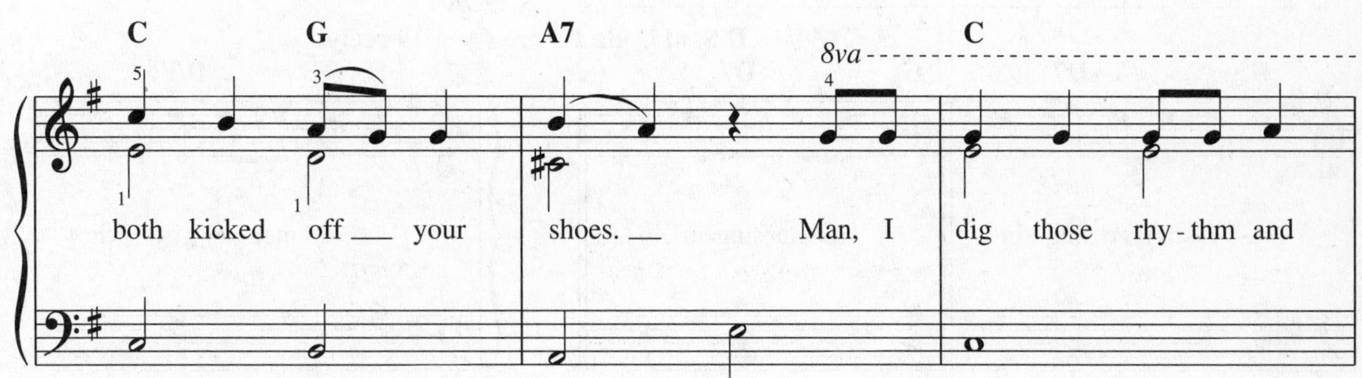
C
G
A7
C
8va
both kicked off your shoes. Man, I dig those rhy - thm and

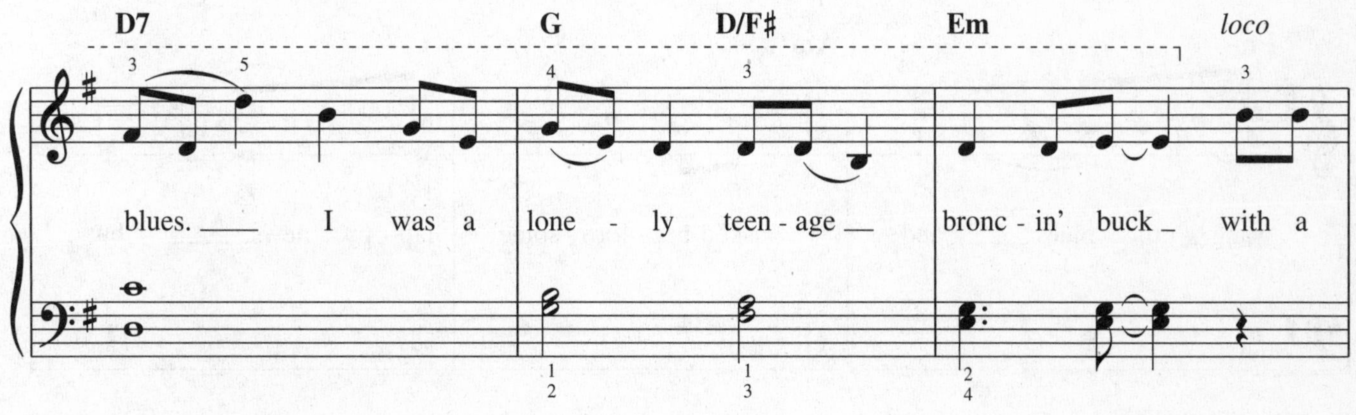
D7
G
D/F#
Em
loco
blues. I was a lone - ly teen - age bronc - in' buck with a

Am
C
G
D/F#
pink car - na - tion and a pick - up truck. But I knew I was

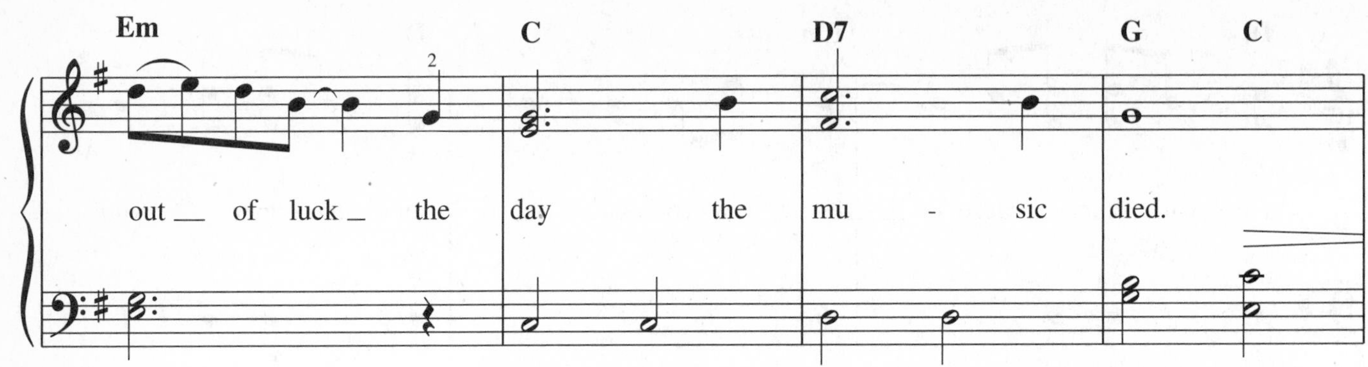
Em
C
D7
G
C
out of luck the day the mu - sic died.

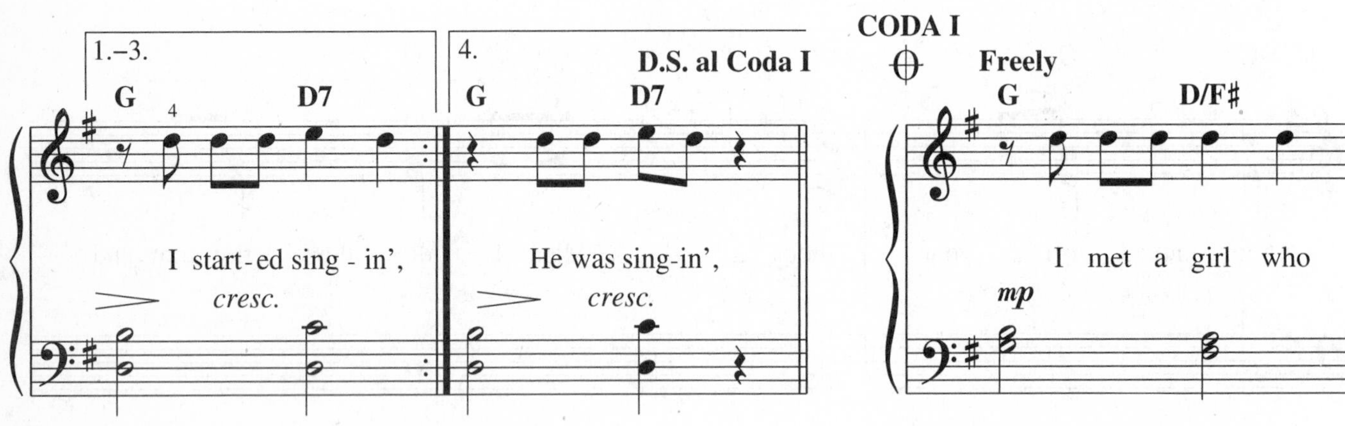
1.–3.
4.
D.S. al Coda I
CODA I
Freely
G
D7
G
D7
G
D/F♯
I start-ed sing - in',
cresc.
He was sing-in',
cresc.
I met a girl who
mp

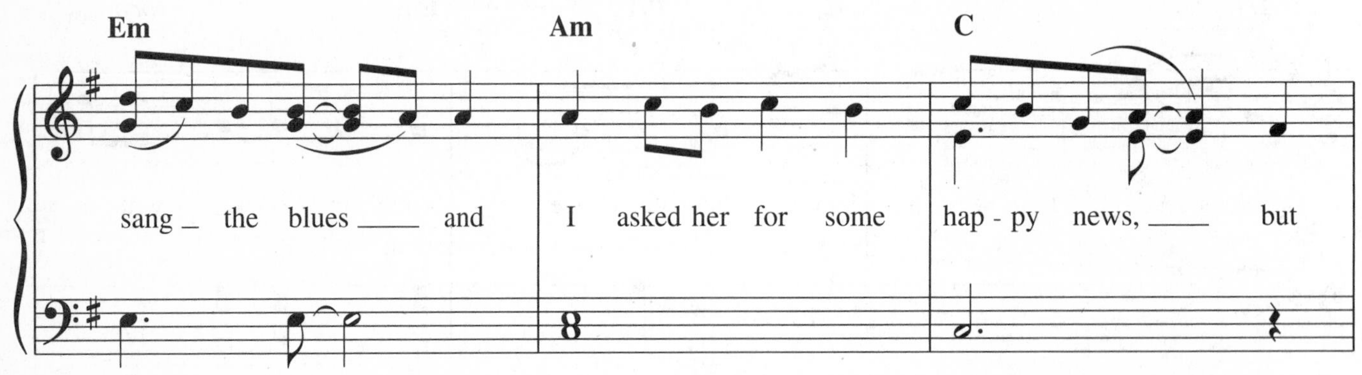
Em
Am
C
sang the blues and I asked her for some hap - py news, but

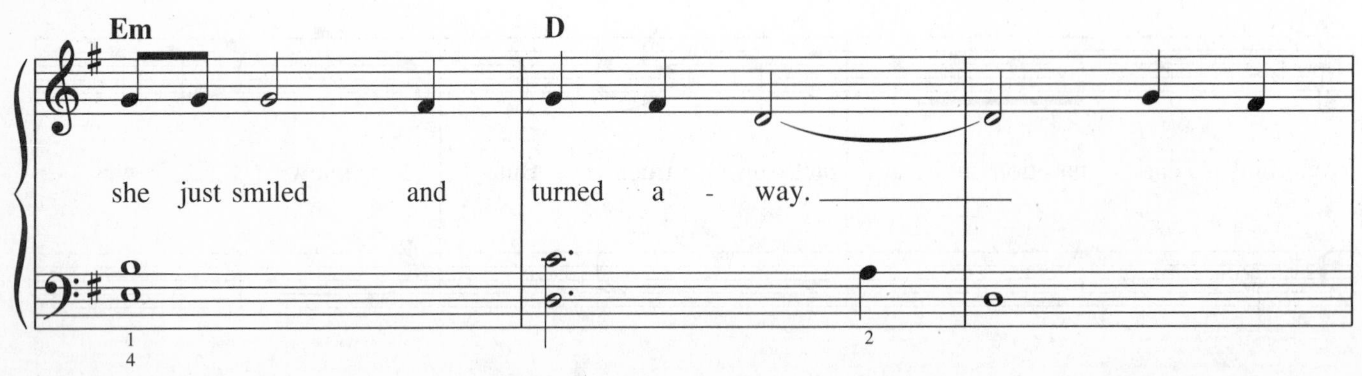
Em
D
she just smiled and turned a - way.

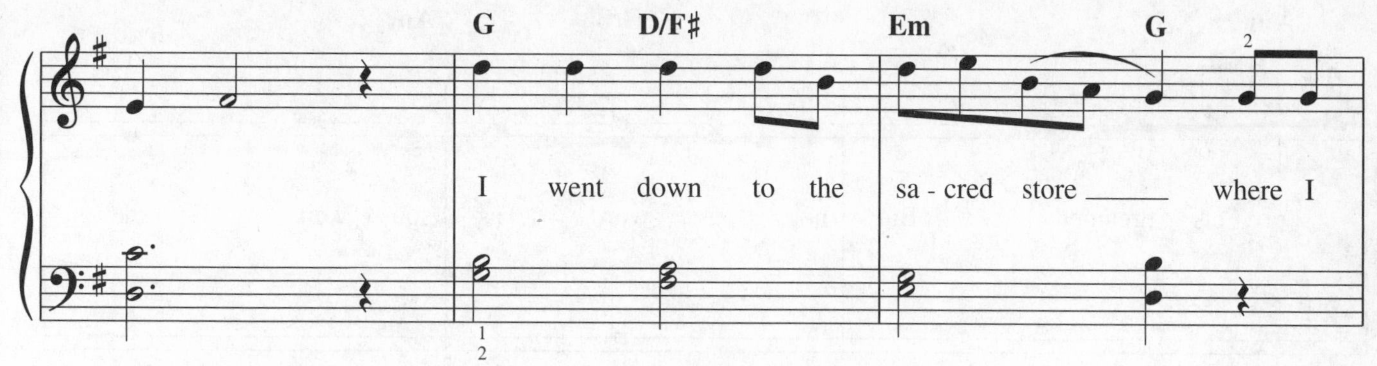
G
D/F#
Em
G
I went down to the sa - cred store where I

Am
G/B
C
Em
heard the mu - sic years be - fore, but the man there said the

C
D
mu - sic would-n't play.
And

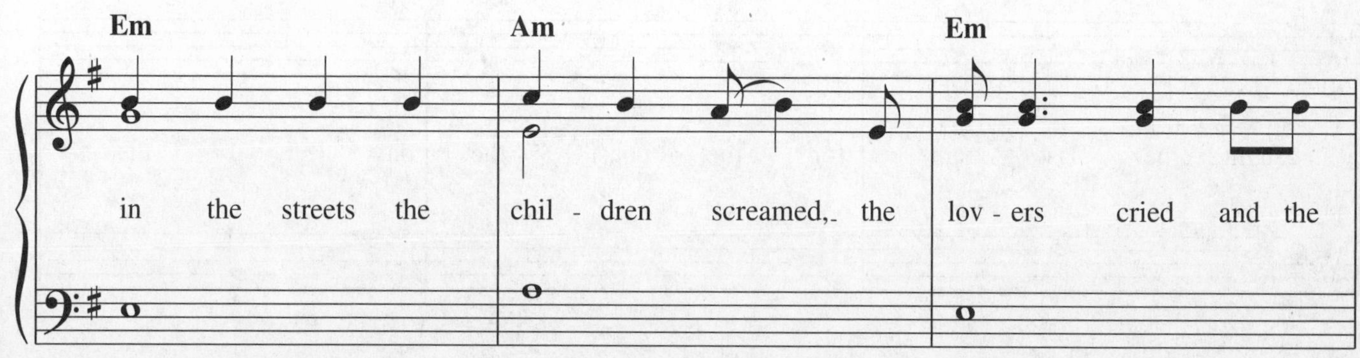
Em
Am
Em
in the streets the chil - dren screamed, the lov - ers cried and the

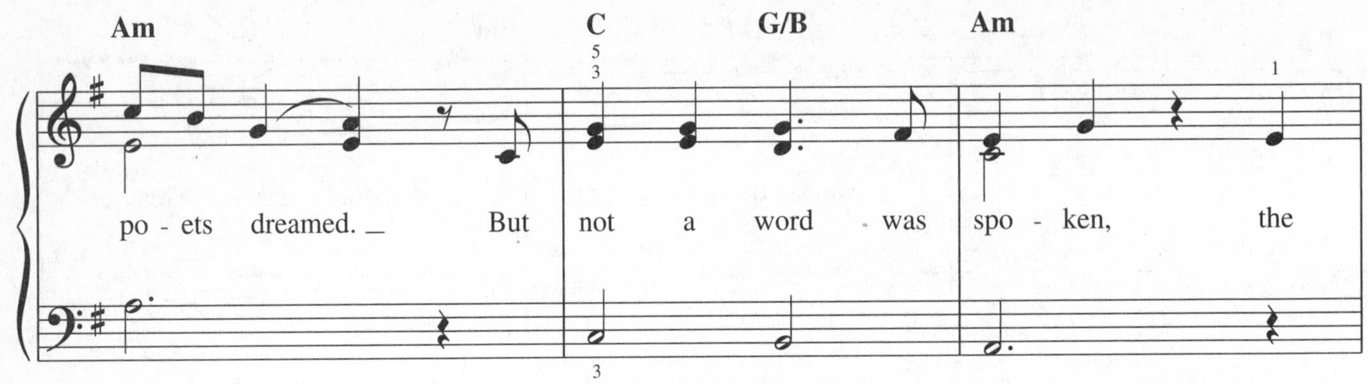
Am
C
G/B
Am
po - ets dreamed. _ But
not a word - was
spo - ken, the

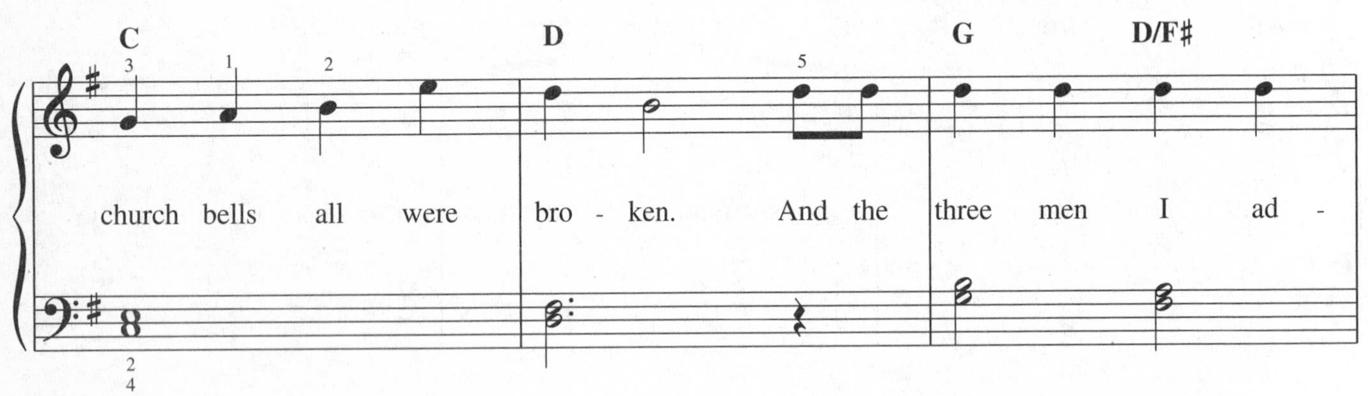
C
D
G
D/F♯
church bells all were
bro - ken. And the
three men I ad -

Em
G/D
C
D7
mire most, the
Fa - ther, Son and the
Ho - ly Ghost, they

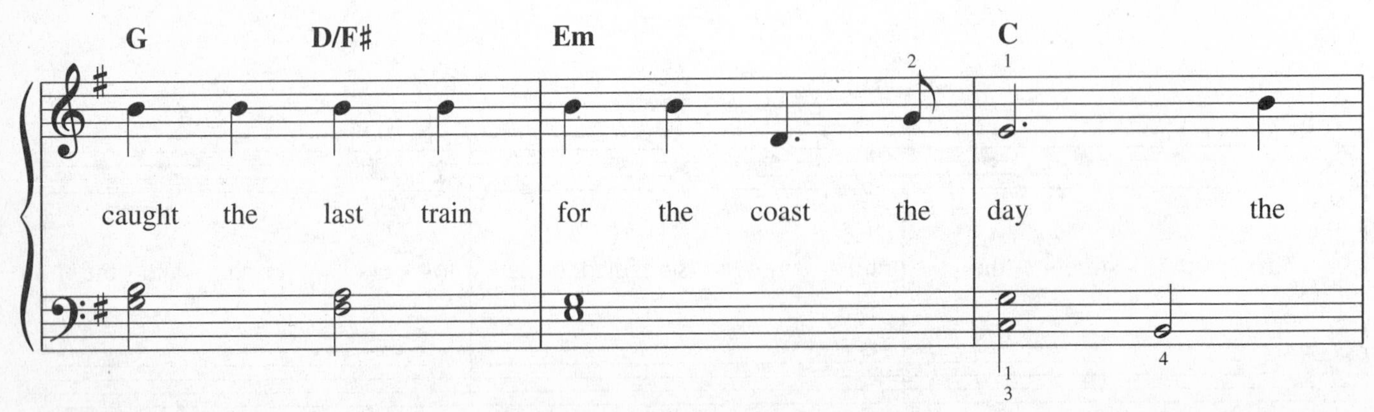
G
D/F♯
Em
C
caught the last train
for the coast the
day the

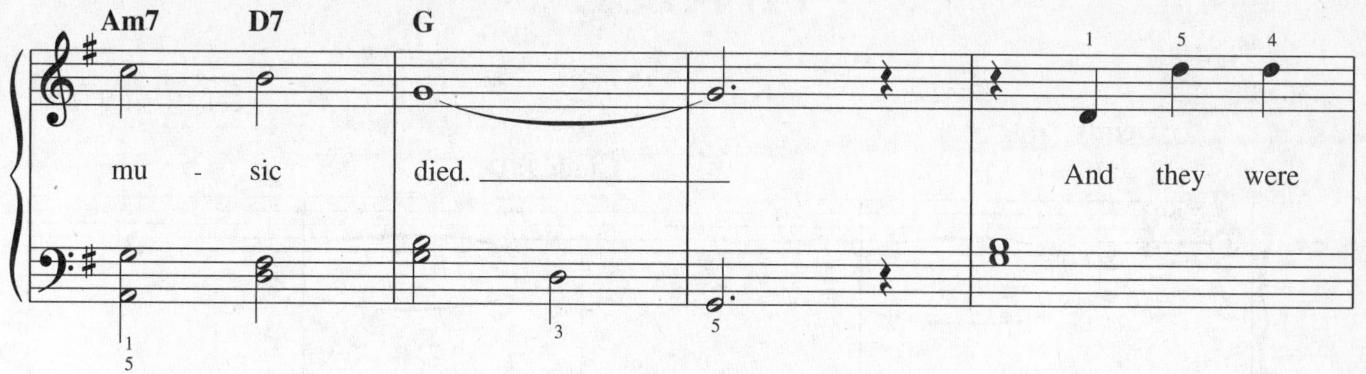

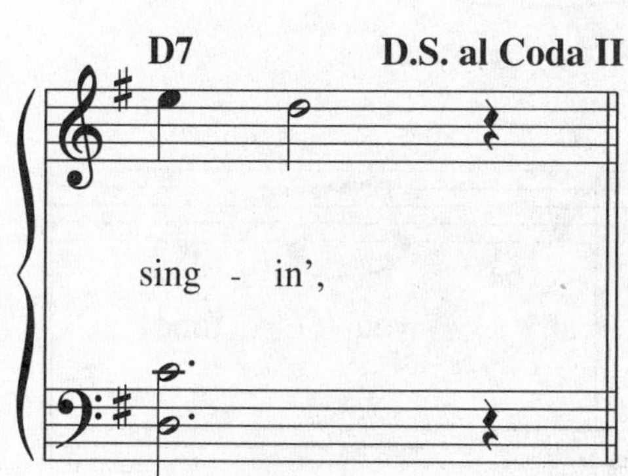

Additional Lyrics

2. Now for ten years we've been on our own,
   And moss grows fat on a rollin' stone
   But that's not how it used to be
   When the jester sang for the king and queen
   In a coat he borrowed from James Dean
   And a voice that came from you and me
   Oh and while the king was looking down,
   The jester stole his thorny crown
   The courtroom was adjourned,
   No verdict was returned
   And while Lenin read a book on Marx
   The quartet practiced in the park
   And we sang dirges in the dark
   The day the music died
   We were singin'... bye-bye... etc.

3. Helter-skelter in the summer swelter
   The birds flew off with a fallout shelter
   Eight miles high and fallin' fast,
   It landed foul on the grass
   The players tried for a forward pass,
   With the jester on the sidelines in a cast
   Now the half-time air was sweet perfume
   While the sergeants played a marching tune
   We all got up to dance
   But we never got the chance
   'Cause the players tried to take the field,
   The marching band refused to yield
   Do you recall what was revealed
   The day the music died
   We started singin'... bye-bye... etc.

4. And there we were all in one place,
   A generation lost in space
   With no time left to start again
   So come on, Jack be nimble, Jack be quick
   Jack Flash sat on a candlestick
   'Cause fire is the devil's only friend
   And as I watched him on the stage
   My hands were clenched in fists of rage
   No angel born in hell
   Could break that Satan's spell
   And as the flames climbed high into the night
   To light the sacrificial rite
   I saw Satan laughing with delight
   The day the music died
   He was singin'... bye-bye... etc.

ANGEL

Words and Music by
SARAH McLACHLAN

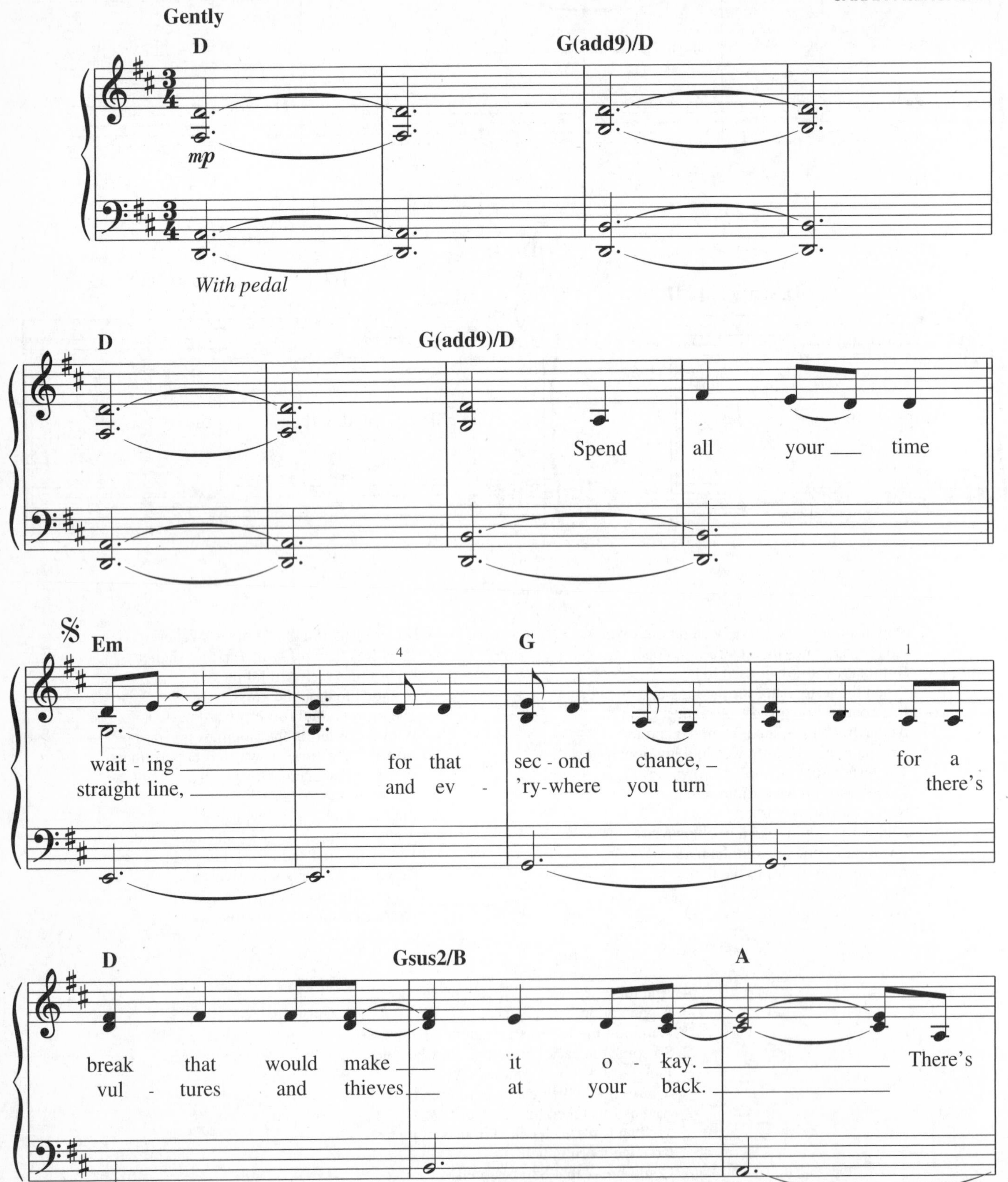

Em7
al - ways some rea - son to feel
Storm keeps on twist - ing. Keep on
G
D
2
not good e - nough, and it's hard at the end
build - ing the lies that you make up for all
Gsus2/B
A
of the day. I need some dis -
that you lack. It don't make no
Em7
G
trac - tion, oh, beau - ti - ful re - lease.
dif - f'rence es - cap - ing one last time.

D Gsus2/B

Memory seep from my
It's easier to be-

A Em

veins. Let me be empty,
lieve in this sweet madness,

G

oh, and weightless, and maybe I'll
oh, this glorious sadness that

D
D6
3
in the arms of the an -

D
2
F♯m
- gel. Fly a - way

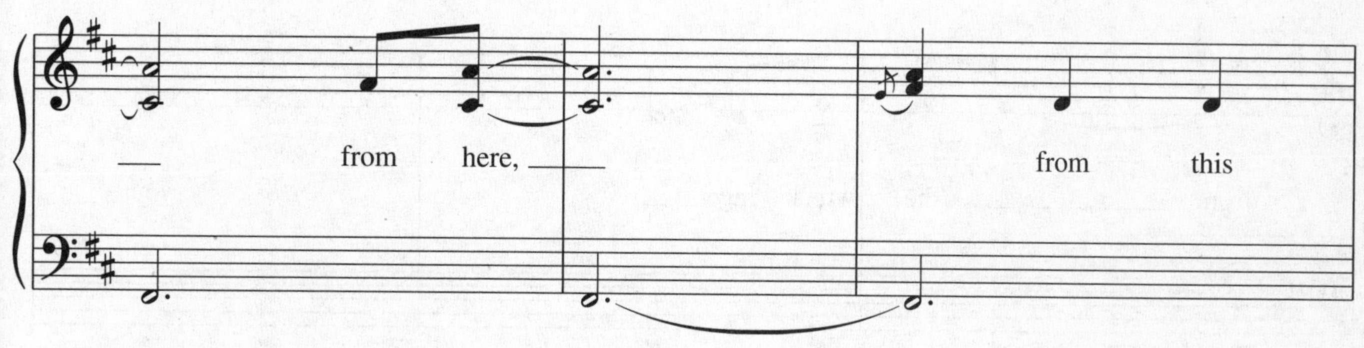
from here, from this

G
dark, cold ho - tel room

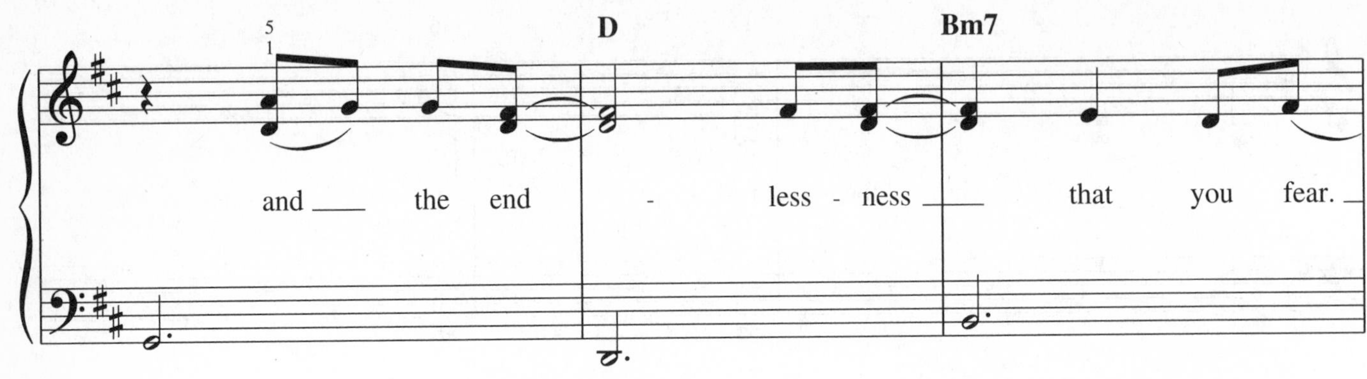
D
Bm7
and the end - less - ness that you fear.

A7
A7sus
D
You are pulled

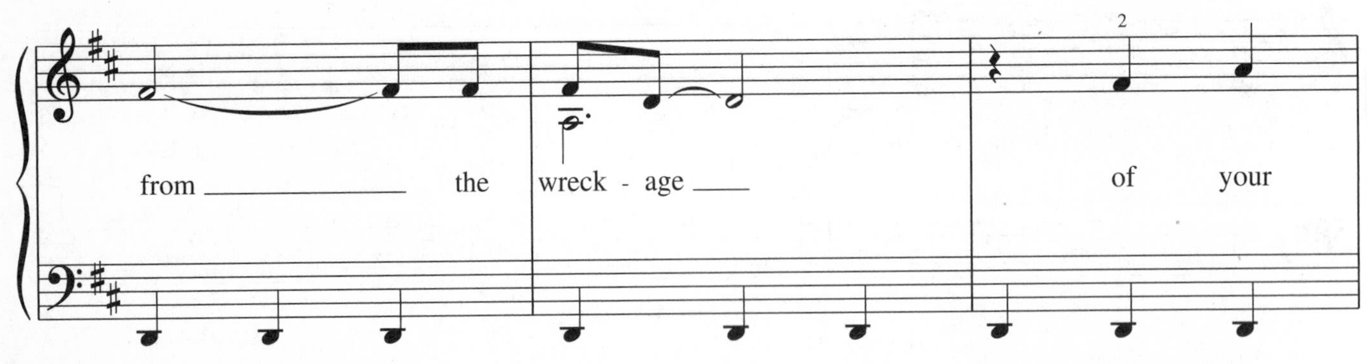
from the wreck - age of your

F♯m
si - lent rev - er - ie.

G
Gsus
You're in the arms of the

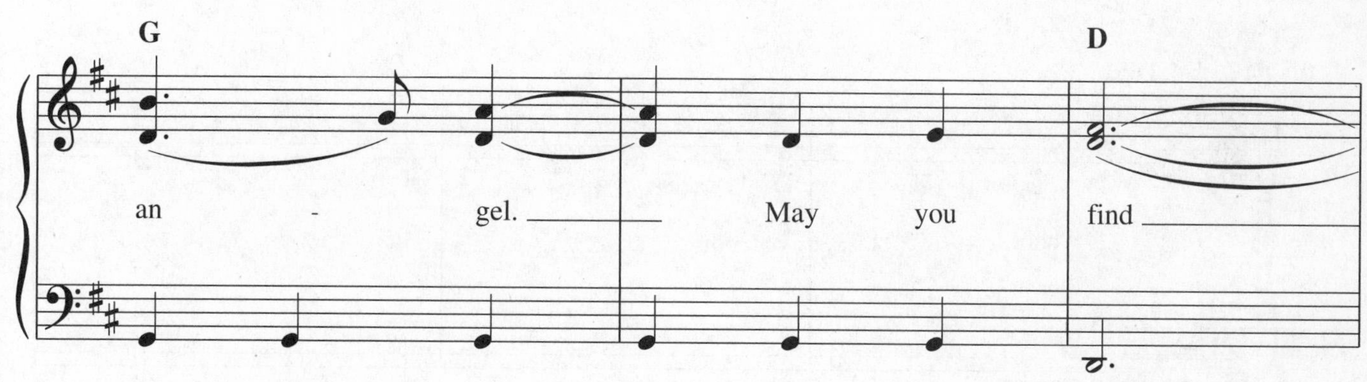
G
D
an - gel. May you find

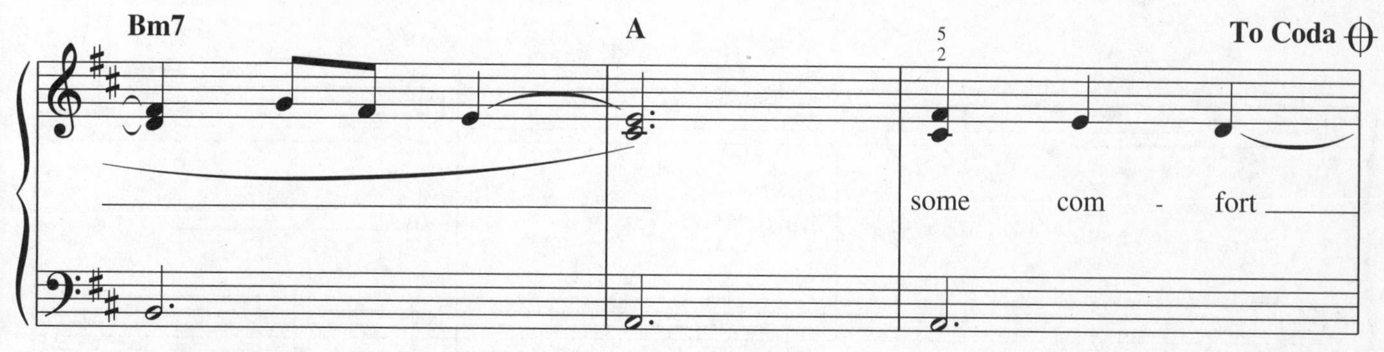
Bm7
A
To Coda
some com - fort

D
G/B
here.

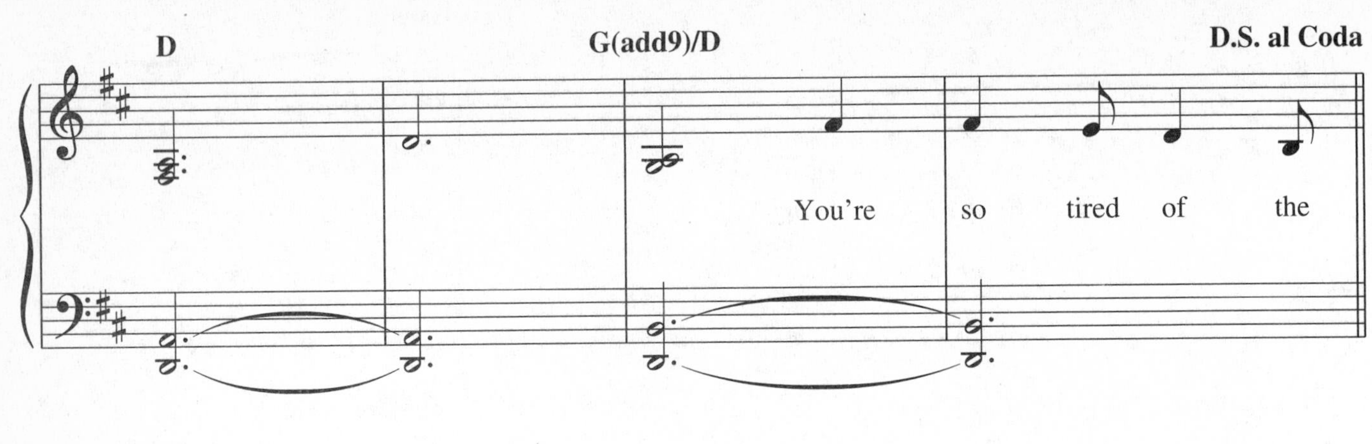
D
G(add9)/D
D.S. al Coda
You're so tired of the

CODA
D
here.

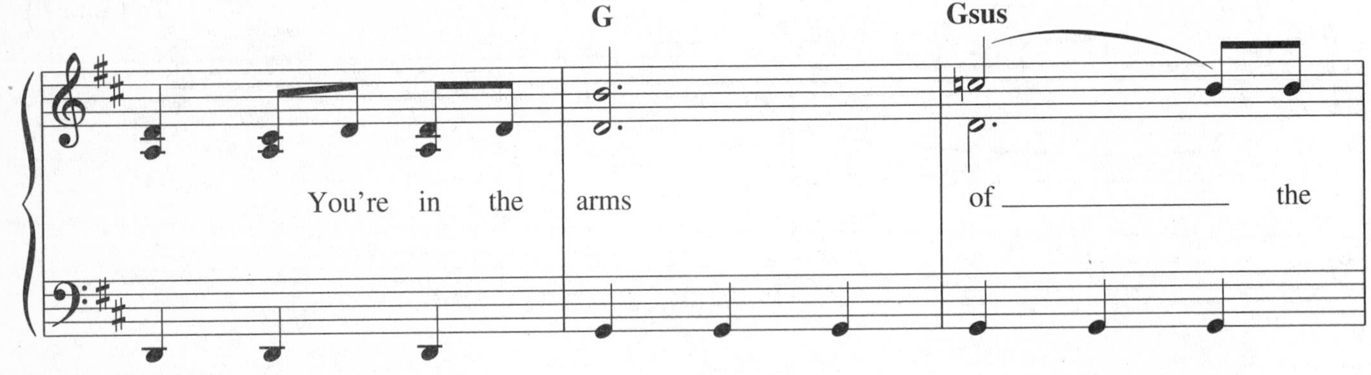
G
Gsus
You're in the arms of the

G
D
an - gel. May you find

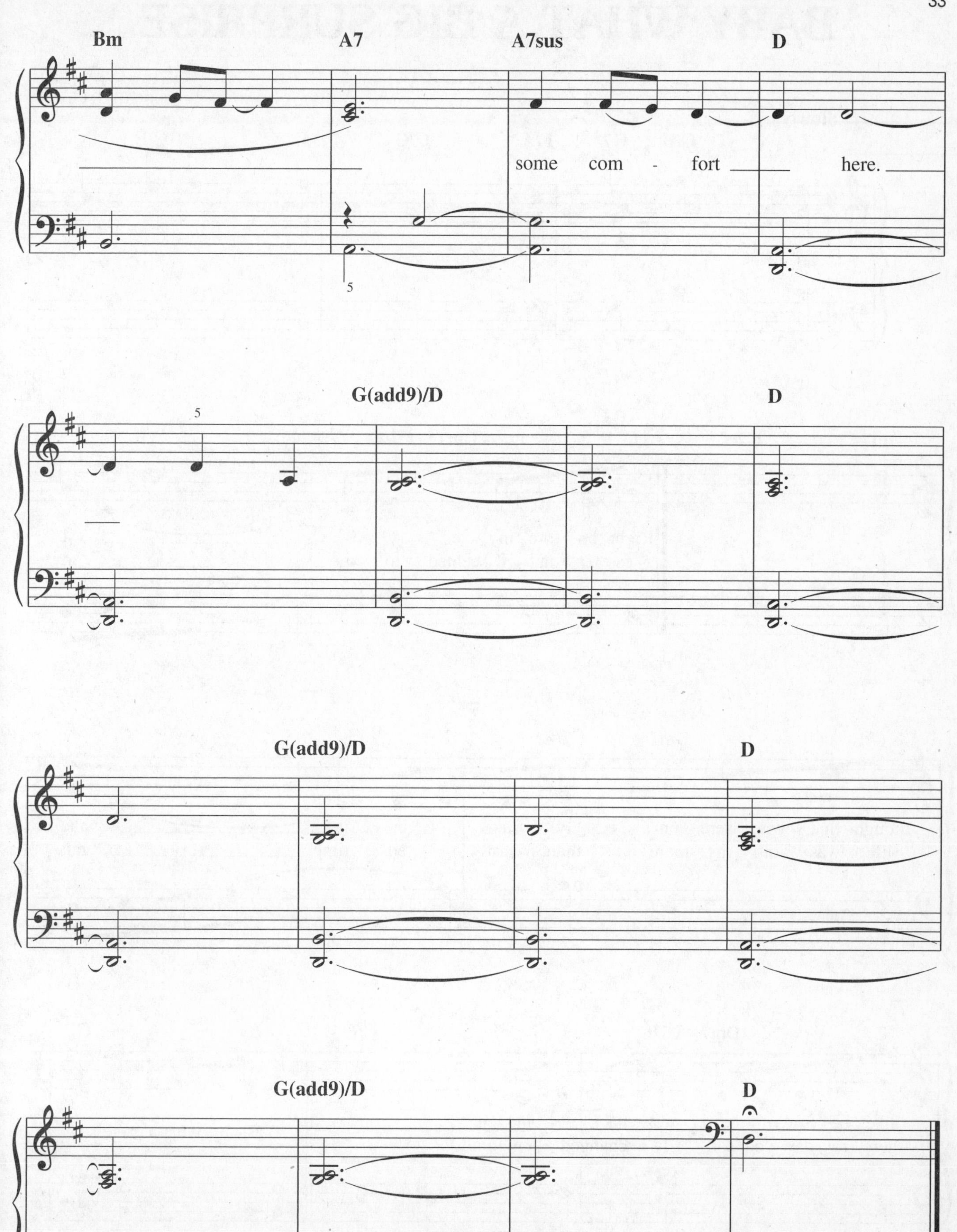
Bm
A7
A7sus
D
some com - fort here.
G(add9)/D
D
G(add9)/D
D
G(add9)/D
D

BABY WHAT A BIG SURPRISE

Words and Music by
PETER CETERA

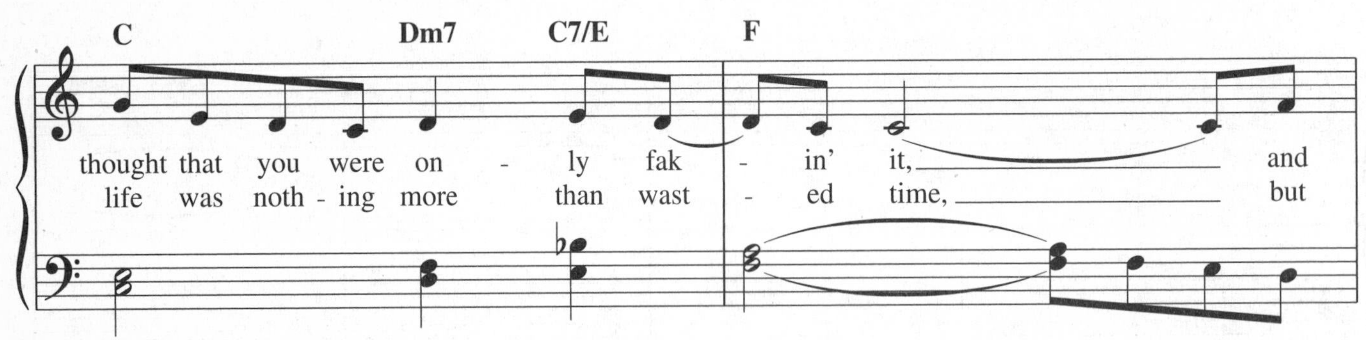

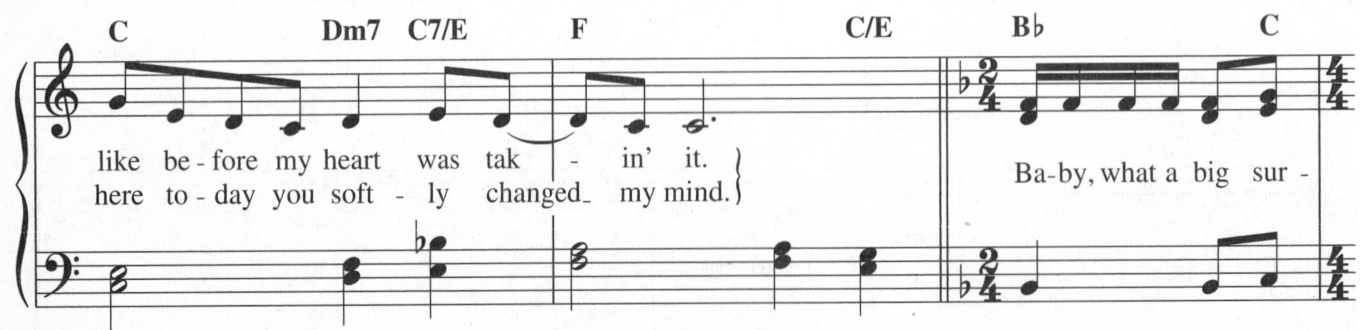

F
C/E
Dm7
B♭
C
F
prise;
right be-fore my ver - y eyes, oh, oh,

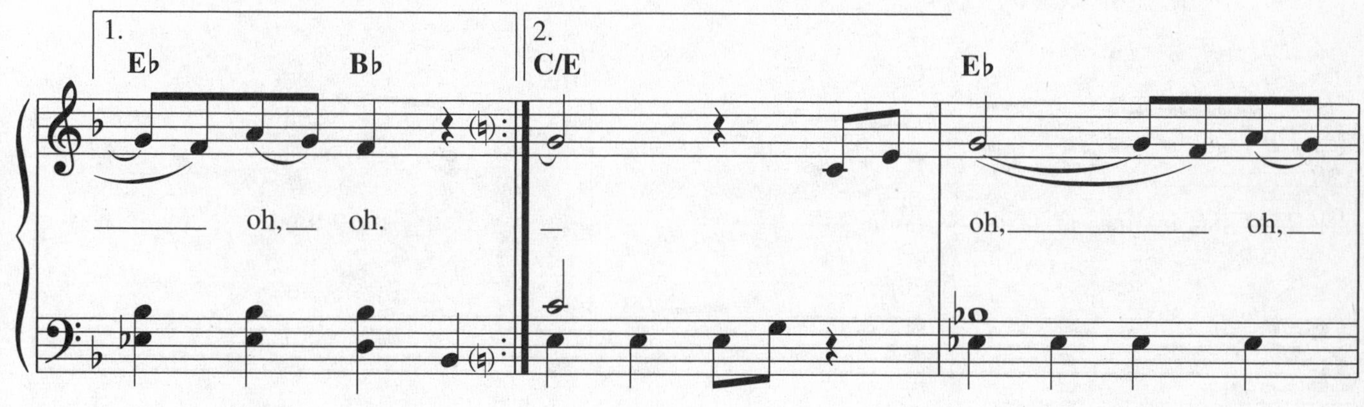
1.
E♭
B♭
2.
C/E
E♭
oh, oh.
oh, oh,

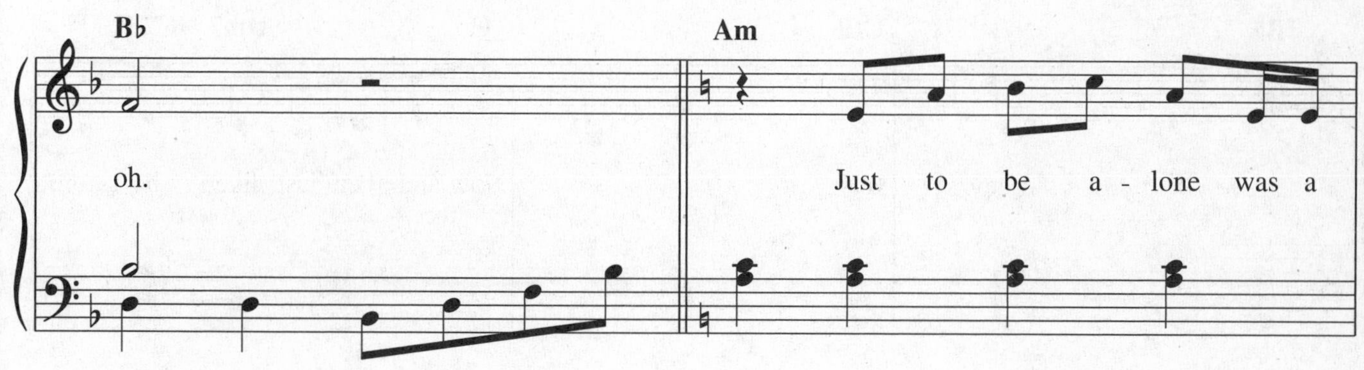
B♭
Am
oh.
Just to be a - lone was a

G
C
Am
G
lit - tle more than I could take,
then you came to stay.

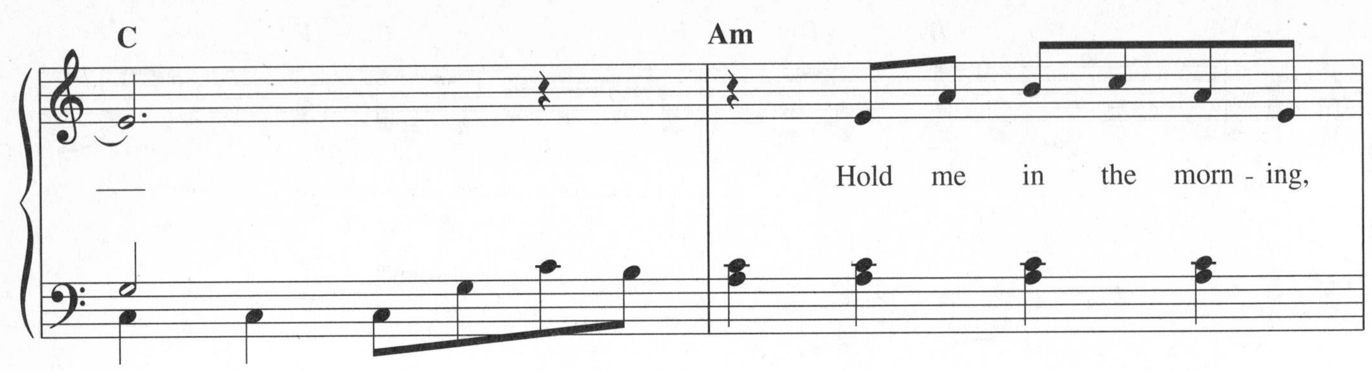
C
Am
Hold me in the morn - ing,

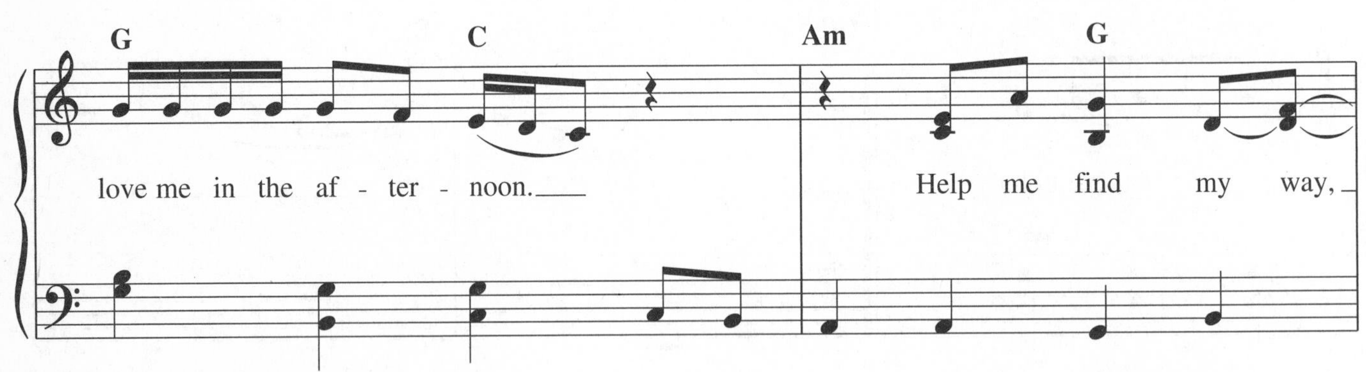
G
C
Am
G
love me in the af - ter - noon.
Help me find my way,

B♭
G/B
C
Dm7
C7/E
hey,
yeah.
Now and then just like be - fore

F
C
Dm7
C7/E
I
think a - bout the love I've thrown

F
C
Dm7
C7/E
— a - way, ——— but
now it does - n't mat - ter an -

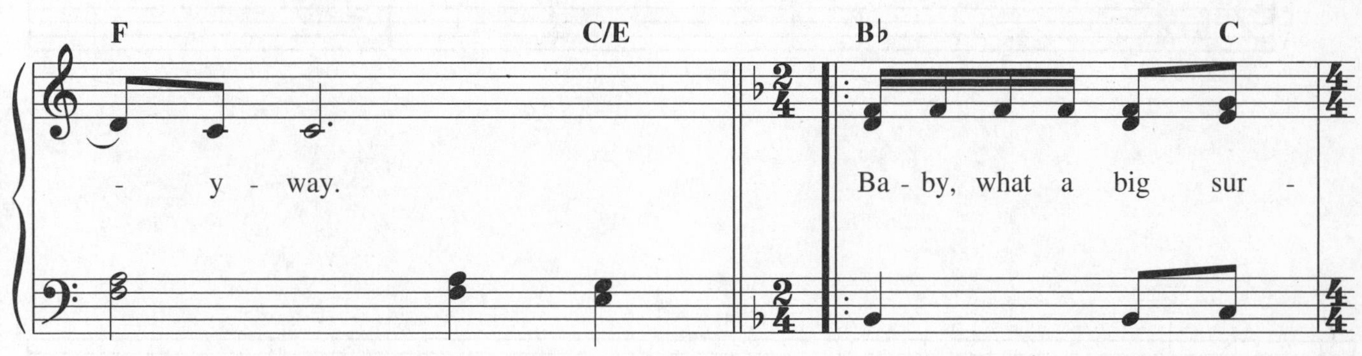
F
C/E
B♭
C
- y - way.
Ba - by, what a big sur -

F
C/E
Dm7
B♭
C
F
prise;
right be - fore my ver - y eyes, oh, oh, —

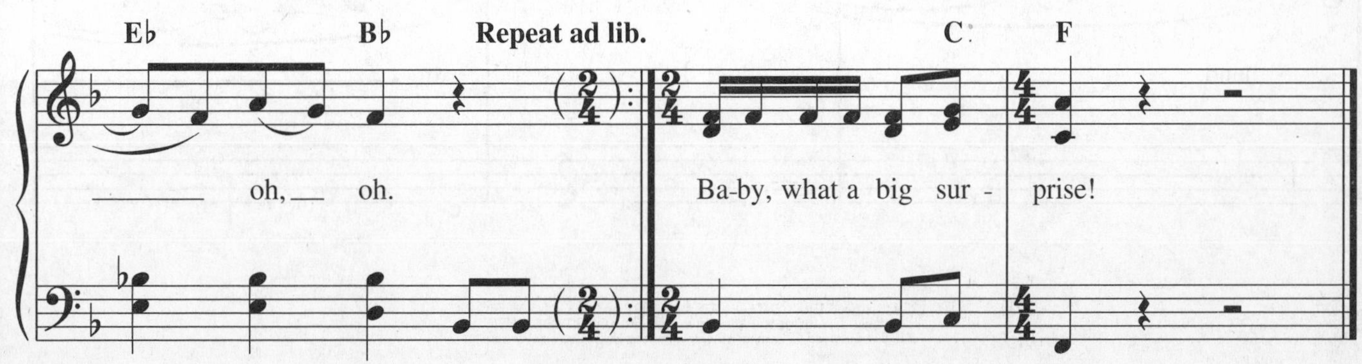
E♭
B♭
Repeat ad lib.
C
F
——— oh, — oh.
Ba-by, what a big sur - prise!

BARBARA ANN

Words and Music by
FRED FASSERT

Bright Rock tempo

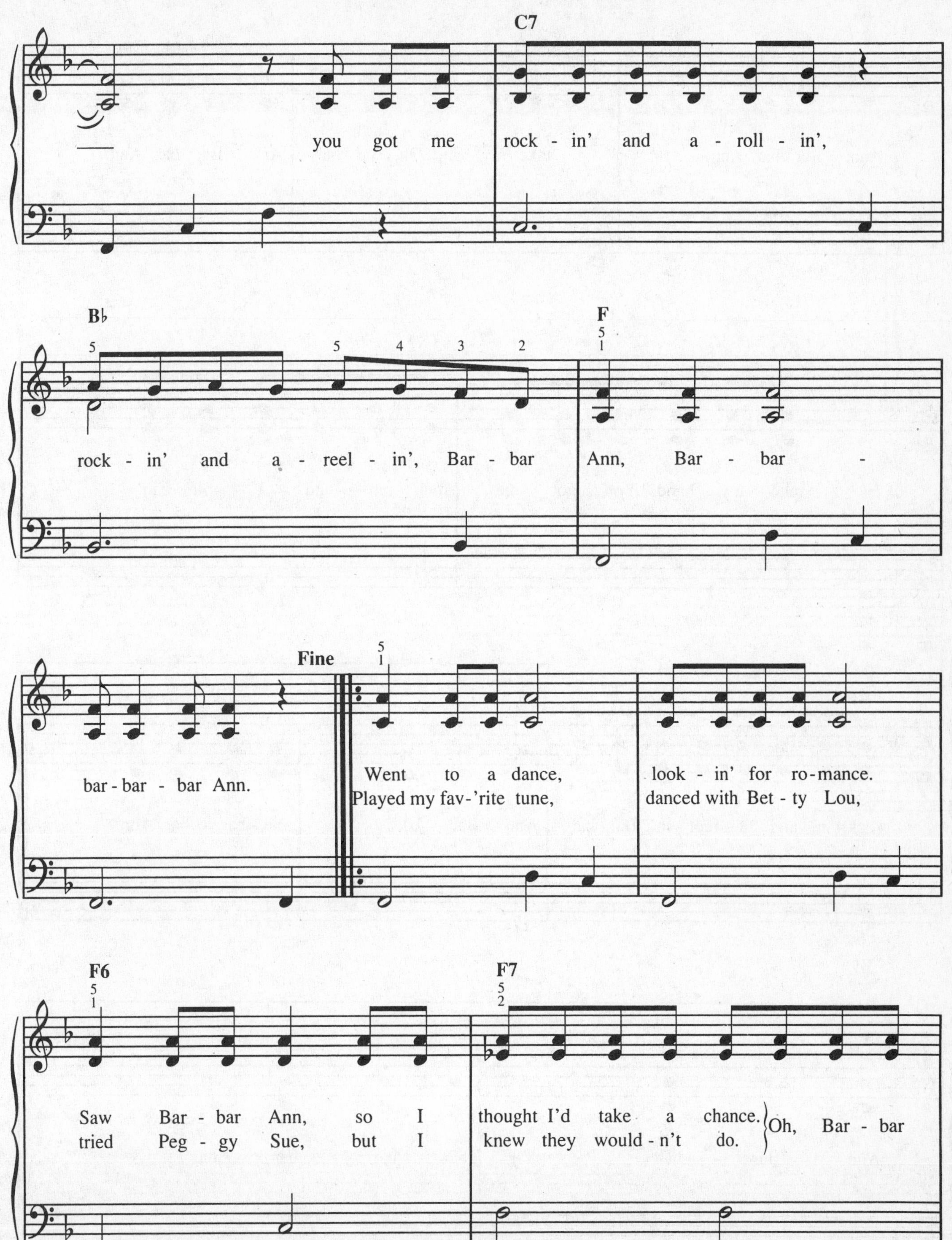
C7
you got me rock - in' and a - roll - in',
B♭
F
rock - in' and a - reel - in', Bar - bar Ann, Bar - bar -
Fine
bar - bar - bar Ann.
Went to a dance, look - in' for ro - mance.
Played my fav-'rite tune, danced with Bet - ty Lou,
F6
F7
Saw Bar - bar Ann, so I thought I'd take a chance.
tried Peg - gy Sue, but I knew they would - n't do.
Oh, Bar - bar

B♭
5
1
F
5
1
Ann, Bar - bar Ann,
take my hand. Oh, Bar - bar
Ann, Bar - bar Ann,
C7
5
1
take my hand. You got me
rock - in' and a - roll - in'
B♭
1.
F
rock - in' and a - reel - in', Bar - bar
Ann, Bar - bar -
bar - bar - bar Ann.
2.
F
D.C. al Fine
Ann, Bar - bar -
bar - bar - bar Ann.

DON'T CRY OUT LOUD

(We Don't Cry Out Loud)

Words and Music by PETER ALLEN
and CAROLE BAYER SAGER

Slowly

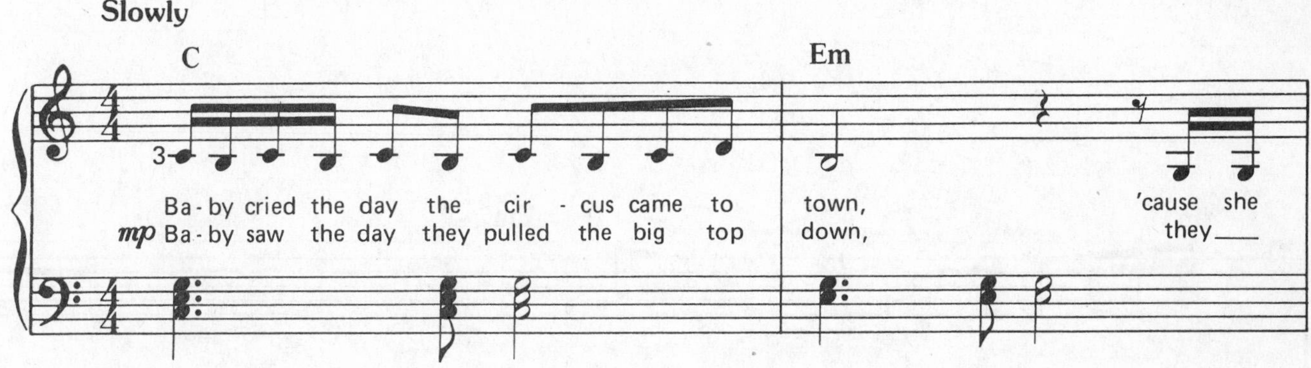

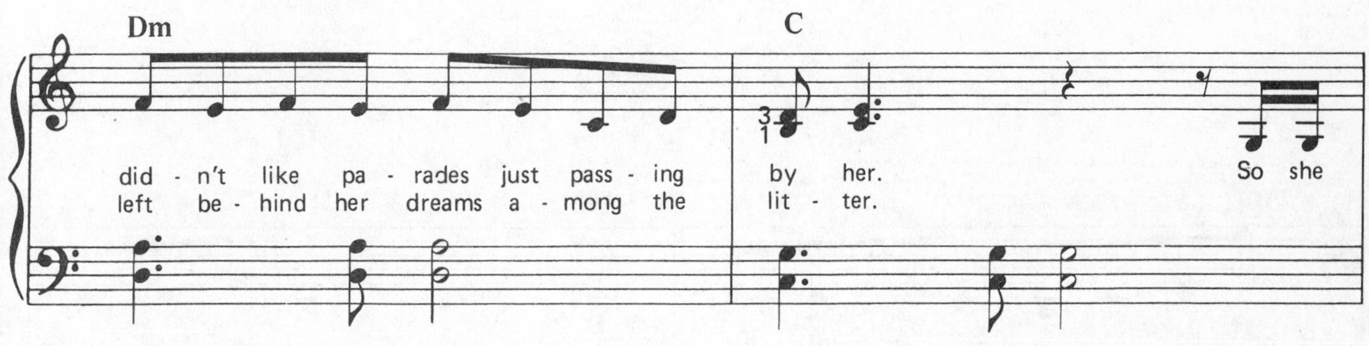

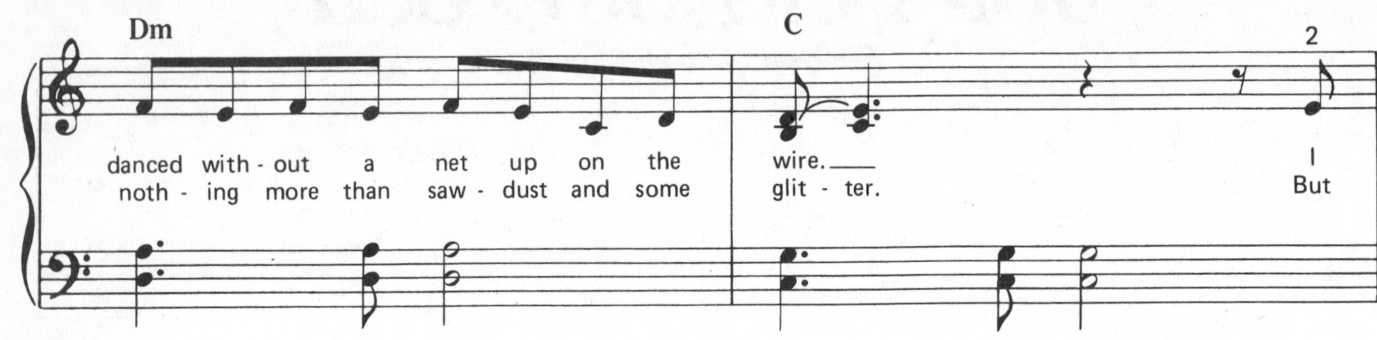
Dm
C
danced with - out a net up on the
nothing - ing more than saw - dust and some
wire.
glit - ter.
I
But

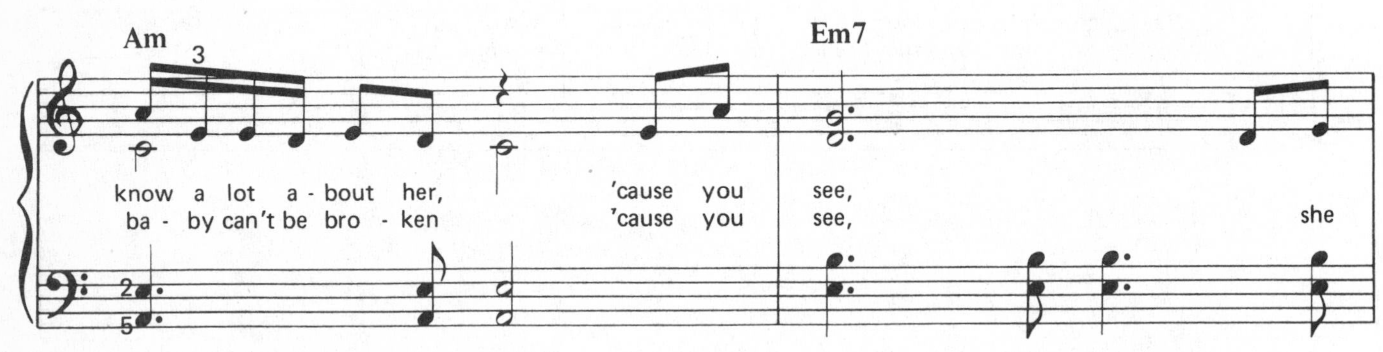
Am
Em7
know a lot a - bout her, 'cause you
ba - by can't be bro - ken 'cause you
see,
see,
she

Am7
D7
Gsus
G7
ba - by is an aw - ful lot like
had the fin - est teach - er that's
me.
me.
I told her,

C
G/B
Am
Dm
Don't cry out loud, Just keep it in - side, learn how to

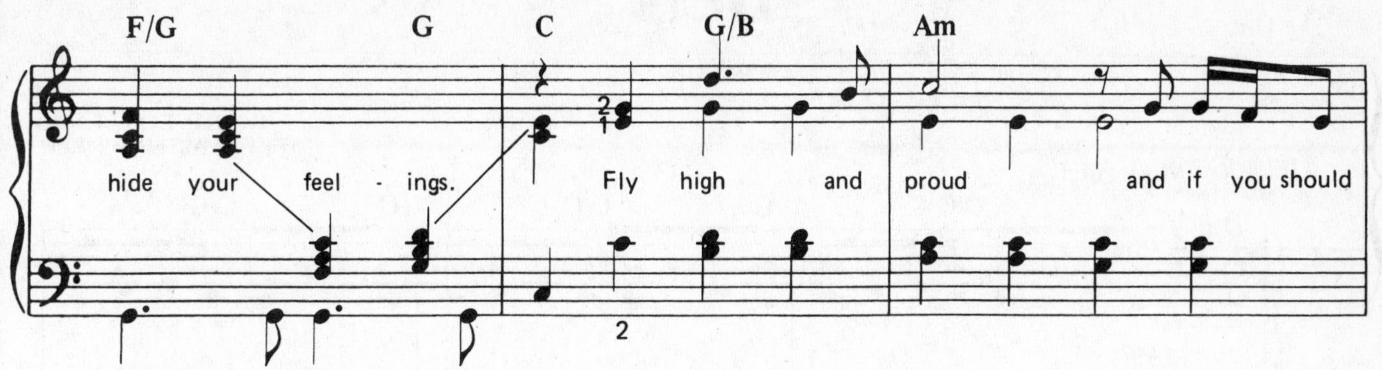
F/G
G
C
G/B
Am
hide your feel - ings. Fly high and proud and if you should
2

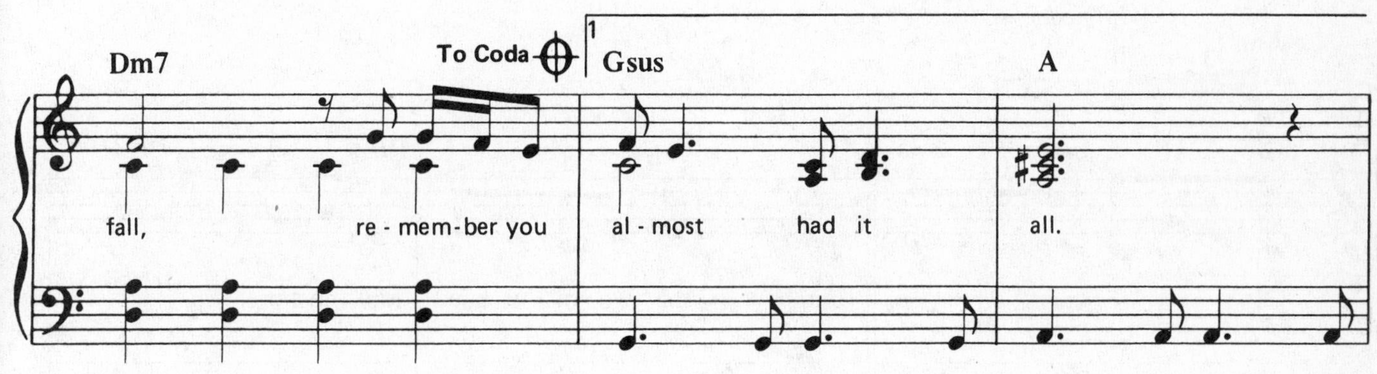
Dm7
To Coda
1
Gsus
A
fall, re - mem - ber you al - most had it all.

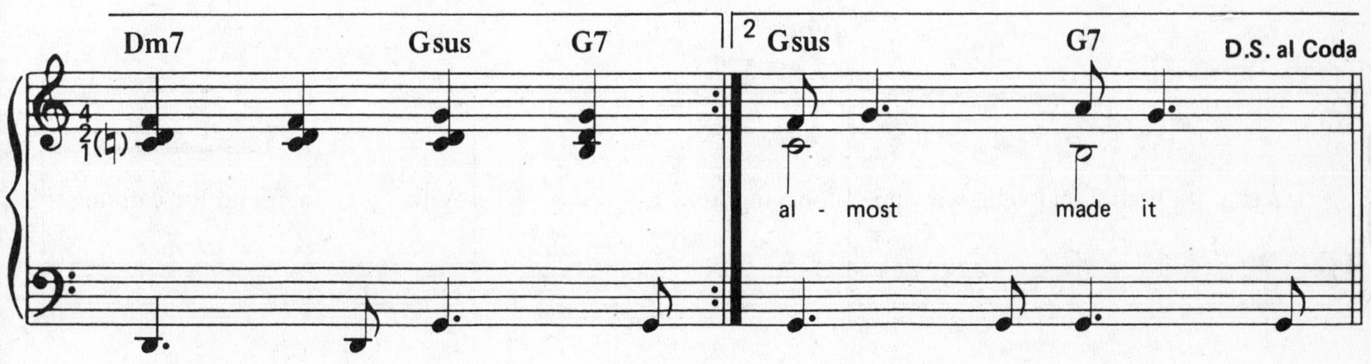
Dm7
Gsus
G7
2 Gsus
G7
D.S. al Coda
al - most made it

CODA
Gsus
G7
C
al - most had it all.
1

BEN

Words by DON BLACK
Music by WALTER SCHARF

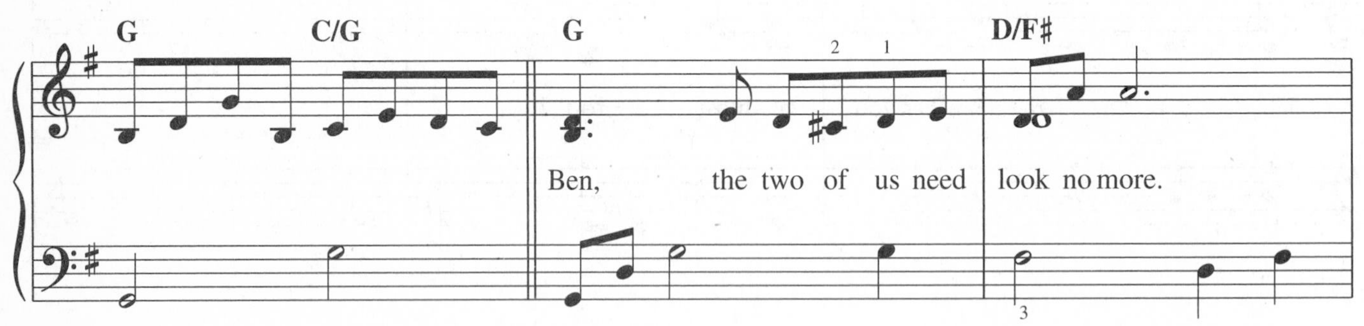

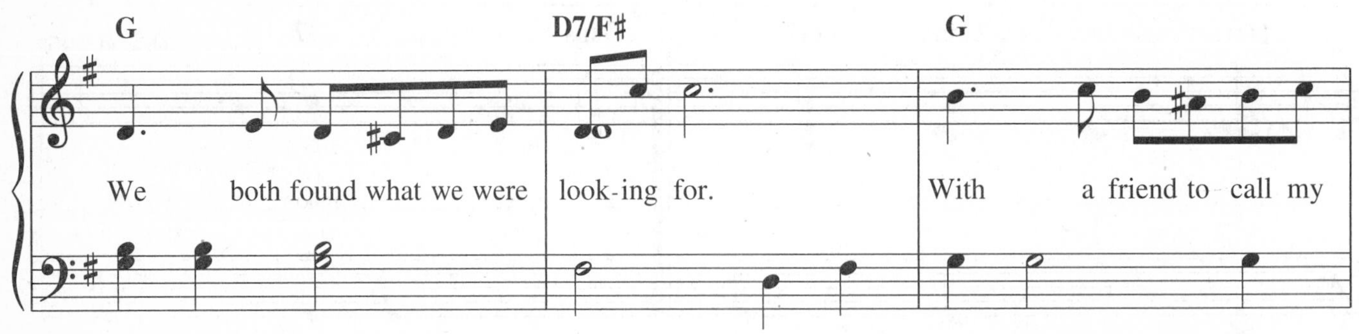

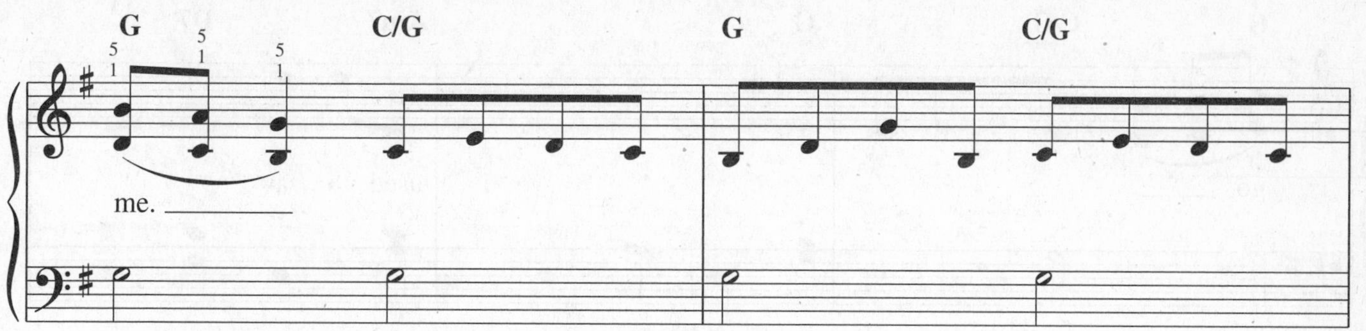
G
C/G
G
C/G
me.

Gm
D/F♯
Gm
Ben, you're al - ways run - ning here and there.
You feel you're not want - ed

D7/F♯
G
B7
an - y - where.
If you ev - er look be - hind and don't like what you

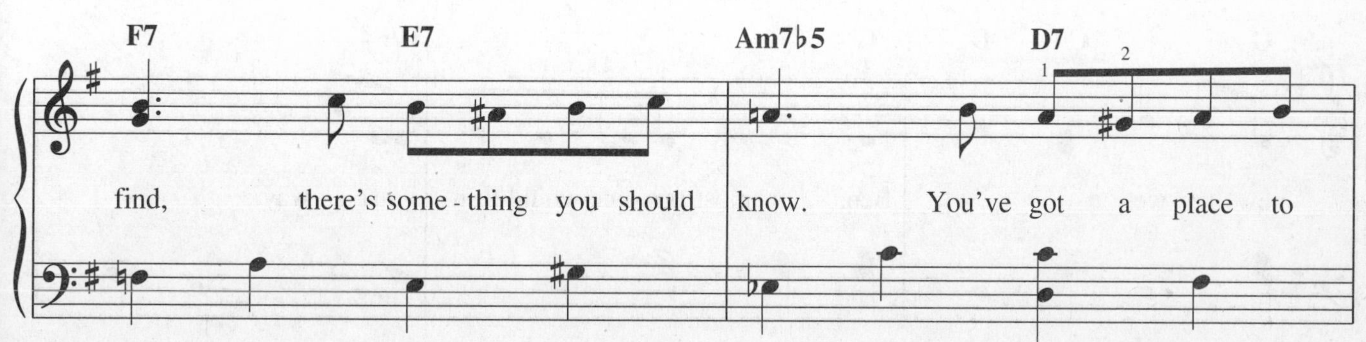
F7
E7
Am7♭5
D7
find, there's some - thing you should know.
You've got a place to

G
C/G
G
Am7
D7
go.
I
used to say

G
G6
Am7
D7
G
I and me.
Now it's us,
now it's we.
I

Am7
D7
G
G6
Am7
D7
used to say
I and me.
Now it's us,

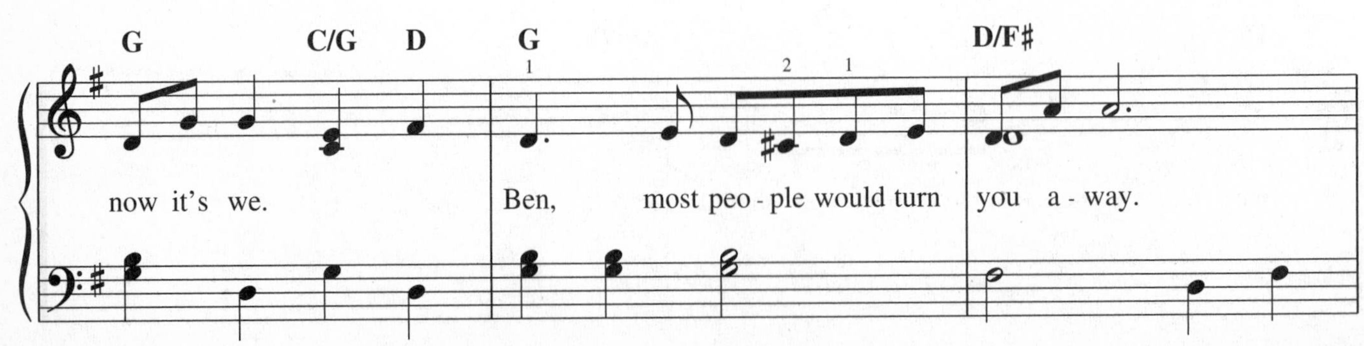
G
C/G
D
G
D/F♯
now it's we.
Ben, most peo - ple would turn
you a - way.

G
D7/F#
G
4
I don't lis - ten to a
word they say.
They don't see you as I

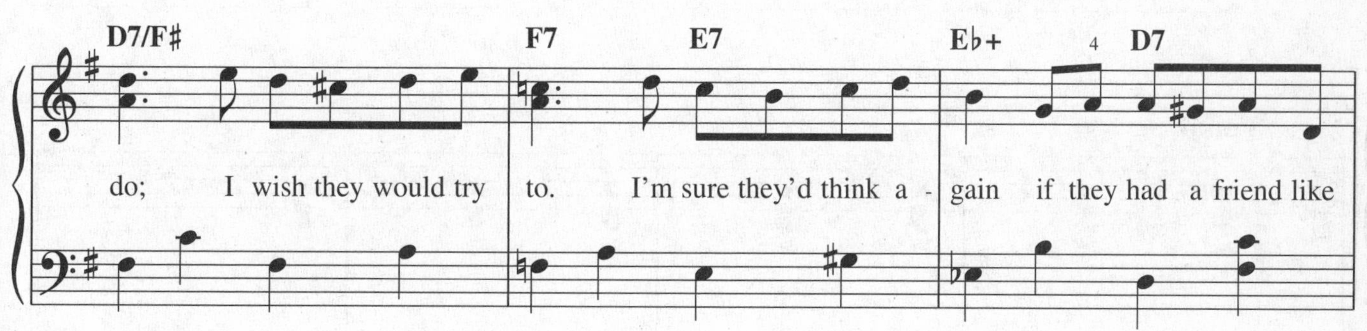
D7/F#
F7
E7
Eb+
4
D7
do; I wish they would try
to. I'm sure they'd think a -
gain if they had a friend like

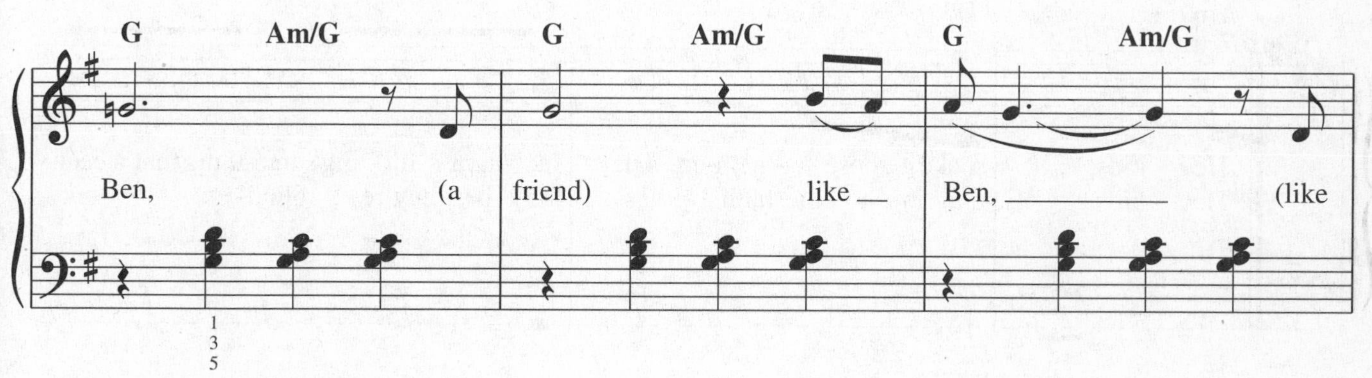
G
Am/G
G
Am/G
G
Am/G
Ben, (a
friend) like
Ben, (like
1
3
5

G
Am/G
G
Ben,) like
Ben.
rit.

BENNIE AND THE JETS

Words and Music by ELTON JOHN
and BERNIE TAUPIN

Em
Am
round. ___
long ___
You're gon - na hear e - lec - tric
where we fight our par - ents out in the

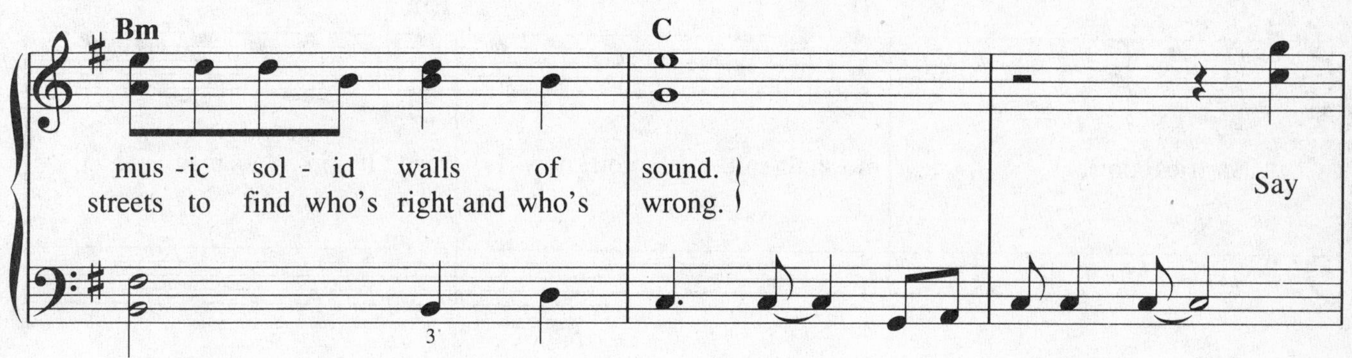
Bm
C
mus - ic sol - id walls of sound.
streets to find who's right and who's wrong.
Say
3

G
Am
4
Can - dy and Ron - nie, have you seen them yet, but they're so spaced out, ___

C
G
Ben - nie and the Jets.
But _ they're weird _ and they're

Am
wonder - der - ful, oh Ben-nie she's real - ly keen. She's got e -

C
D
Em
lec-tric boots, a mo-hair suit, you know I read it in a mag - a -

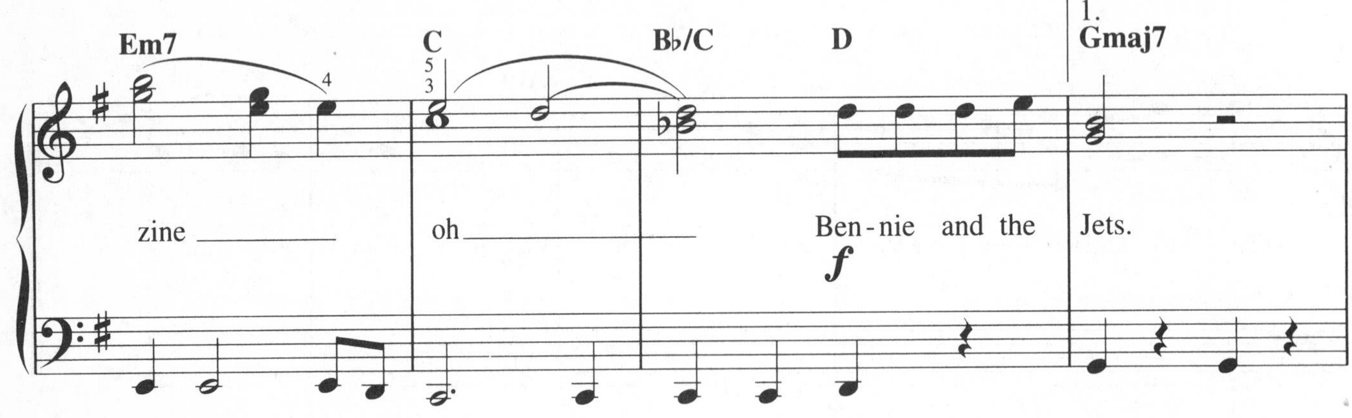
Em7
C
B♭/C
D
1.
Gmaj7
zine oh Ben-nie and the Jets.
f

Fmaj7

2.
Gmaj7
Jets.
Gmaj7
Ben - nie,
ff
Ben - nie
Ben - nie Ben - nie
Fmaj7
1.
Ben - nie Ben - nie and the Jets
2.
Gmaj7

CRIMSON AND CLOVER

Words and Music by TOMMY JAMES
and PETER LUCIA

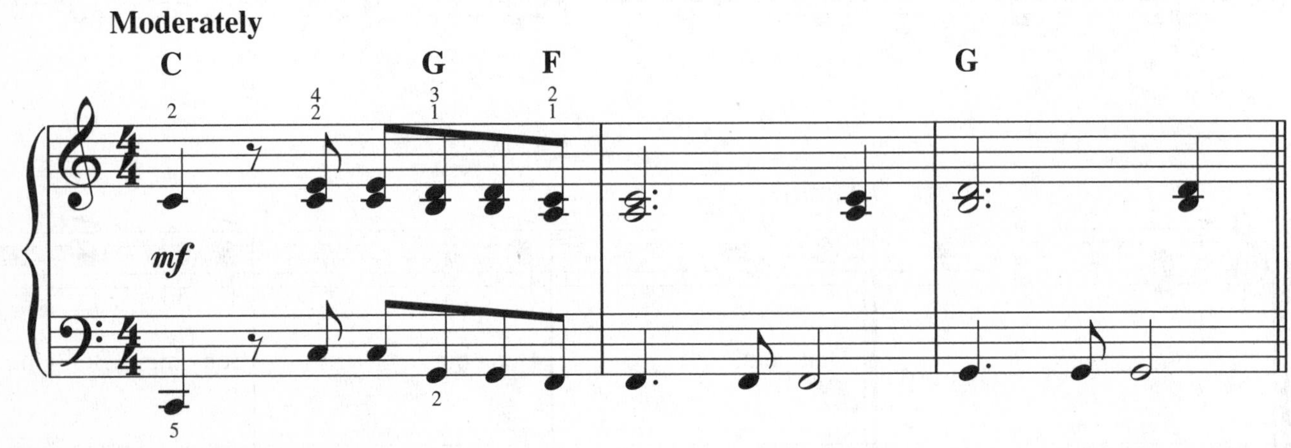

C G F G C G F
clo - ver.
Ah,

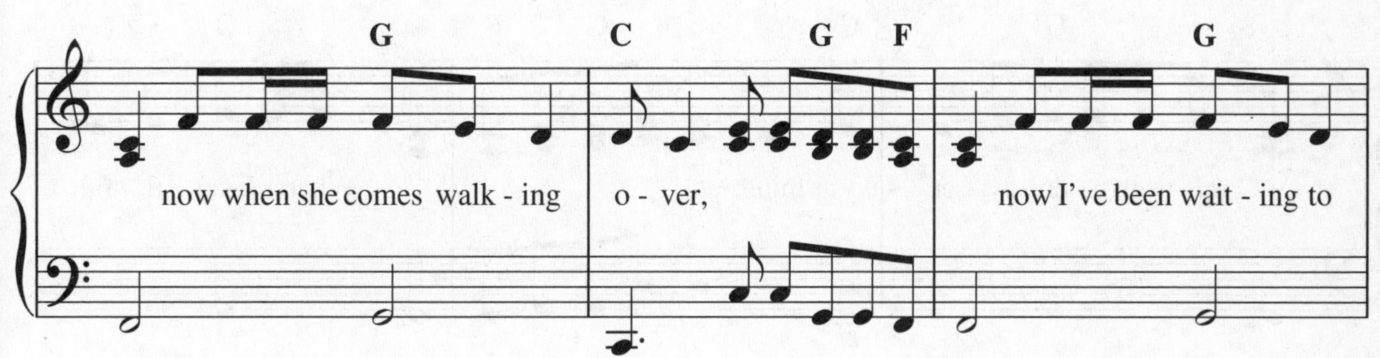
G C G F G
now when she comes walk - ing
o - ver,
now I've been wait - ing to

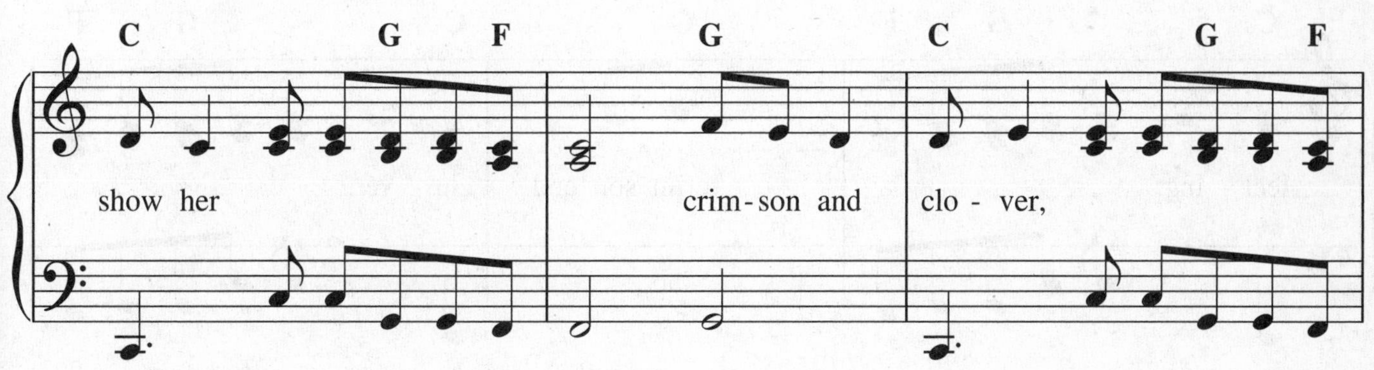
C G F G C G F
show her
crim - son and
clo - ver,

G C G F G
o - ver and
o - ver.

C G F G C G F
Yeah, my, my, such a sweet thing.

G C G F G
I wan-na do ev - er - y - thing. What a beau - ti - ful

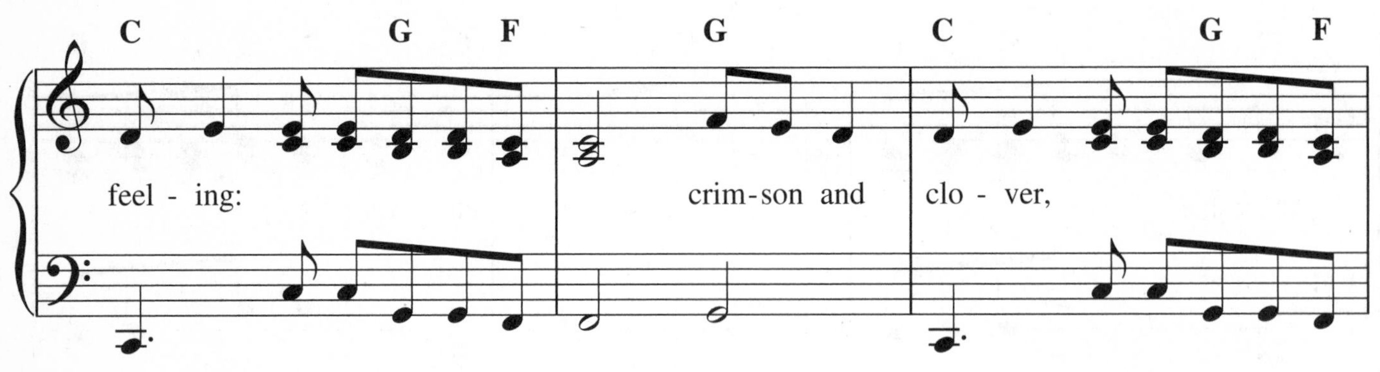
C G F G C G F
feel - ing: crim-son and clo - ver,

G
o - ver and o - ver.

C
G
F
G
C
G
Crim - son and clo - ver,

F
G
C
G
F
G
o - ver and o - ver.
Crim - son and clo - ver,
o - ver and o - ver.

C
G
F
G
C
G

F
G
C

DIZZY

Words and Music by TOMMY ROE
and FREDDY WELLER

Eb
Ab
Bb
Ab
diz - zy.
I

Eb
Ab
Bb
Ab
First time that I saw you, girl, I knew that I just had to make you
fi - n'lly got to talk to you, and told you just ex - act - ly how I

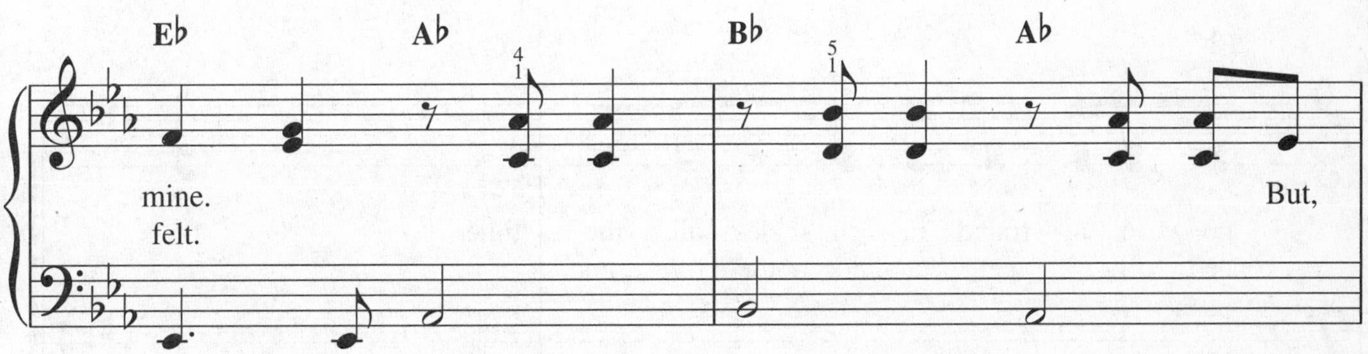
Eb
Ab
Bb
Ab
mine.
felt.
But,

Eb
Ab
Bb
Ab
it's so hard to talk to you with fel - lows hang - in' 'round you all the
Then I held you close to me and kissed you, and my heart be - gan to

E♭

1.

G

go - in' a - round in cir - cles all the time.

need to call a doc - tor for some

2.

G C F A

help. Diz - zy, I'm so

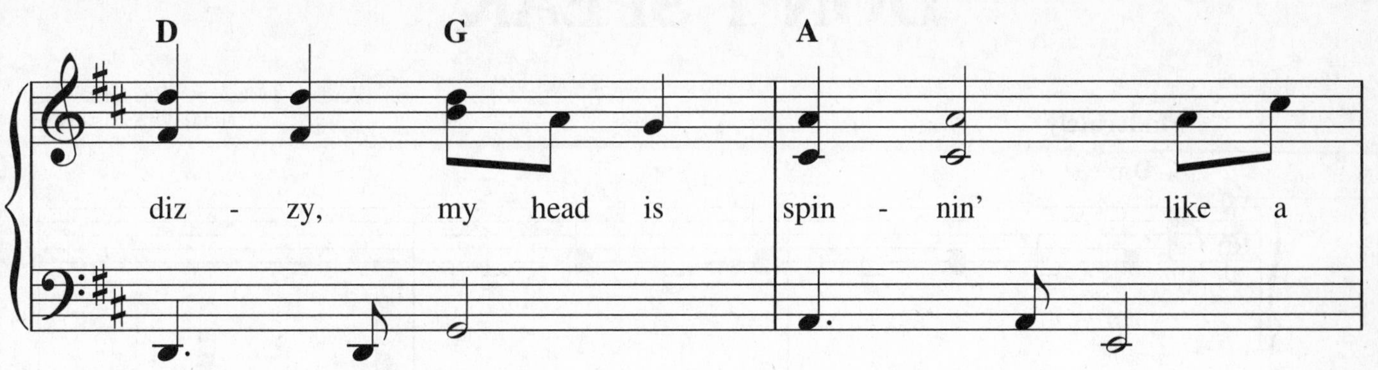
D
G
A
diz - zy, my head is spin - nin' like a

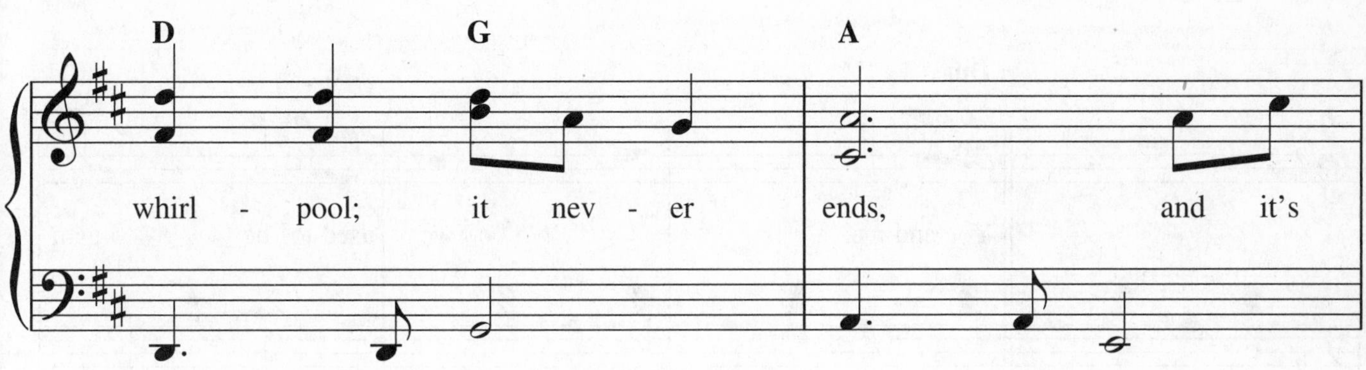
D
G
A
whirl - pool; it nev - er ends, and it's

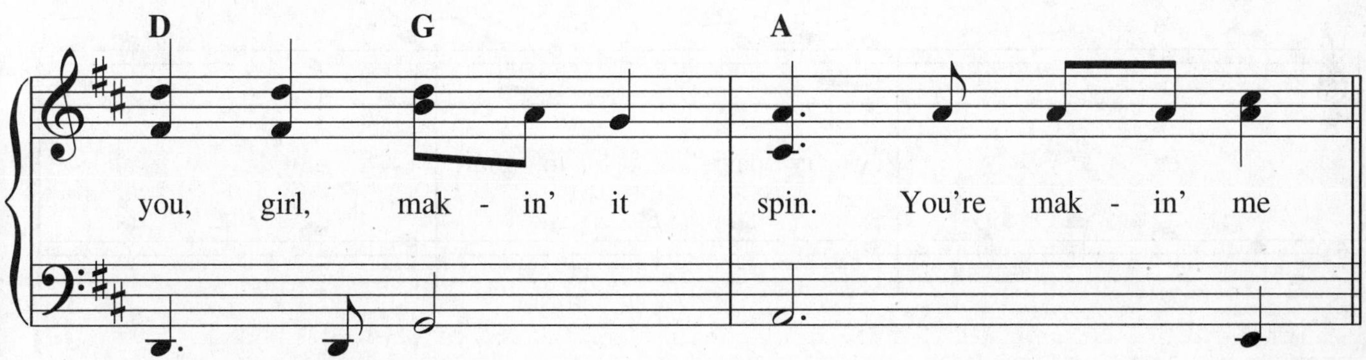
D
G
A
you, girl, mak - in' it spin. You're mak - in' me

D
G
A
Play 3 times
D
diz - zy. You're mak - in' me diz - zy.

DON'T SPEAK

Words and Music by ERIC STEFANI
and GWEN STEFANI

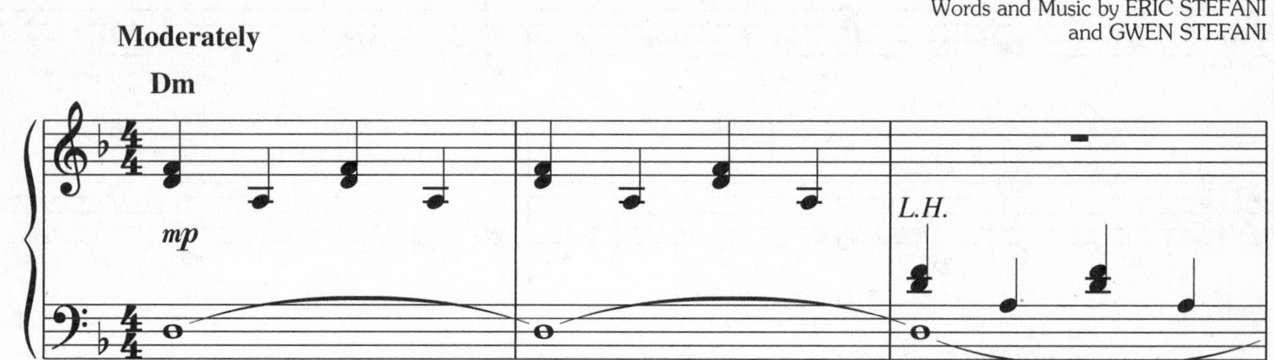

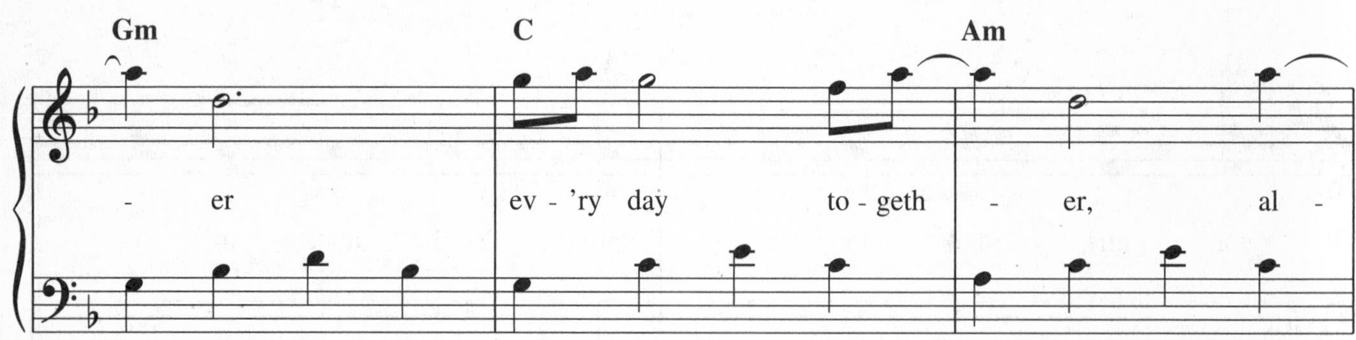

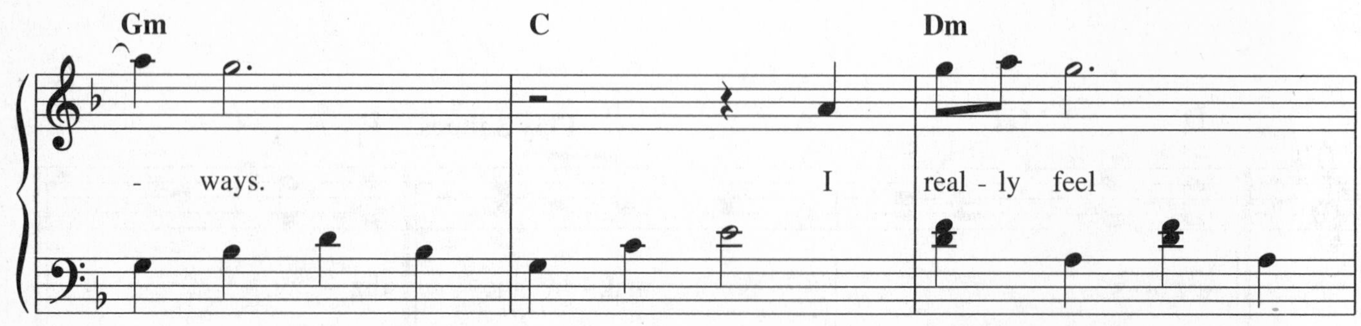

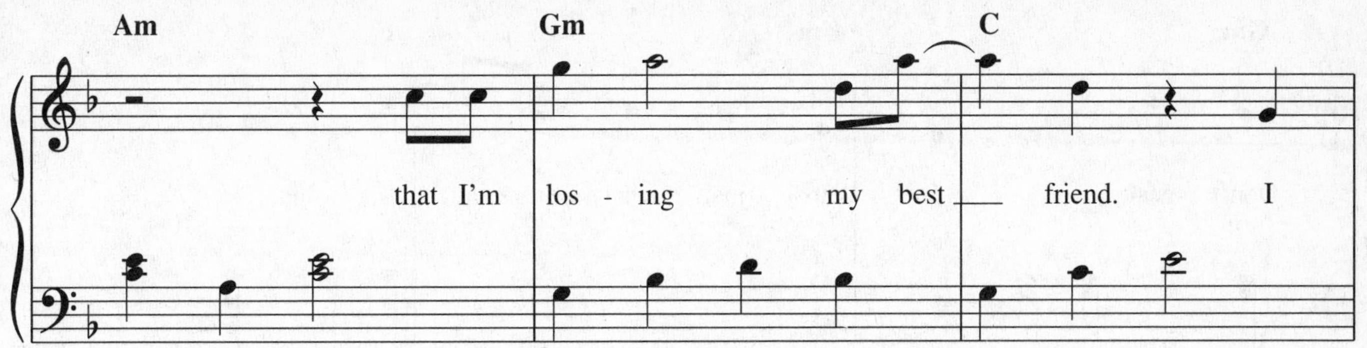
Am
Gm
C
that I'm los - ing my best friend. I

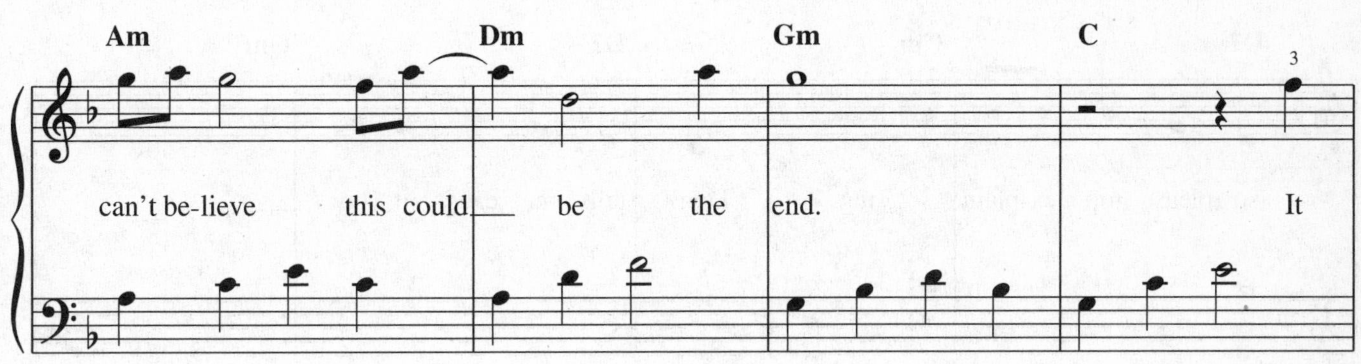
Am
Dm
Gm
C
3
can't be-lieve this could be the end. It

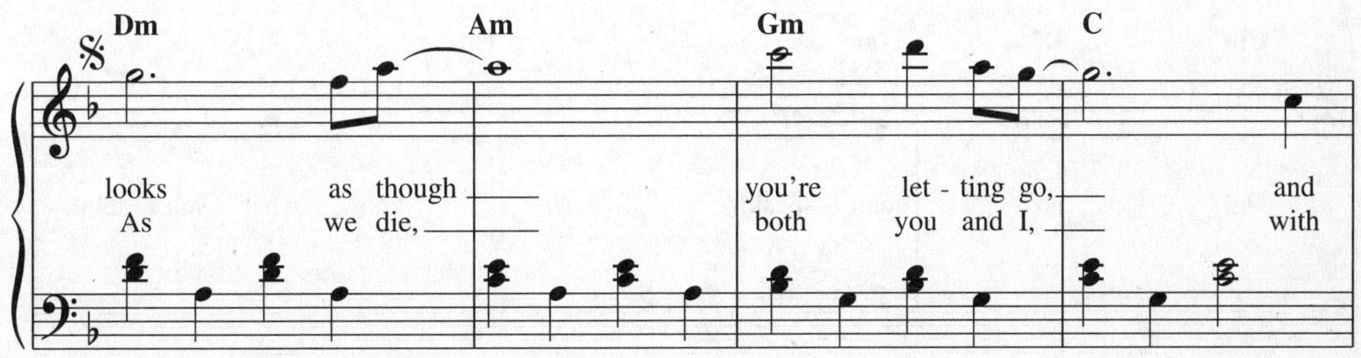
Dm
Am
Gm
C
looks as though you're let - ting go, and
As we die, both you and I, with

F
C
D
if it's real, well, I don't want to know.
my head in my hands I sit and cry.

Gm
Cm
F
Don't speak, I know just what you're say - ing,

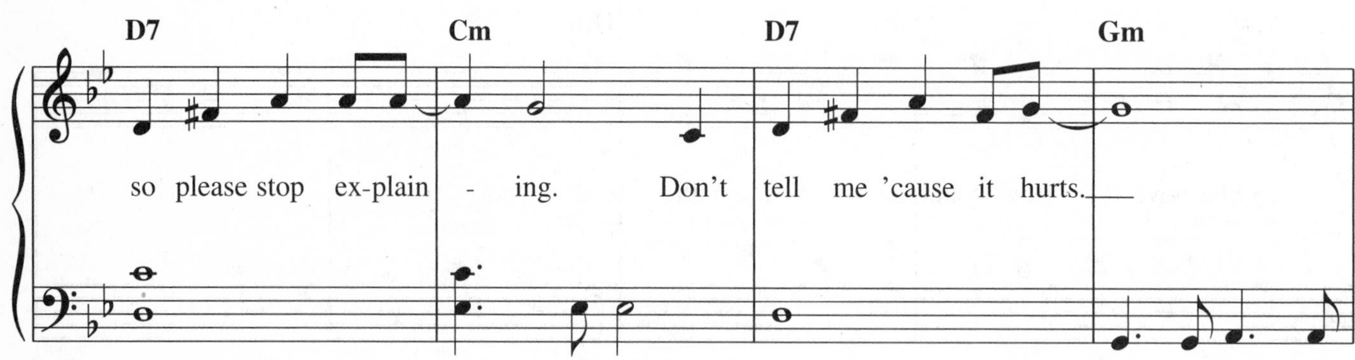
D7
Cm
D7
Gm
so please stop ex-plain - ing. Don't tell me 'cause it hurts.

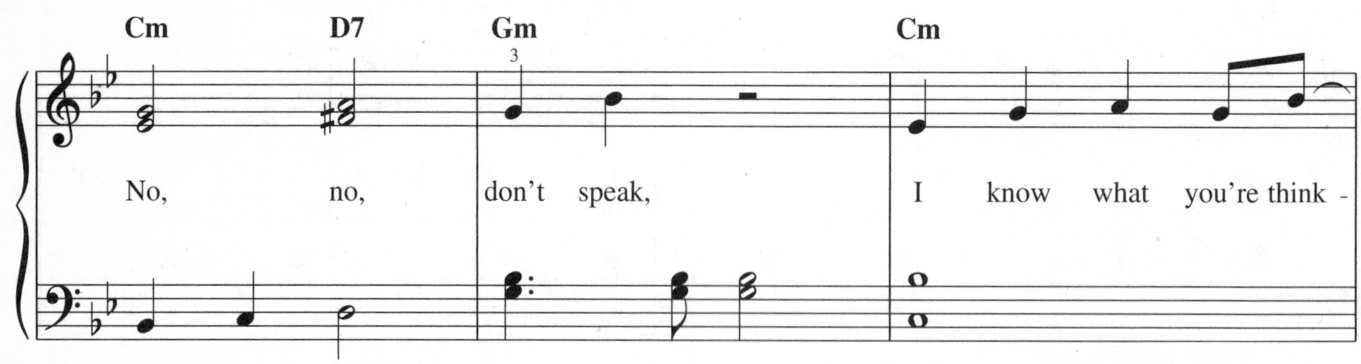
Cm
D7
Gm
Cm
No, no, don't speak, I know what you're think -

F
D7
Cm
- ing. I don't need your rea - sons. Don't

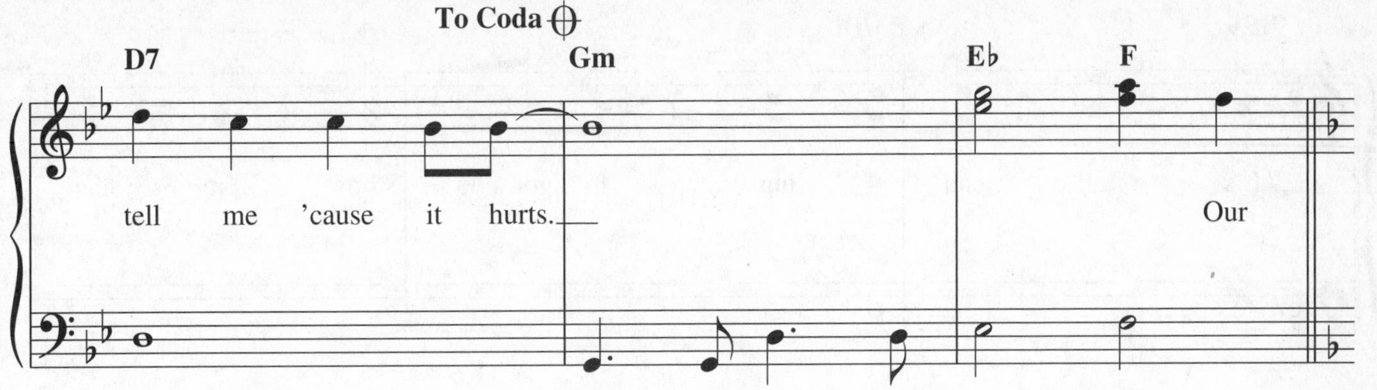
To Coda
D7
Gm
E♭
F
tell me 'cause it hurts.
Our

Dm
Am
mem - or - ies,
they can be in - vit -

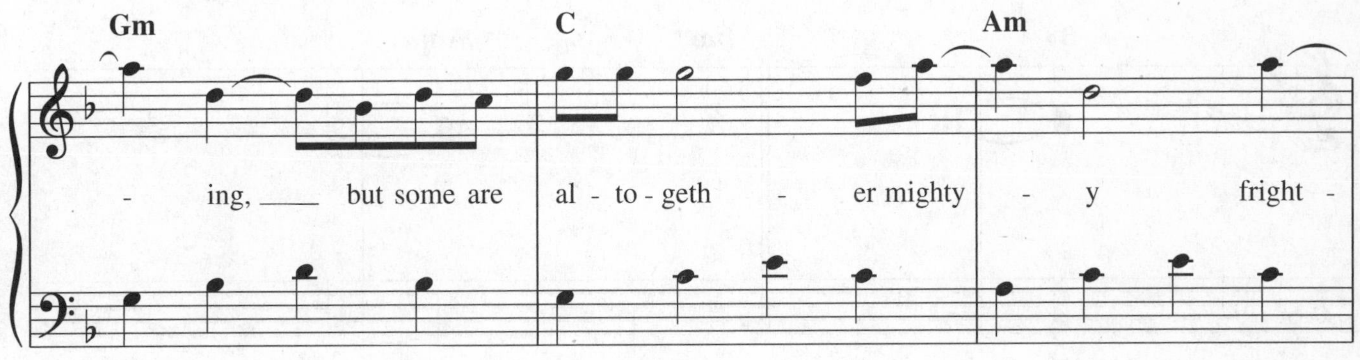
Gm
C
Am
- ing, but some are al - to - geth - er mighty - y fright -

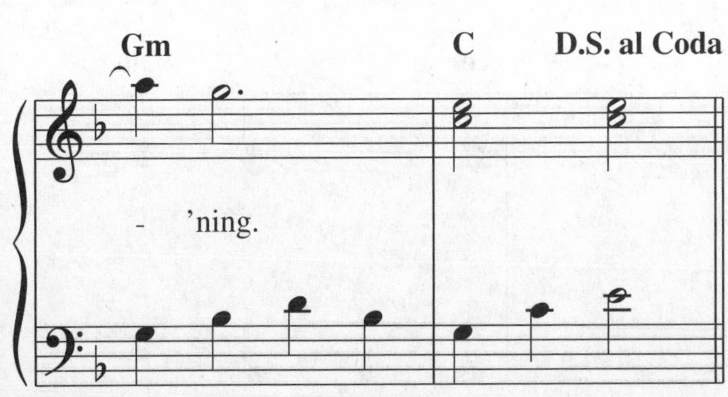
Gm
C
D.S. al Coda
- 'ning.

CODA
Gm

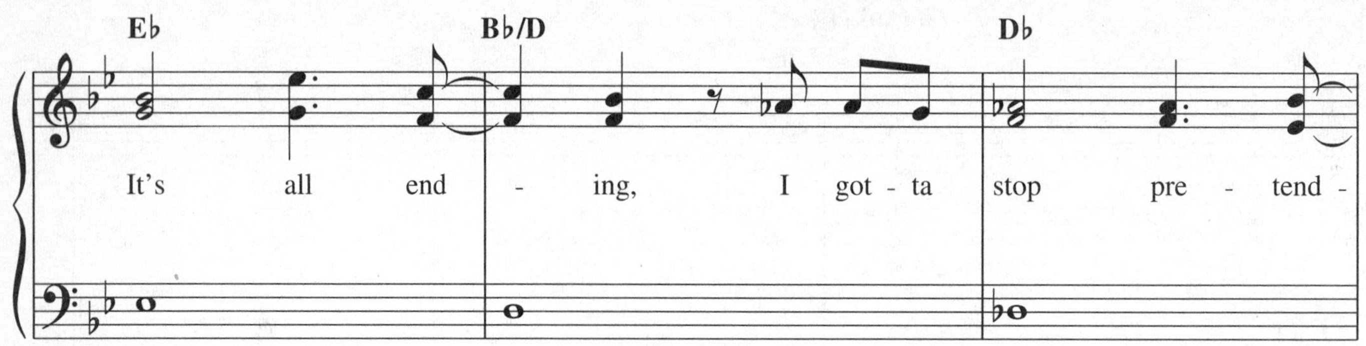
E♭
B♭/D
D♭
It's all end - ing, I got - ta stop pre - tend -

A♭/C
C♭
C♭(♭5)
- ing who we are.

B♭
Dm
Am

Gm
C
Am
Dm

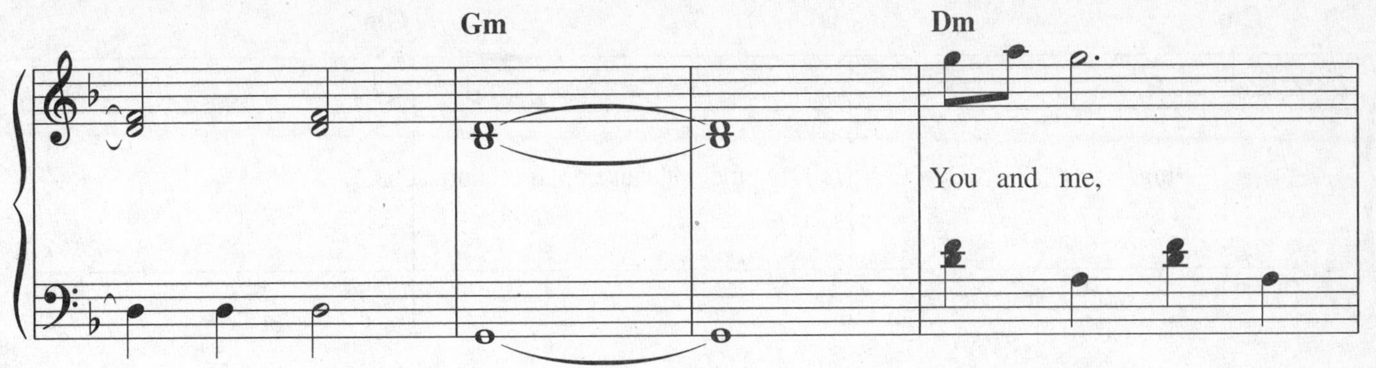
Gm
Dm
You and me,

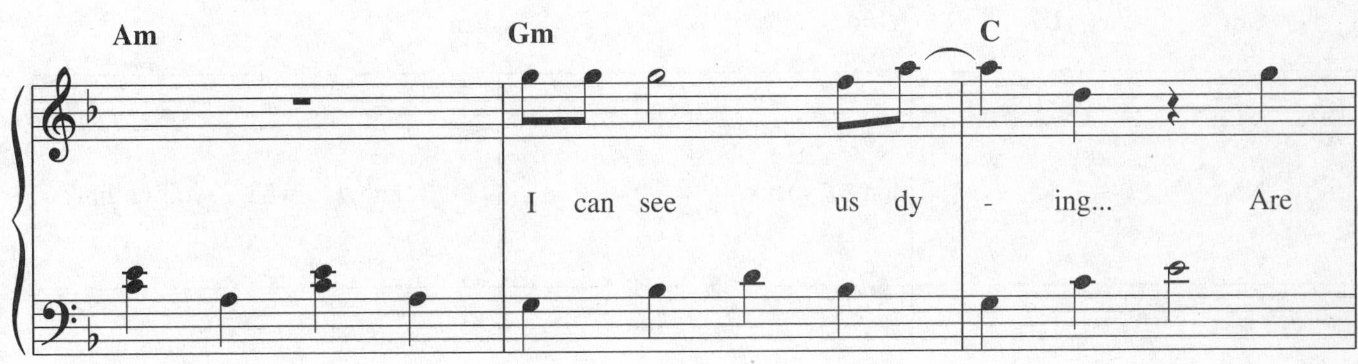
Am
Gm
C
I can see us dy - ing... Are

Gm
C
Gm
3
we?
Don't speak, I

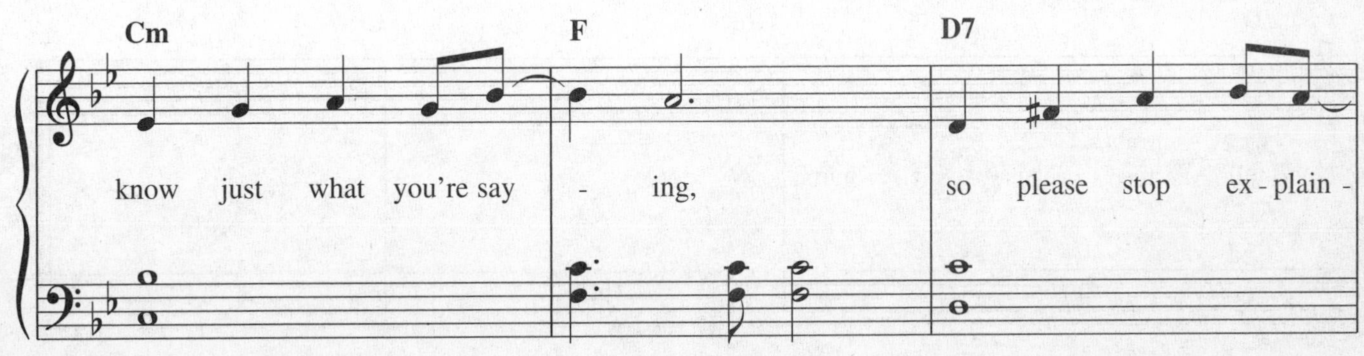
Cm
F
D7
know just what you're say - ing, so please stop ex - plain -

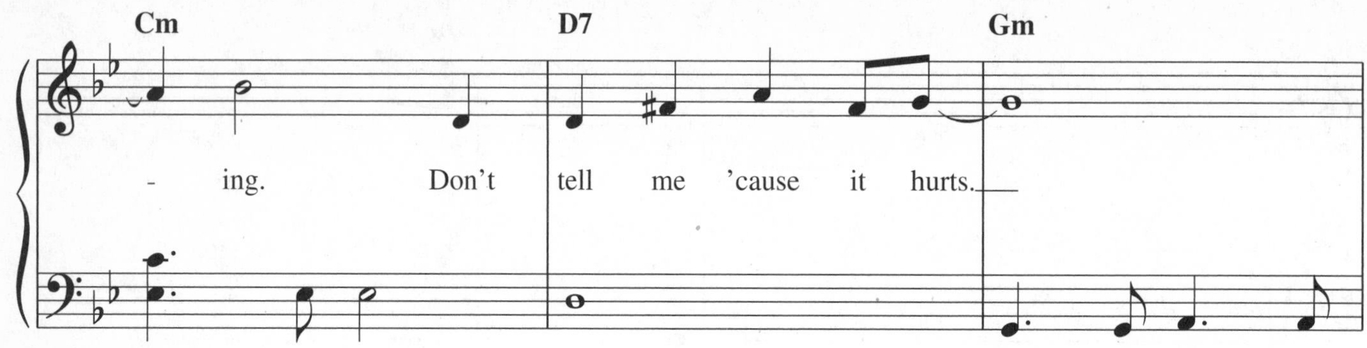
Cm
D7
Gm
- ing. Don't
tell me 'cause it hurts.

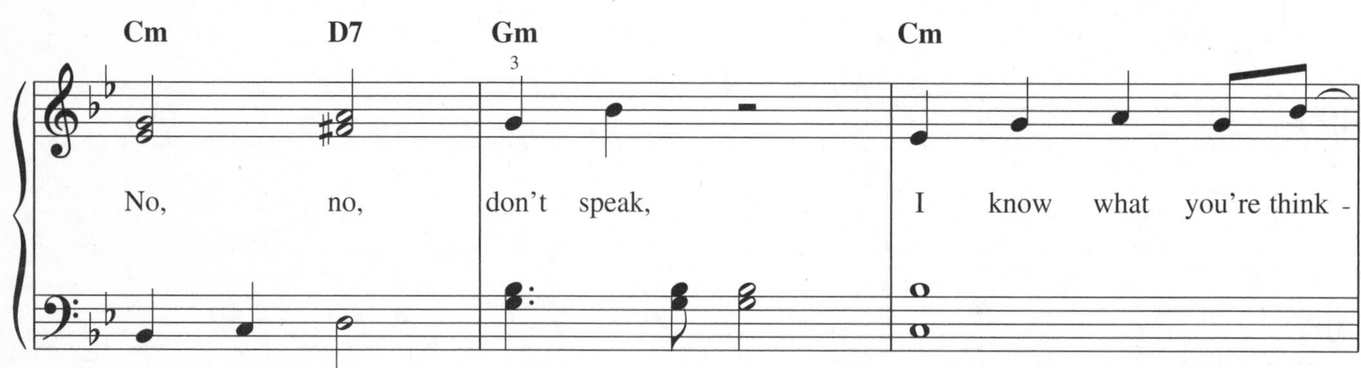
Cm
D7
Gm
Cm
No, no,
don't speak,
I know what you're think -

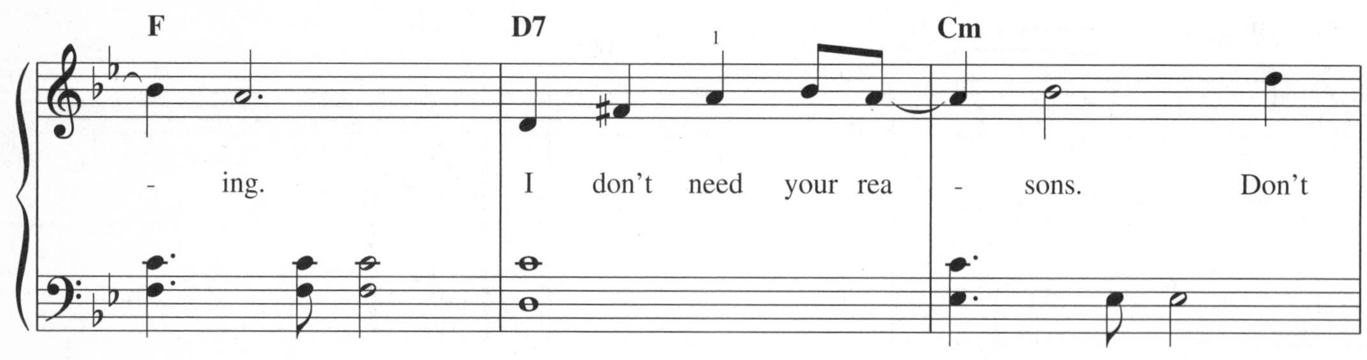
F
D7
Cm
- ing.
I don't need your rea
- sons. Don't

Repeat and Fade
D7
Gm
Cm7
D7
tell me 'cause it hurts.

DUST IN THE WIND

Words and Music by
KERRY LIVGREN

Moderate Folk style

C Am

mf

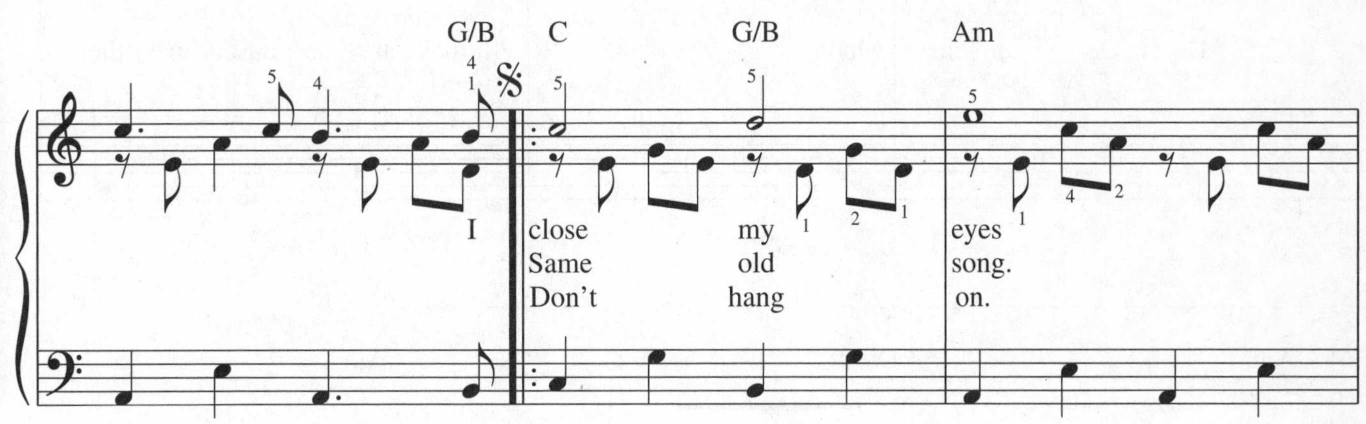

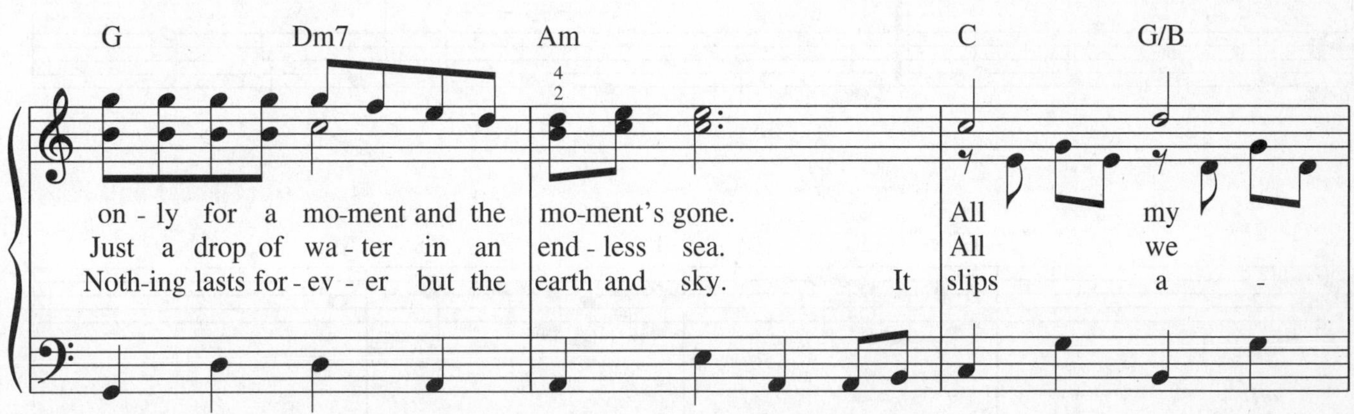

Am
G
Dm7
Am
To Coda
dreams
do
way.
pass be - fore my eyes a cu - ri - os - i - ty.
crum-bles to the ground though we re - fuse to see.
All your mon-ey won't an - oth - er min-ute buy.
D/F#
G
Am
Am/G
1.
Dust in the wind.
All they are is dust in the
wind.
2.
All we are is dust in the wind.
F
mp

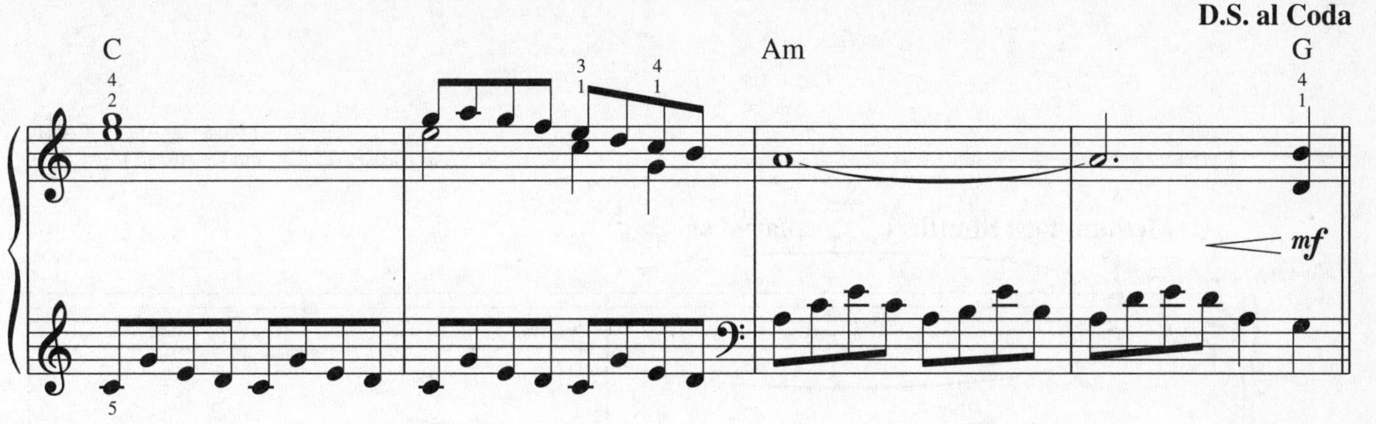
D.S. al Coda
C
Am
G
mf

CODA
D/F#
G
Am
Am/G
Dust ___ in the wind.

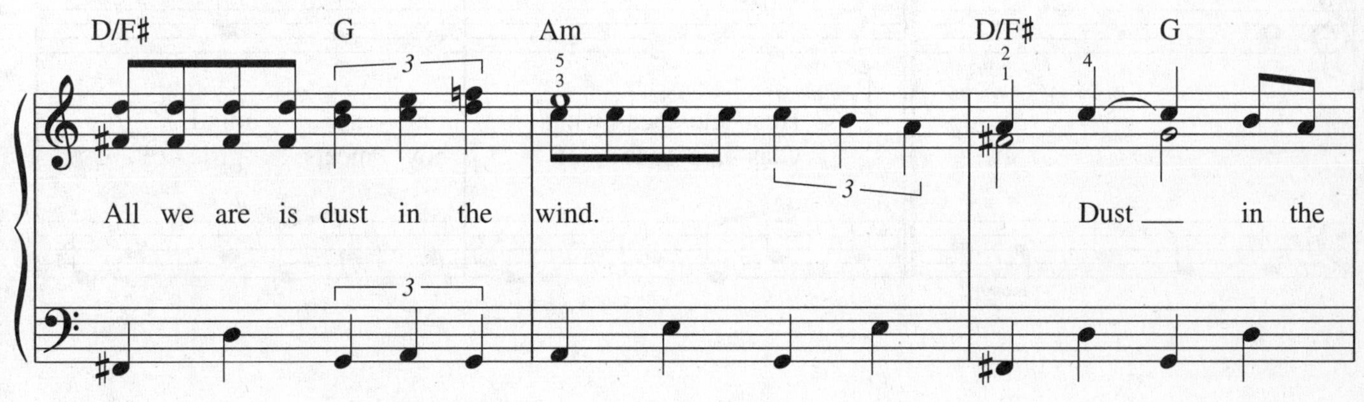
D/F#
G
Am
D/F#
G
All we are is dust in the wind.
Dust ___ in the

Am
D/F#
G
Am
wind.
Ev - 'ry-thing is dust in the wind.
rit.

EVERY HEARTBEAT

Words and Music by AMY GRANT,
WAYNE KIRKPATRICK and CHARLIE PEACOCK

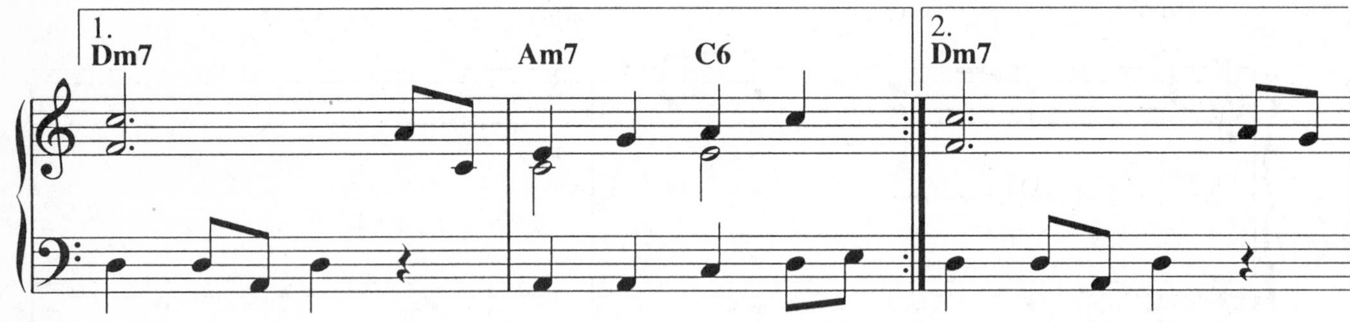

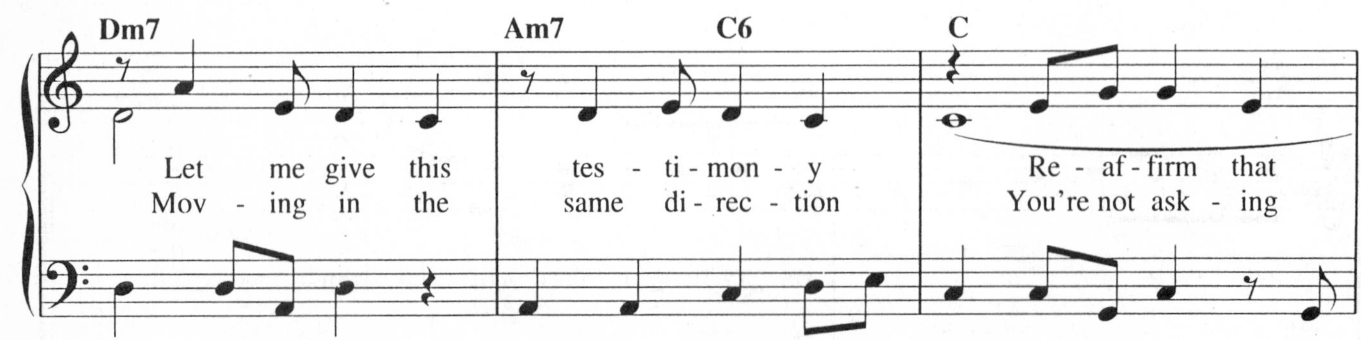

Dm7
Am7
C6
you will find that you are my one and on - ly.
for the world, I'm not ask - ing for per - fec - tion.
Dm7
B♭maj7
No ex - cep - tion to this rule. I'm sim - ple but
Just a love that's well de - signed. For pass - ing the
Dm7
3
I'm no fool. I've got a wit - ness hap - py to say,
test of time. I'm here to tell you I'm here to stay
C
C/B♭
Am7
C/G
Am7
G/F
ev - er - y ho - ur, ev - er - y day. Ev - ery heart - beat

Em7
F
C
G
Am7
F
bears your name.
Loud and clear they
stake my claim.
C
G/F
Em7
F
C/E
To Coda
1.,3. My red blood_ runs true_ blue
2. Ask an - y - one and they'll tell you it's true
and ev - er - y ___ heart - beat be-
1.
F
Gsus
N.C.
3
longs to you.
2.
F
Gsus
D.S. al Coda
longs to you.

CODA
F
Gsus
Gm
longs to you.
Woo.

D/F#
Gm
C
Ooh. Ah.

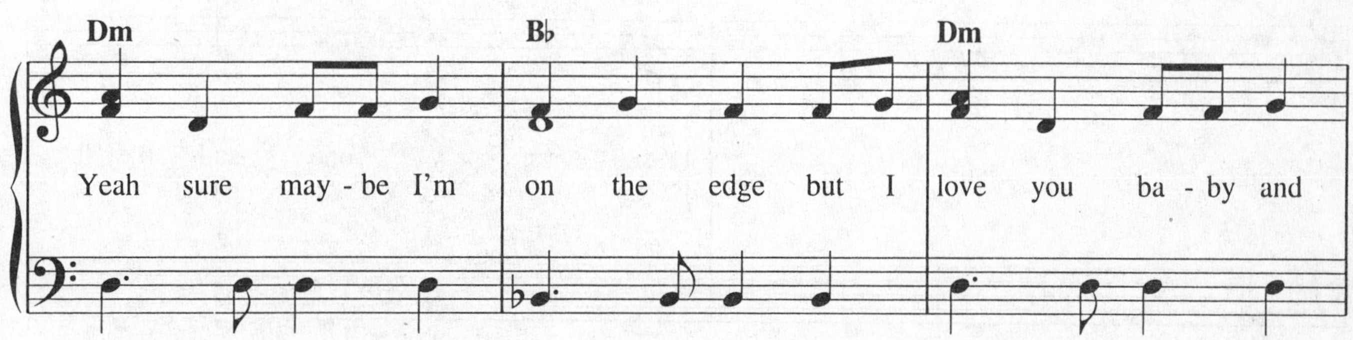
Dm
B♭
Dm
Yeah sure may - be I'm
on the edge but I
love you ba - by and

B♭
C
B♭maj7
3
like I said,
I'm here to tell you,
I'm here to stay,
3

Am7
Gsus
ev - er - y ho - ur ev - er - y day.
Am7 G/F Em7 F C G
Ev - er - y heart - beat bears your name. Loud and clear they
Am7 F C G/F
stake my claim.
Ask an - y one and they'll
My red blood
Repeat and Fade
Em7 F C/E F Gsus
tell you its true that
runs the blue.
Ev - er - y heart - beat be - longs to you.

GOOD VIBRATIONS

Words and Music by BRIAN WILSON
and MIKE LOVE

Moderately

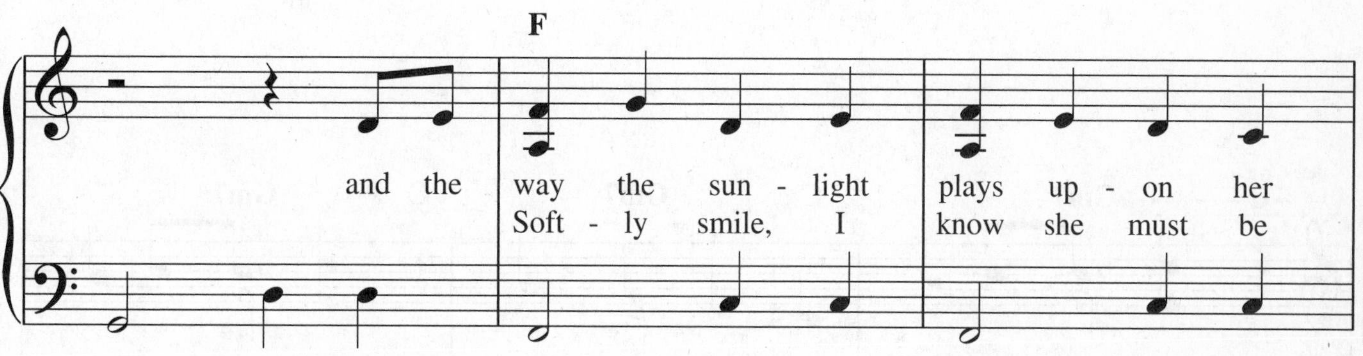

G
F
gen - tle word,
on the wind that lifts her
in her eyes,
she goes with me to a

E7
G7
per - fume through the air.
blos - som world.
4

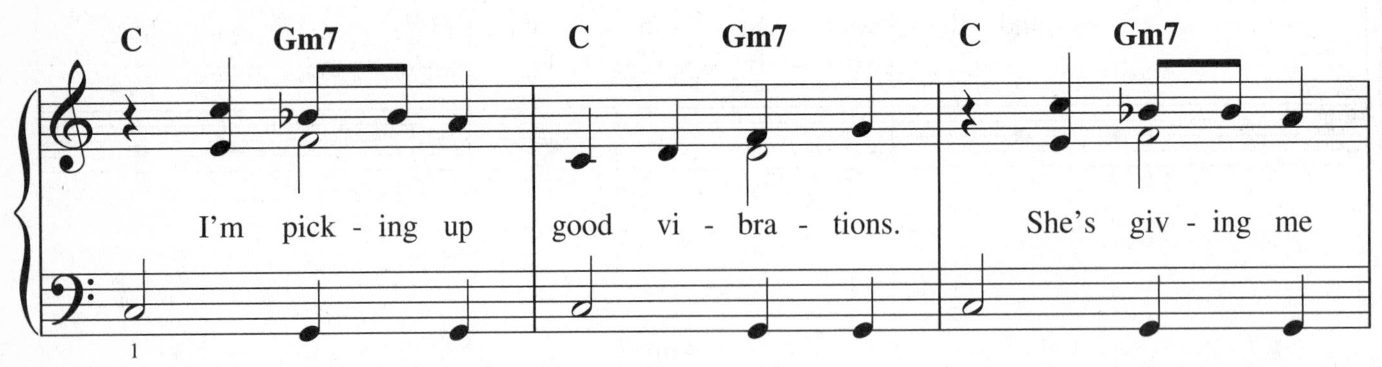
C Gm7 C Gm7 C Gm7
I'm pick - ing up good vi - bra - tions. She's giv - ing me
1

C Gm7 C Gm7 C Gm7
ex - ci - ta - tions. I'm pick - ing up good vi - bra - tions.

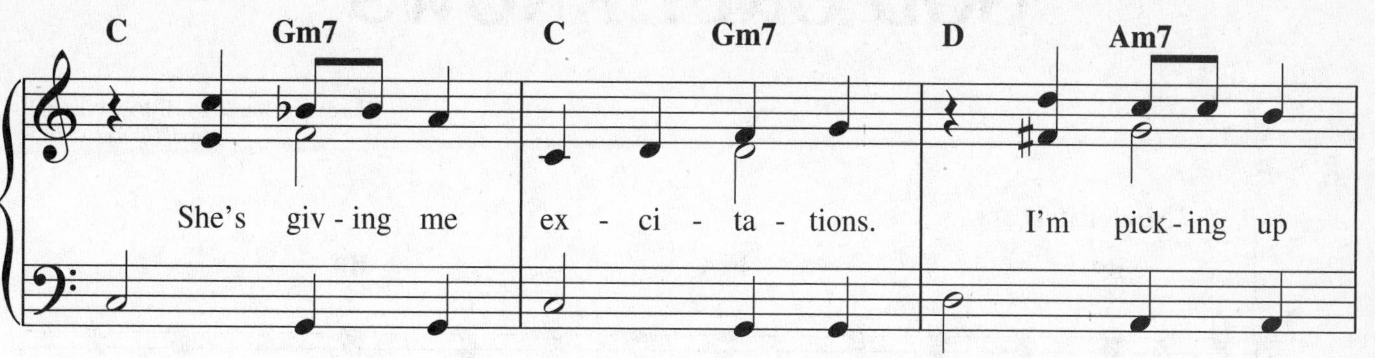
C
Gm7
C
Gm7
D
Am7
She's giv - ing me
ex - ci - ta - tions.
I'm pick - ing up

D
Am7
D
Am7
D
Am7
good vi - bra - tions.
She's giv - ing me
ex - ci - ta - tions.

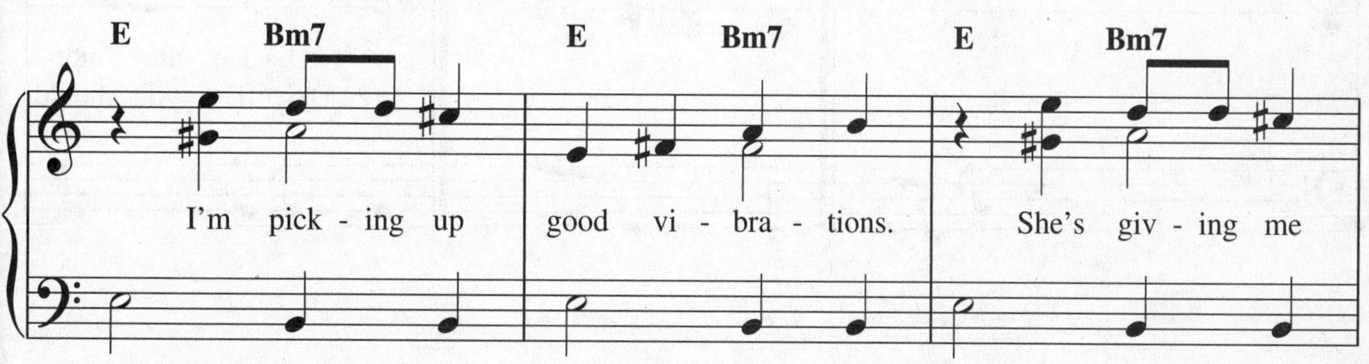
E
Bm7
E
Bm7
E
Bm7
I'm pick - ing up
good vi - bra - tions.
She's giv - ing me

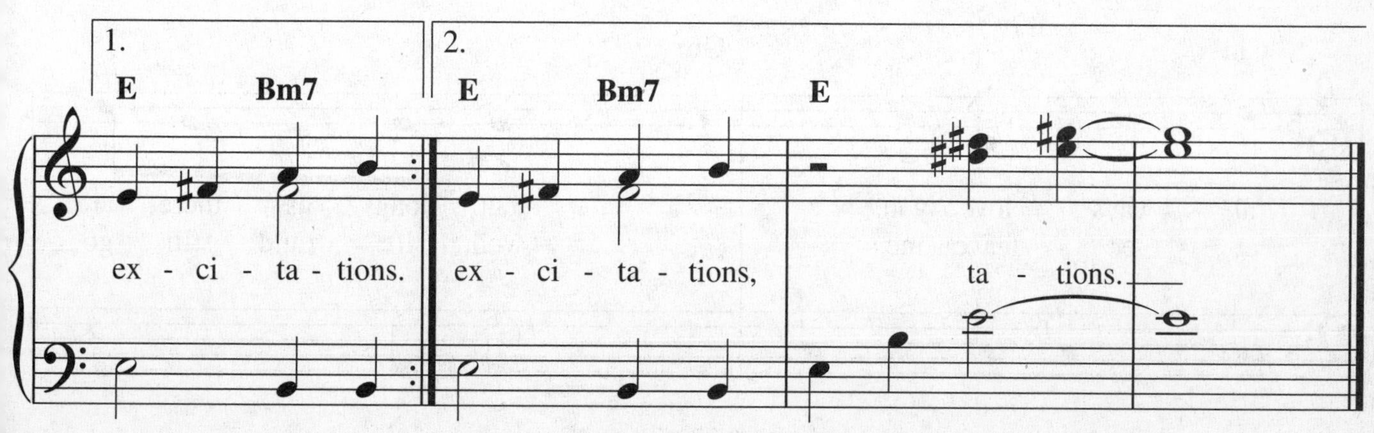
1.
2.
E
Bm7
E
Bm7
E
ex - ci - ta - tions.
ex - ci - ta - tions,
ta - tions.

GOD ONLY KNOWS

Words and Music by BRIAN WILSON
and TONY ASHER

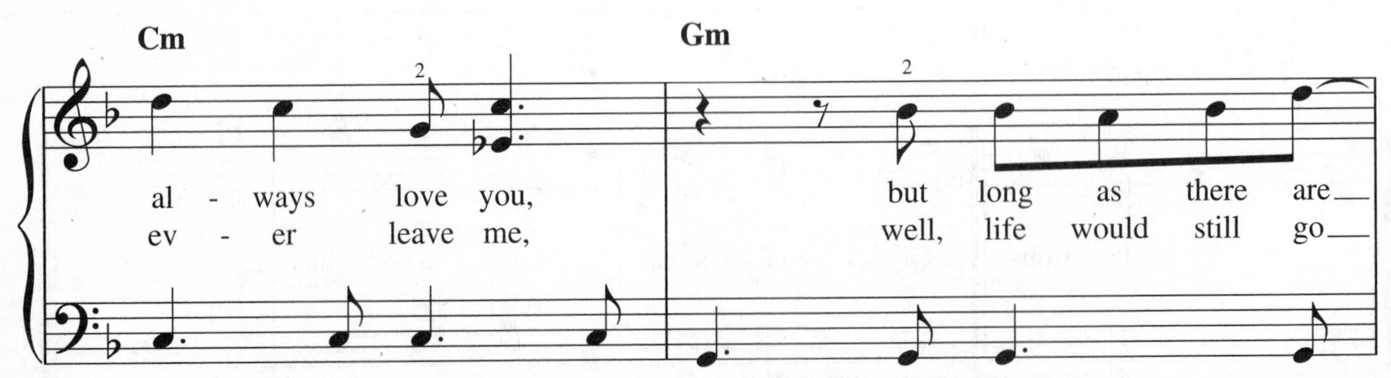

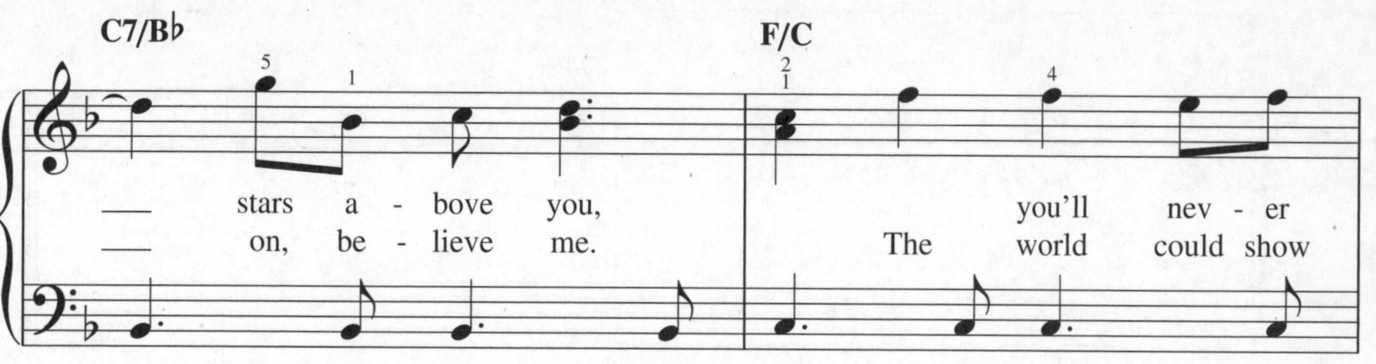
C7/B♭
F/C
stars a - bove you,
on, be - lieve me.
you'll nev - er
The world could show

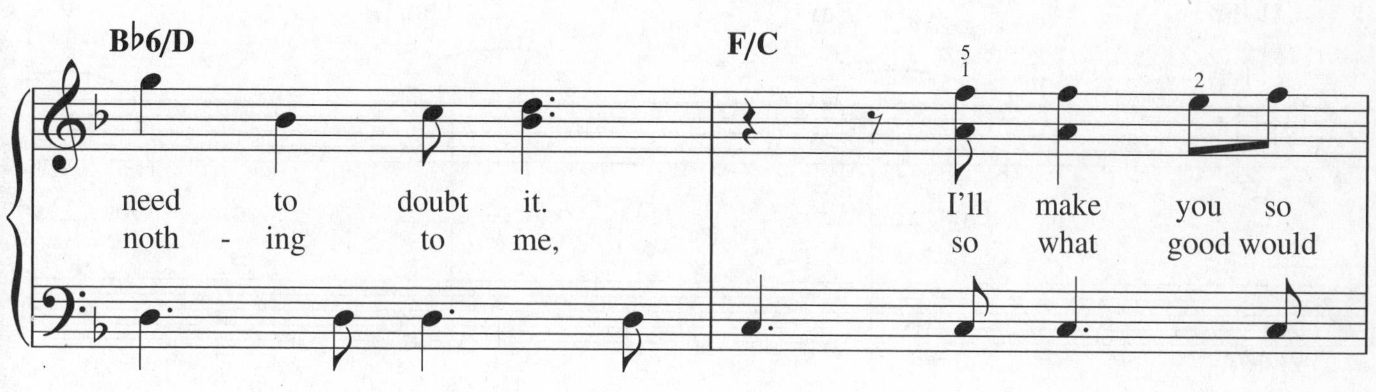
B♭6/D
F/C
need to doubt it.
noth - ing to me,
I'll make you so
so what good would

G9
B♭
sure a - bout it.
liv - ing do me?
God on - ly

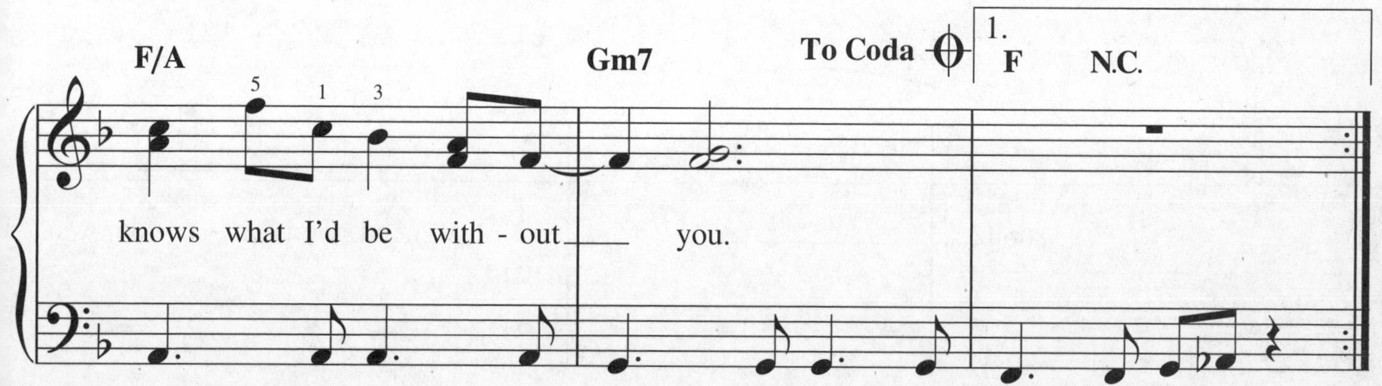
F/A
Gm7
To Coda
1.
F
N.C.
knows what I'd be with - out you.

2.
N.C.
Ab
Ab/Eb
Fm
Cm/G
Ooh,
ooh.
Ooh,
F/Eb
Bb/F
Adim/F#
ooh.
Ooh,
ooh,
Bb/F
Em7b5
Eb
ooh.
And God on - ly knows

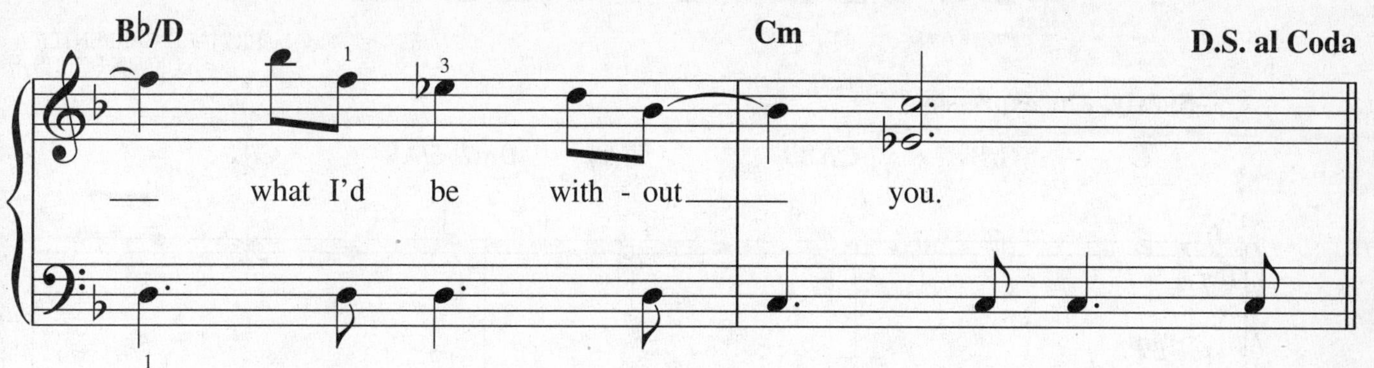
B♭/D
Cm
D.S. al Coda
what I'd be with - out you.

CODA
F/A
B♭
F/A
God on - ly knows what I'd be with - out

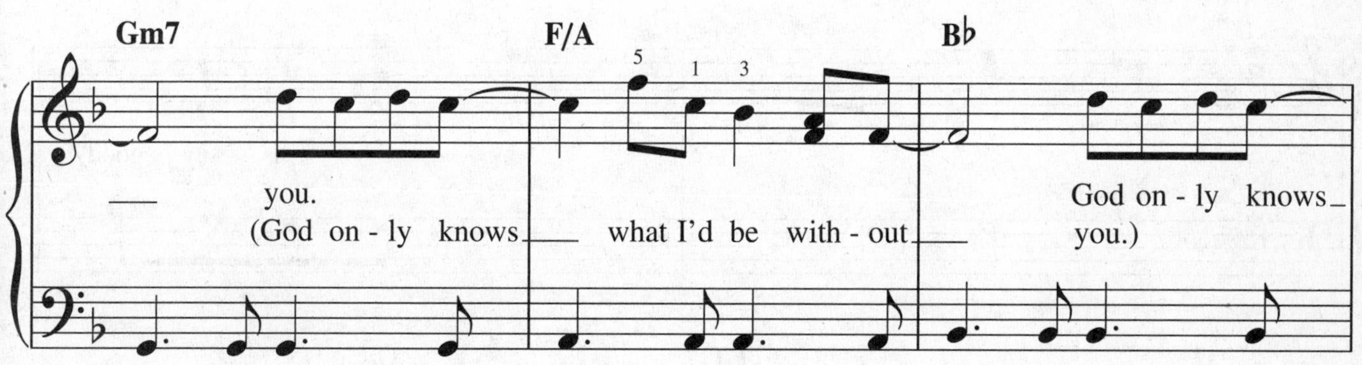
Gm7
F/A
B♭
you.
(God on - ly knows what I'd be with - out you.)
God on - ly knows

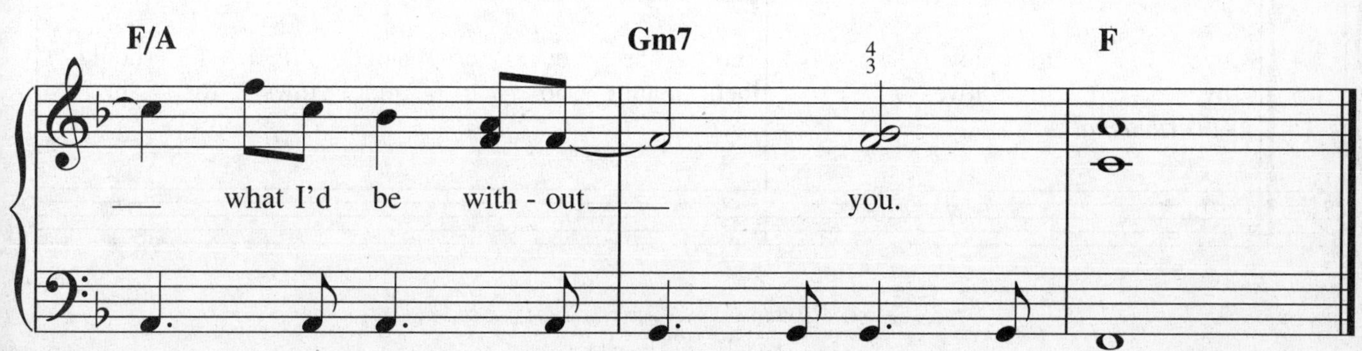
F/A
Gm7
F
what I'd be with - out you.

GOODBYE TO LOVE

Words and Music by RICHARD CARPENTER
and JOHN BETTIS

C
G/C
Csus
G/C
live or die, time and time a - gain the chance for
heart of mine, sure - ly time will lose these bit - ter

E
Am
F♯m7♭5
C/G
Dm7/G
love has passed me by and all I know of love is how to live with -
mem - 'ries and I'll find that there is some - one to be - lieve in and to

Em7/G
E/G♯
Am
F♯m7♭5
out it. I just can't seem to find it.
live for, some - thing I could live for.
(End instrumental)

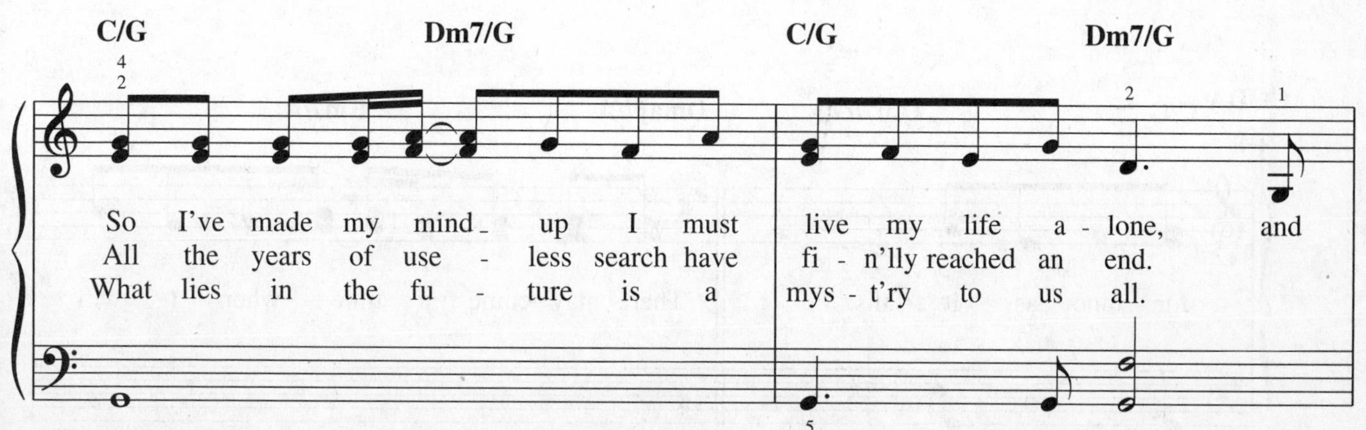
C/G
Dm7/G
C/G
Dm7/G
So I've made my mind up I must live my life a - lone, and
All the years of use - less search have fi - n'lly reached an end.
What lies in the fu - ture is a mys - t'ry to us all.

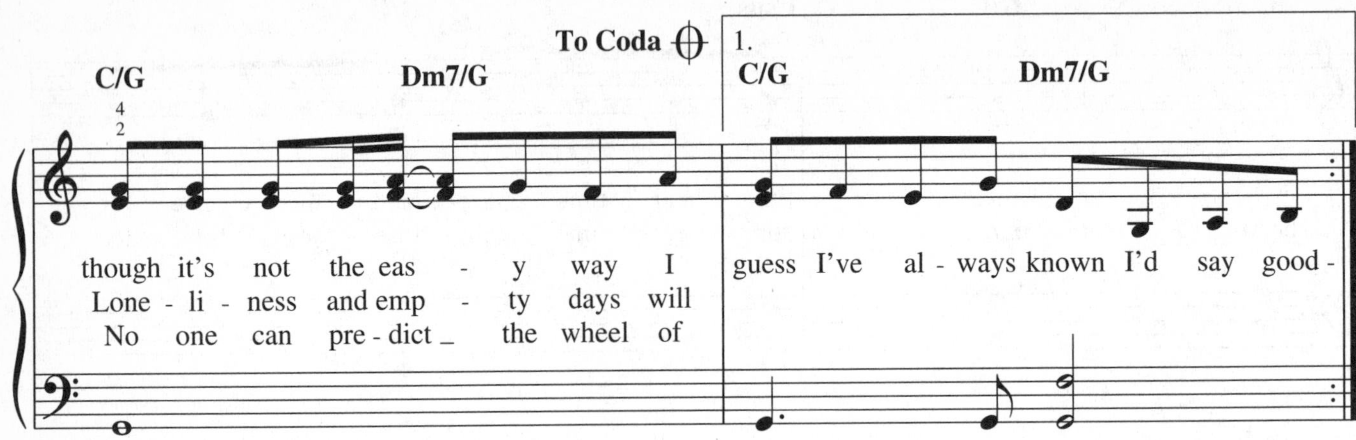
To Coda
1.
C/G
Dm7/G
C/G
Dm7/G
though it's not the eas - y way I
Lone - li - ness and emp - ty days will
No one can pre - dict _ the wheel of
guess I've al - ways known I'd say good -

2.
C/G
Dm7/G
Em7
A7
be my on - ly friend. From this
day love is for - got - ten, I'll go

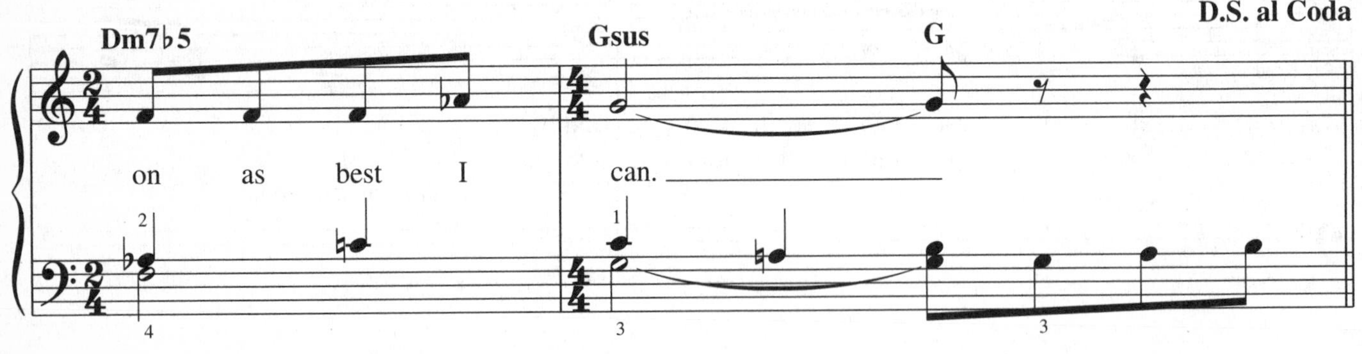
D.S. al Coda
Dm7♭5
Gsus
G
on as best I
can. _

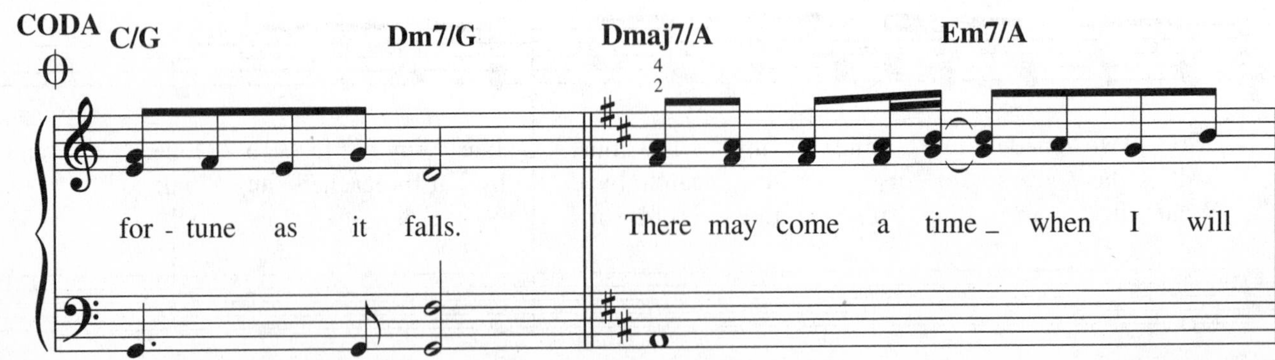
CODA
C/G
Dm7/G
Dmaj7/A
Em7/A
for - tune as it falls.
There may come a time _ when I will

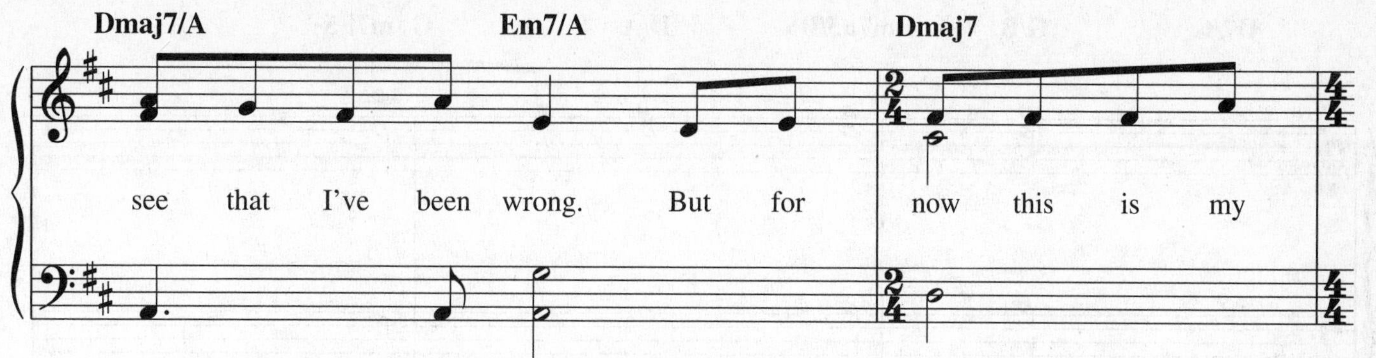
Dmaj7/A
Em7/A
Dmaj7
see that I've been wrong. But for now this is my

Em7
A7
D
song. And it's good - bye to love.

G/A
D
I'll say good - bye to love.

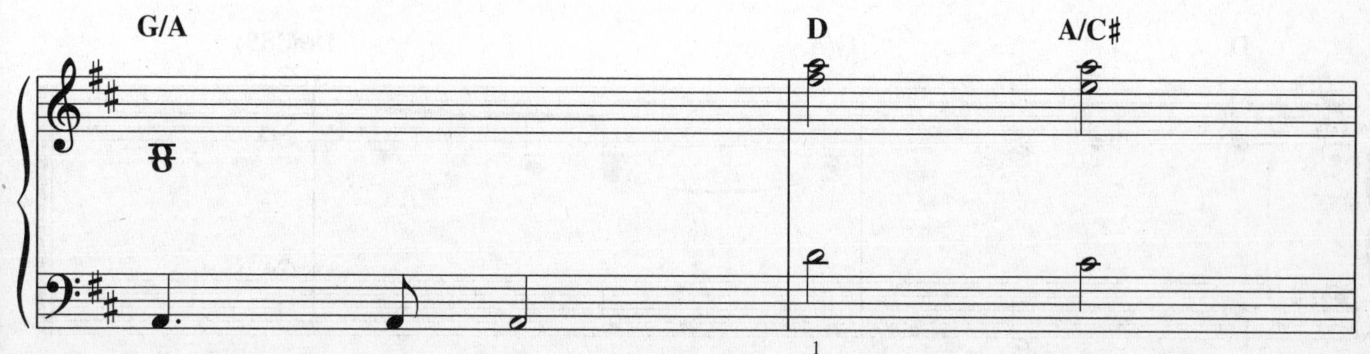
G/A
D
A/C♯
1

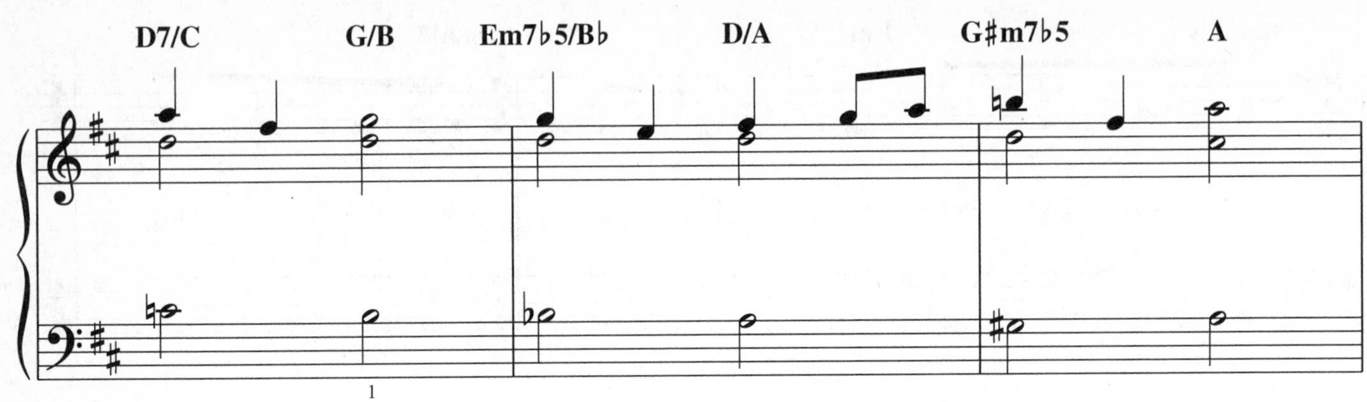
D7/C
G/B
Em7♭5/B♭
D/A
G♯m7♭5
A
1

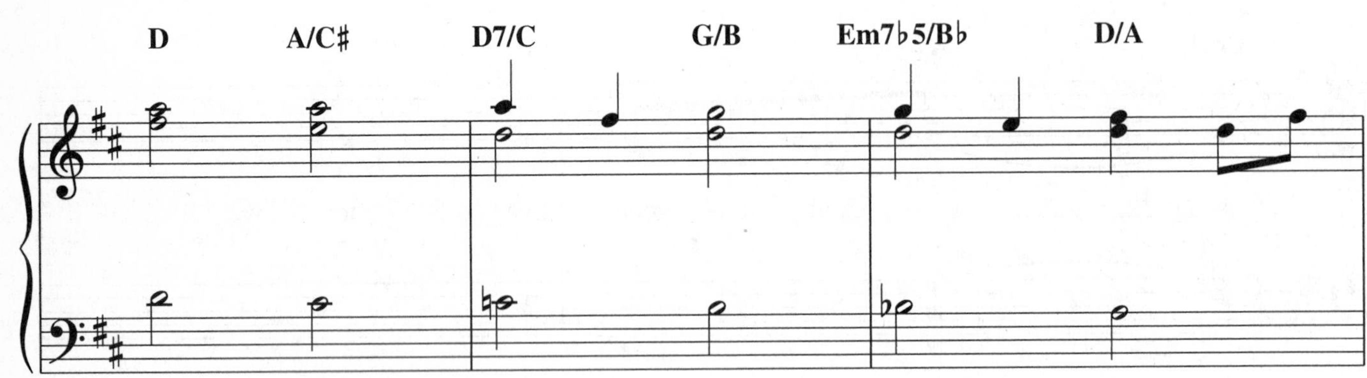
D
A/C♯
D7/C
G/B
Em7♭5/B♭
D/A

G♯m7♭5
A
D
G/A

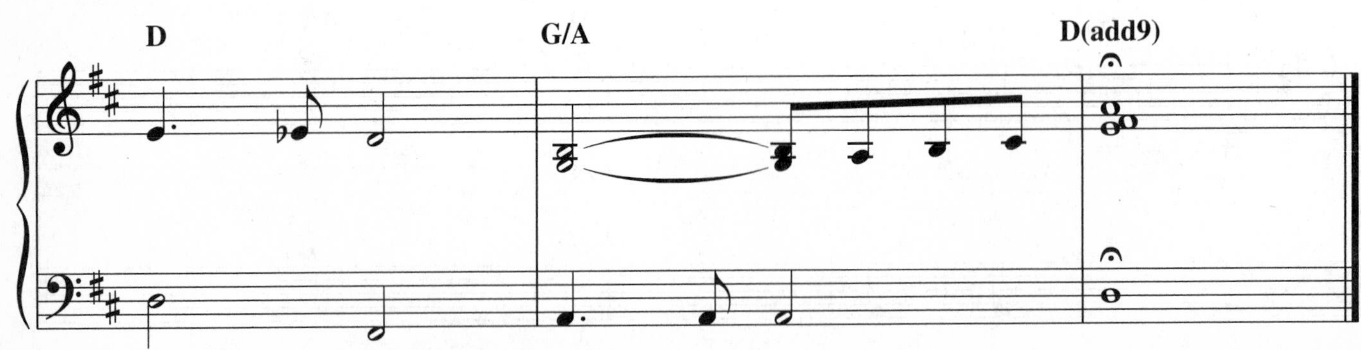
D
G/A
D(add9)

THE GREAT PRETENDER

Words and Music by
BUCK RAM

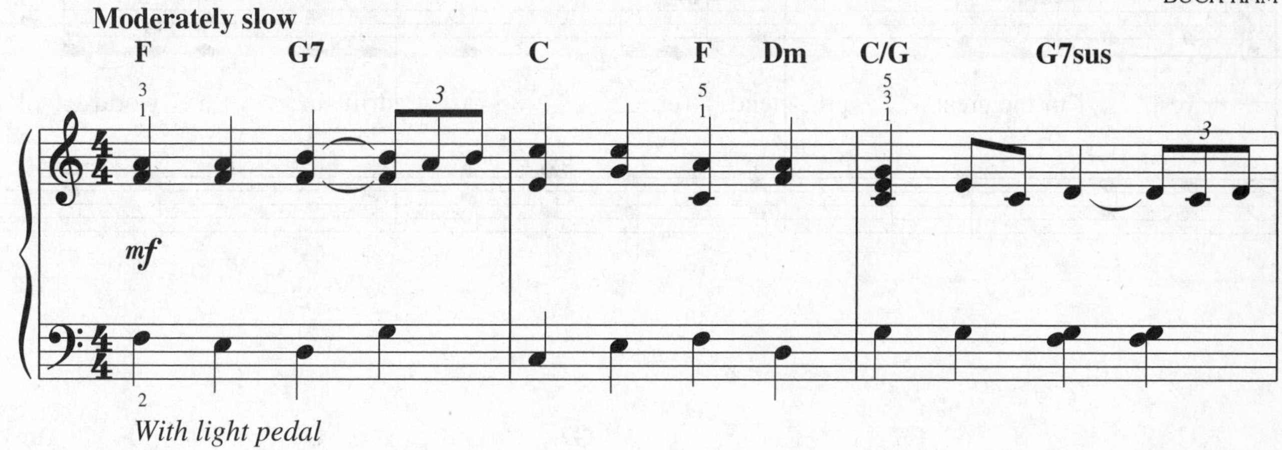

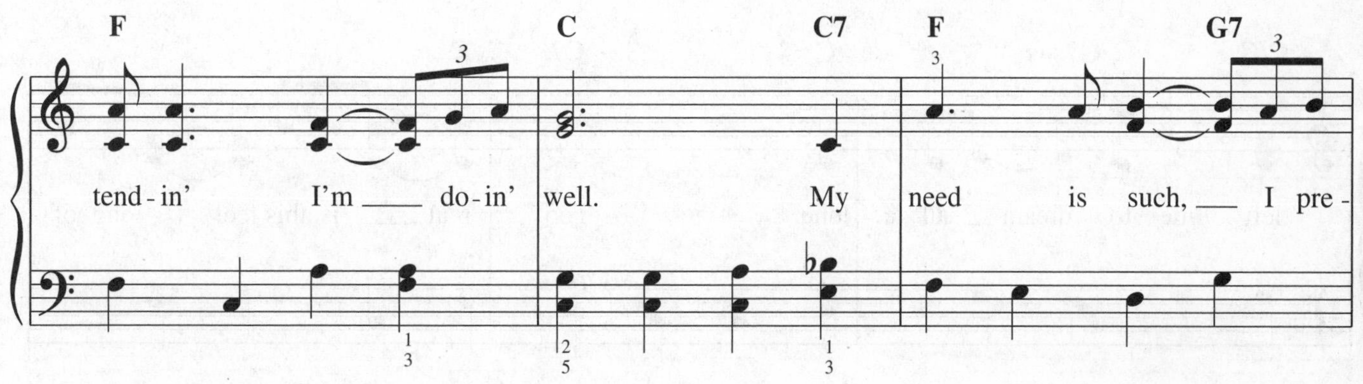

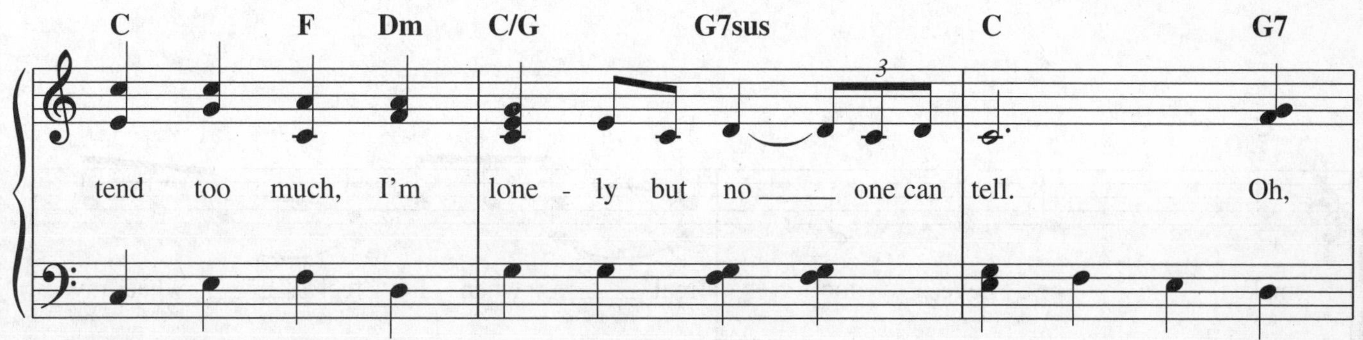

C
F
Dm/G
C
C7
F
3
yes, ___ I'm the great
pre - tend - er, ___
a - drift in
a
world ___ of my

C
C7
F
G7
C
F
Dm
own.
I
play
the
game ___ but, to
my
real
shame, you've

C/G
G7sus
C
C7
F
left
me
to
dream ___ all
a - lone.
Too
real ___ is this feel - ing of

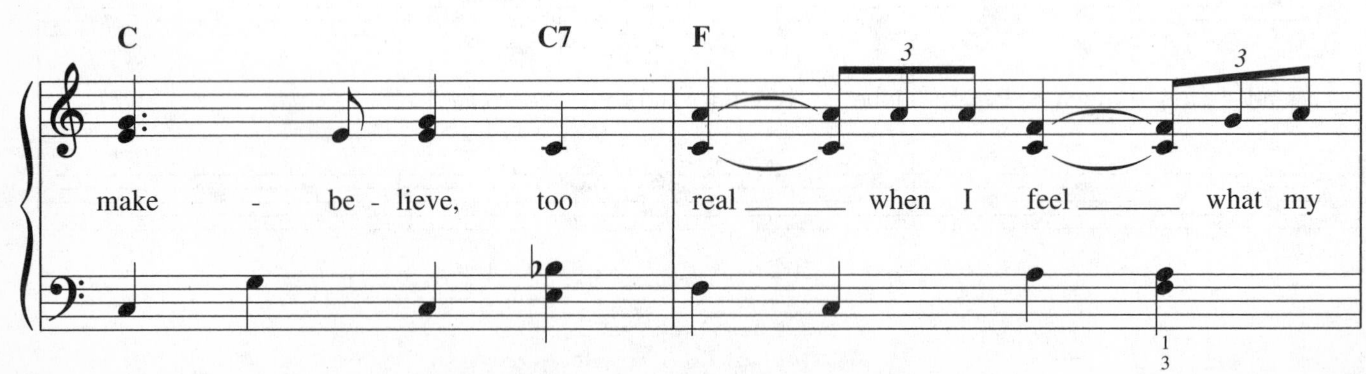
C
C7
F
make - be - lieve,
too
real ______ when I
feel ______ what my

C/G G7 C F Dm/G C C7
heart __ can't con-ceal. Oh, __ yes, __ I'm the great pre - tend - er, __ just

F C C7 F G7
laugh - in' and gay __ like a clown. I seem to be __ what I'm

C F Dm C/G Dm E G7
not, you see, I'm wear-in' my heart __ like a crown; pre -

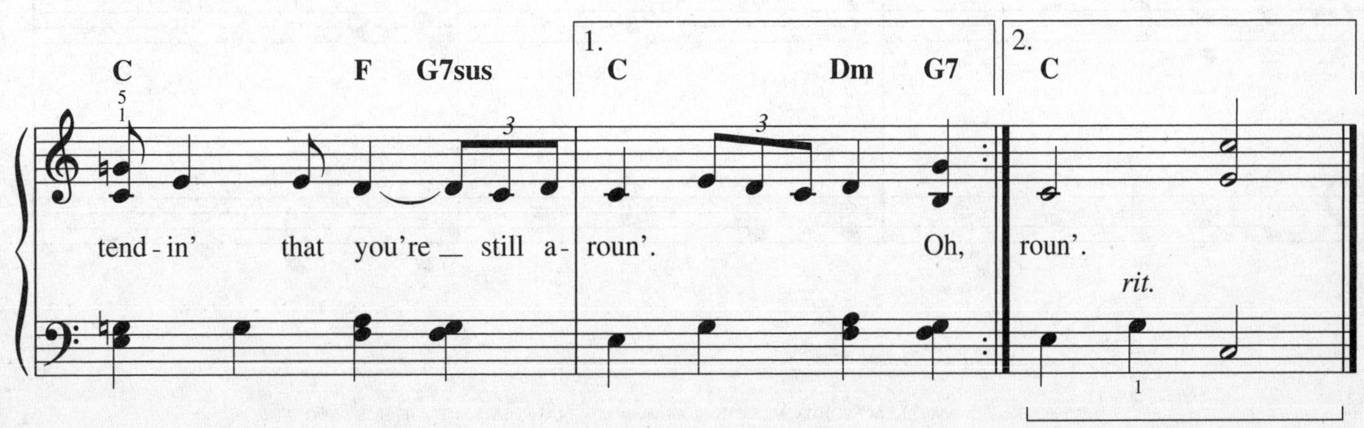
C F G7sus 1. C Dm G7 2. C
tend-in' that you're __ still a- roun'. Oh, roun'.
rit.

GREEN ONIONS

Written by AL JACKSON, JR.,
LEWIS STEINBERG, BOOKER T. JONES
and STEVE CROPPER

Am

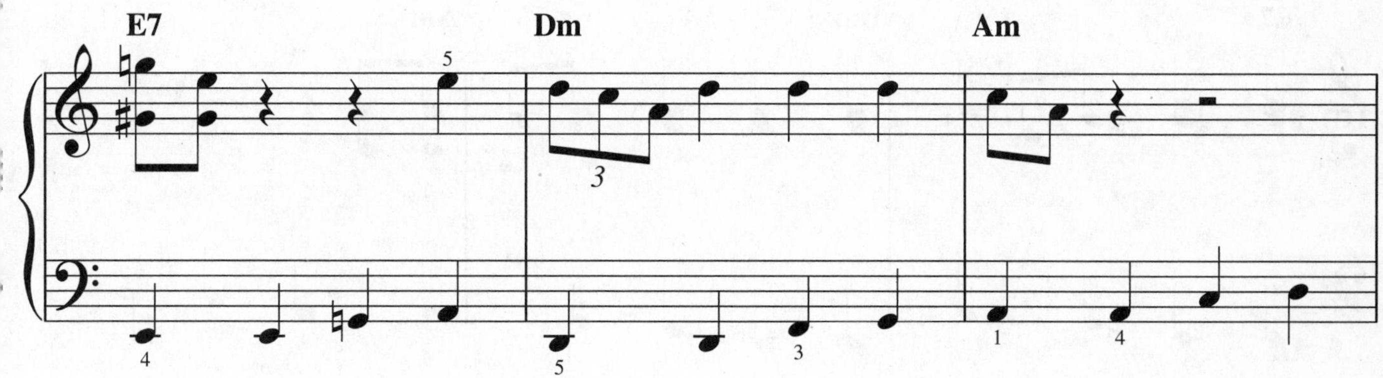
E7
Dm
Am

To Coda

Dm

Am

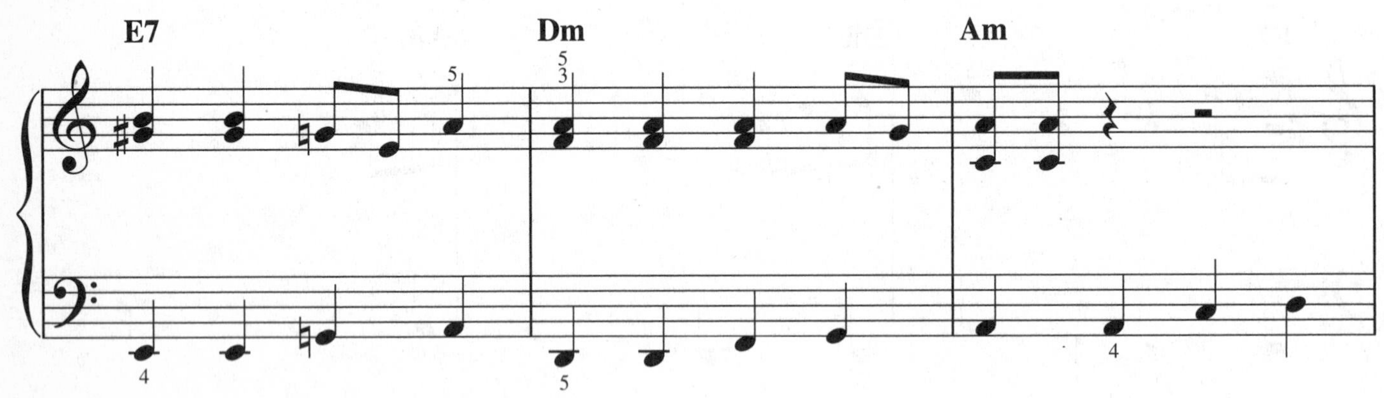
E7
Dm
Am

Am

Dm

Am
5
5
4

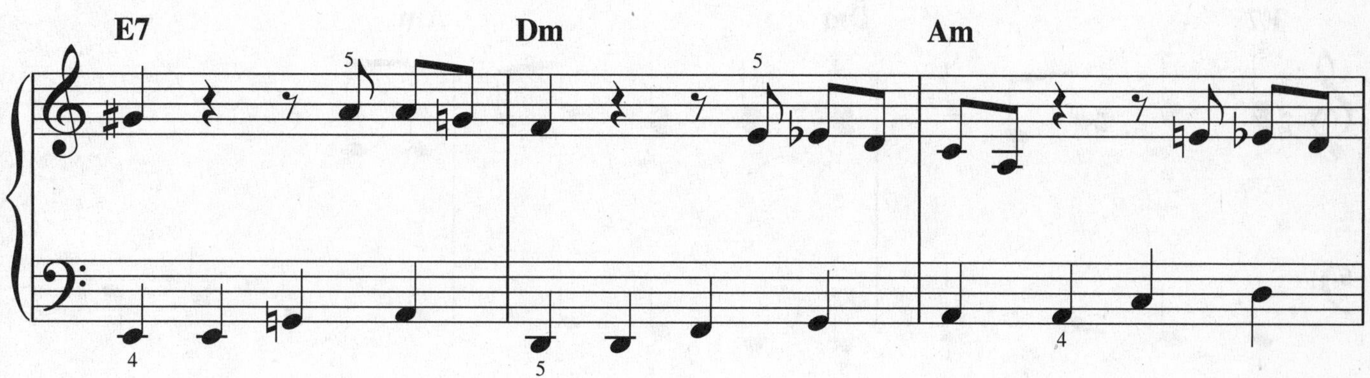
E7
Dm
Am
5
5
4
5
4

1
3

Dm
3
1

Am
5
1

E7
Dm
Am
4
2
5
4
5
4

D.S. al Coda
1
4

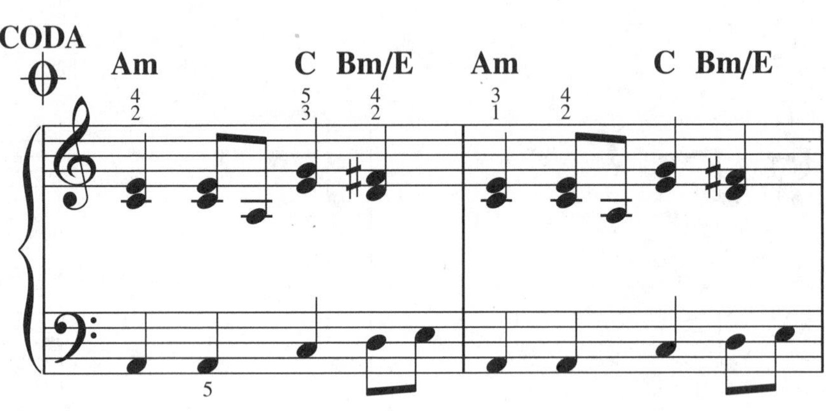
CODA
Am
C
Bm/E
Am
C
Bm/E
4
2
5
3
4
2
3
1
4
2
5

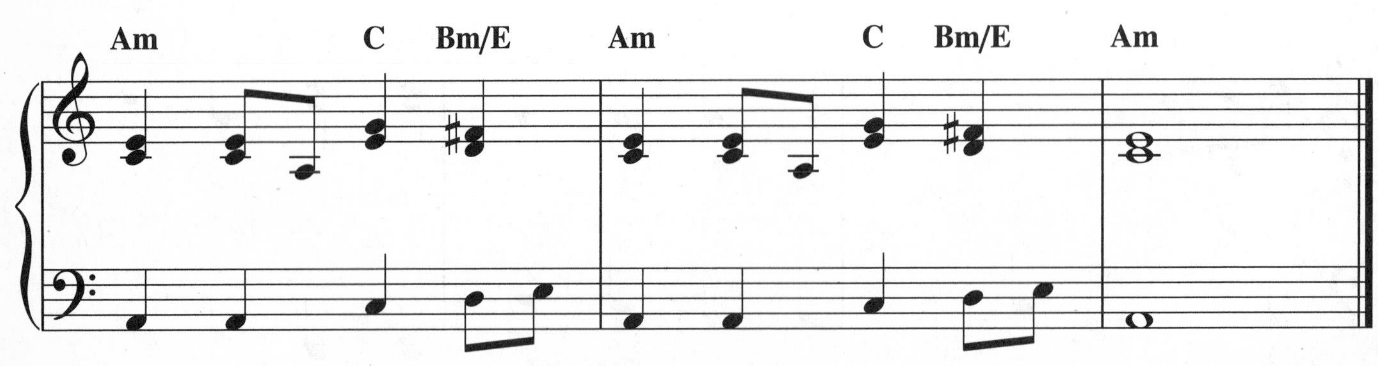
Am
C
Bm/E
Am
C
Bm/E
Am

I DON'T WANT TO WAIT

Words and Music by
PAULA COLE

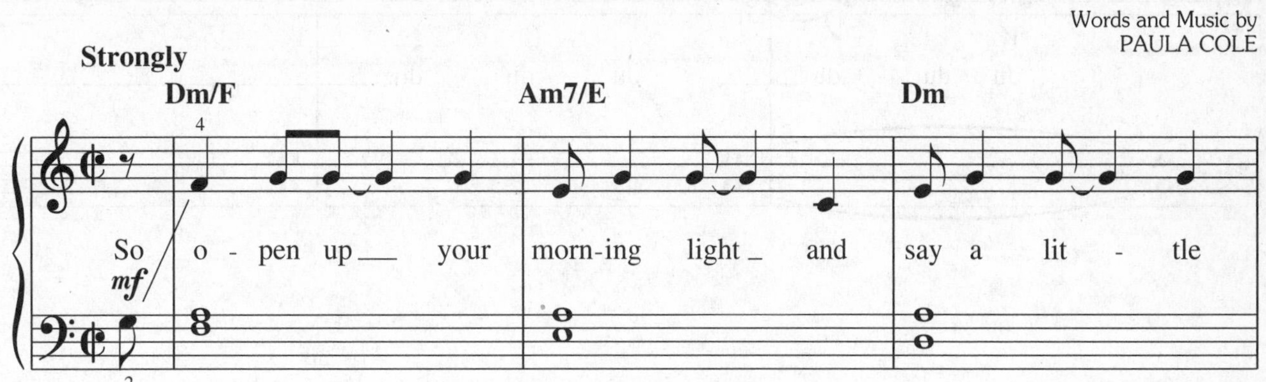

C
du du du du du du.

G
She had two ba - bies, one was six
He showed up all wet on the rain -

C6
months, one was three, in the war of for - ty four.
- y front step wear - ing shrap - nel in his skin.

G
5
2
Ev - 'ry tel - e-phone ring, ev - 'ry heart -
And the war he saw lives in - side

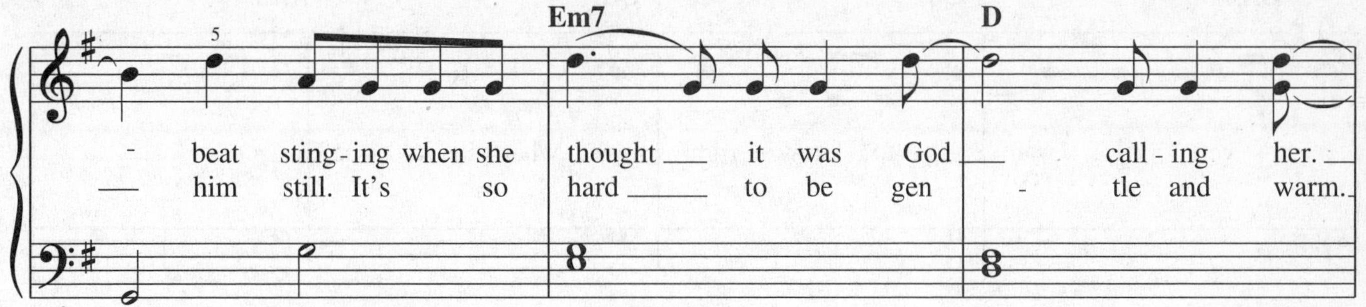
Em7
D
5
- beat sting - ing when she thought it was God call - ing her.
him still. It's so hard to be gen - tle and warm.

C
Em
D
4
Oh, would her son grow to know his fa -
The years pass by, and now he has grand -

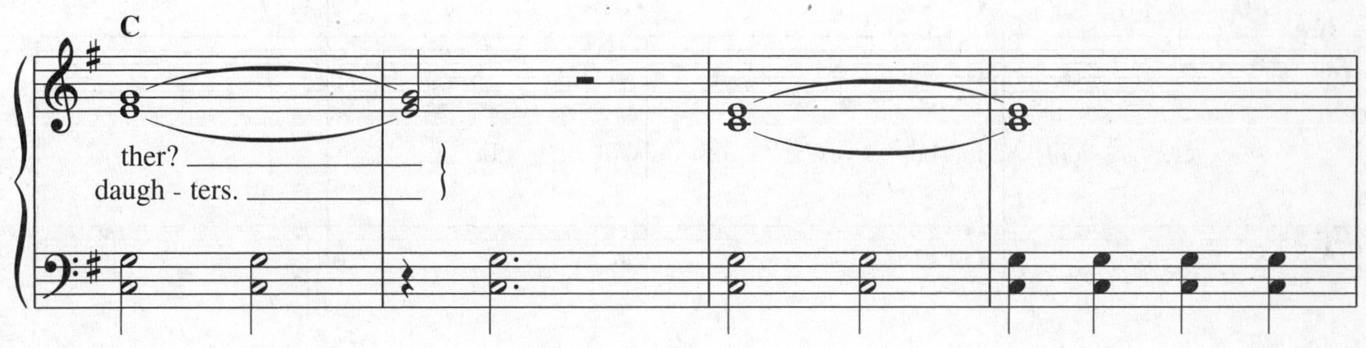
C
ther?
daugh - ters.

G
G/F#
Em
2
I don't want to wait for our lives to be o -

G/D
C
G/B
Am7
5
- ver. I want to know right now, what will it be?

Dsus
G
G/F♯
Em
2
I don't want to wait for our lives to be o -

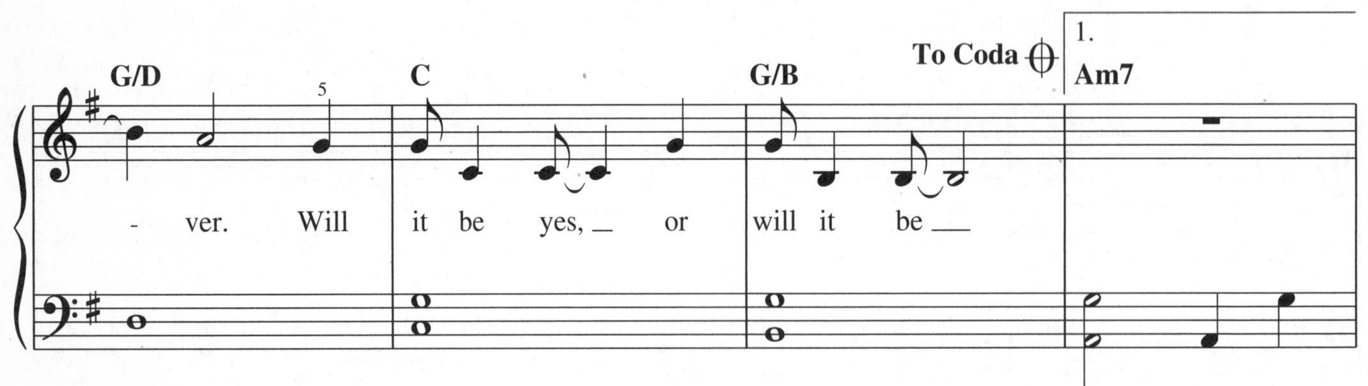
G/D
C
G/B
To Coda
1.
Am7
5
- ver. Will it be yes, or will it be

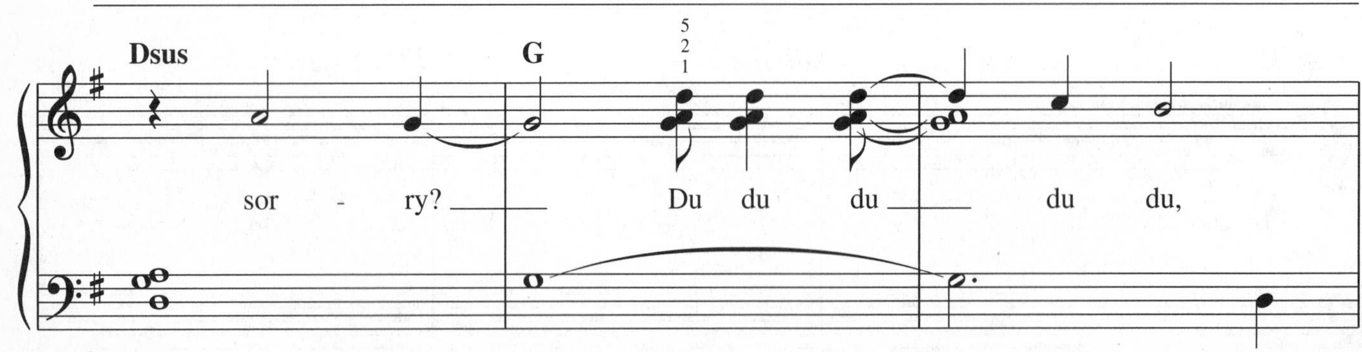
Dsus
G
5
2
1
sor - ry? Du du du du du,

C
du du du du du, du du du

2.
Am7
du du du.

G7(add4)
Oh, so you look at me from a - cross

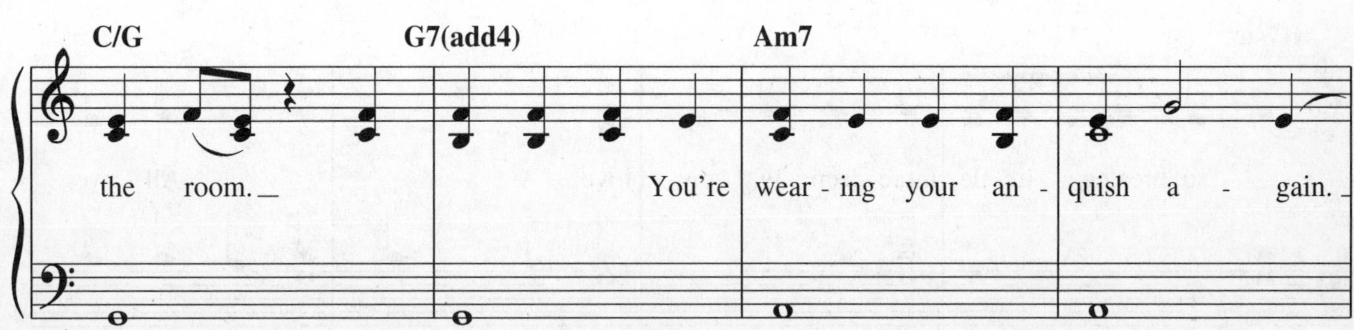
C/G
G7(add4)
Am7
the room. You're wear - ing your an - quish a - gain.

B♭
3
Be - lieve me, I know the feel -

Fsus
- ing; it sucks you in - to the jaws of an -

C
ger.
Oh,

G7sus
so breathe a lit - tle more deep - ly, my love.
All we

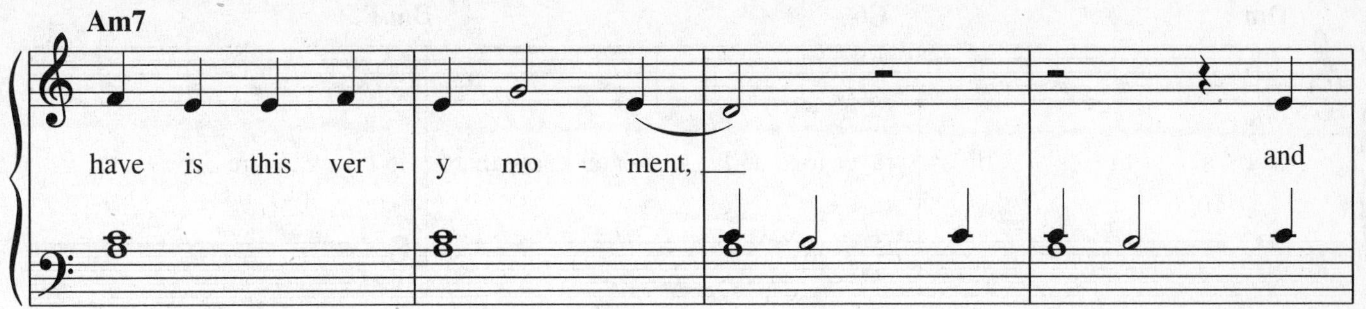
Am7
have is this ver - y mo - ment,
and

B♭(add2)
Fsus
I don't want to do what his fa - ther and his fa - ther and his fa - ther did. I

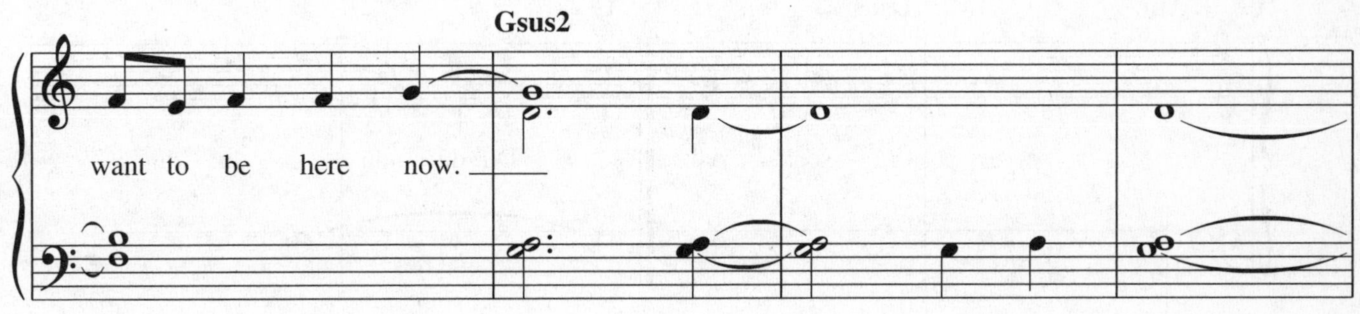
Gsus2
want to be here now.

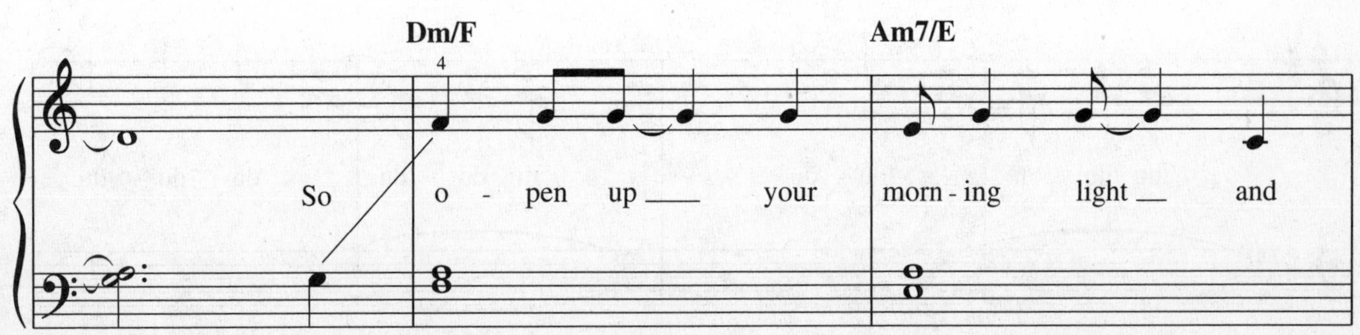
Dm/F
Am7/E
4
So o - pen up your morn - ing light and

Dm
C6
Dm/F
say a lit - tle prayer for I. You know that if we are to

Am7/E
Dm7
C6
D.S. al Coda
stay a - live, then see the peace in ev - 'ry eye.

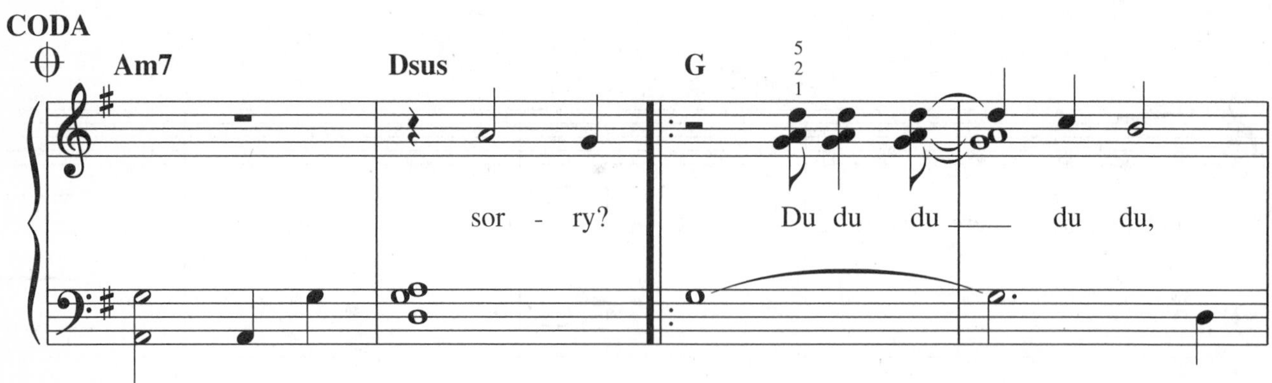
CODA
Am7
Dsus
G
sor - ry? Du du du du du,

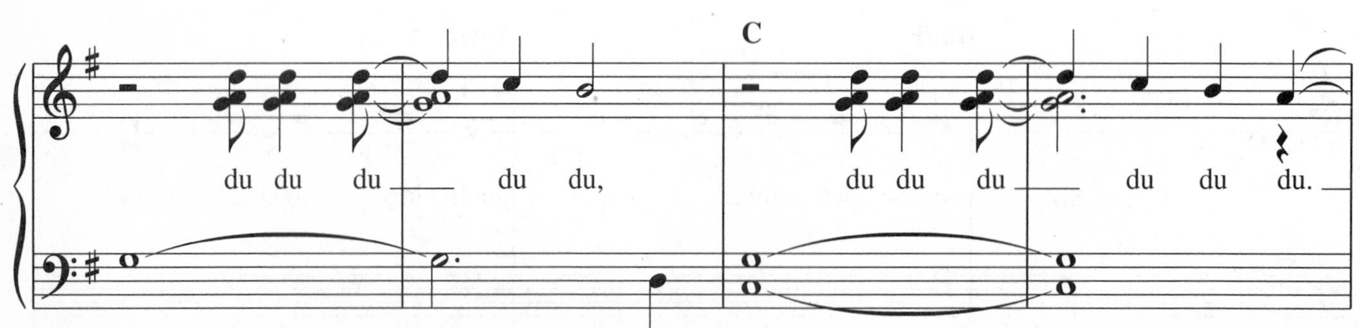
C
du du du du du, du du du du du du.

1.
2.
So

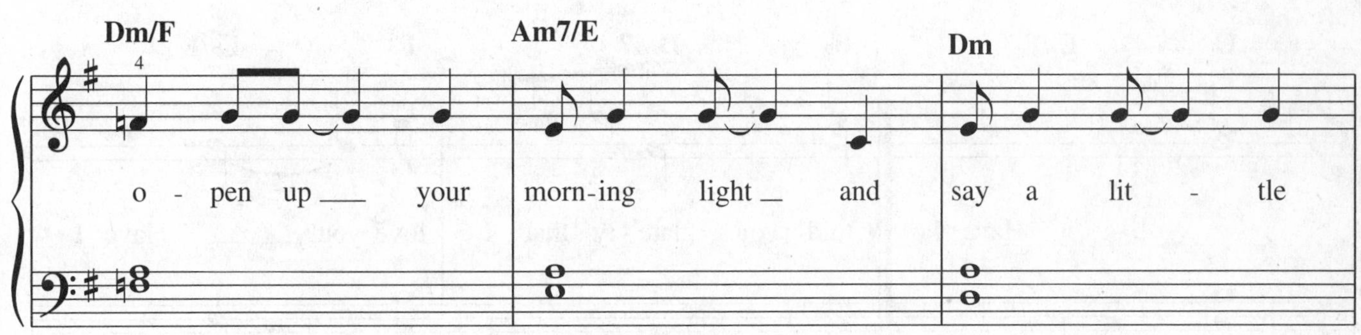
Dm/F
Am7/E
Dm
4
o - pen up ___ your morn-ing light ___ and say a lit - tle

C6
Dm/F
Am7/E
prayer for I. ___ You know that if we are ___ to stay a - live, ___ then

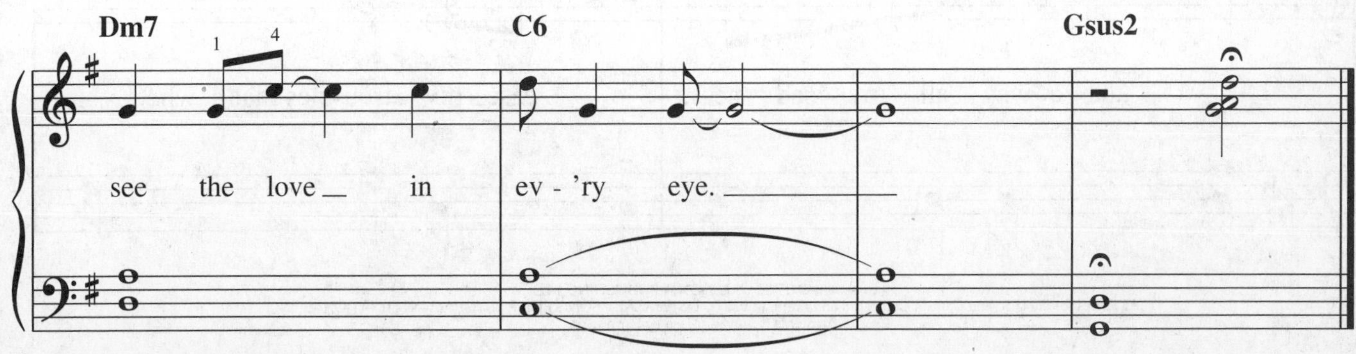
Dm7
C6
Gsus2
1 4
see the love ___ in ev - 'ry eye. ___

HAVE I TOLD YOU LATELY

Words and Music by
VAN MORRISON

B♭ E♭/F B♭ Dm7 E♭ E♭/F
do. 1. For the morn - in' sun in all its glo - ry greets the
2. Instrumental solo
B♭ Dm7 E♭ E♭/F E♭maj7
day with hope and com-fort, too. You fill my life with laugh-ter
Dm7 Cm7 E♭/F
and some-how you make it bet - ter, ease my trou-bles that's what you
B♭ Cm7 B♭/D E♭maj7
do. There's a love that's di-vine and it's yours and it's mine
Solo ends

Dm7
Cm7 Dm7 E♭maj7
___ like the sun.
And at the end of the day
we should give thanks and pray
Dm7
to the one, ___
1.
E♭/F
to the one. _ Have I
2.
E♭/F
to the one. _ And have I
B♭
Dm7
told you late-ly that I
E♭
E♭/F
love you? Have I
B♭
Dm7
told you there's no one else a - bove you? ______
E♭
E♭/F

E♭maj7
Dm7
Cm7
E♭/F
You fill my heart with glad-ness, take a-way my sad-ness, ease my trou-bles that's what you
B♭
Cm7
B♭/D
E♭maj7
Dm7
do. Take a-way all my sad-ness, fill my life with glad-ness,
Cm7
E♭/F
B♭
Cm7
B♭/D
E♭maj7
ease my trou-bles that's what you do. Take a-way all my sad-ness,
Dm7
Cm7
E♭/F
B♭
fill my heart with glad-ness, ease my trou-bles that's what you do.

HERO

Words and Music by MARIAH CAREY
and WALTER AFANASIEFF

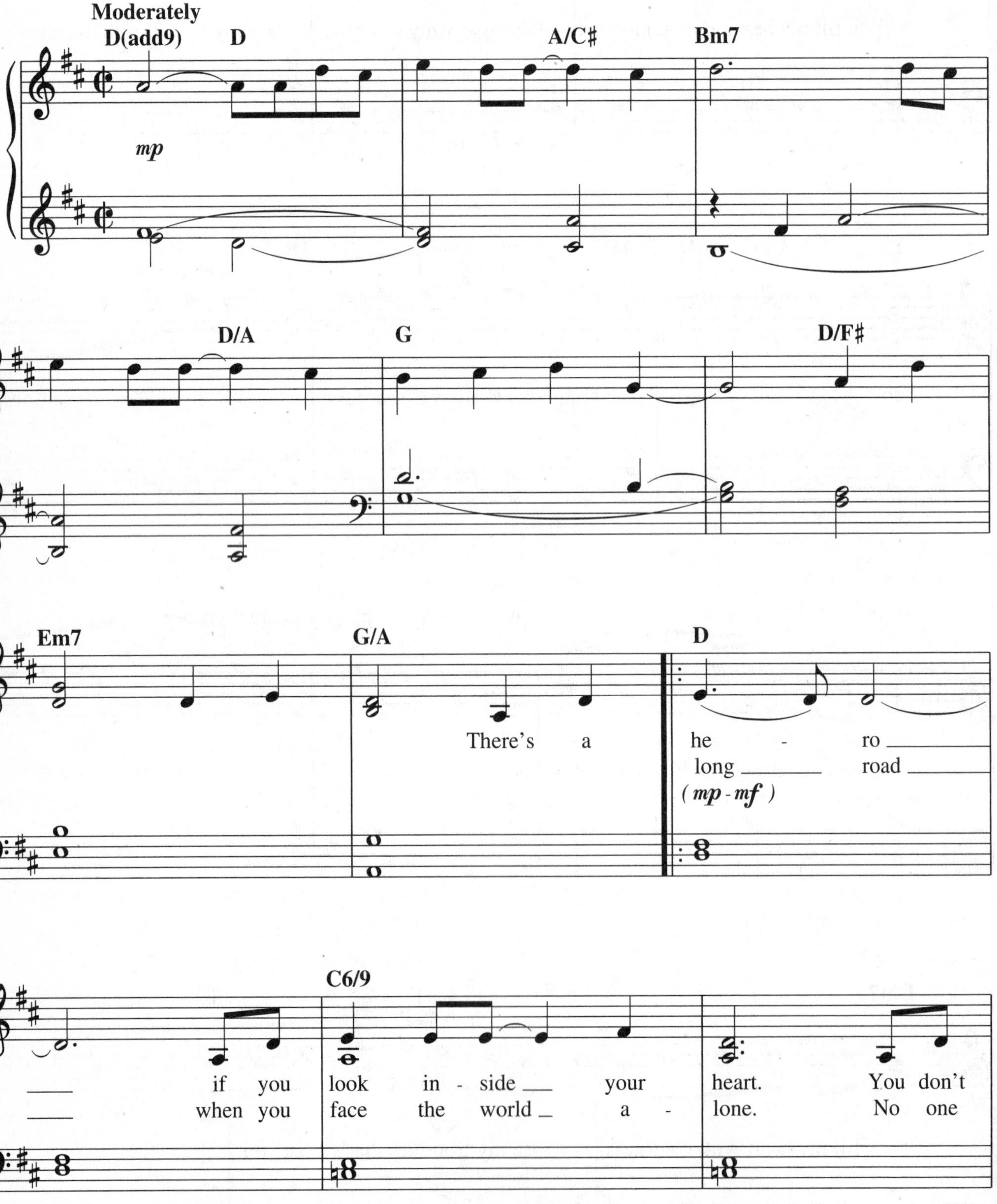
Moderately
D(add9)
D
A/C♯
Bm7
mp
D/A
G
D/F♯
Em7
G/A
D
There's a
he - ro
long road
(mp - mf)
C6/9
if you look in - side your heart. You don't
when you face the world a - lone. No one

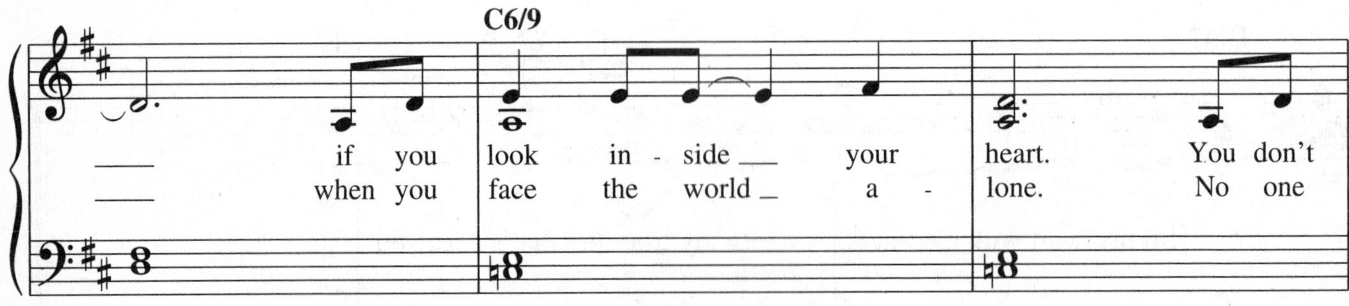

Bm7
G/A
have to be a - fraid of what you are.
reach - es out a hand for you to hold.

A
D
There's an an - swer if you
You can find love if you

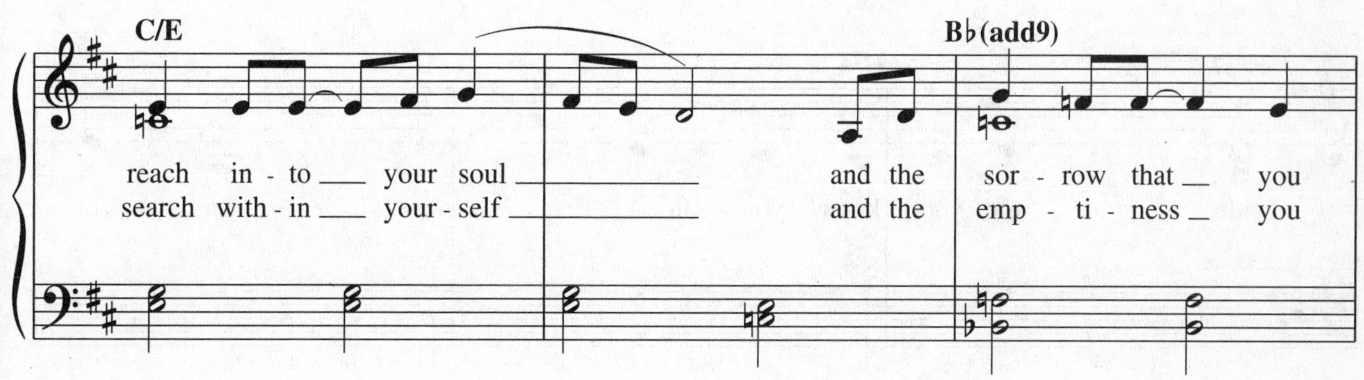
C/E
B♭(add9)
reach in - to your soul and the sor - row that you
search with - in your - self and the emp - ti - ness you

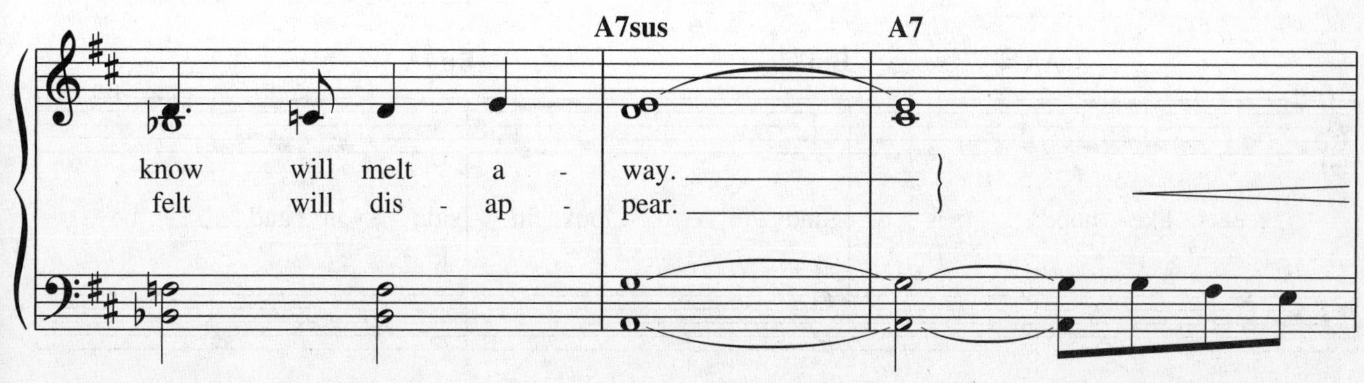
A7sus
A7
know will melt a - way.
felt will dis - ap - pear.

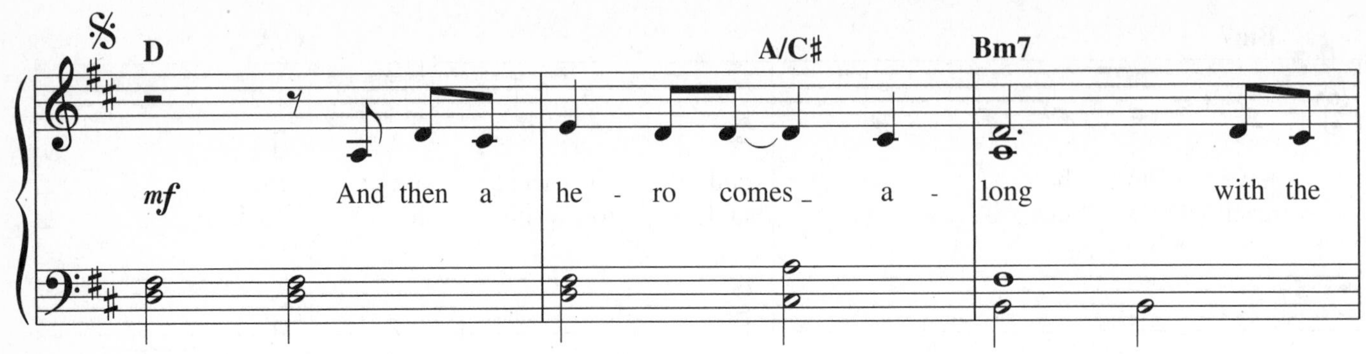
D
A/C♯
Bm7
mf
And then a
he - ro comes _ a -
long with the

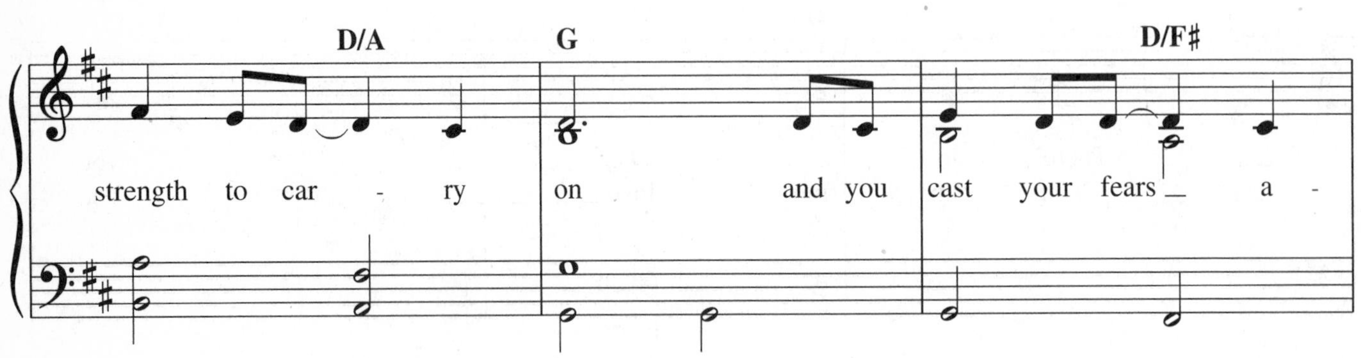
D/A
G
D/F♯
strength to car - ry
on and you
cast your fears _ a -

Em7
G/A
D
side, and you
know you can _ sur -
vive. So when you

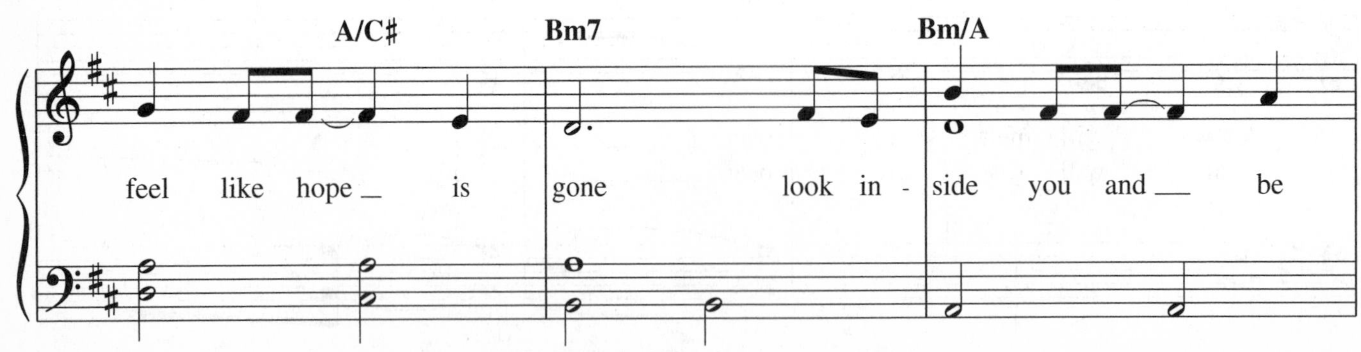
A/C♯
Bm7
Bm/A
feel like hope _ is
gone look in -
side you and _ be

G
D/F♯
Em7
strong and you'll fin - 'lly see the truth that a

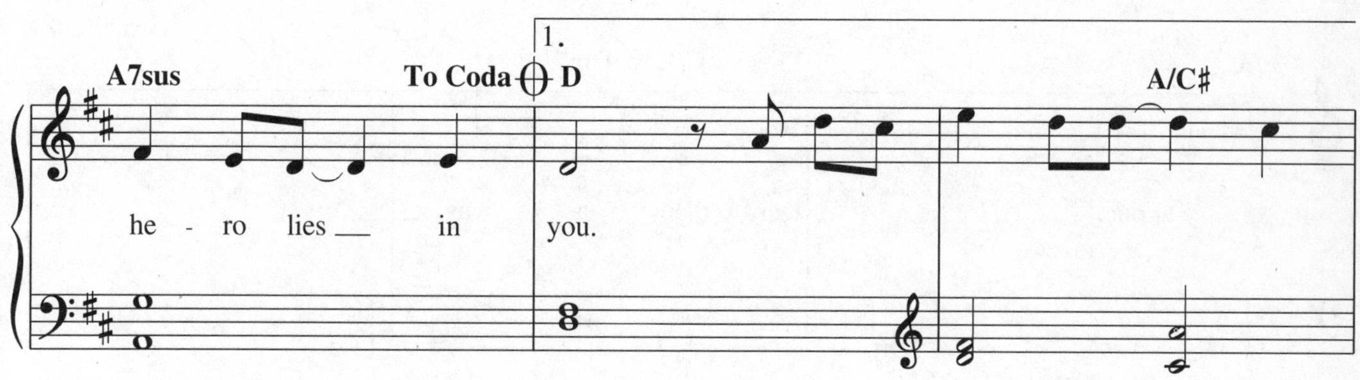
1.
A7sus
To Coda
D
A/C♯
he - ro lies in you.

2.
Bm
D/A
G
D
It's a you.

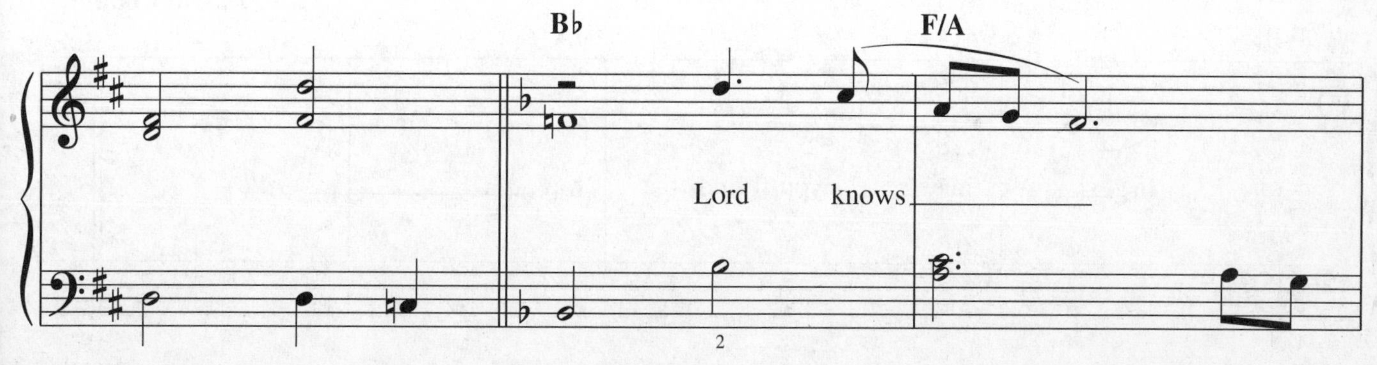
B♭
F/A
Lord knows

F
C
B♭
dreams are hard to fol - low,
but don't let

F/A
F C/E Dm7 C
an - y - one
tear them a - way.

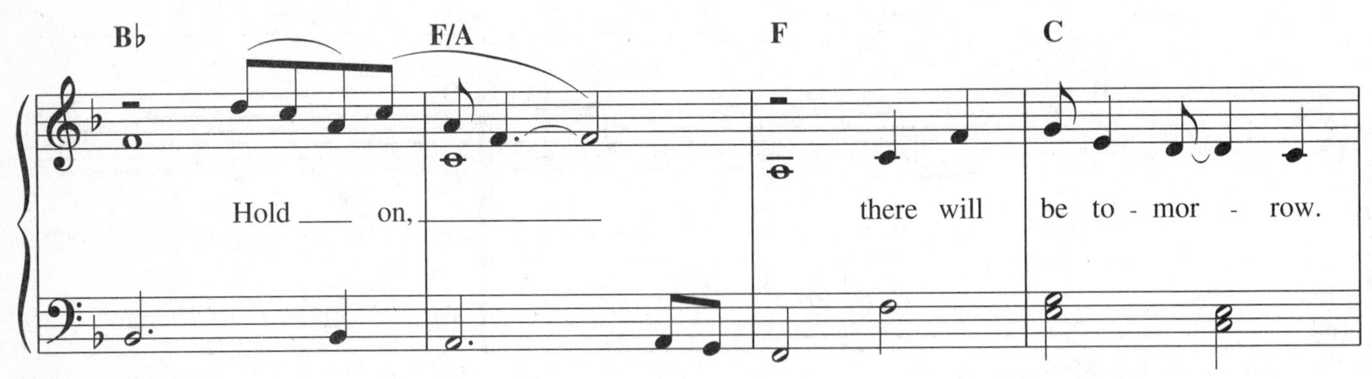
B♭
F/A
F
C
Hold on,
there will be to - mor - row.

D.S. al Coda
B♭
F/A
G/A
A
3
In time you'll find the way.
rall.

CODA
G
D/F#
Em7
you.
That a
molto rall.

A7sus
A7
D
A/C#
he - ro lies in
you.
mp a tempo

Bm7
D/A
G
That a
rit.

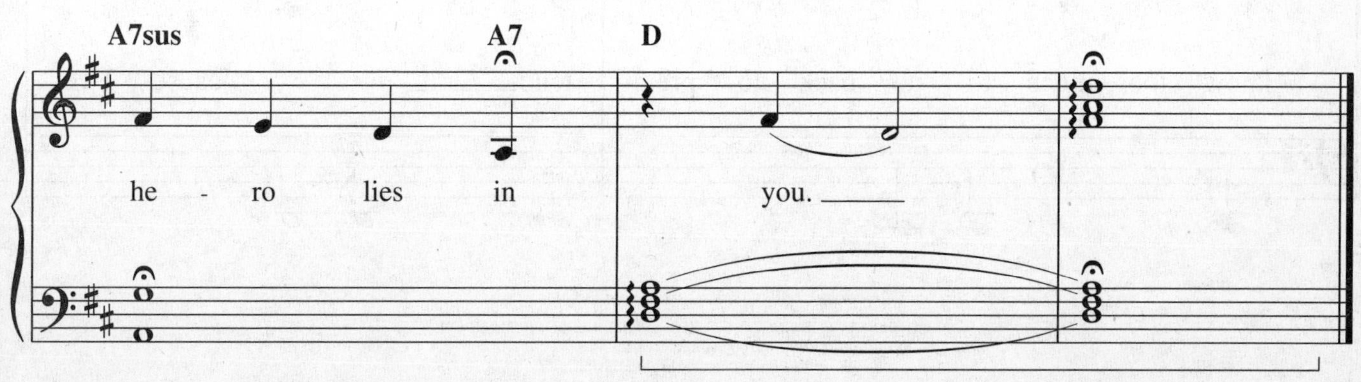
A7sus
A7
D
he - ro lies in
you.

I AM WOMAN

Words by HELEN REDDY
Music by RAY BURTON

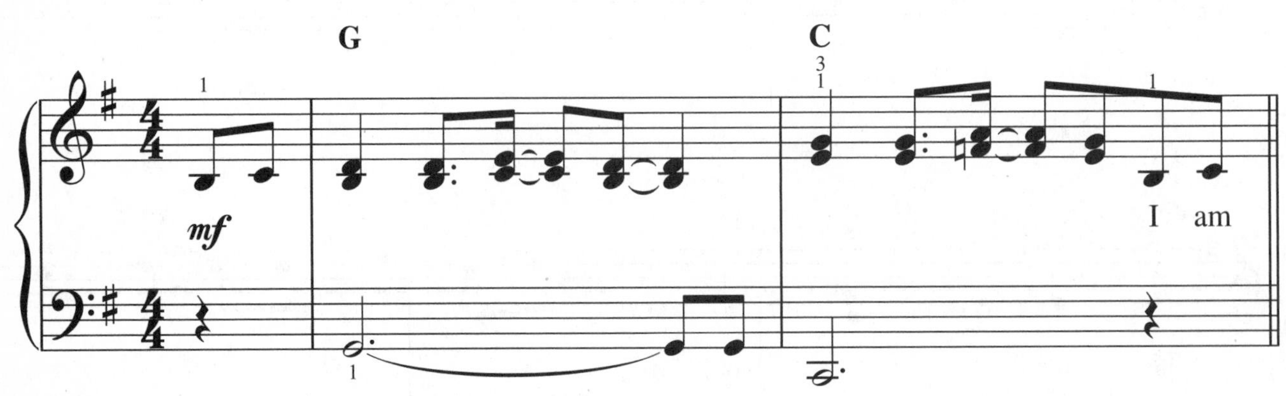

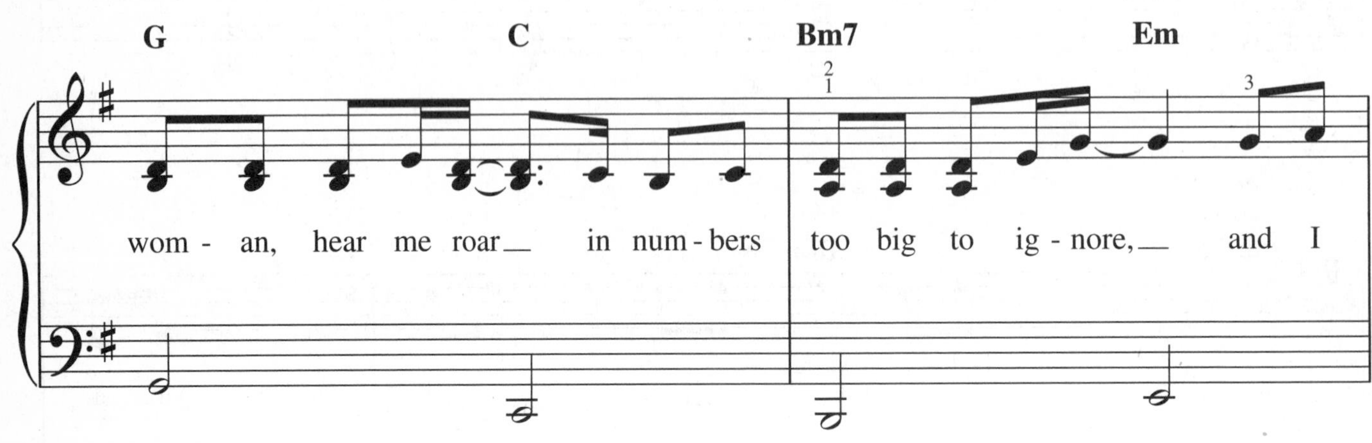

G
C
G
C
heard it all be - fore and I've been down there on the floor, no one's

A7
D
C7
ev - er gon - na keep me down a - gain. Oh,

F
B♭
yes, I am wise but it's wis - dom born of pain.

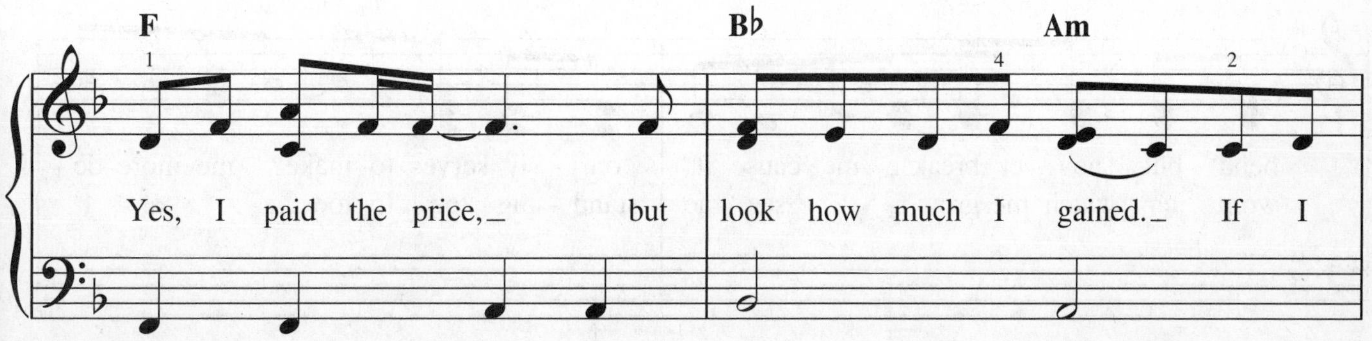
F
B♭
Am
Yes, I paid the price, but look how much I gained. If I

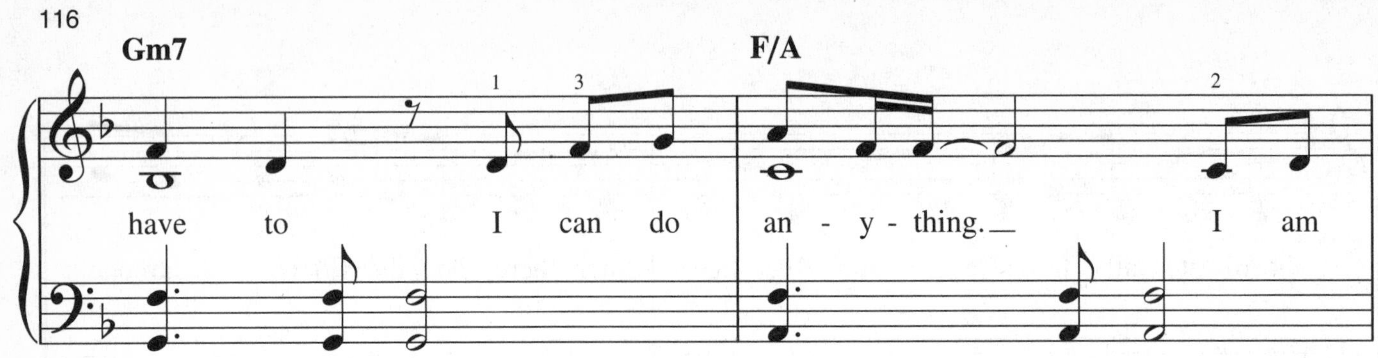
Gm7
F/A
have to I can do an - y - thing. I am

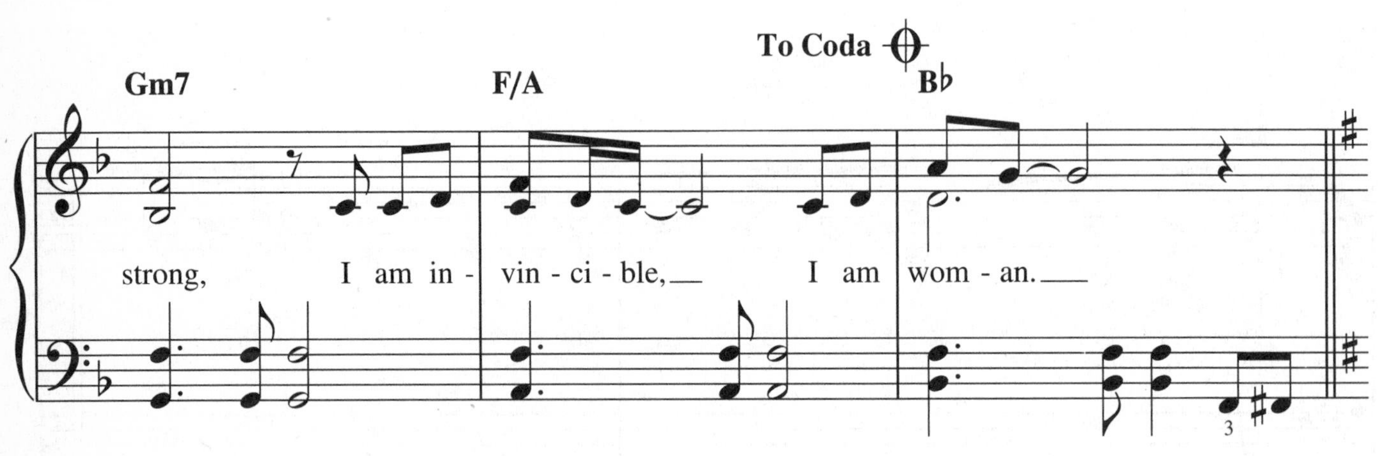
To Coda
Gm7
F/A
B♭
strong, I am in - vin - ci - ble, I am wom - an.

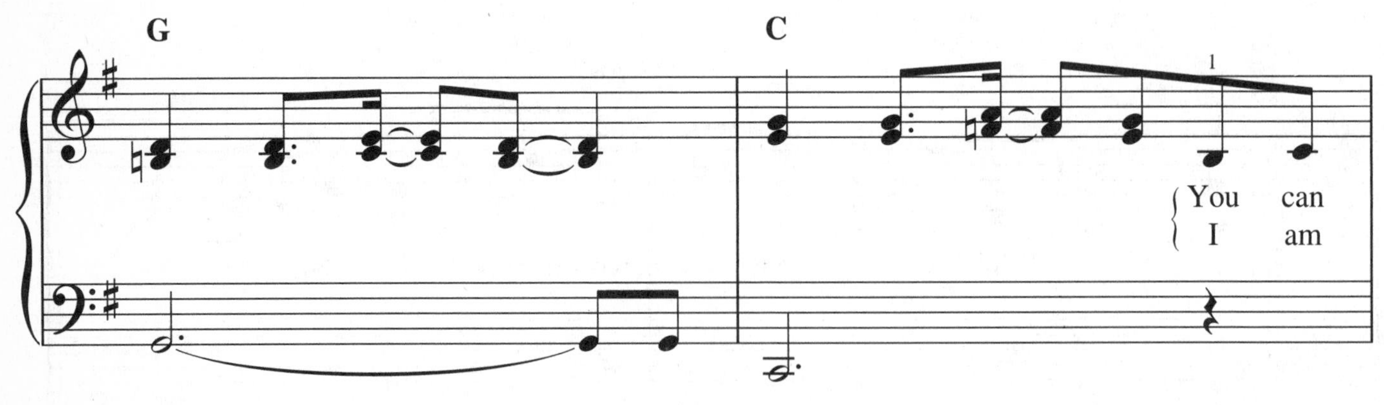
G
C
You can
I am

G
C
Bm7
Em
bend but nev - er break me 'cause it on - ly serves to make me more de -
wom - an, watch me grow see me stand - ing toe to toe as I

C
Dsus
D
ter - mined to a - chieve my fi - nal goal. And I
spread my lov - in' arms a - cross the land. But I'm
G
C
G
C
come back e - ven strong - er, not a nov - ice an - y long - er, 'cause you've
still an em - bry - o with a long, long way to go un -
A7
1.
D
C7
deep - ened the con - vic - tion in my soul. Oh,
til I make my broth - er un - der -
2.
D
C7
D.S. al Coda
CODA
B♭maj9
B♭6
F
stand. Oh,
wom - an!

I HEARD IT THROUGH THE GRAPEVINE

Words and Music by NORMAN J. WHITFIELD and BARRETT STRONG

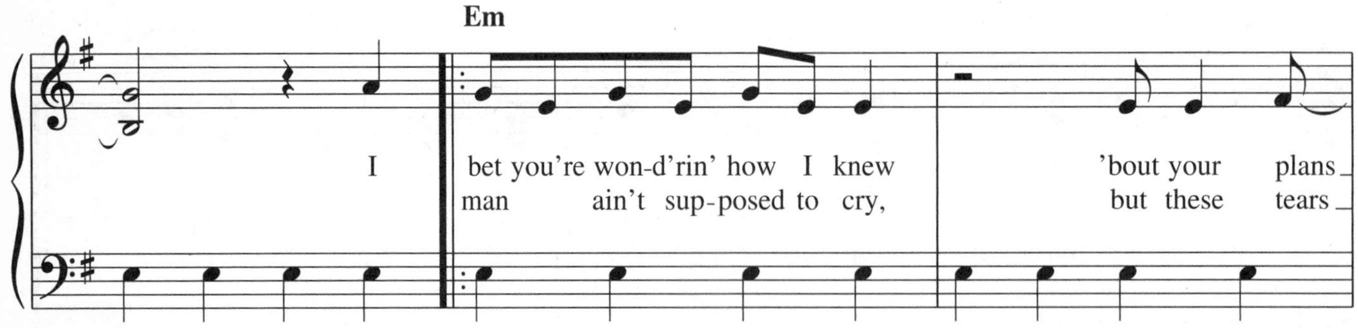

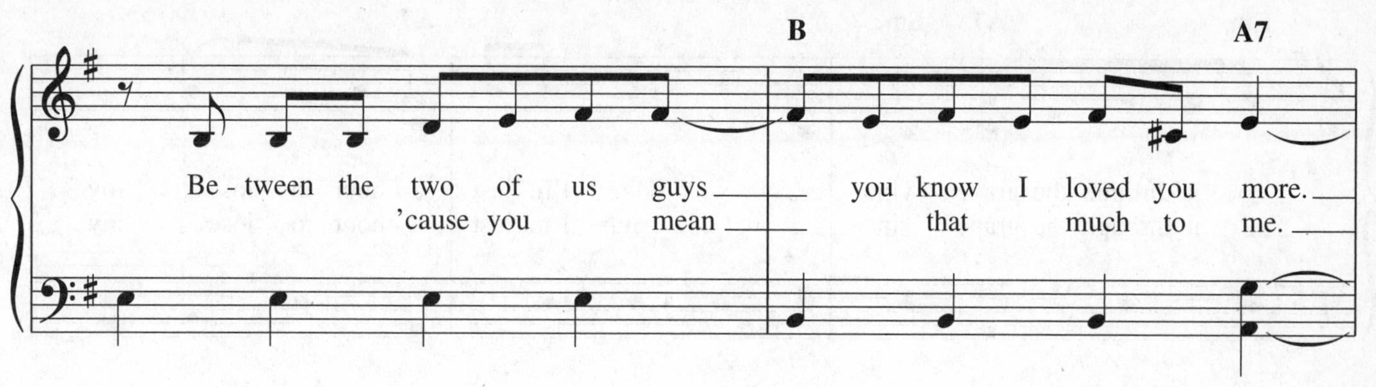
B
A7
Be - tween the two of us guys you know I loved you more.
'cause you mean that much to me.

C♯m
A7
It took me by sur - prise I must say when I
You could have told me your - self that you

Em
A7
Em
A7
Em
found out yes - ter - day. Don't you know that I heard it through the grape - vine,
loved some - one else. In - stead I heard it through the grape - vine,

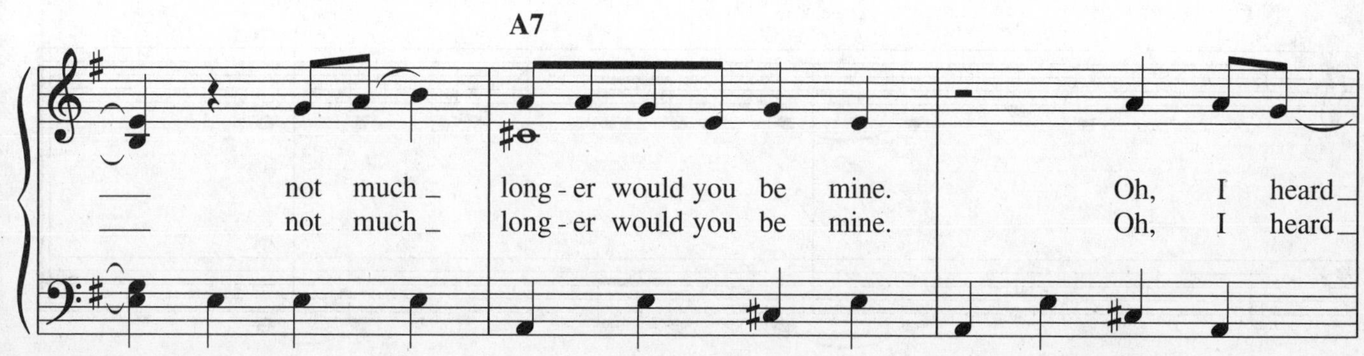
A7
not much long - er would you be mine. Oh, I heard
not much long - er would you be mine. Oh, I heard

Em
A7
Em
A7
it through the grape - vine.
Oh, I'm just
a - bout to lose my
it through the grape - vine.
And I'm just
a - bout to lose my

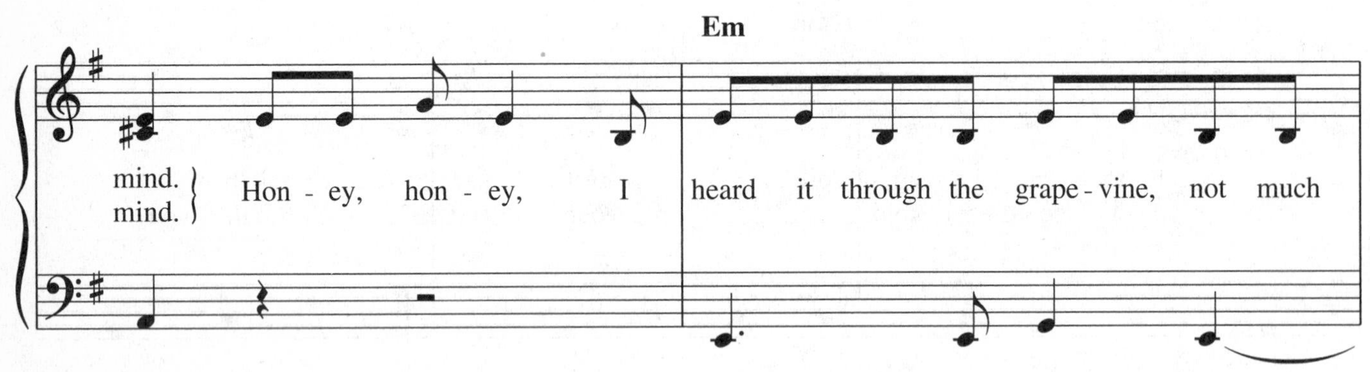
Em
mind.
mind.
Hon - ey, hon - ey, I
heard it through the grape - vine, not much

1.
2.
long-er would you be mine, ba - by.
I know a

N.C.

I HOPE YOU DANCE

Words and Music by TIA SILLERS
and MARK D. SANDERS

- ways keep that hun - ger. May you
of least re - sis - tance. Liv - in'

F
4
1
nev - er take one sin - gle breath for grant - ed.
might mean tak - in' chanc - es if they're worth tak - in'.

G
God for - bid love ev - er leaves you emp - ty - hand -
Lov - in' might be a mis - take but it's worth mak -

F
G
- ed. I hope you still feel small when you
- in'. Don't let some hell - bent

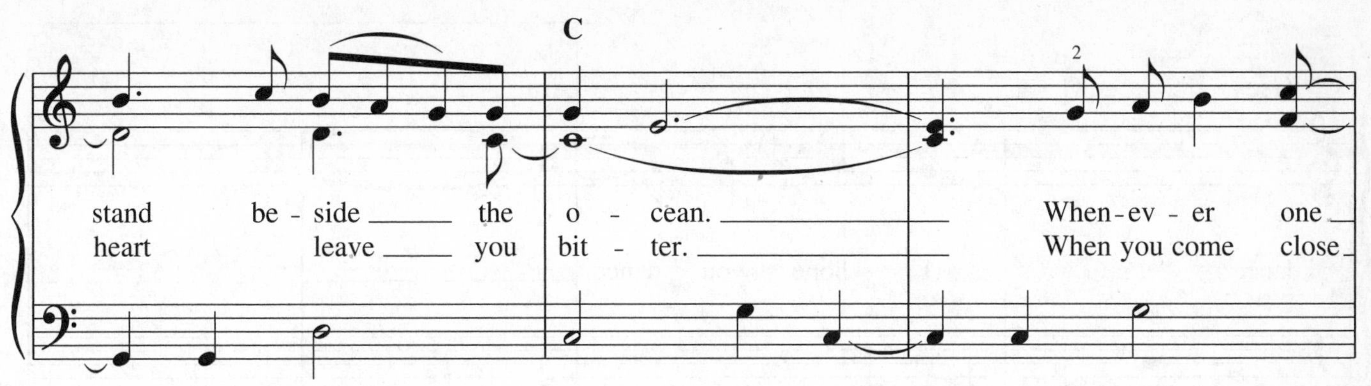
C
2
stand be - side the o - cean. When-ev - er one
heart leave you bit - ter. When you come close

F
G
C
5
1
4
1
door clos - es, I hope one more o - pens.
to sell - in' out, re - con - sid - er.

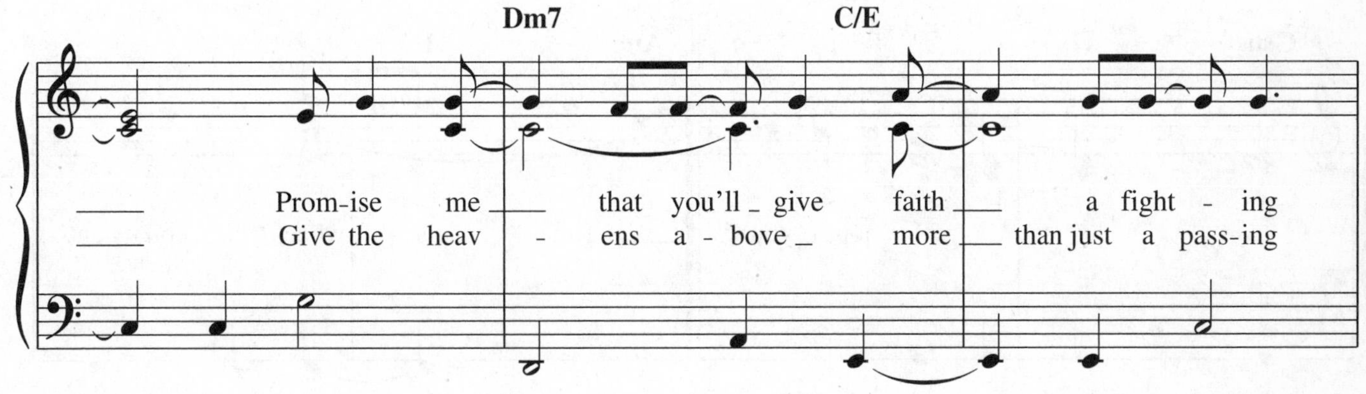
Dm7
C/E
Prom-ise me that you'll give faith a fight - ing
Give the heav - ens a - bove more than just a pass-ing

F
To Coda
2
chance.
glance.
And when you get the choice to sit it out or

1.
Gsus
G
Am
F
dance.
I hope _ you dance.

C
G/B
Am
F
I hope _ you
dance.

2.
Gsus
G
Am
F
I hope _ you
Time is a wheel in con - stant

C
G/B
Am
F
mo - tion al - ways roll - ing us

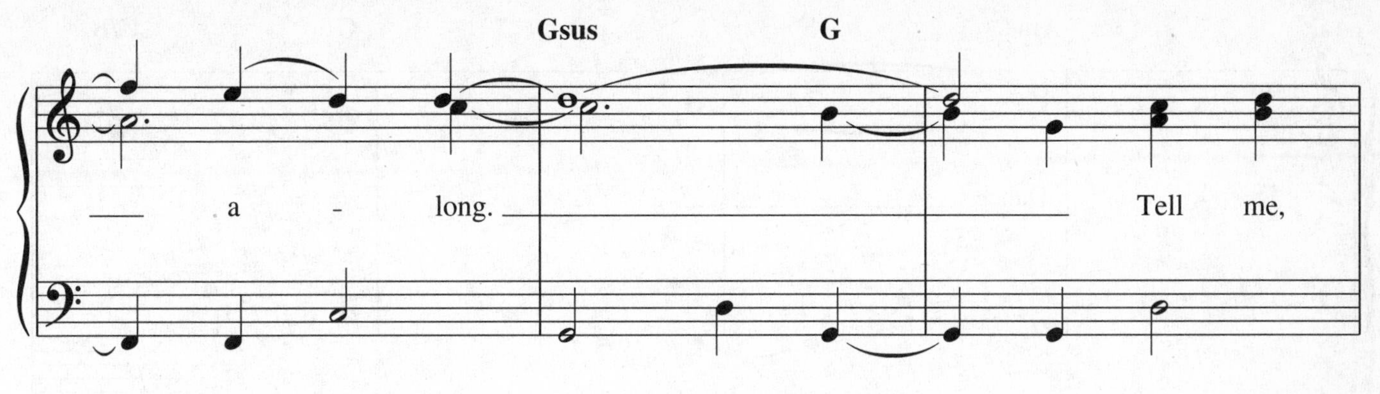
Gsus
G
a - long.
Tell me,

Am
F
C
G/B
who wants to look back on their youth and won -

Am
F
- der where those years have gone?

Gsus
G
D.S. al Coda
(Verse 1)
I hope you still

CODA
Gsus
dance.

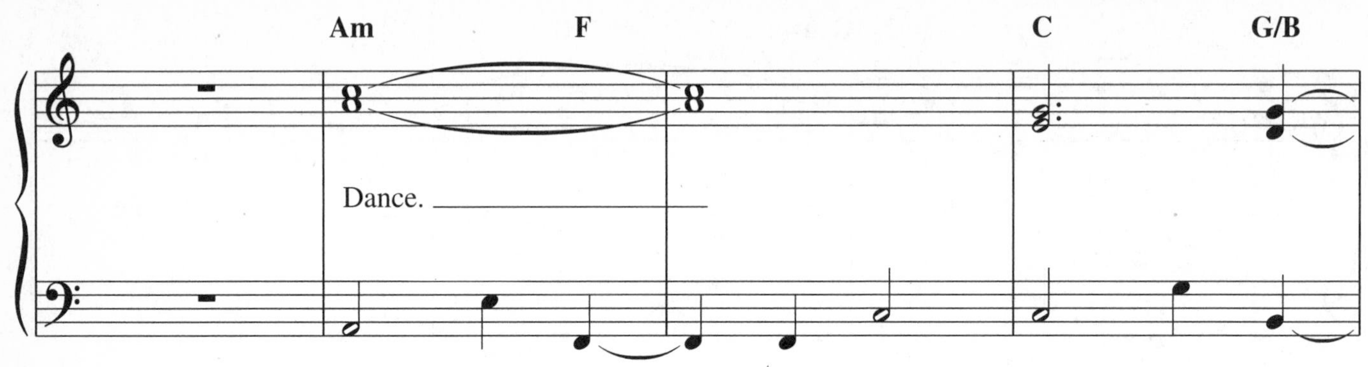
Am
F
C
G/B
Dance.

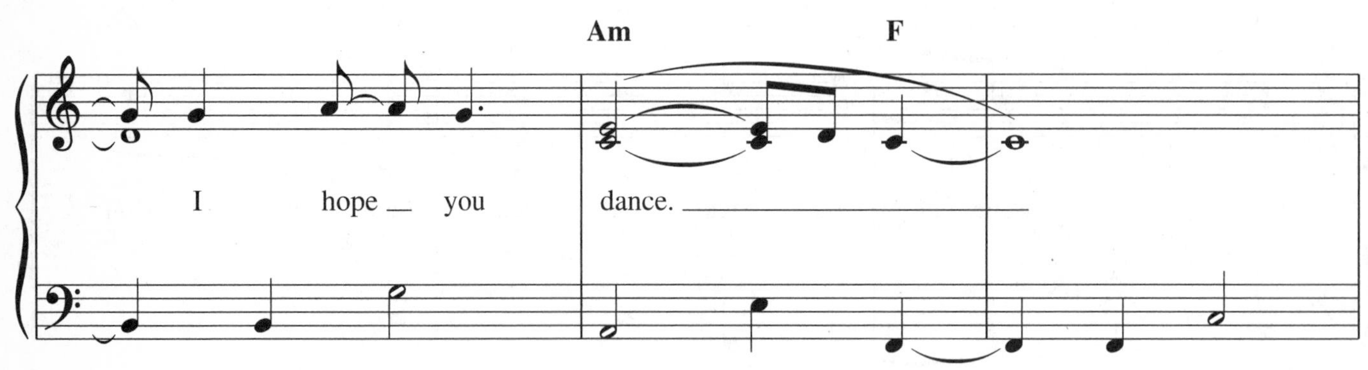
Am
F
I hope you
dance.

Gsus
G
Am
F
I hope you dance. Time is a

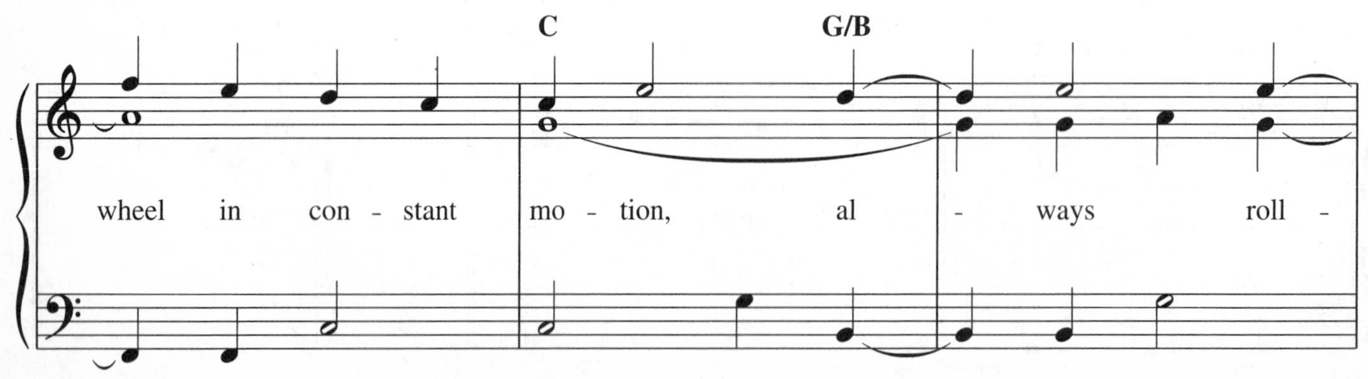
C
G/B
wheel in con - stant mo - tion, al - ways roll -

Am
F
Gsus
G
- ing
us
a
-
long.
Am
F
Tell
me,
who
wants
to
look
back
on
their
C
G/B
Am
F
youth
and
won
-
der
where
those
years
Gsus
G
C
have
gone?

I'M EASY

from NASHVILLE

Words and Music by
KEITH CARRADINE

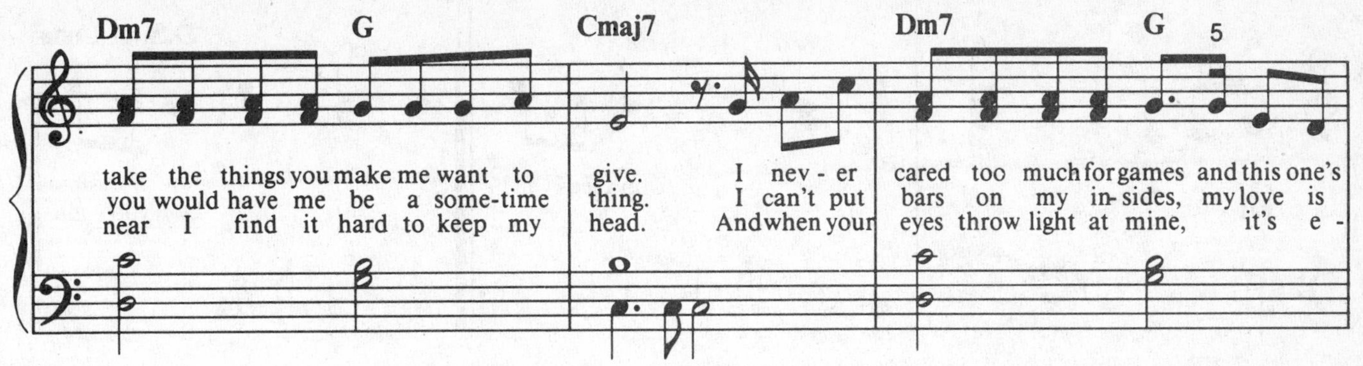
Dm7 G Cmaj7 Dm7 G
take the things you make me want to give. I nev - er cared too much for games and this one's
you would have me be a some-time thing. I can't put bars on my in-sides, my love is
near I find it hard to keep my head. And when your eyes throw light at mine, it's e -

Cmaj7 Fmaj7 Dm7
3rd time to Coda
driv - ing me in - sane; You're not half as free to wan - der as you
some - thing I can't hide; It still hurts when I re - call the times I
nough to change my mind, Make me leave my cau - tious words and ways be -

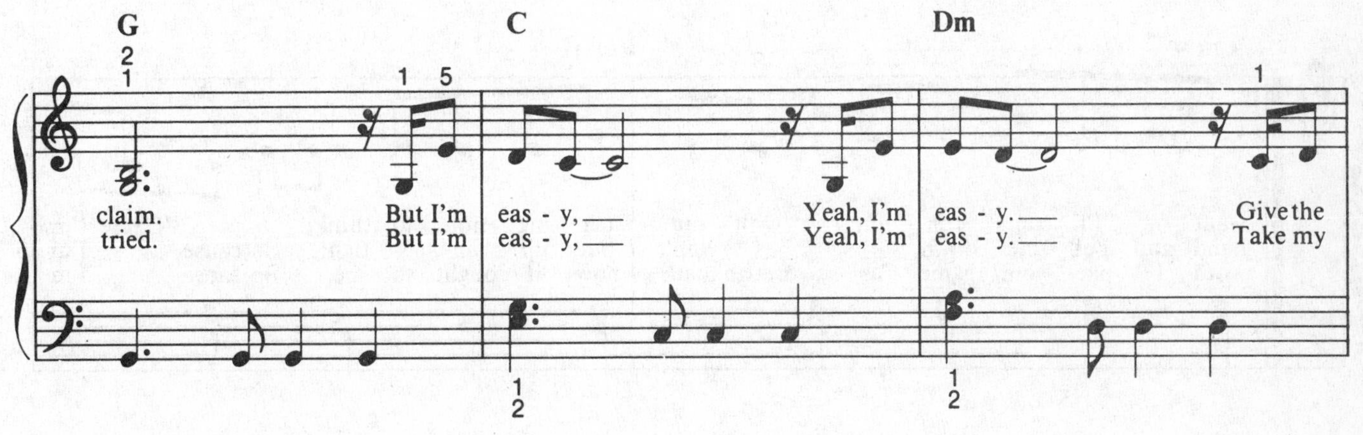
G C Dm
claim. But I'm eas - y, Yeah, I'm eas - y. Give the
tried. But I'm eas - y, Yeah, I'm eas - y. Take my

Em Fmaj7
word I'll play the game as though that's how it ought to be Be-cause I'm
hand and pull me down, I won't put up an - y fight Be-cause I'm

C
1.
2.
D.S. al Coda
eas - y.
eas - y.
Don't lead me
Don't do me

CODA
G
C
Dm
hind. That's why I'm
eas - y, yeah, I'm
eas - y. Say you

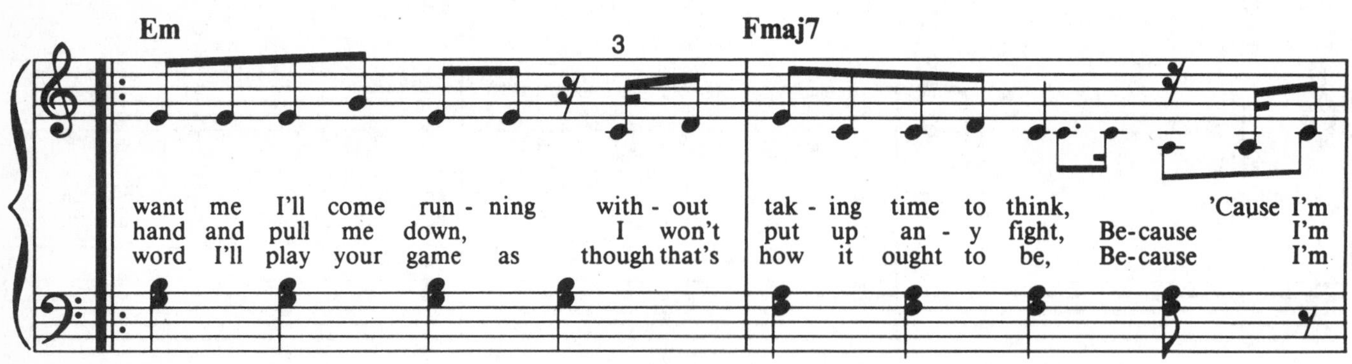
Em
Fmaj7
want me I'll come run - ning with - out
hand and pull me down, I won't
word I'll play your game as though that's
tak - ing time to think, 'Cause I'm
put up an - y fight, Be-cause I'm
how it ought to be, Be-cause I'm

1.,2.
C
Dm
3.
C
Cmaj7
eas - y, yeah, I'm
eas - y, yeah, I'm
eas - y. Take my
eas - y. Give the
eas - y.

IT'S ALL COMING BACK TO ME NOW

Words and Music by
JIM STEINMAN

F
C/G
G
Em
Am
ev - er.
I fin - ished cry - ing in the
Thought you were his - t'ry with the

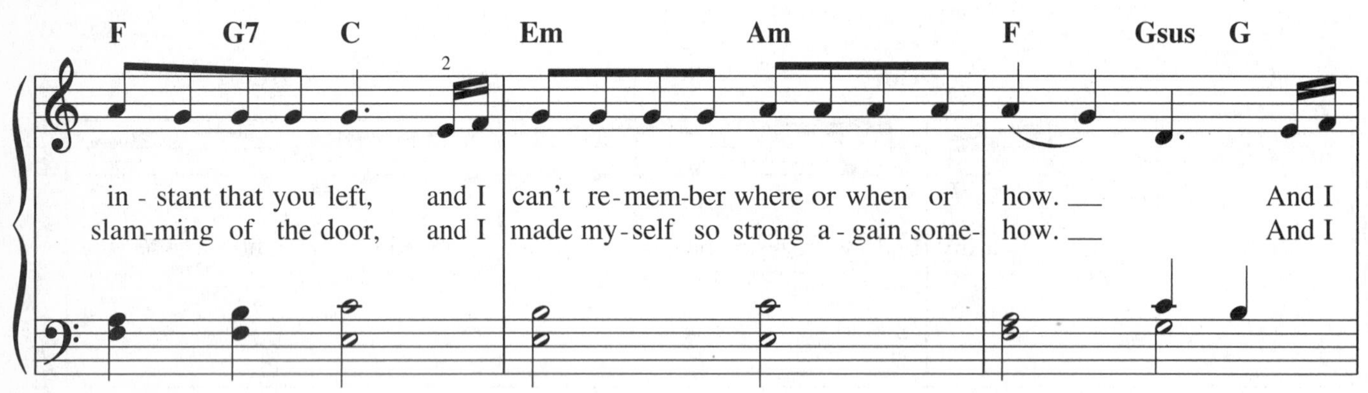
F
G7
C
Em
Am
F
Gsus
G
in - stant that you left, and I can't re - mem - ber where or when or how. And I
slam - ming of the door, and I made my - self so strong a - gain some - how. And I

Em
Am
F
G
F
ban - ished ev - 'ry mem - 'ry you and I had ev - er made.
nev - er was - ted an - y of my time on you since then.
rit.

F/G
C
G/B
But when you touch me like this, and you hold me like that, I just
But if I touch you like this, and if you kiss me like that, it was
a tempo

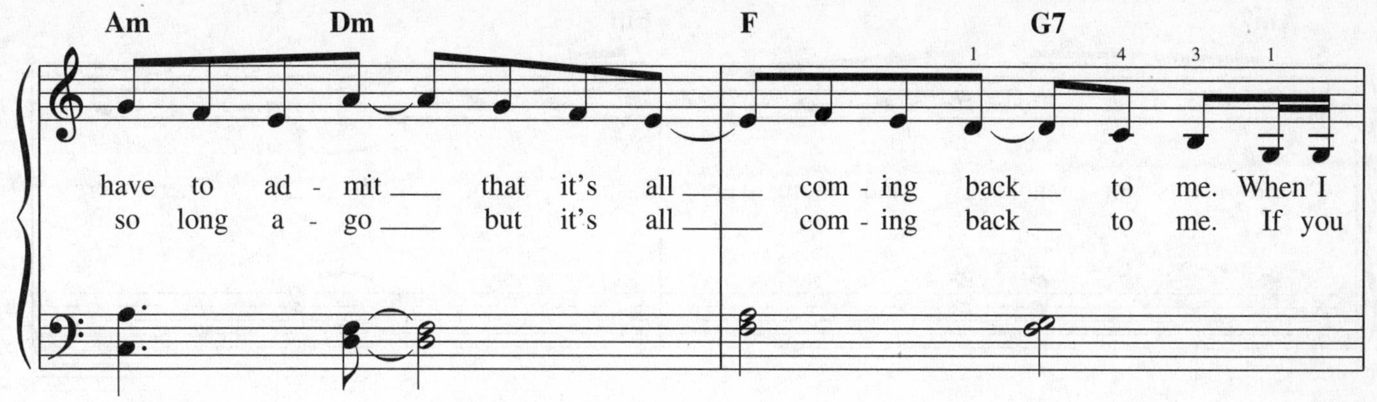
Am
Dm
F
G7
have to ad - mit ___ that it's all ___ com - ing back ___ to me. When I
so long a - go ___ but it's all ___ com - ing back ___ to me. If you

C
G/B
touch you like this, ___ and I hold you like that, ___ it's so
touch me like this, ___ and if I kiss you like that, ___ it was

Am7
Dm
F
G7
hard to be - lieve, ___ but it's all ___ com - ing back ___ to me.
gone with the wind, ___ but it's all ___ com - ing back ___ to me.
It's

C
F
G
all com - ing back, ___ it's all com - ing back to me now. ___ There were

Am7
F
Em
F
mo - ments of gold ___ and there were flash - es of light. ___ There were

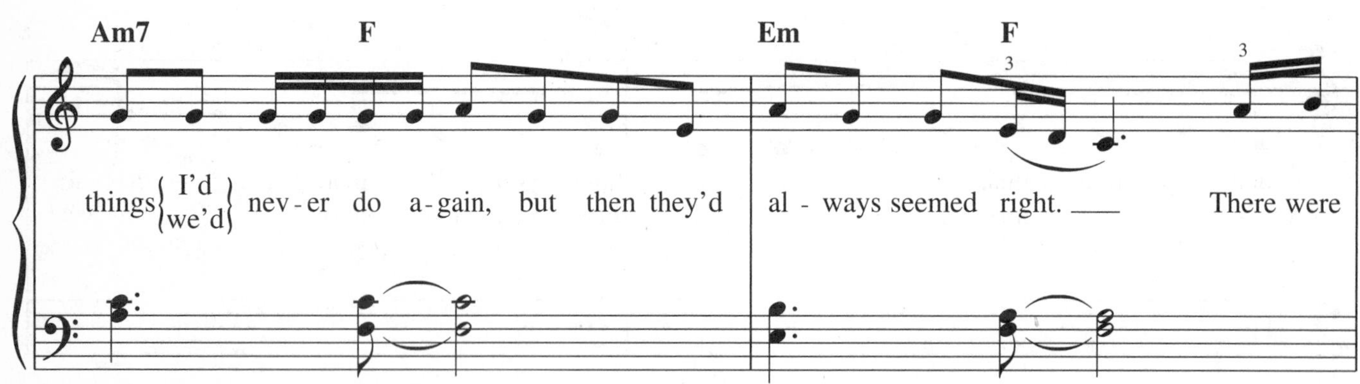
Am7
F
Em
F
things I'd / we'd nev - er do a - gain, but then they'd al - ways seemed right. ___ There were

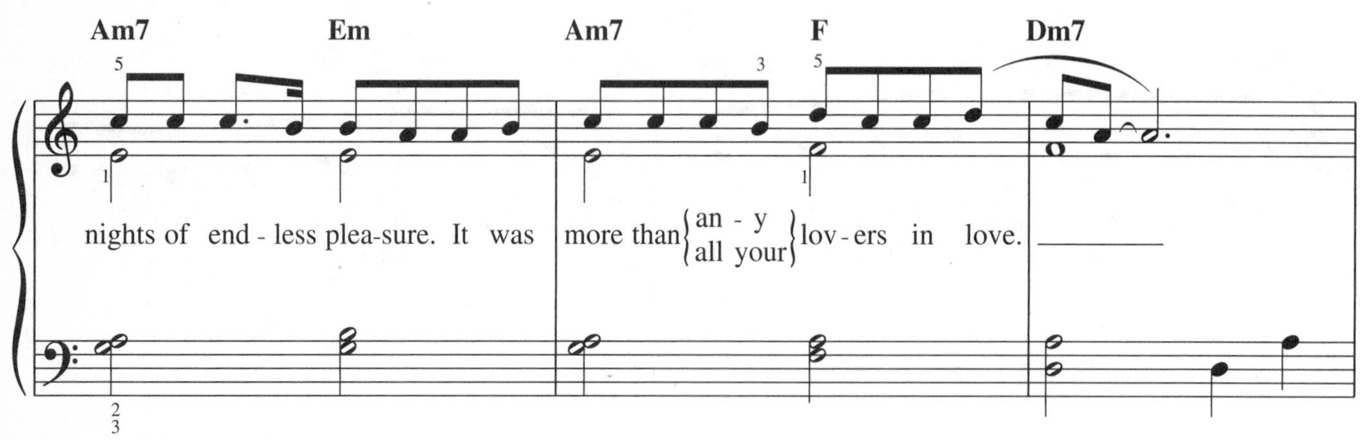
Am7
Em
Am7
F
Dm7
nights of end - less plea - sure. It was more than an - y / all your lov - ers in love. ___

F/G
C
G/B
Ba - by, ba - by, if I kiss you like this, _ and if you whis - per like that, _ it was
Ba - by, ba - by, when you touch me like this, _ and when you hold me like that, _ it was

Am7
Dm
F
G7
lost long a - go, but it's all com - ing back to me. If you
gone with the wind, but it's all com - ing back to me. When you

C
G/B
want me like this, and if you need me like that, it was
see me like this, and when I see you like that, then we've

Am7
Dm
F
G7
that long a - go, but it's all com - ing back to me. It's so
seen what we want, to see all com - ing back to me. The

Am7
Dm
F
G7
hard to re - sist, and it's all com - ing back to me.
flesh and the fan - ta - sies all com - ing back to me.
I can

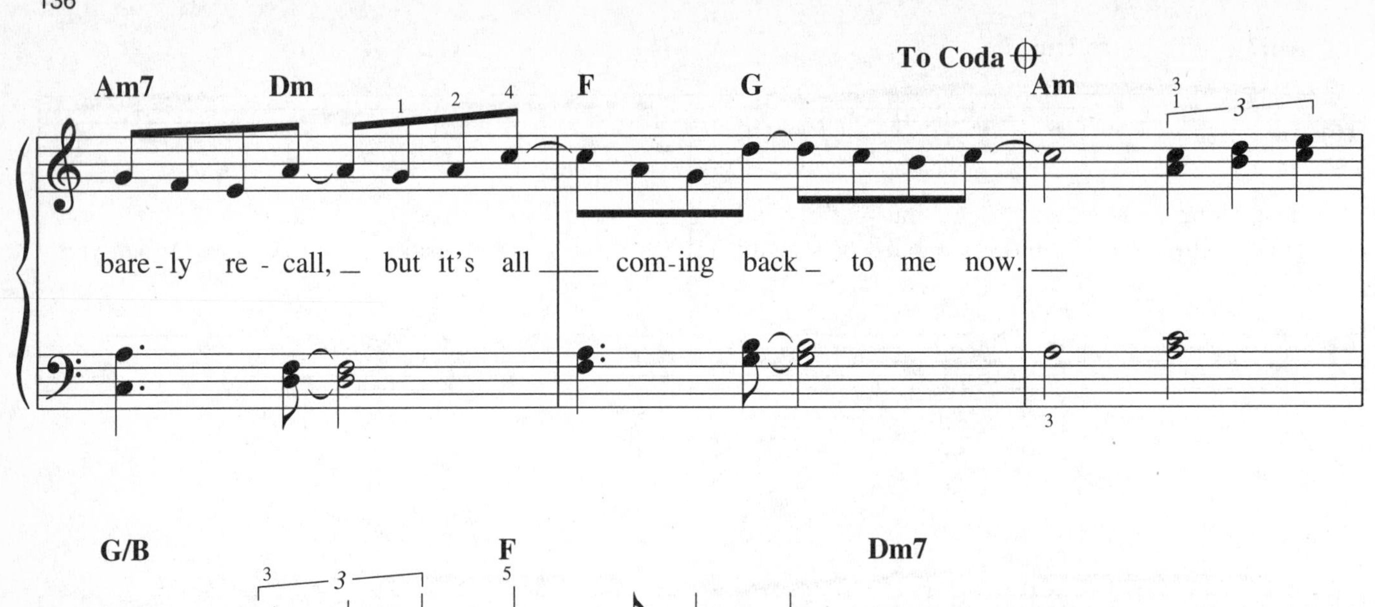
To Coda
Am7
Dm
F
G
Am
bare - ly re - call, _ but it's all ___ com-ing back _ to me now. __

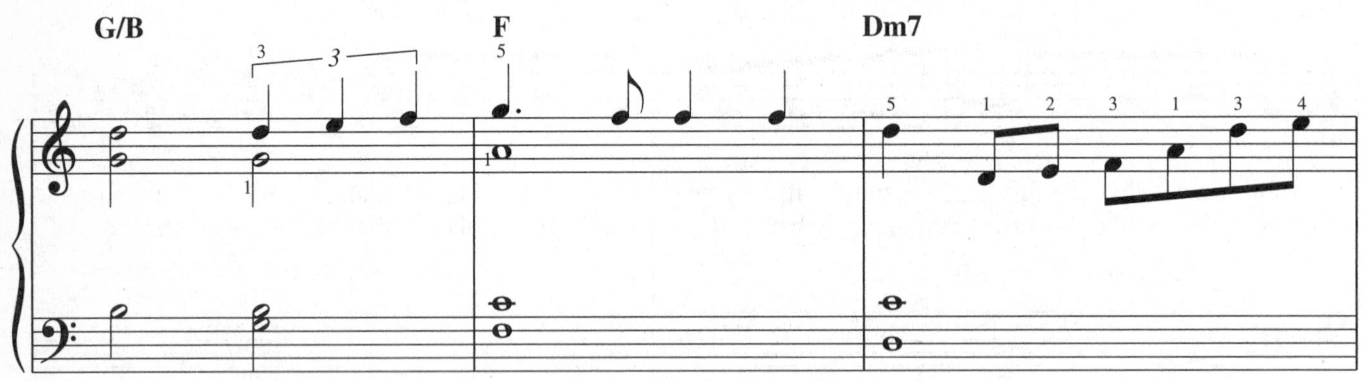
G/B
F
Dm7

D.S. al Coda

CODA
Am
G
F
N.C.
If you for -

C
G/B
give me all this, ___ if I for - give you all that, ___ we for -

Am7 Dm F G7 C
give and for - get, and it's all com-ing back to me now. It's all com-ing

F G C
back to me now. And when I touch you like that, it's all com-ing

F G C
back to me now. And if you do it like this, it's all com-ing

F C
back to me now. And if we...
rit.

IF I EVER LOSE MY FAITH IN YOU

Music and Lyrics by
STING

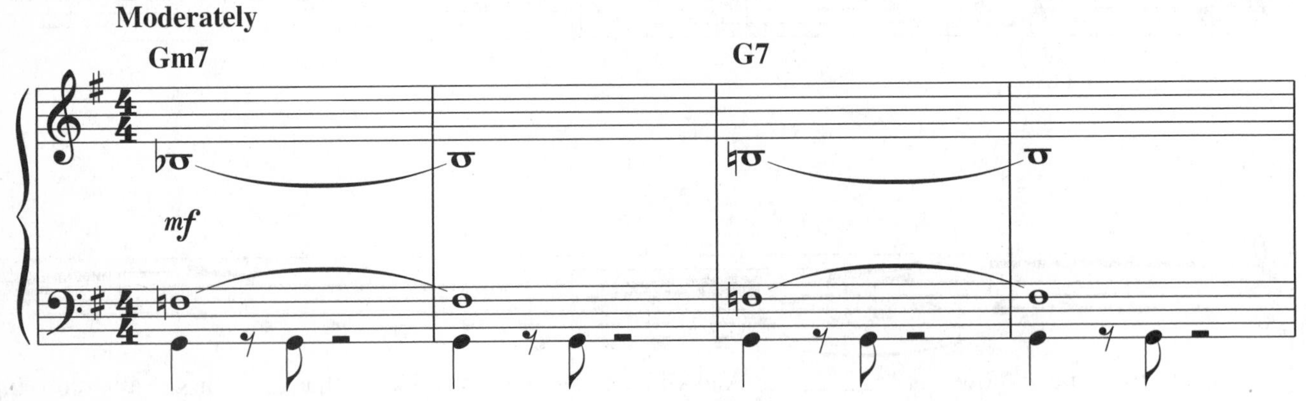

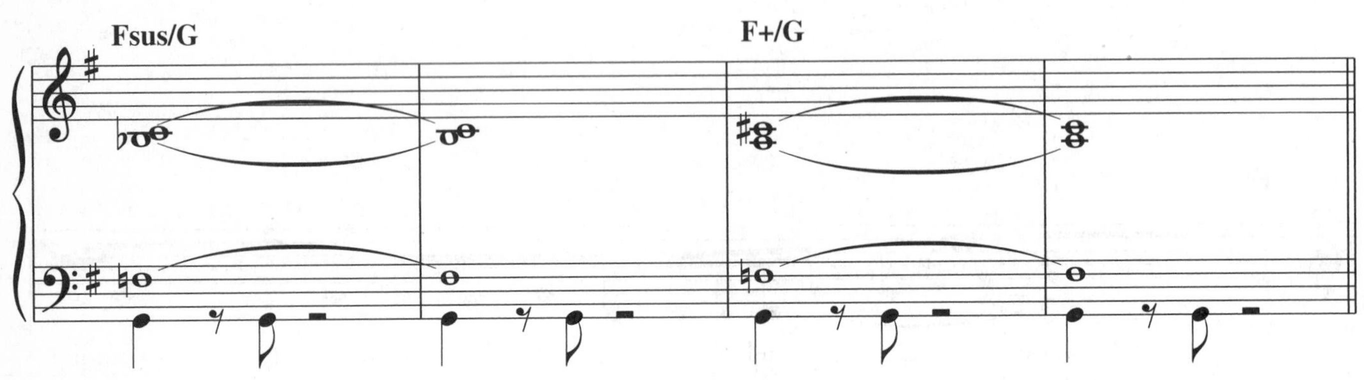

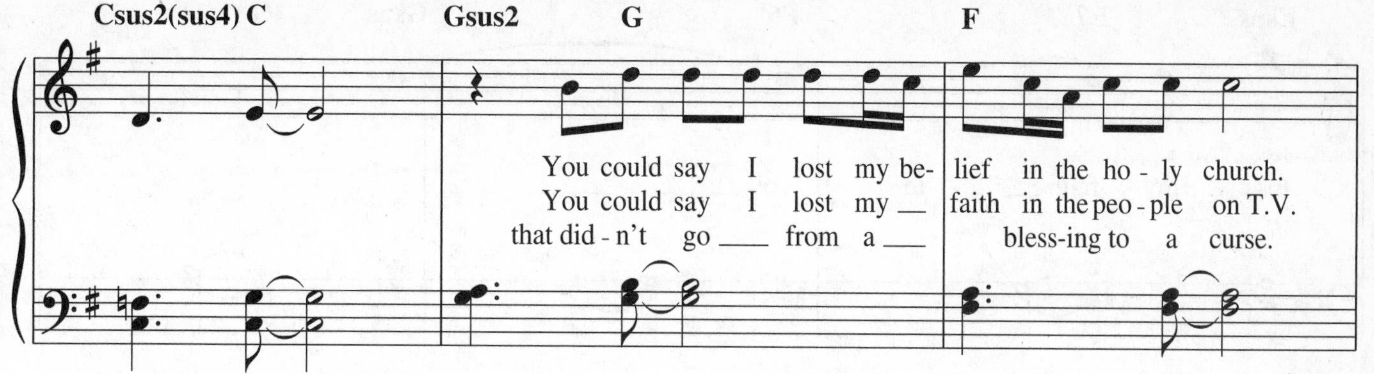
Csus2(sus4) C
Gsus2
G
F
You could say I lost my be- lief in the ho - ly church.
You could say I lost my faith in the peo - ple on T.V.
that did - n't go from a bless-ing to a curse.

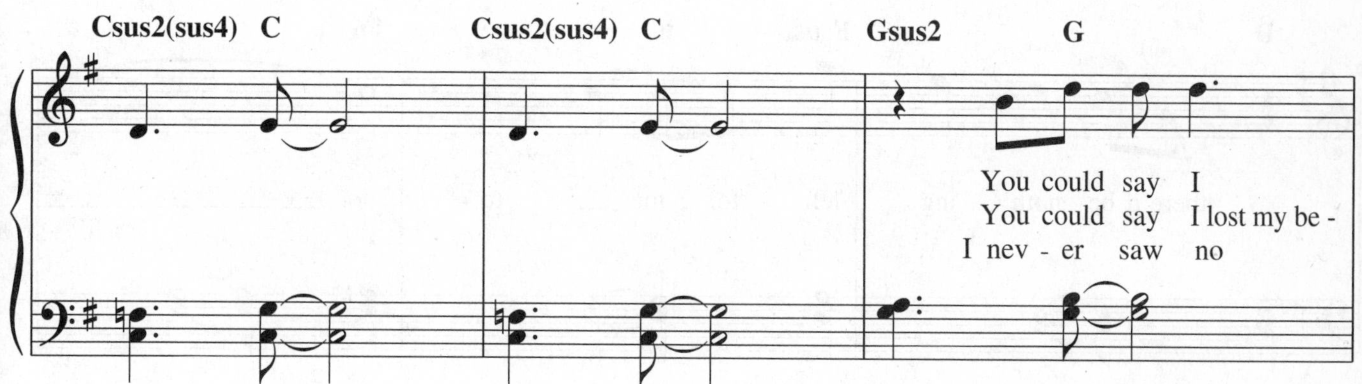
Csus2(sus4) C
Csus2(sus4) C
Gsus2
G
You could say I
You could say I lost my be -
I nev - er saw no

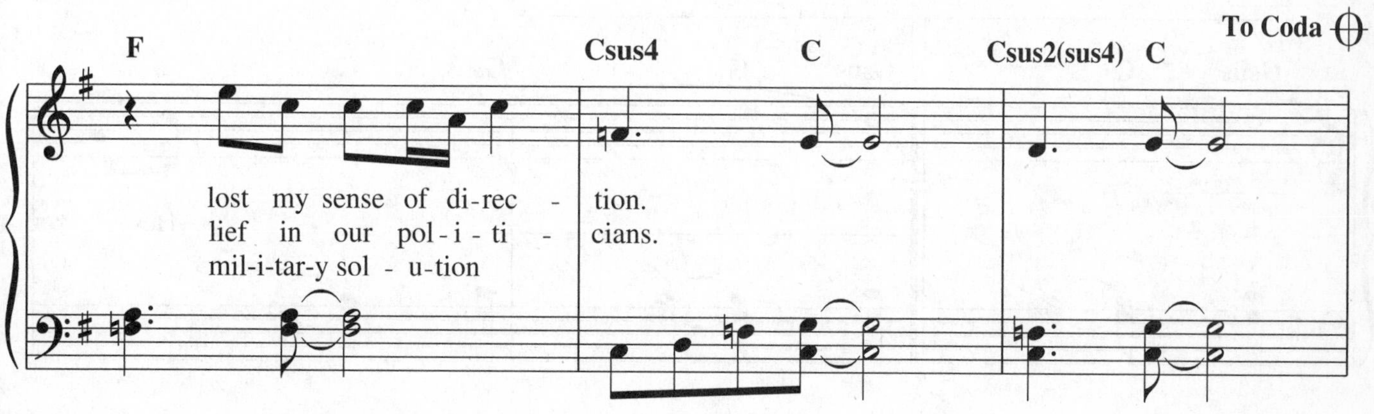
To Coda
F
Csus4
C
Csus2(sus4) C
lost my sense of di-rec - tion.
lief in our pol - i - ti - cians.
mil-i-tar-y sol - u-tion

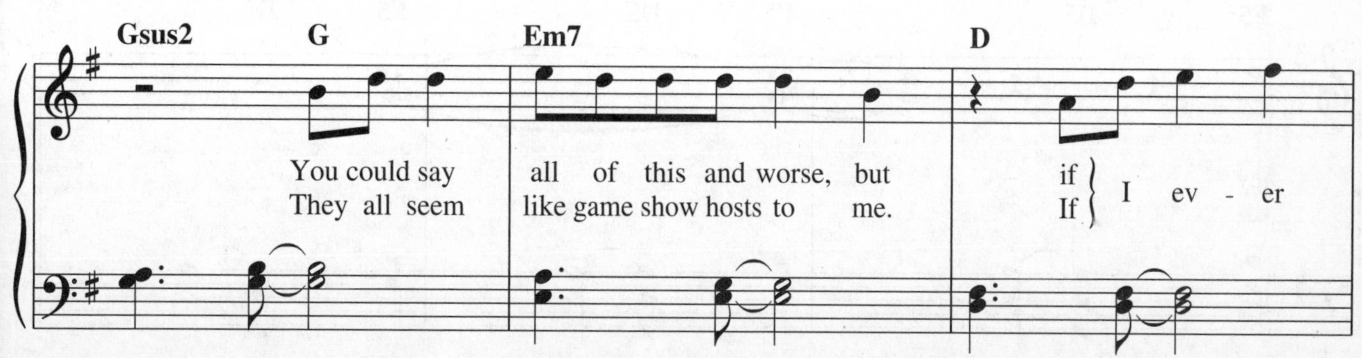
Gsus2
G
Em7
D
You could say all of this and worse, but
They all seem like game show hosts to me.
if
If
I ev - er

Esus
E7
F6
Gsus
G
lose my faith in you

D
Esus
E7
F6
there'd be noth - ing left for me to do.

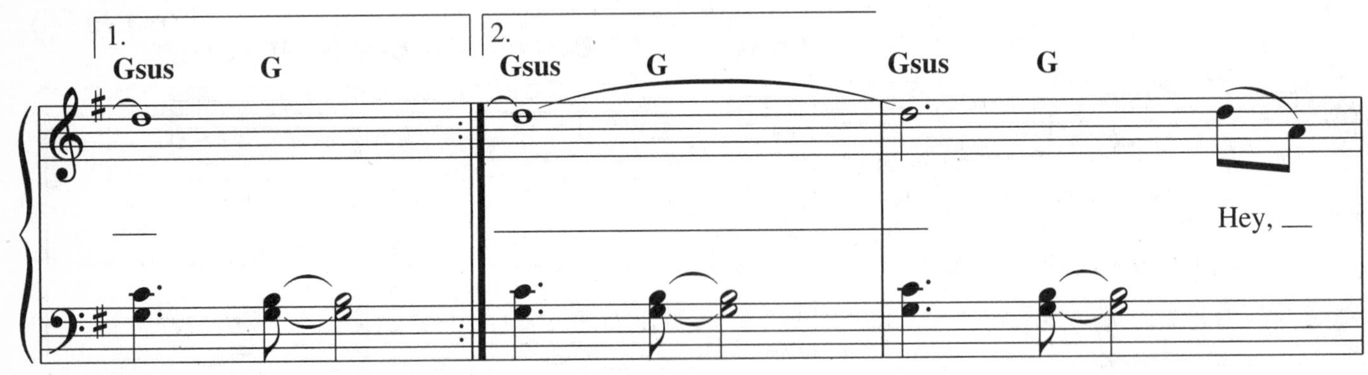
1.
2.
Gsus
G
Gsus
G
Gsus
G
Hey,

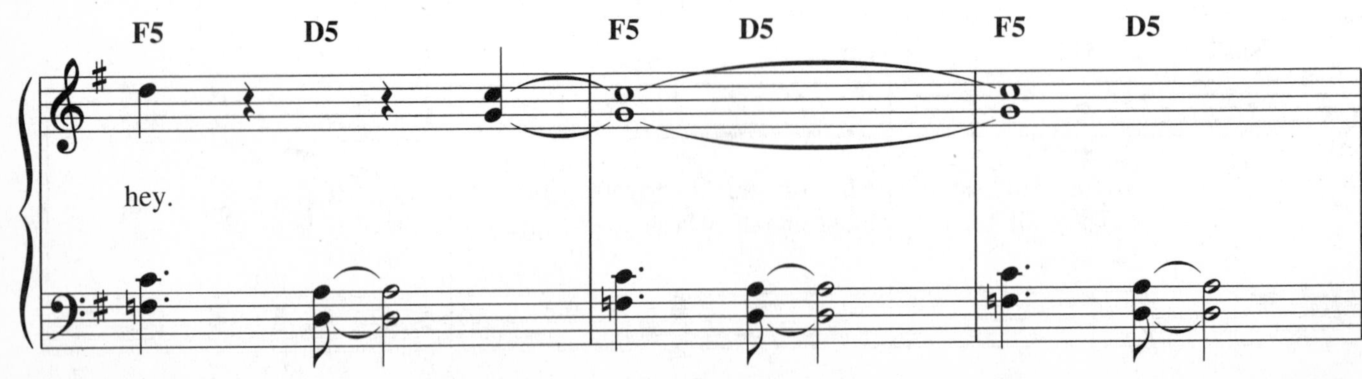
F5
D5
F5
D5
F5
D5
hey.

F5
D5
Em7
F♯m7
I could be lost in - side their

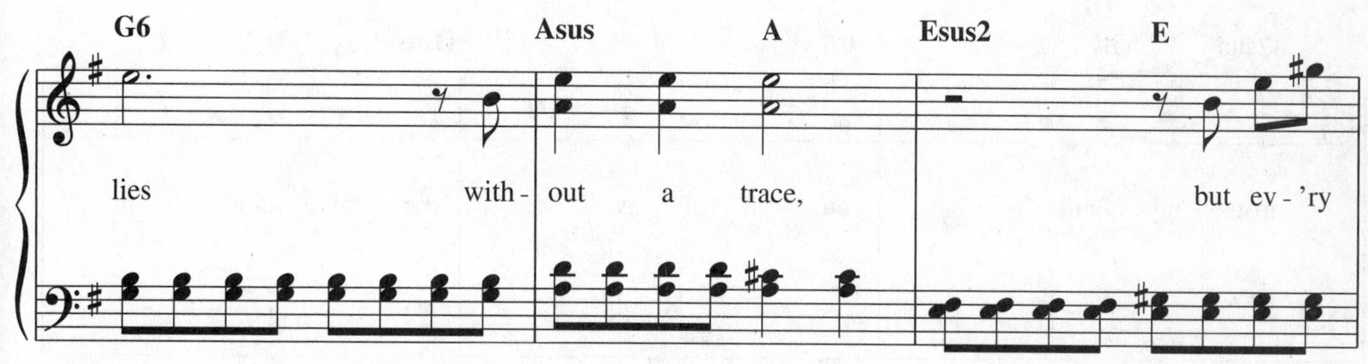
G6
Asus
A
Esus2
E
lies with - out a trace, but ev - 'ry

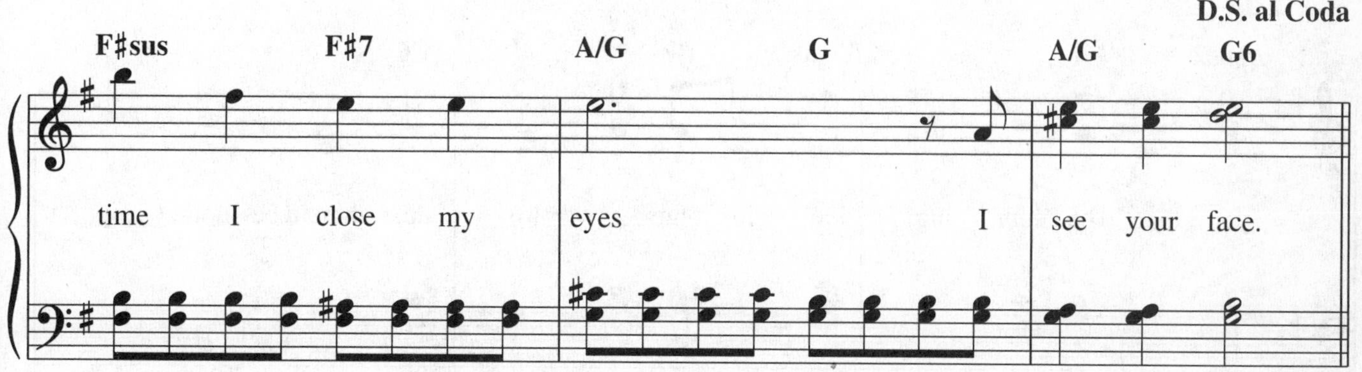
D.S. al Coda
F♯sus
F♯7
A/G
G
A/G
G6
time I close my eyes I see your face.

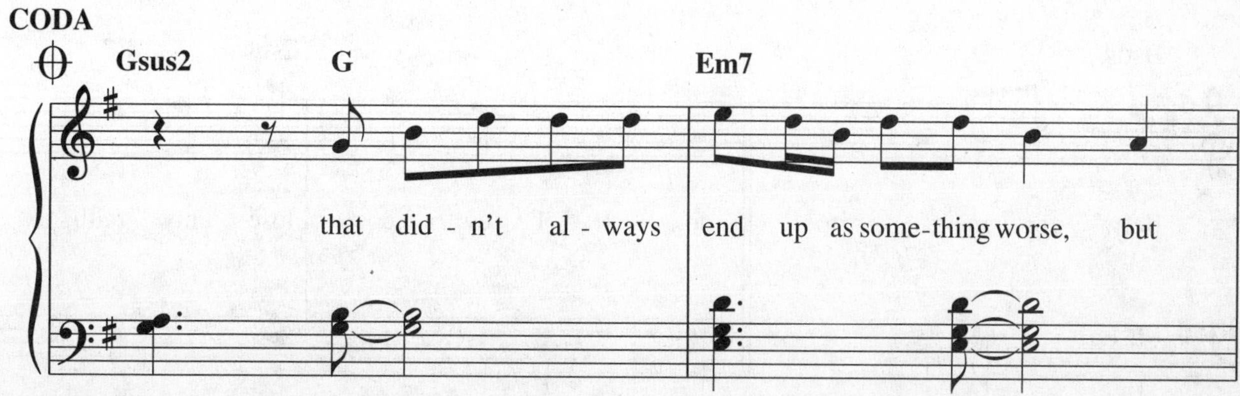
CODA
Gsus2
G
Em7
that did - n't al - ways end up as some-thing worse, but

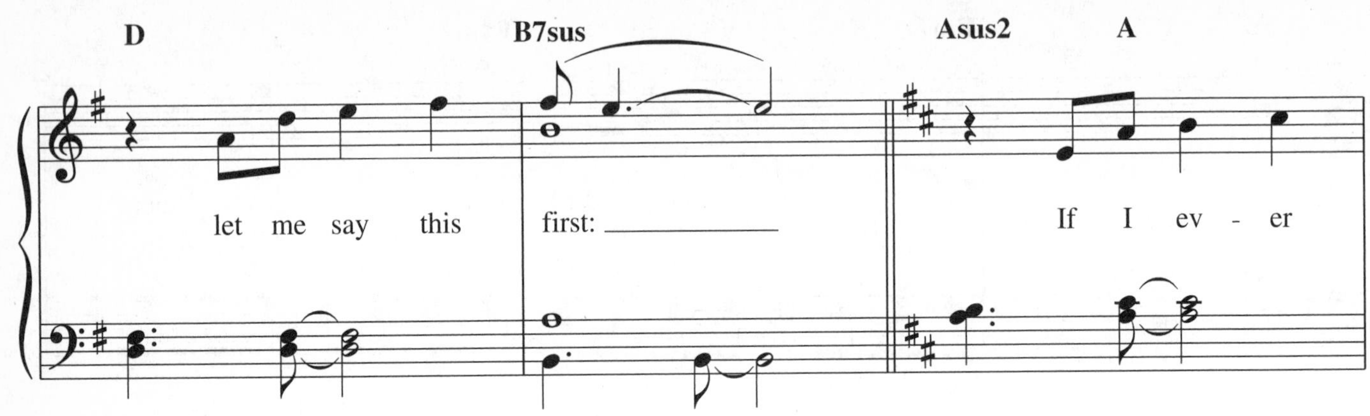
D
B7sus
Asus2
A
let me say this
first:
If I ev - er

B7sus
B7
C6
Dsus
D
lose my faith in
you, if I ev - er
lose my faith in

Asus2
A
B7sus
B7
C6
you there'd be noth - ing
left for me to
do, there'd be noth - ing

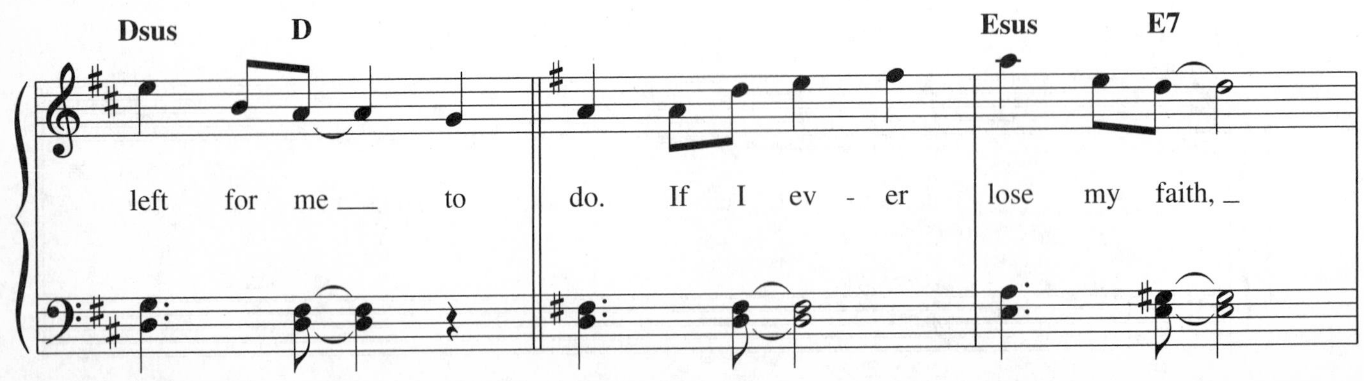
Dsus
D
Esus
E7
left for me to
do. If I ev - er
lose my faith,

F6
Gsus
G/A
D
if I ev - er
lose my faith, _
if I ev - er

Esus
E7
F6
Gsus
G
lose my faith, _
if I ev - er
lose my faith _

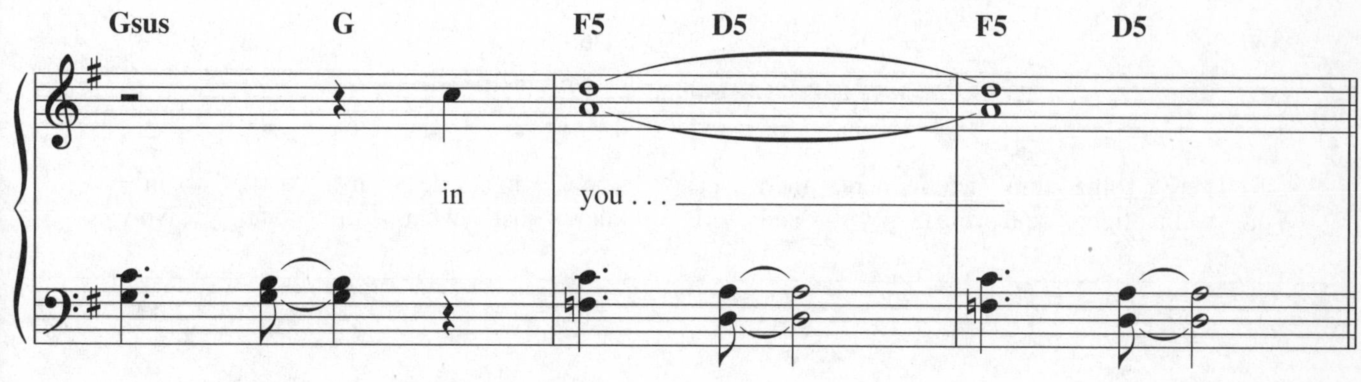
Gsus
G
F5
D5
F5
D5
in
you . . .

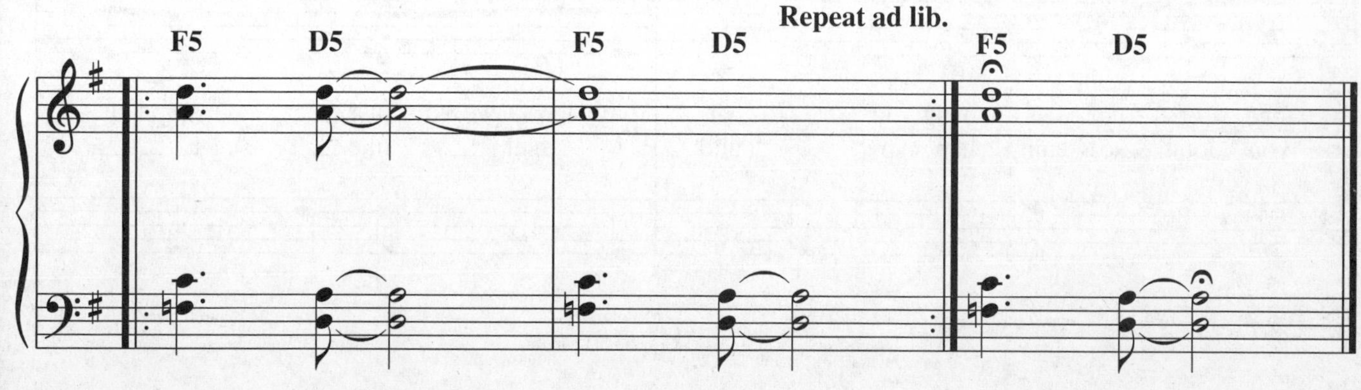
Repeat ad lib.
F5
D5
F5
D5
F5
D5

IT'S TOO LATE

Words and Music by CAROLE KING
and TONI STERN

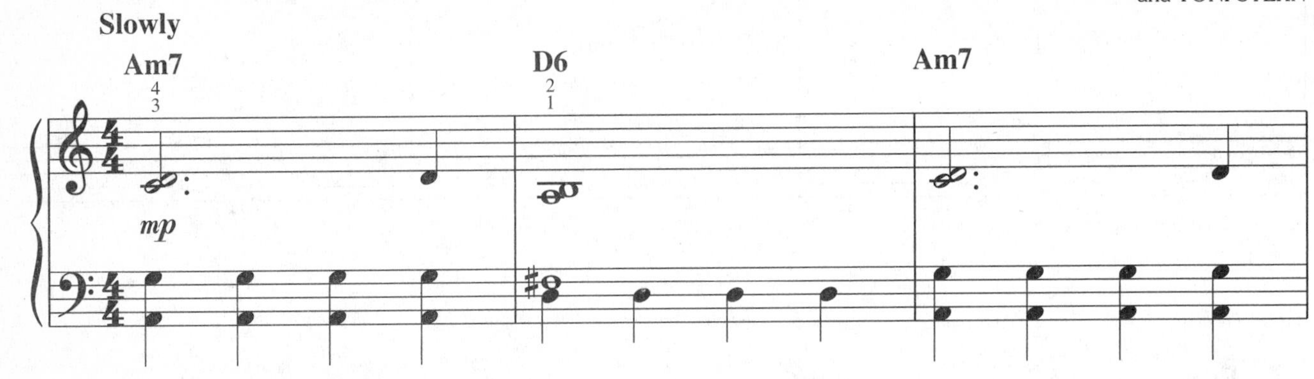

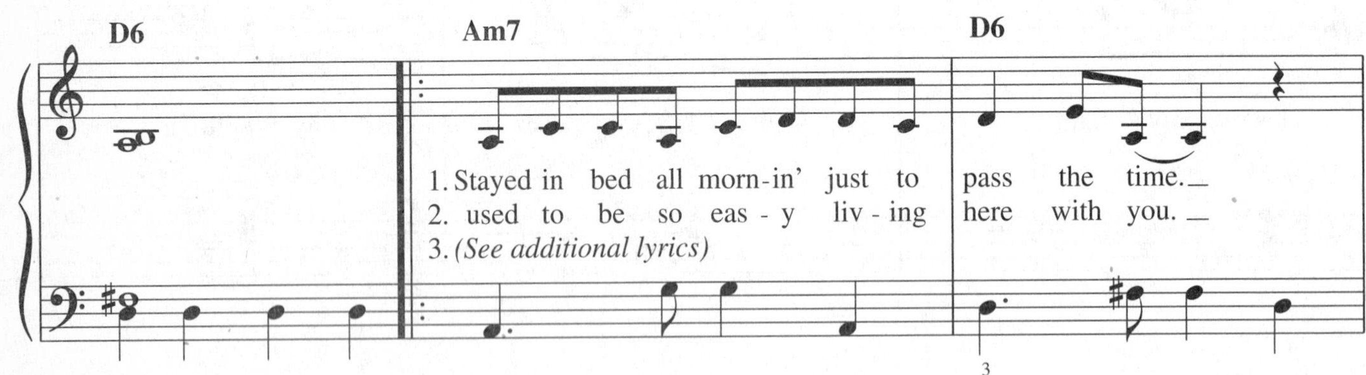

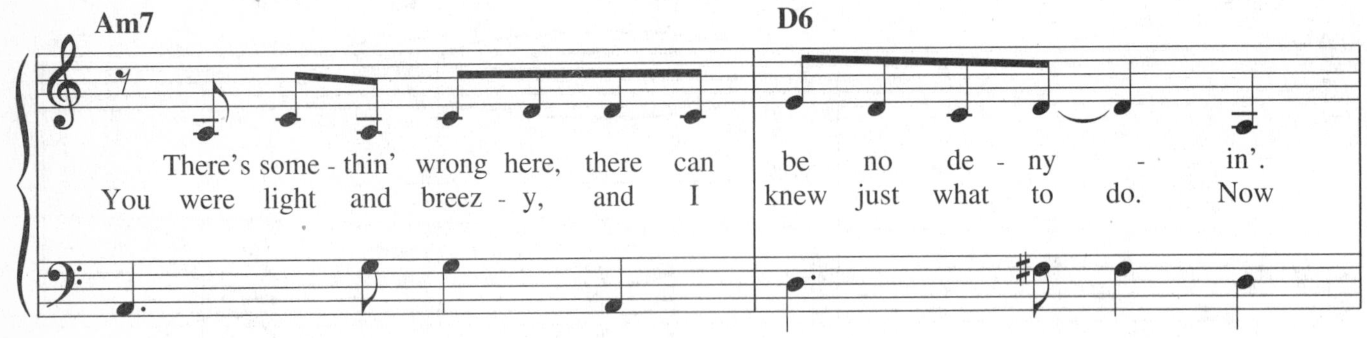

Fmaj7
Chorus
B♭maj7
try - in'.
fool.
And it's
too late, ba - by, now

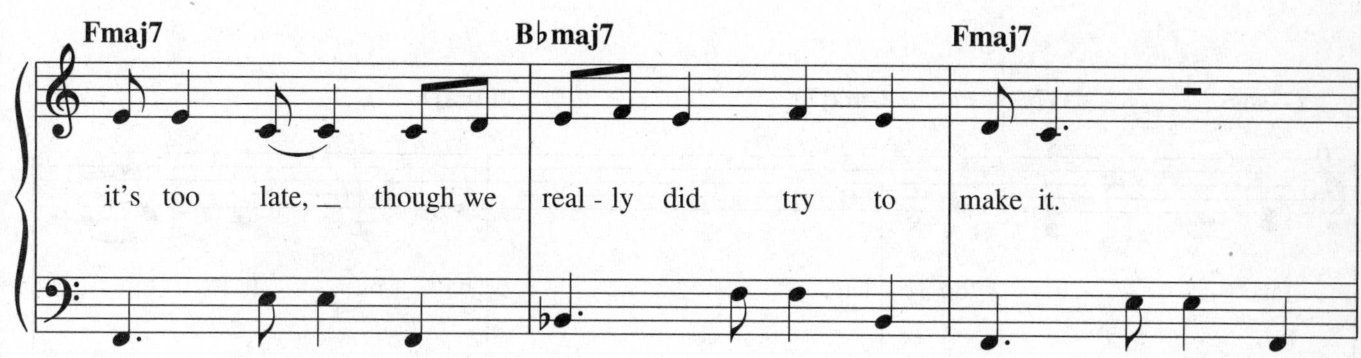
Fmaj7
B♭maj7
Fmaj7
it's too late, though we real - ly did try to make it.

B♭maj7
Fmaj7
1.,2.
Dm7
Fmaj7
Some - thin' in - side has died, and I can't hide and I just can't

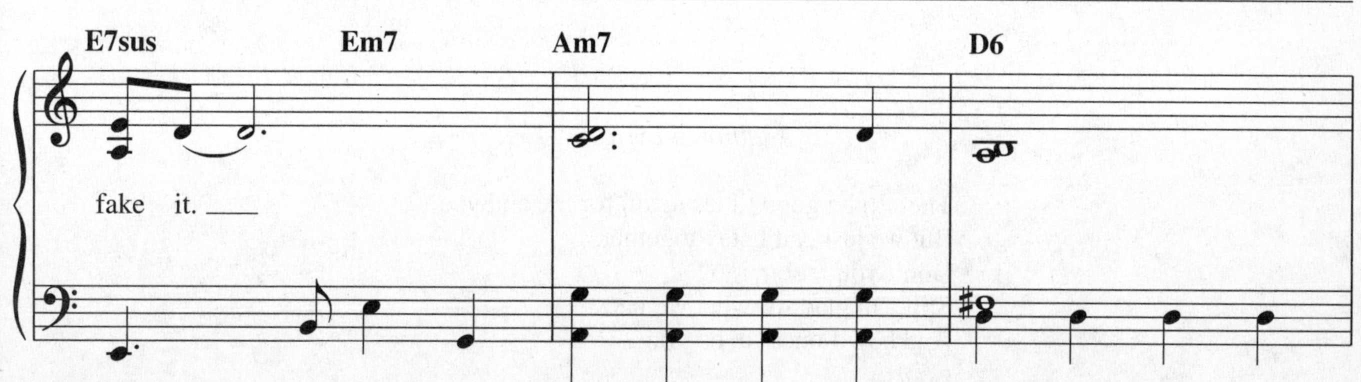
E7sus
Em7
Am7
D6
fake it.

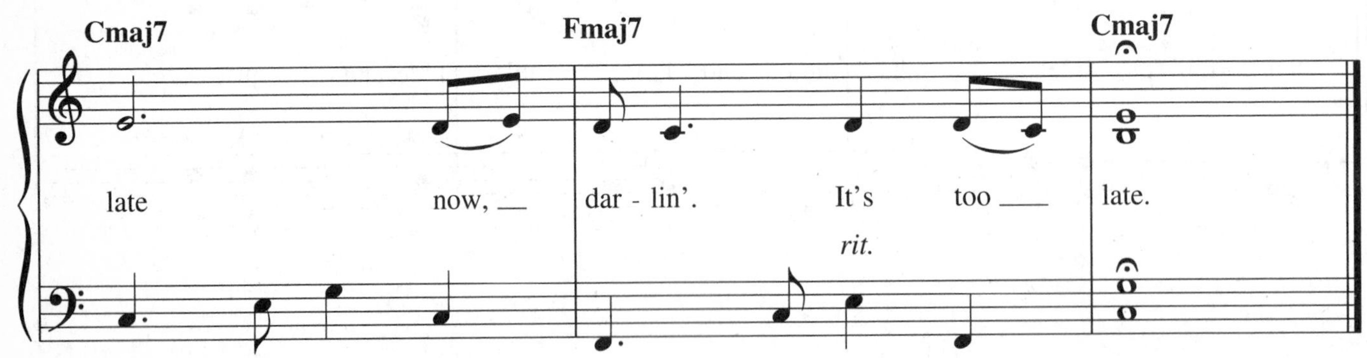

Additional Lyrics

3. There'll be good times again for me and you,
But we just can't stay together.
Don't you feel it, too?
Still I'm glad for what we had
And how I once loved you.
Chorus

JOY TO THE WORLD

Words and Music by
HOYT AXTON

G
C
world.
All ___ the boys and
girls _ now.
5
5

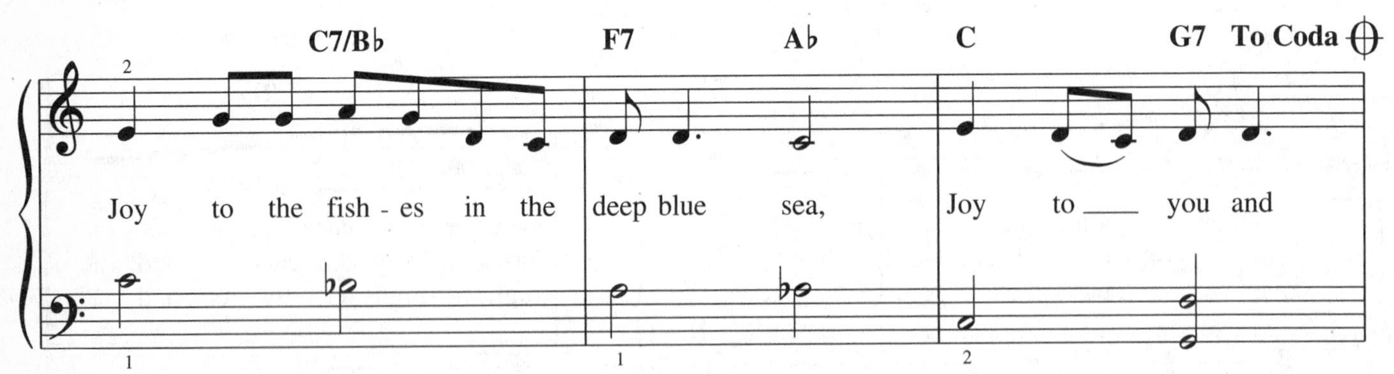
C7/B♭
F7
A♭
C
G7 To Coda
Joy to the fish - es in the
deep blue sea,
Joy to ___ you and
2
1
1
2

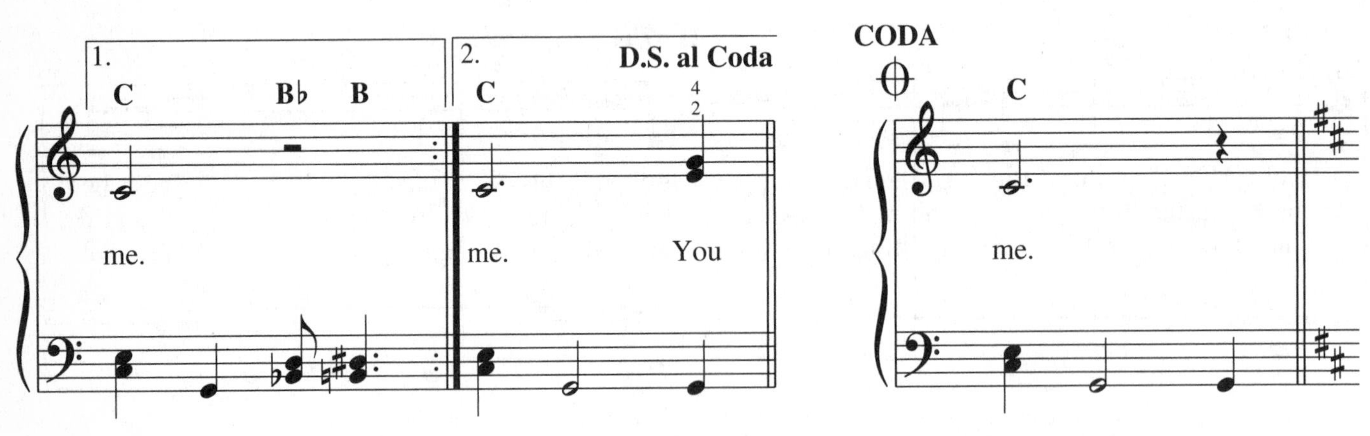
1.
2.
D.S. al Coda
CODA
C
B♭
B
C
C
me.
me.
You
me.
4
2

D
G
D
G
Joy
to the world.
All the
boys and girls. _
5

D G D
Joy to the world, Joy to

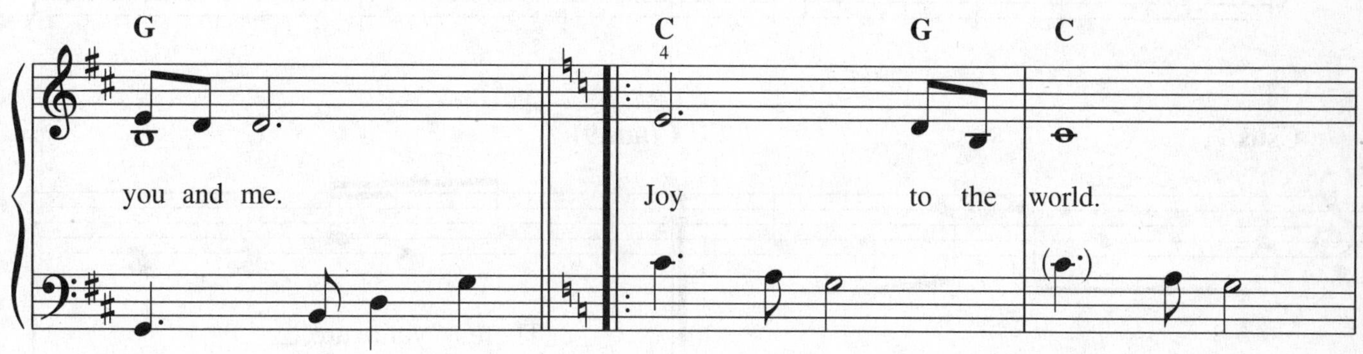
G C G C
you and me. Joy to the world.

G C C7/B♭
All the boys and girls. Joy to the fish - es in the

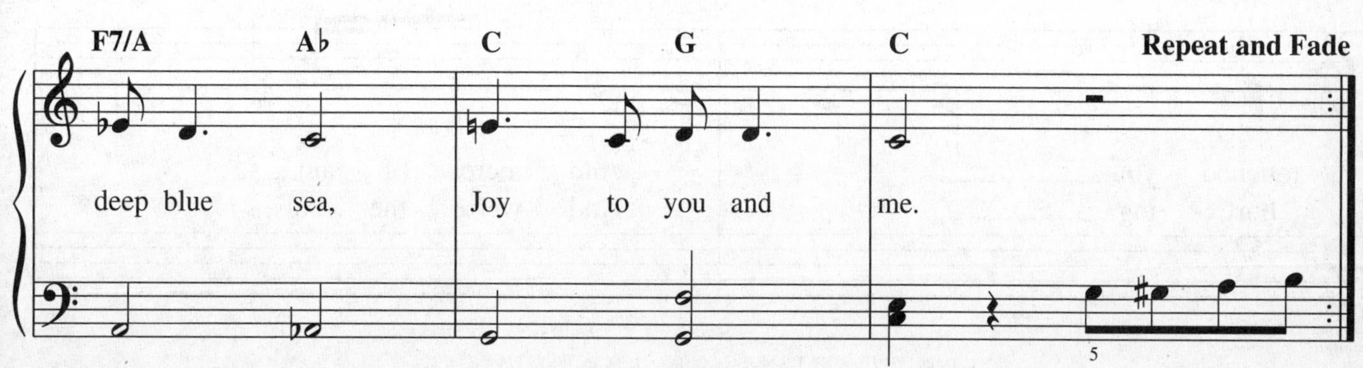
F7/A A♭ C G C
Repeat and Fade
deep blue sea, Joy to you and me.

LOOKS LIKE WE MADE IT

Words and Music by RICHARD KERR
and WILL JENNINGS

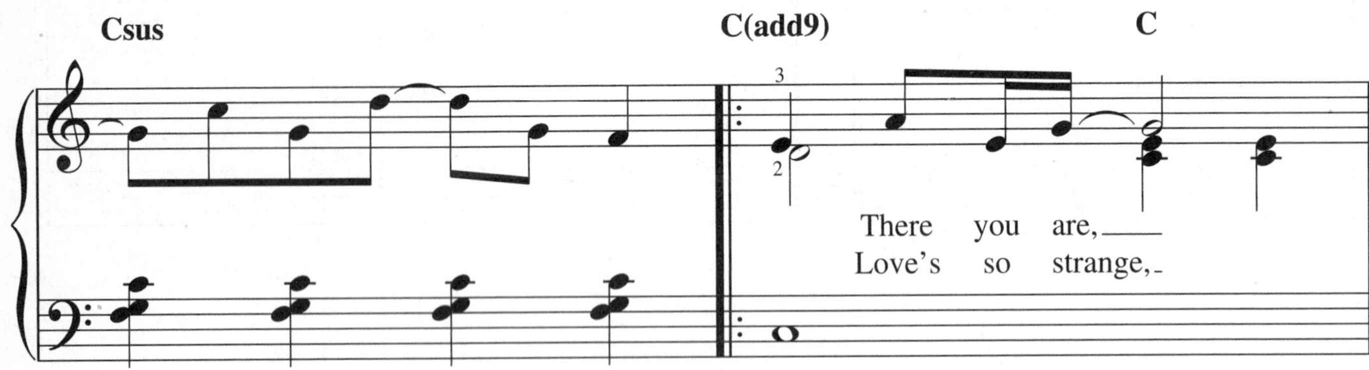

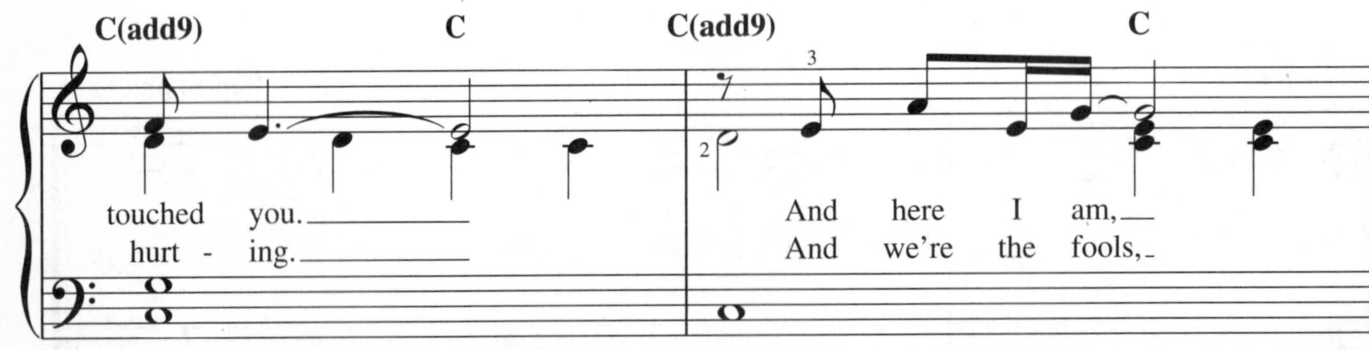

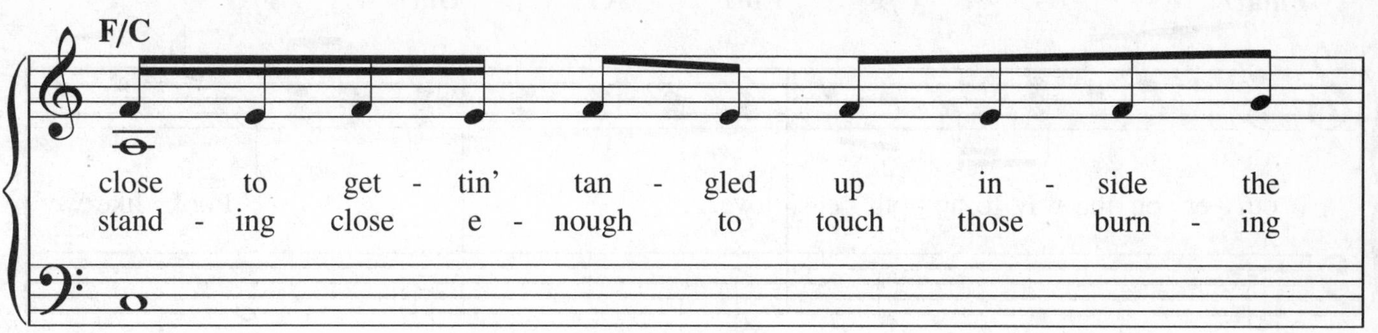
F/C
close to get - tin' tan - gled up in - side the
stand - ing close e - nough to touch those burn - ing

C(add9) C G/B Am D7sus D7
3
thought of you.__ Do you love him as much as I love
mem - o - ries.__ And if you hold him for the sake of all those

G Am D7
her? And will that love be strong when old feel - ings start to
times love made us lose our minds, could I ev - er let you

F/G G C G/C
stir?___ Looks like we made it,
go?___ Oh, no we've made it,
left each

Fmaj7
G
G/F
Em7
A7
Dm7
F/G
oth - er on the way to an - oth - er
love.
Looks like we

C
G/C
F
G
G/F
Em7
Am
3
made it,
or I
thought so till to - day un - til you were
there, ev - 'ry - where, and

1.
Dm7
C/E
F
F/G
C
all I could taste was love the way we
made it.

G/C
F/C
3
2.
Dm7
C/E
F
F/G
all I could taste was love the way we

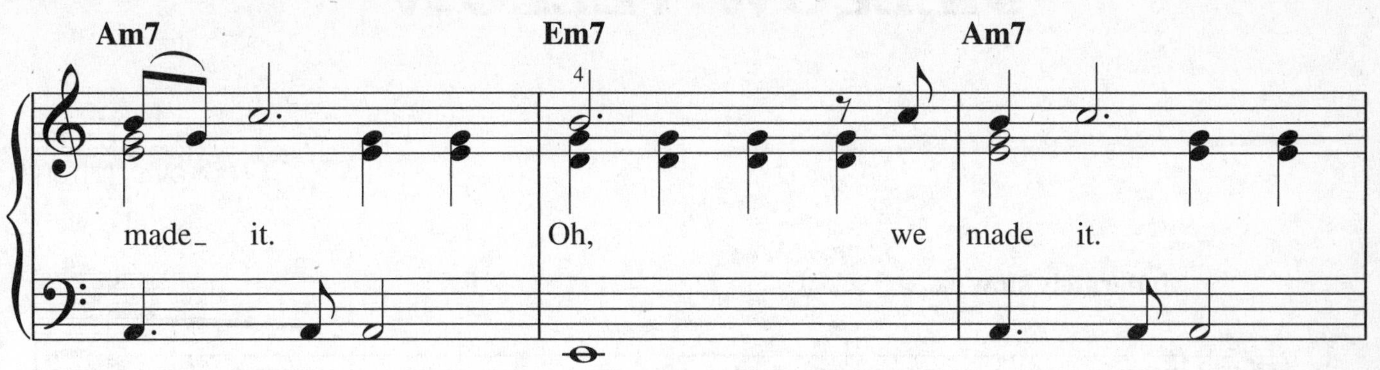
Am7
Em7
Am7
4
made_ it.
Oh,
we
made it.

F/G
C
G/C
Looks like we
made it.

F/C
C
G/C
Looks like we
made it.

F/C
C
Looks like we
made it.

MELLOW YELLOW

Words and Music by
DONOVAN LEITCH

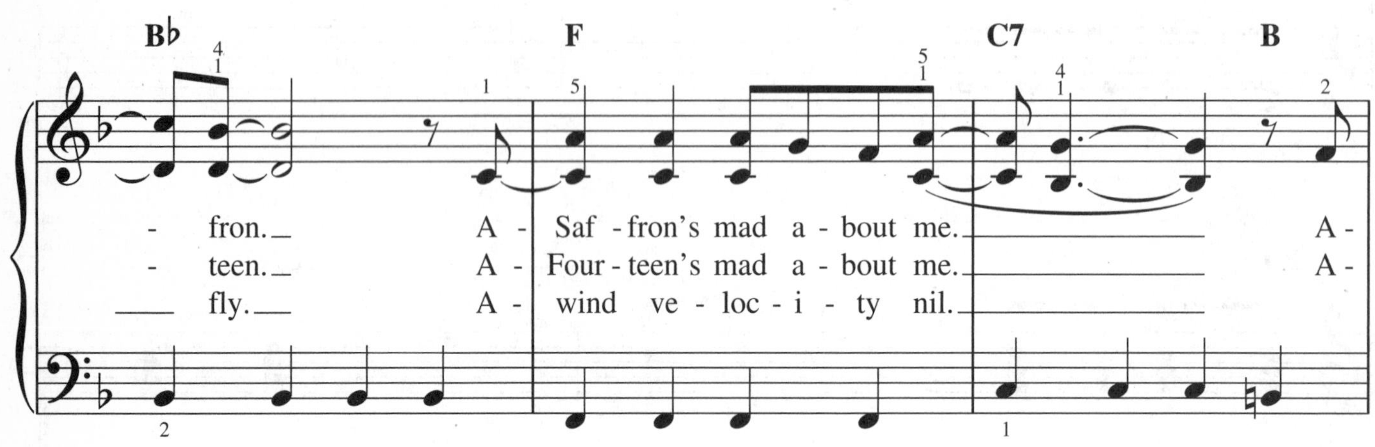

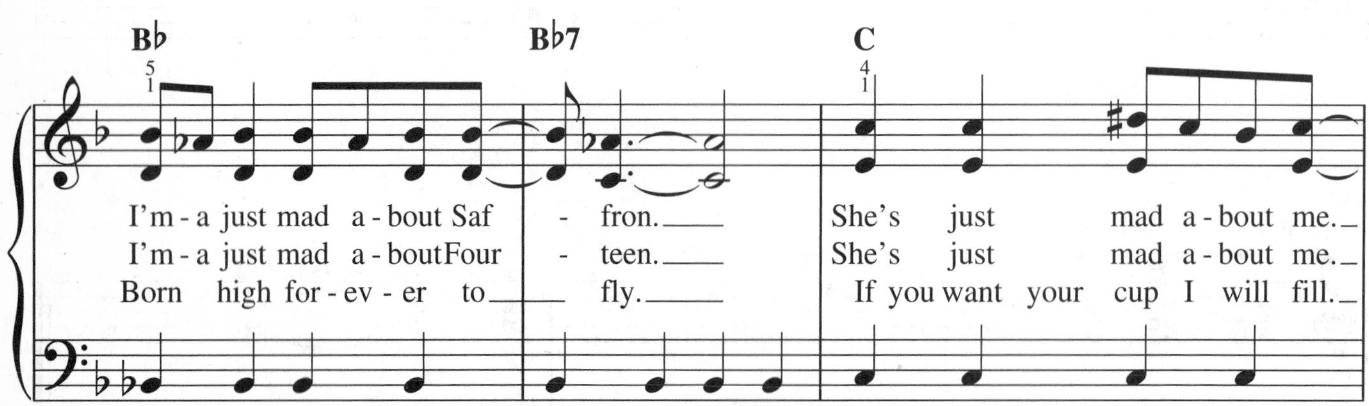

C7
F
B♭
C7
They call me Mel-low Yel-low.
They call me Mel-low
F
B♭
C7
F
Yel-low.
They call me Mel-low Yel-low.
B♭
1.,2.
C
C7
3.
C
F
He's so mel-low, he's so mel-low.
E-lec-tri-cal ba-na-
I'm just mad a-bout Saf-

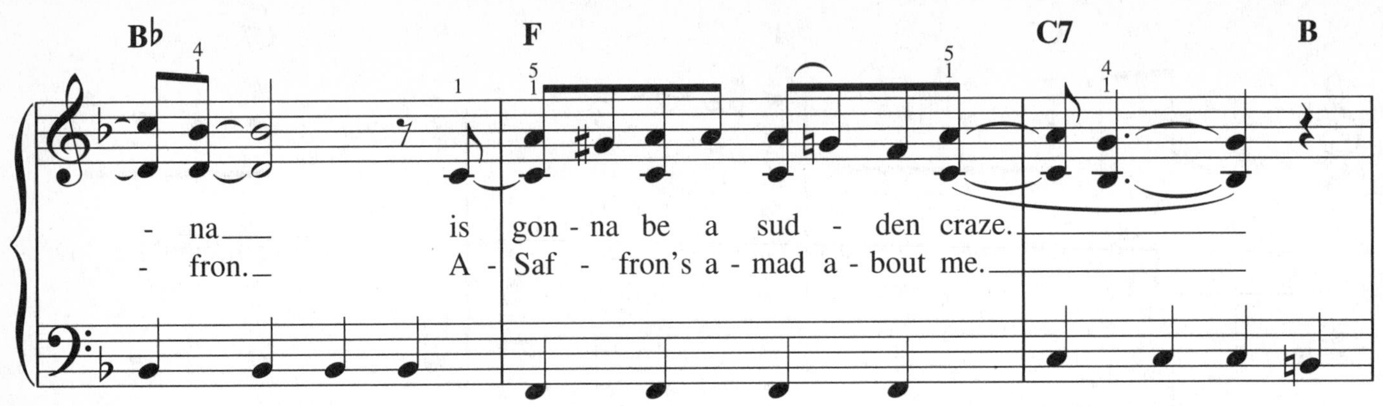
B♭
F
C7
B
- na
is
gon - na be a sud - den craze.
- fron.
A - Saf - fron's a - mad a - bout me.

B♭
C
E - lec - tri - cal ba - na - na
is
bound to be the ver - y next phase.
All the boys are mad a - bout a - Saf - fron.
A - Saf - fron's a - mad a - bout me.

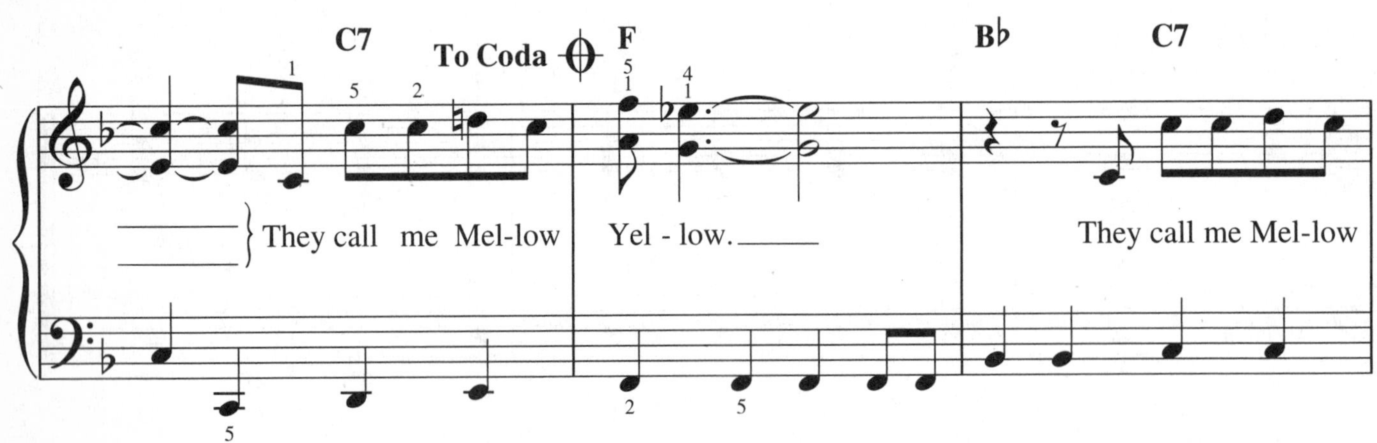
C7
To Coda
F
B♭
C7
They call me Mel-low
Yel - low.
They call me Mel-low

F
B♭
C7
F
Yel - low.
They call me Mel-low
Yel - low.

B♭
C
C7
D.S. al Coda

CODA
F
B♭
C7
F
Yel - low.
They call me Mel-low
Yel - low.

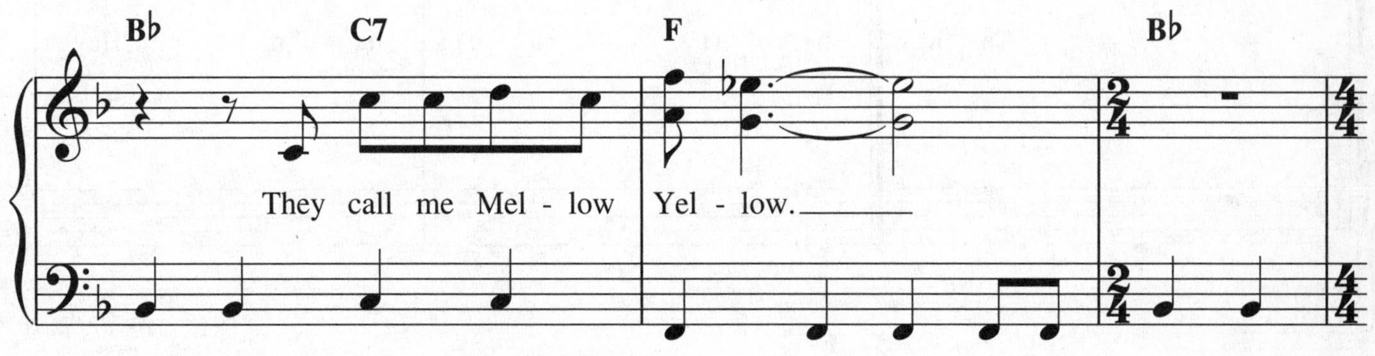
B♭
C7
F
B♭
They call me Mel - low
Yel - low.

C
C7
F

NA NA HEY HEY KISS HIM GOODBYE

Words and Music by ARTHUR FRASHUER DALE,
PAUL ROGER LEKA and GARY CARLA

Gm7
C
F
Gm7
C
love you the way that I love you,
near you to com - fort and cheer you.
F
Dm
Gm
'cause if he did no, no, he would-n't make you
When all those sad tears are falling baby
C
B♭
A
cry.
from your eyes.
He might be thrill - ing bab - by, but
Dm
Gm
F
my love's so dog - gone will - ing. So kiss him,

B♭
B♭m
C
F
go on and kiss him, good - bye. Na na
A♭
1.
E♭
F
na na, Hey Hey Hey, good - bye. Na na
2.
E♭
F
hey, hey, Good - bye. Na na na na, na na
A♭
E♭
F
Repeat and Fade
na na, Hey Hey Hey, Good - bye. Na na

PLEASE COME TO BOSTON

Words and Music by
DAVE LOGGINS

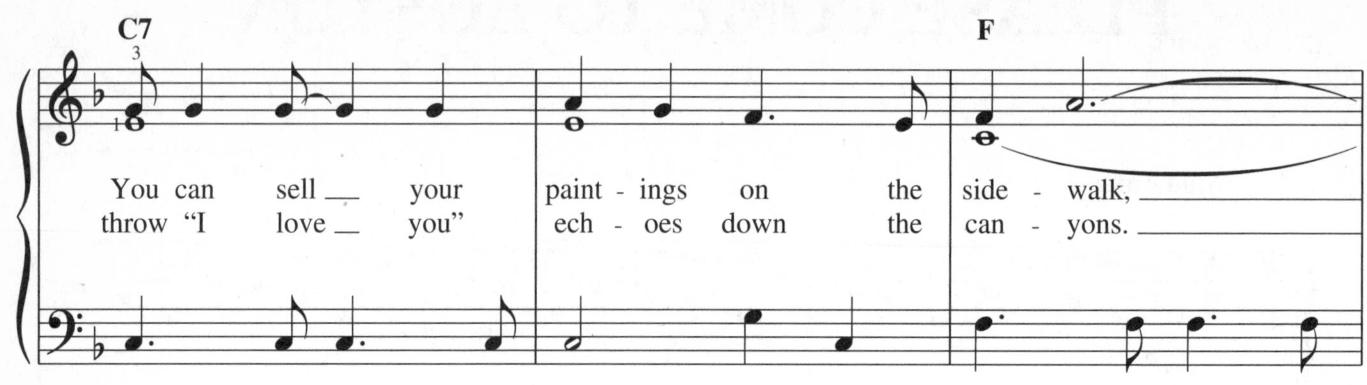
C7
F
You can sell __ your paint - ings on the side - walk, ___
throw "I love __ you" ech - oes down the can - yons. ___

Dm
___ by a ca - fé where I hope to be
___ And then lie a - wake at night un - til they come

B♭
F
work - ing soon. ___
back a - round. ___
Please come to

C7
Bos - ton.
Den - ver.
L. A.
She said, "no, but you come home to

F
C7
F
me."
And she said, _
"Hey ram - blin 'boy, _ now won't you

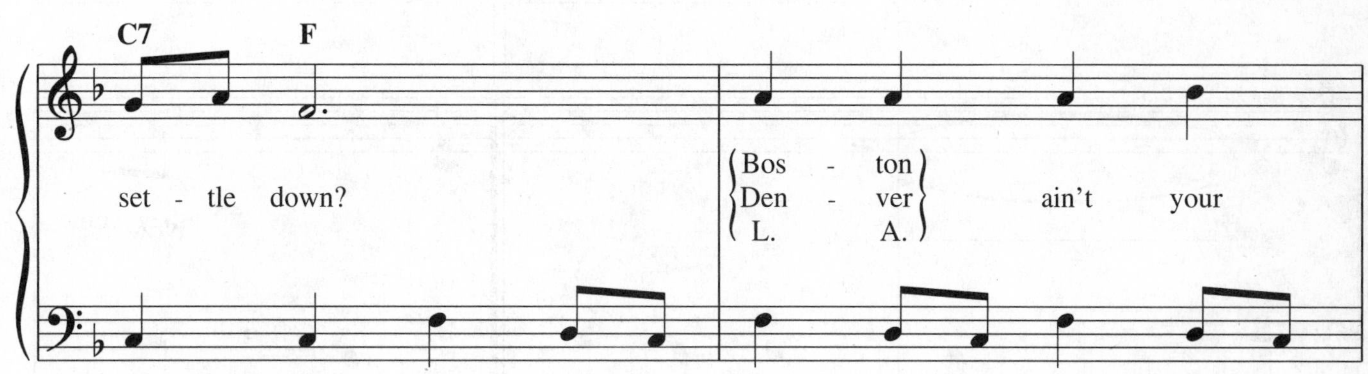
C7
F
set - tle down?
Bos - ton
Den - ver
L. A.
ain't your

C7
F
kind of town. _
There ain't no gold _ and there

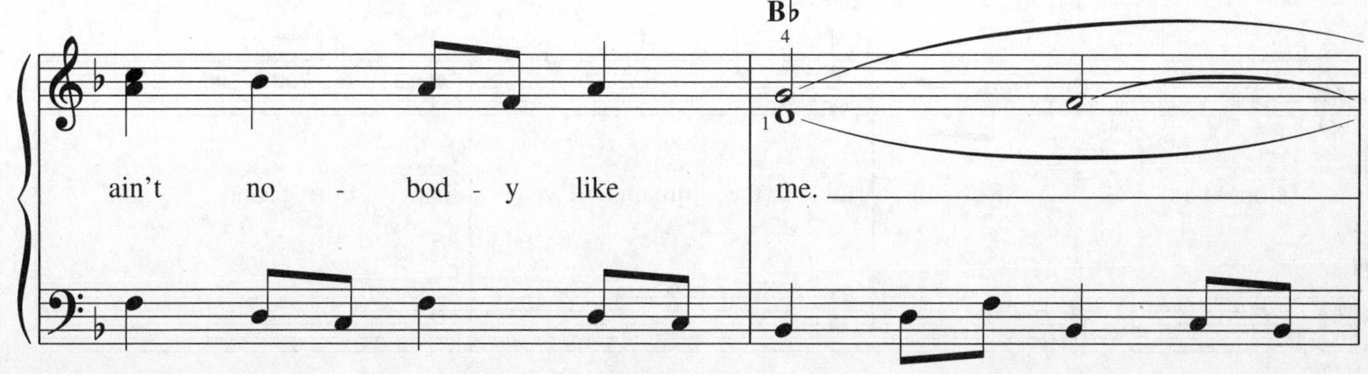
B♭
ain't no - bod - y like
me. _

Gm7
C7
To Coda
I'm the num-ber one fan of the man from Ten - nes -

F
1.
2.
see."
Now this

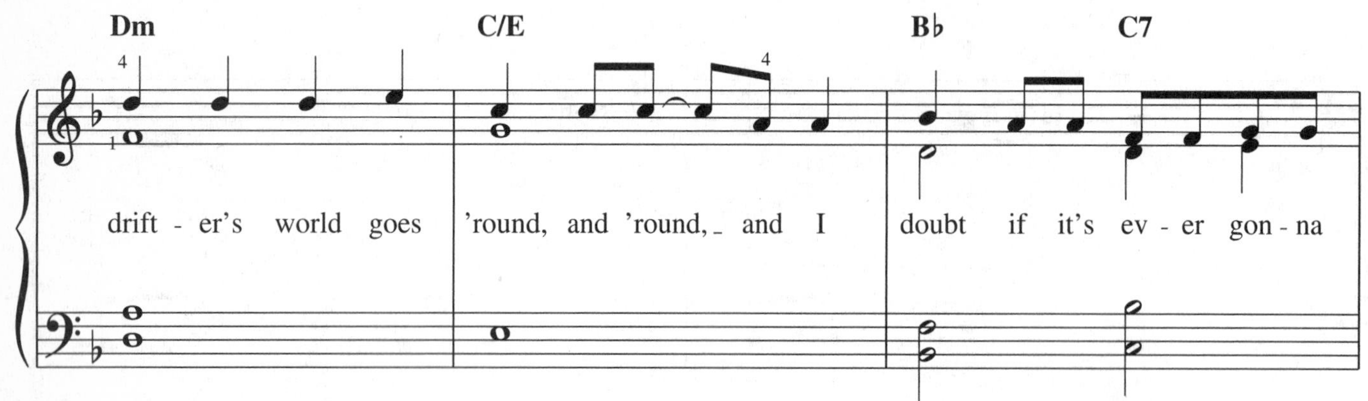
Dm
C/E
B♭
C7
drift - er's world goes 'round, and 'round, and I doubt if it's ev - er gon - na

F
Dm
C/E
stop. But of all the dreams I've lost or found and

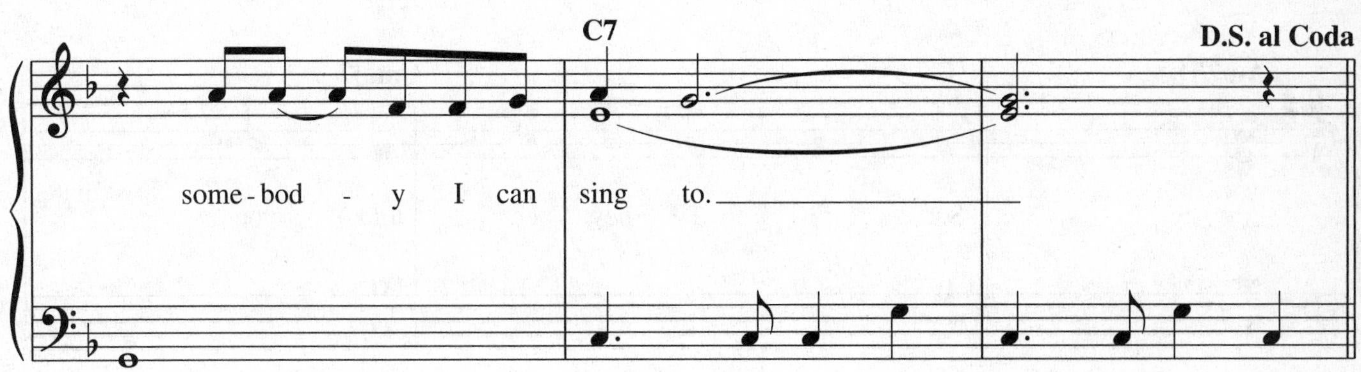

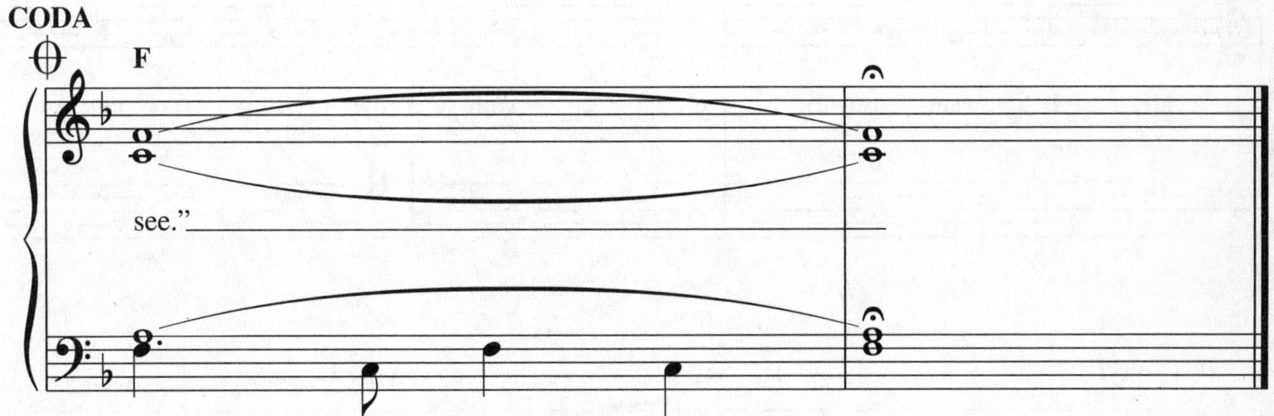

Additional Lyrics

Please come to L.A. to live forever.
A California life alone is just too hard to build.
I live in a house that looks out over the ocean,
and there's some stars that fell from the sky
living up on the hill.
Please come to L.A. She just said, "no,
boy, won't you come home to me?"
Chorus

ONE SWEET DAY

Words and Music by MARIAH CAREY, WALTER AFANASIEFF, SHAWN STOCKMAN,
MICHAEL McCARY, NATHAN MORRIS and WANYA MORRIS

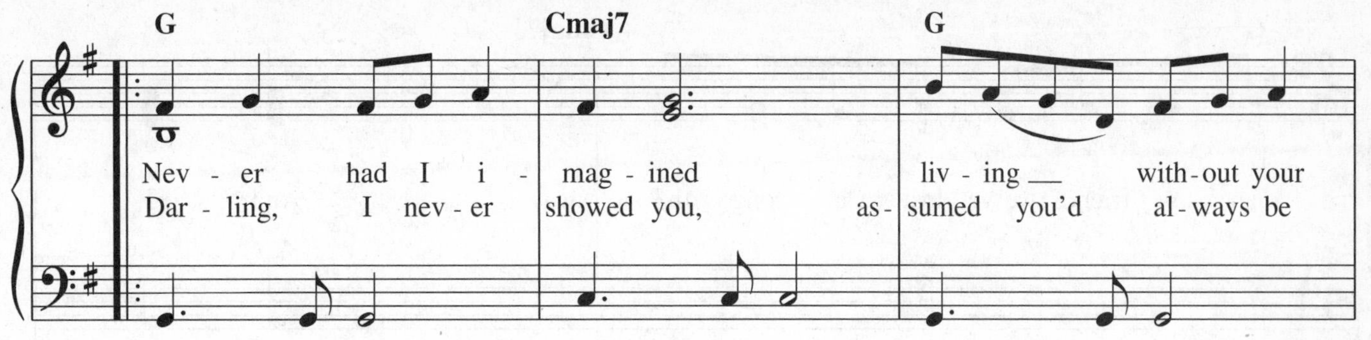
G
Cmaj7
G
Nev - er had I i - mag - ined liv - ing __ with-out your
Dar - ling, I nev - er showed you, as- sumed you'd al - ways be

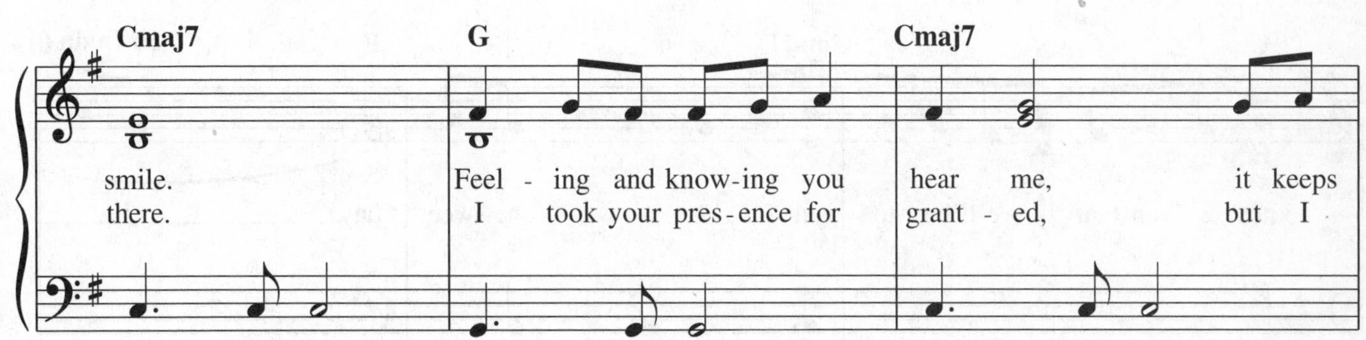
Cmaj7
G
Cmaj7
smile. Feel - ing and know-ing you hear me, it keeps
there. I took your pres-ence for grant - ed, but I

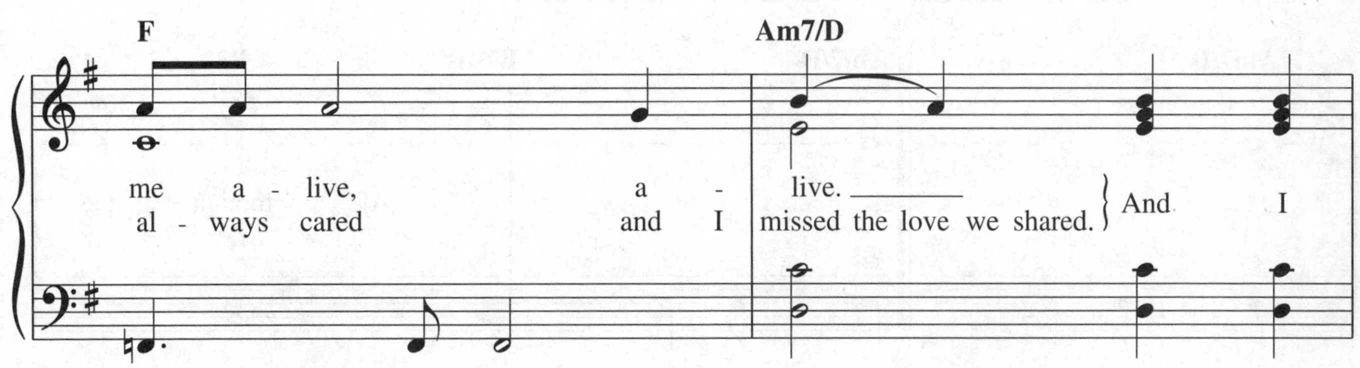
F
Am7/D
me a - live, a - live. ____
al - ways cared and I missed the love we shared.
And I

G
Cmaj7
know you're shin - ing down on me from heav - en like so

G
Cmaj7
many - y friends we've lost a - long the way. ___ And I

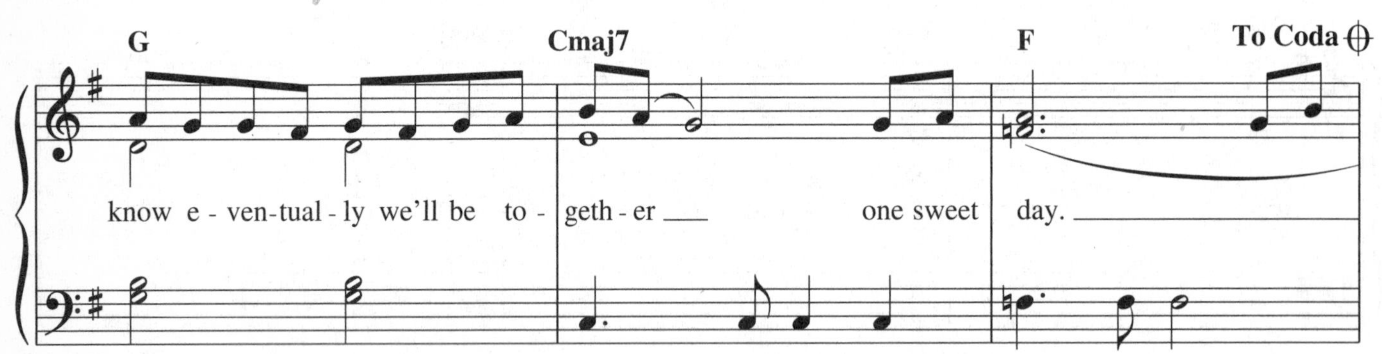
G
Cmaj7
F
To Coda
know e - ven-tual - ly we'll be to - geth - er ___ one sweet day. ___

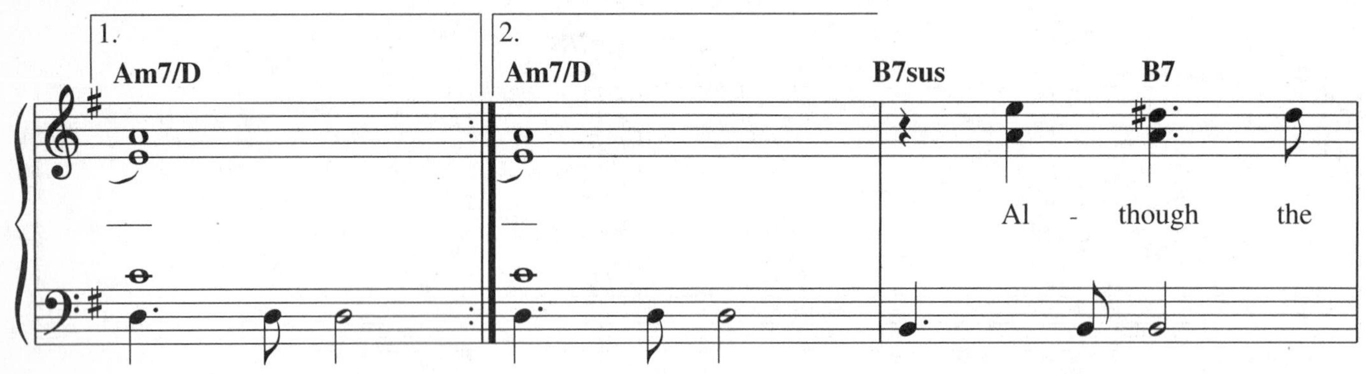
1.
2.
Am7/D
Am7/D
B7sus
B7
Al - though the

Em
Cmaj7
D7
G
sun will nev - er shine the same, _ I'll al-ways look to a bright-er day. ___

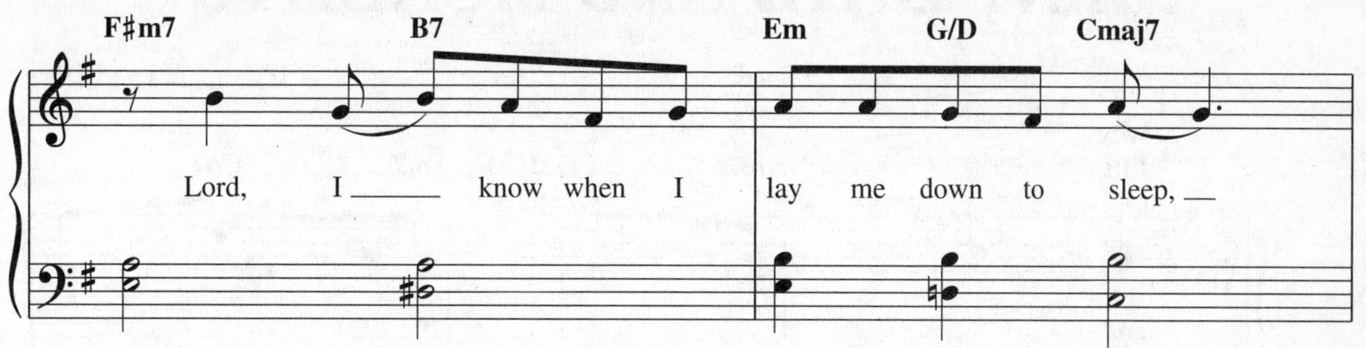
F♯m7
B7
Em
G/D
Cmaj7
Lord, I ___ know when I lay me down to sleep, ___

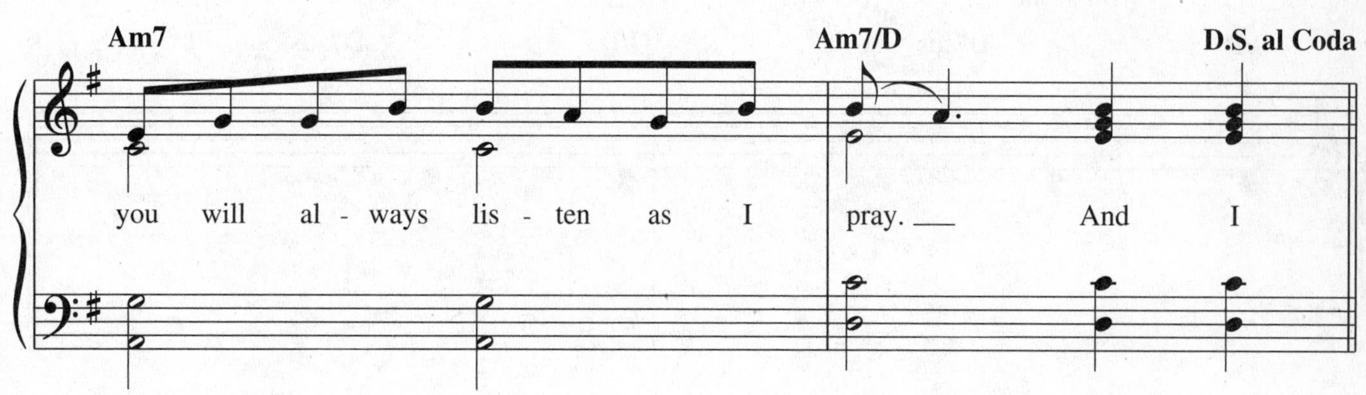
Am7
Am7/D
D.S. al Coda
you will al - ways lis - ten as I pray. ___ And I

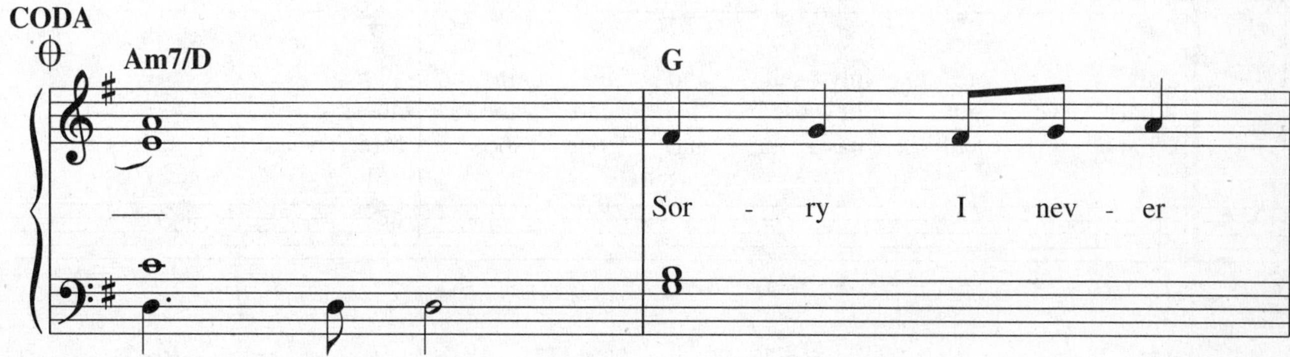
CODA
Am7/D
G
___ Sor - ry I nev - er

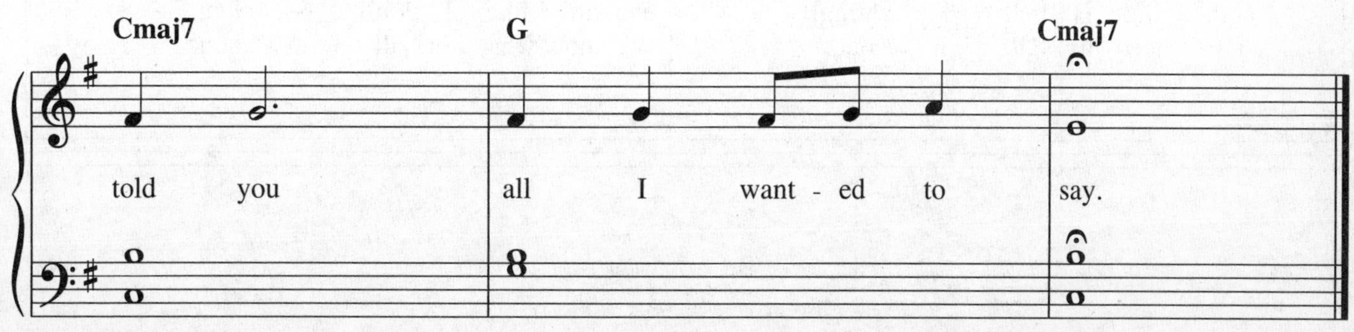
Cmaj7
G
Cmaj7
told you all I want - ed to say.

RAINY DAYS AND MONDAYS

Lyrics by PAUL WILLIAMS
Music by ROGER NICHOLS

Em7
Cmaj7
Am7
C/D
G
Hang - in' a - round noth - ing to do but frown;
Walk - in' a - round some kind of lone - ly clown;
Hang - in' a - round noth - ing to do but frown;
Am7
C/D
G/D
D7sus
1.
G/D
D7sus
rain-y days and Mon-days al - ways get me down.
2.,3.
G/D
B/D#
Em7
Cmaj7
Am7
D7
Gmaj7
Fun - ny but it seems I al - ways wind up here with you,
Bm7
Cmaj7
C/D
D
B7/D#
nice to know some-bod - y loves me.

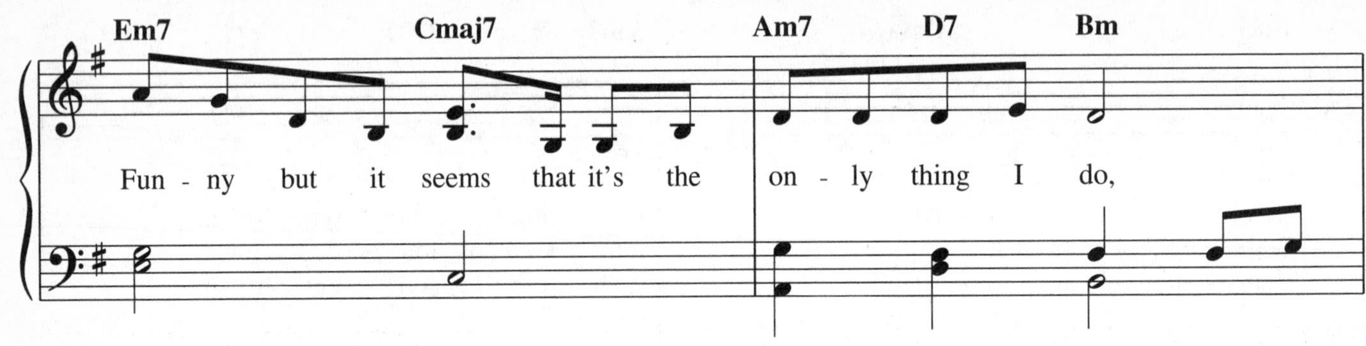
Em7
Cmaj7
Am7
D7
Bm
Fun - ny but it seems that it's the on - ly thing I do,

To Coda
D.S. al Coda
Bm7
Cmaj7
D7sus
D7
Am7/D
D7
run and find the one who loves _ me.

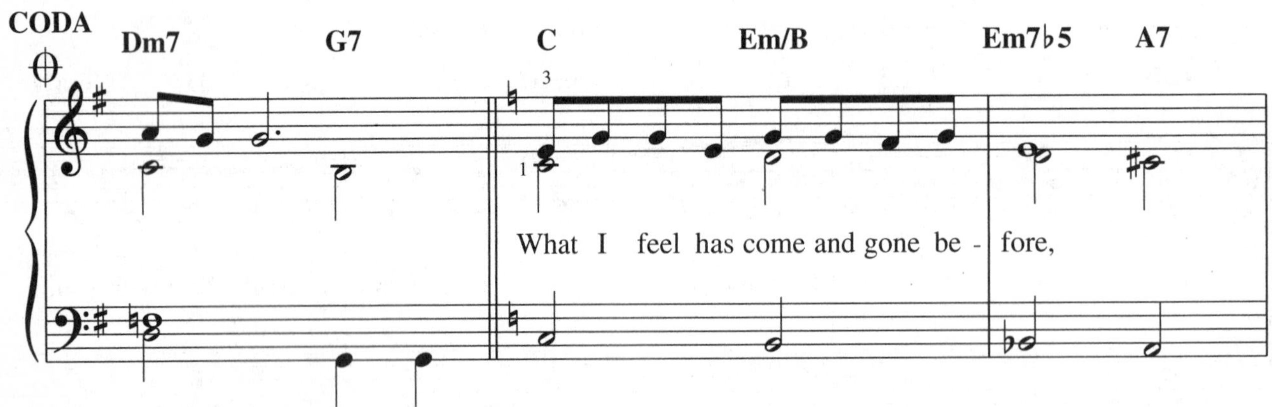
CODA
Dm7
G7
C
Em/B
Em7♭5
A7
What I feel has come and gone be - fore,

Dm11
Em7
Fmaj7
Em7
no need to talk it out, we know what it's all a - bout.

Am7
Fmaj7
Dm7
F/G
C
3
1
2
3
1
Hang - in' a - round noth - in' to do but frown;
1.
Dm7
F/G
C/G
E/G#
rain - y days and Mon - days al - ways get me down.
2.
Dm7
F/G
C/G
rain - y days and Mon - days al - ways get me down.
G7sus
C/G
G7sus
Cmaj7

RESPECT

Words and Music by
OTIS REDDING

F7
C7
F7
- by when you come home.
Re - spect.
G
F
G
3. I'm out to give you
4. (See additional lyrics)
all my mon - ey
but all I'm ask - in'
F
G
F
in re - turn, hon - ey,
is to give me
my pro - per re - spect when you get
C7
F7
C7
home.
Yeah, ba - by, when you get
home.

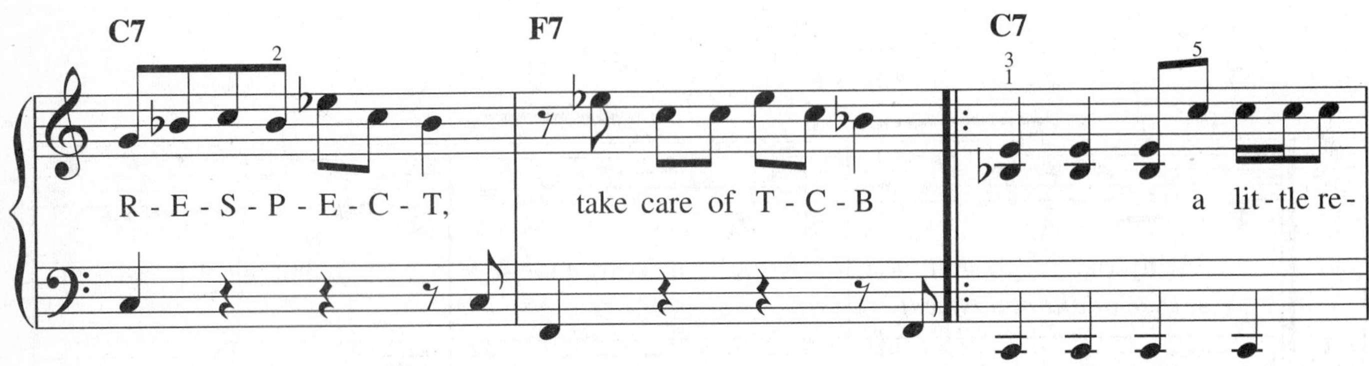

Additional Lyrics

2. I ain't gonna do you wrong while you gone.
   I ain't gonna do you wrong 'cause I don't wanna.
   All I'm askin' is for a little respect, when you come home.
   Baby, when you come home, respect.

4. Ooh, your kisses, sweeter than honey,
   And guess what so here's my money,
   All I want you to do for me is give it to me when you get home.
   Yeah, baby, when you get home.

SHEILA

Words and Music by
TOMMY ROE

C
D
G
C
G
D
like a lit - tle Shei - la;
her name
drives me in - sane.
G
D
C
D
G
C
Sweet lit - tle girl,
that's my lit - tle Shei - la,
man, this lit - tle girl is fine.
G
D
Me and Shei - la
go for a ride, oh,
C
G
D
oh, oh, oh, I feel - a
fun - ny in - side.
Then lit - tle Shei - la

C
G
whis - pers in my ear, oh, oh, oh, oh. I love you, Shei - la dear.
D
C
D
G
C
Shei - la said she loved me, she said she'd nev - er leave me. True love will
G
D
G
D
C
D
nev - er die. We're so dog-gone hap - py, just bein' a - round to - geth - er.
G
C
1.
G
2.
G
Man, this lit - tle girl is fine.

RESPECT YOURSELF

Words and Music by MACK RICE
and LUTHER INGRAM

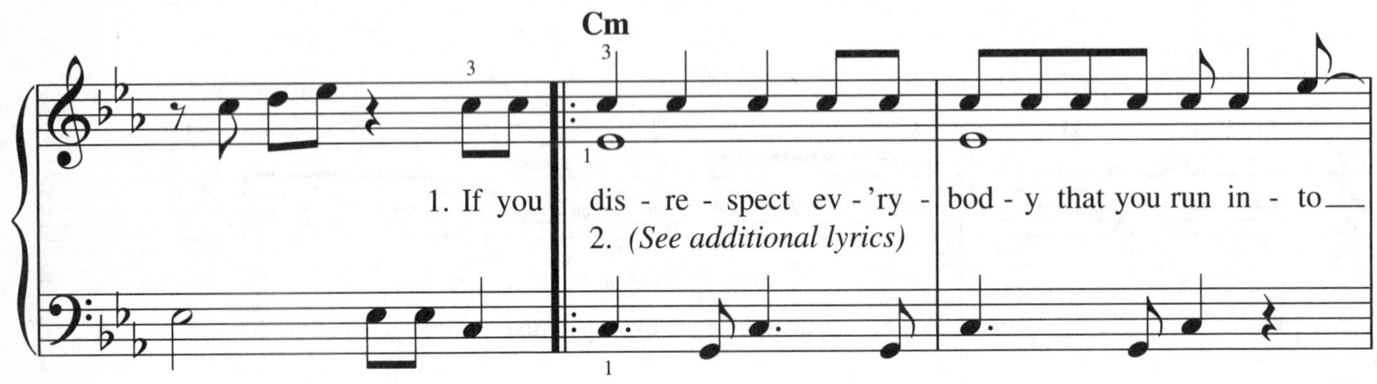

5
2
1
bod - y 'sposed to re - spect you?
If you

3
don't give a heck a - bout the man with the Bi - ble in his hand,

5
just get out the way and let the gen - tle - man do his thing.

5
1
You the kind of gen - tle - man

want ev - 'ry - thing your way. Take the

sheet off your face, boy, it's a brand new day.

Chorus
Re - spect your - self, re - spect your - self.

G+
'Cause if you don't re - spect your - self ain't no - bod - y

Additional Lyrics

2. If you're walking around thinking that the world
Owes you something 'cause you're here,
You're going out the world backward like you did
When you first came 'ere.
Keep talking about the president won't stop air pollution.
Put your hand over your mouth when you cough; that'll help the solution.
You cuss around women folk, don't even know their name,
Then you're dumb enough to think it makes you a big ole man.
To Chorus:

RIKKI DON'T LOSE THAT NUMBER

Words and Music by WALTER BECKER
and DONALD FAGEN

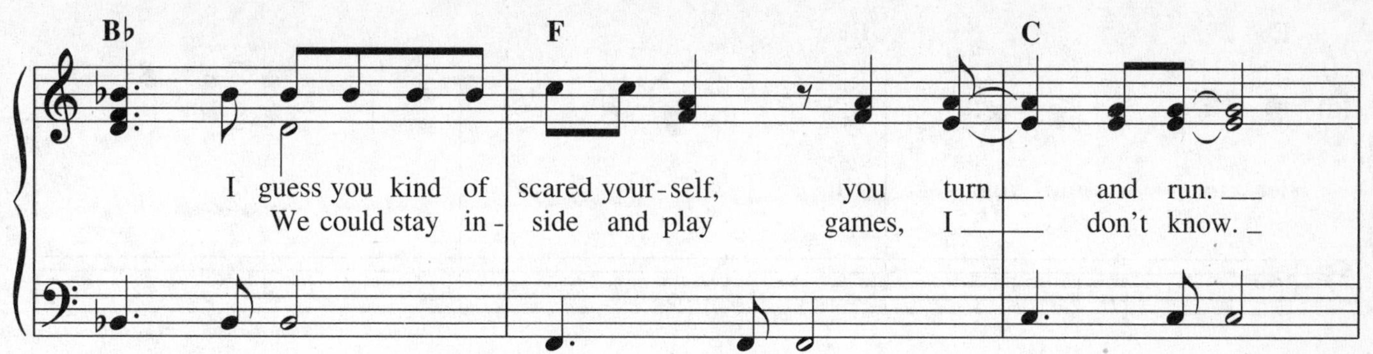

B♭
F
C
I guess you kind of scared your-self, you turn and run.
We could stay in-side and play games, I don't know.

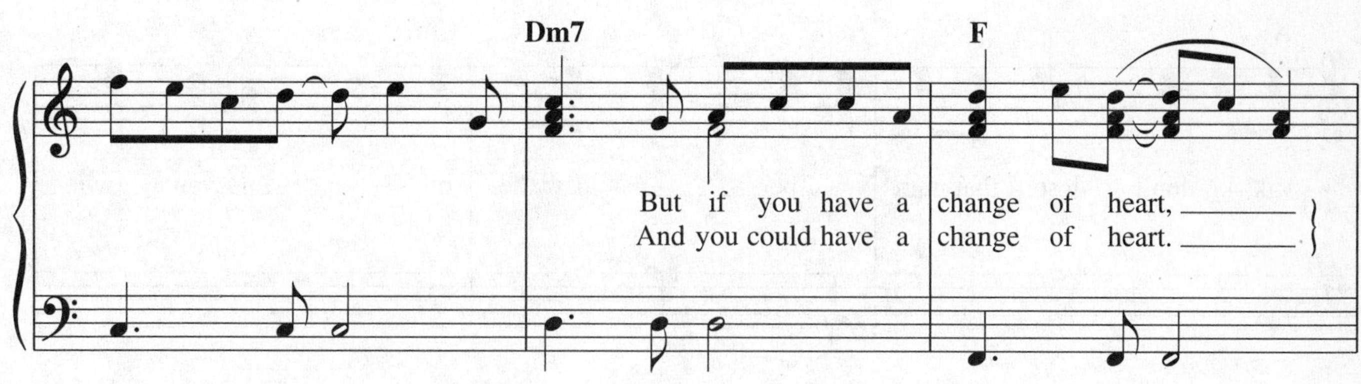

Dm7
F
But if you have a change of heart,
And you could have a change of heart.

N.C.
C
Rik-ki, don't lose that num - ber; you don't wan-na

E♭
F
call no-bod - y else. Send it off in a

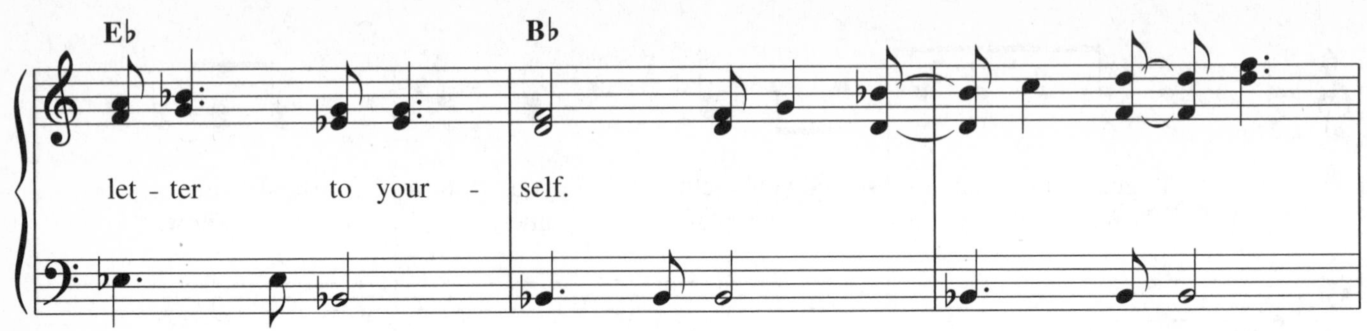
E♭
B♭
let - ter to your - self.

A♭
Cm
Rik - ki, don't lose that num - ber; it's the on - ly one you own.

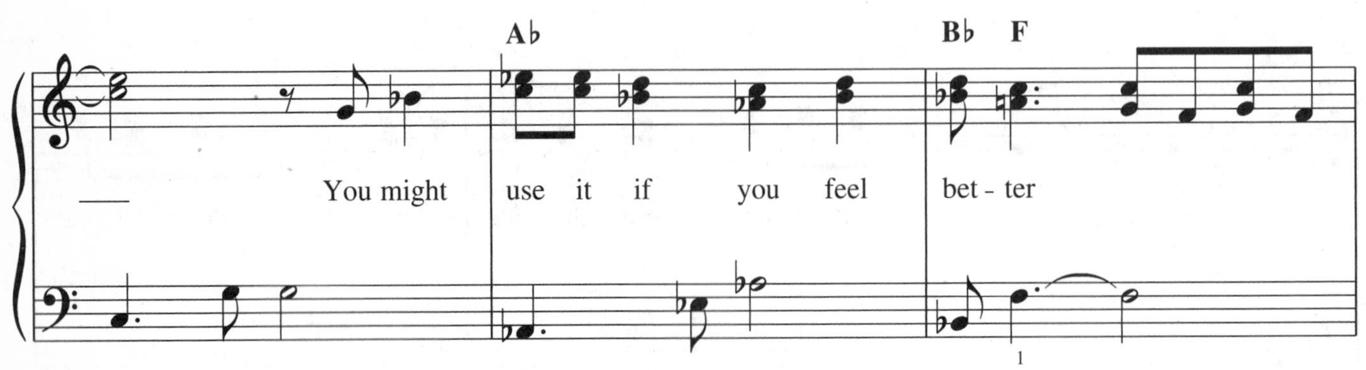
A♭
B♭ F
You might use it if you feel bet - ter

To Coda
N.C.
C
when you get home.

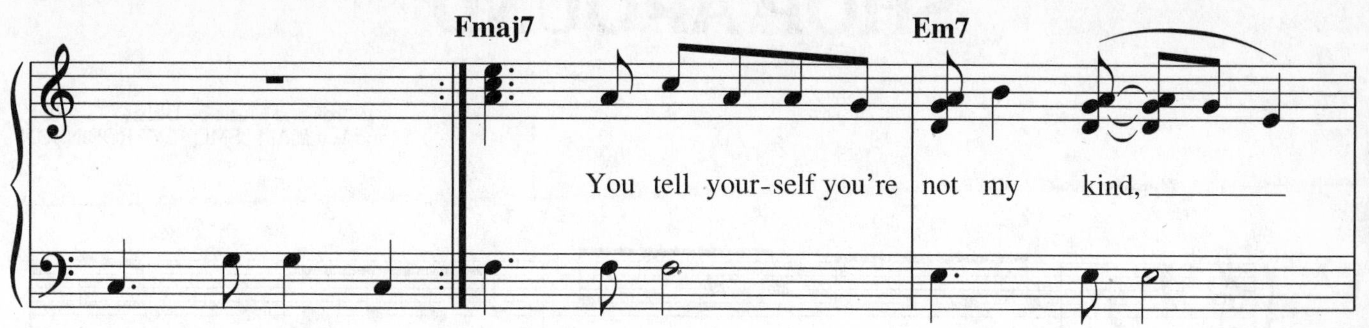
Fmaj7
Em7
You tell your-self you're not my kind,

Fmaj7
Am7
Dm7
but you don't e - ven know your mind.
And you could have a

F
N.C.
D.S. al Coda
change of heart.

CODA
C7
Rik - ki, don't lose that num -

- ber,
Rik - ki, don't lose that num - ber.

SHOP AROUND

Words and Music by BERRY GORDY
and WILLIAM "SMOKEY" ROBINSON

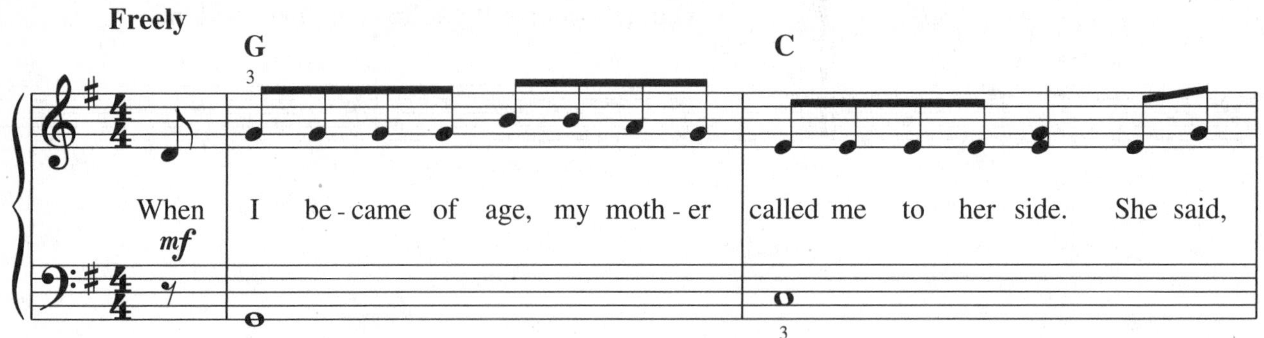

G7
C7
A7
Keep your free-dom for as long as you can now.
Be-fore you tell 'em that you love 'em so now,
My ma-ma told

D7
N.C.
G7
me you bet-ter shop a-round, oh

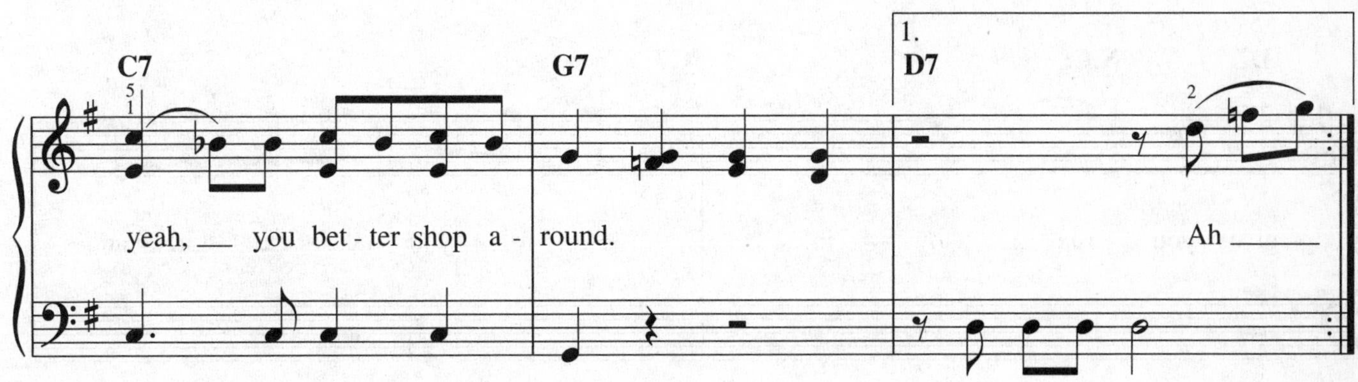
C7
G7
1.
D7
yeah, you bet-ter shop a-round.
Ah

2.
D7
C7
Try to get your-self a

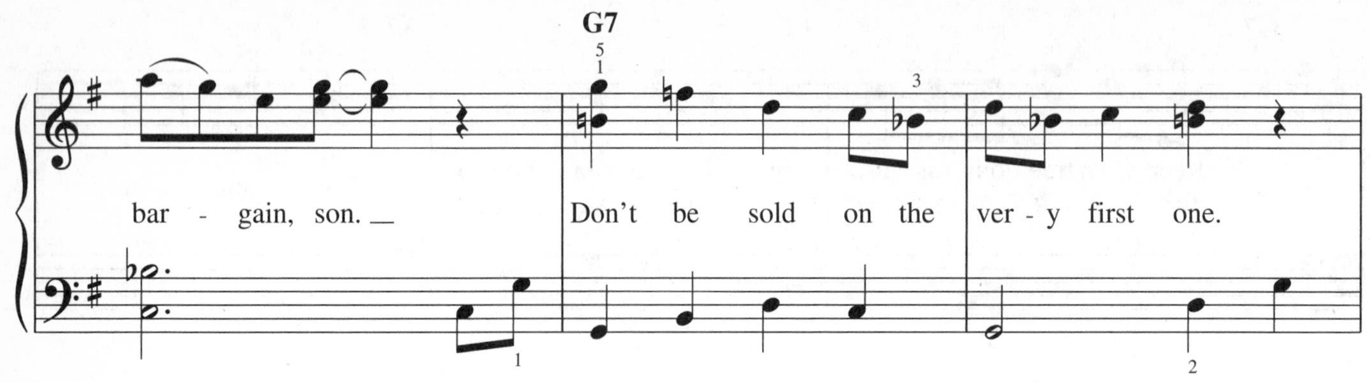
G7
bar - gain, son. __
Don't be sold on the
ver - y first one.

C7
A7
N.C.
Pret - ty girls come a
dime a doz - en. A -
try to find one who's gon - na

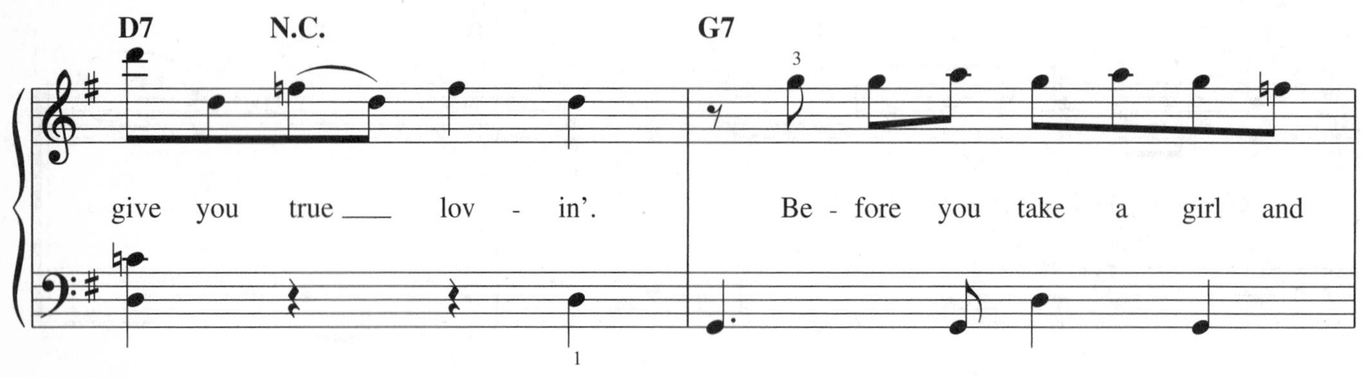
D7
N.C.
G7
give you true ___ lov - in'.
Be - fore you take a girl and

C7
G7
C7
To Coda
say, "I do" now,
make sure she's in
love with _ you now.

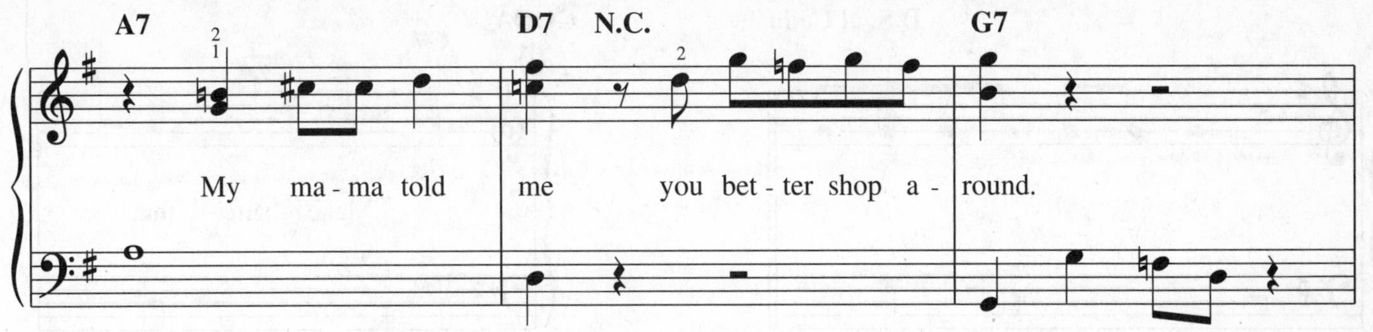
A7
D7 N.C.
G7
My ma-ma told me you bet-ter shop a-round.

C7
G7
C7

G7
C7
G7

D.S. al Coda

CODA
G7
Make sure that her

C7
G7
love is true now.
I hate to see you feel - in'

C7
A7
D7 N.C.
sad and blue now.
My ma - ma told
me you bet - ter shop a -

G7
C7
G
round.

THE SIGN

Words and Music by buddha, joker,
jenny and linn

C
D
G
Am
D
you're not the one for me?
I see a lot of stars?
Is e - nough e-nough?

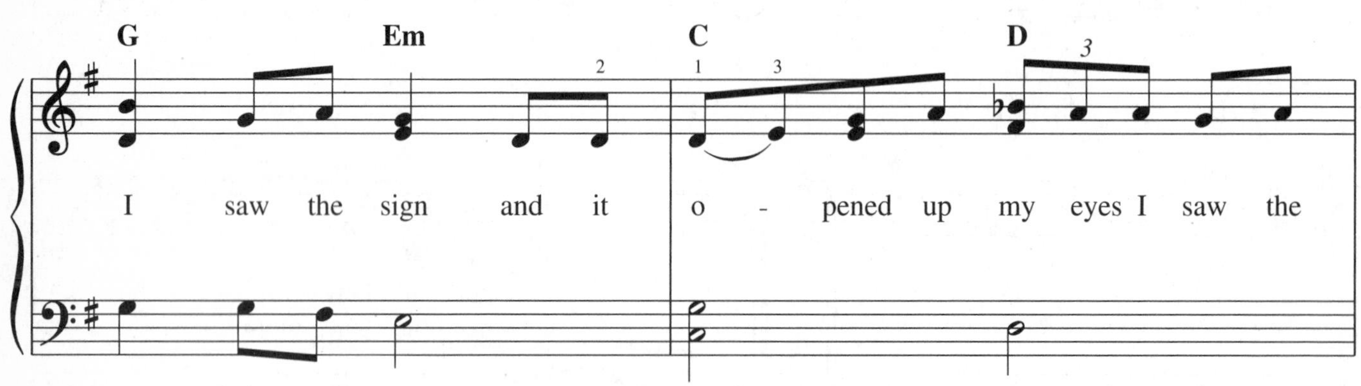
G
Em
C
D
I saw the sign and it o - pened up my eyes I saw the

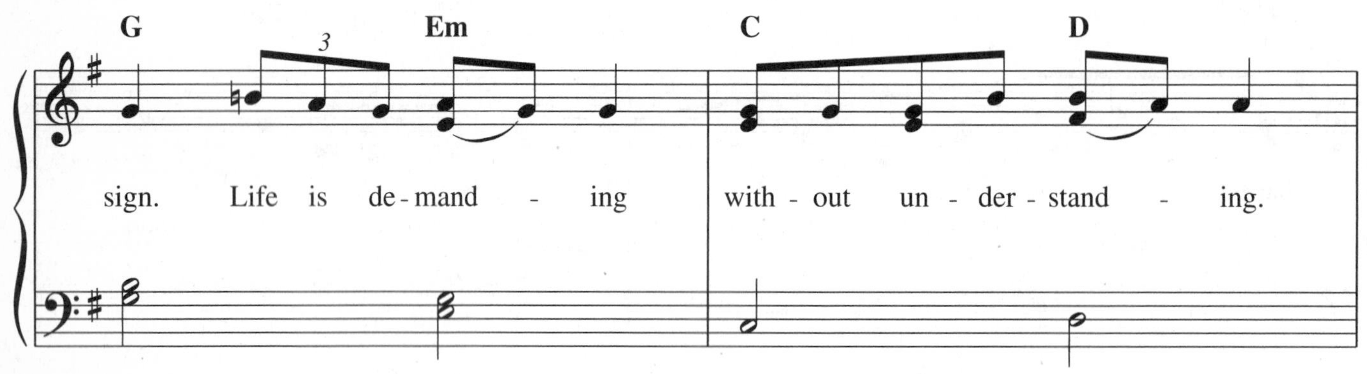
G
Em
C
D
sign. Life is de - mand - ing with - out un - der - stand - ing.

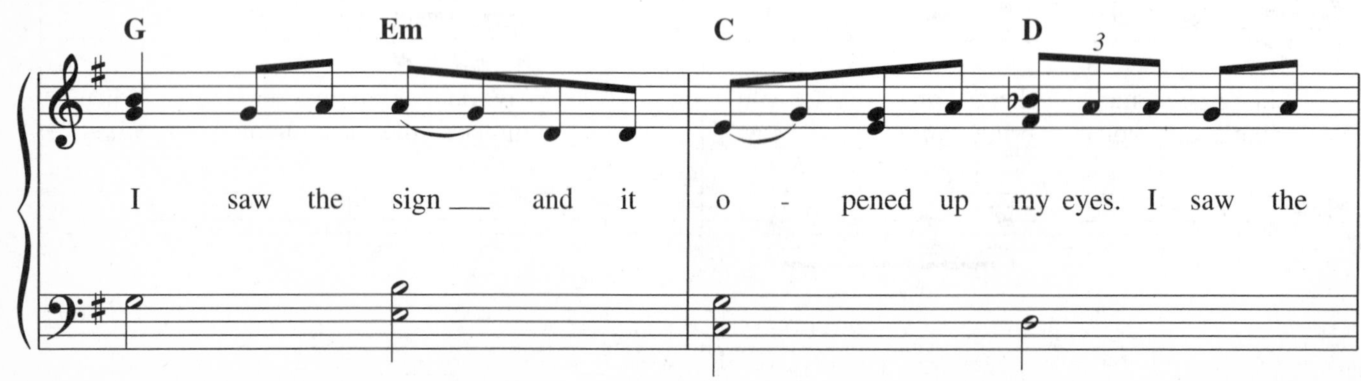
G
Em
C
D
I saw the sign and it o - pened up my eyes. I saw the

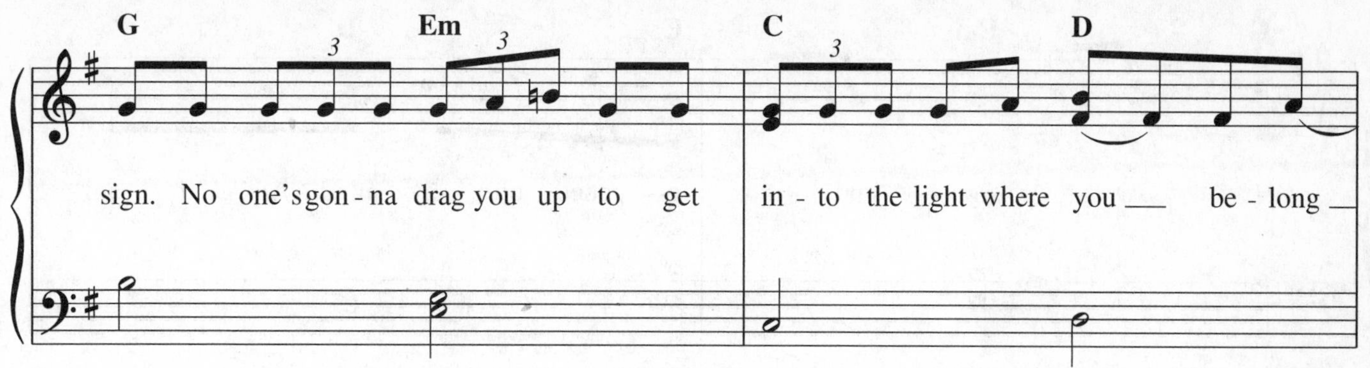
G
Em
C
D
sign. No one's gon - na drag you up to get
in - to the light where you be - long

C
D
Gm
E♭
F
Gm
E♭
F
(But where do you be - long?)

Gm
E♭
F
1.
Gm
E♭
D
2.
Gm
E♭
F
Gm
E♭
F

Gm
E♭
F
Gm
E♭
F
Gm
E♭
F

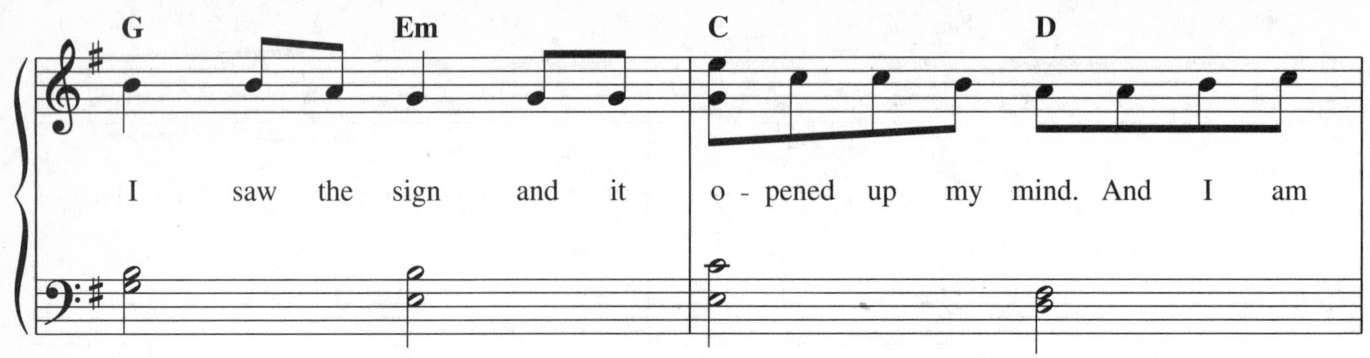
G
Em
C
D
I saw the sign and it o - pened up my mind. And I am

G
3
3
Em
C
3
D
hap - py now liv - in' with-out you. I loved you, oh, oh, oh.

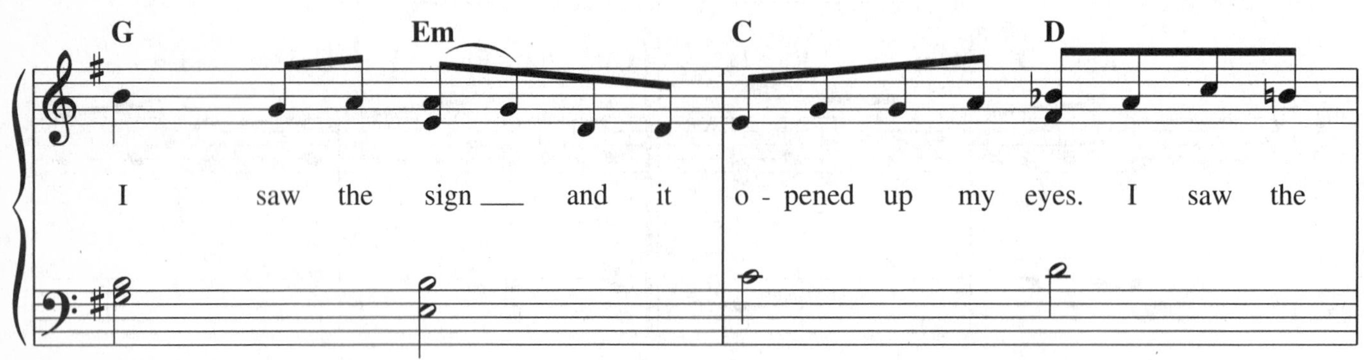
G
Em
C
D
I saw the sign and it o - pened up my eyes. I saw the

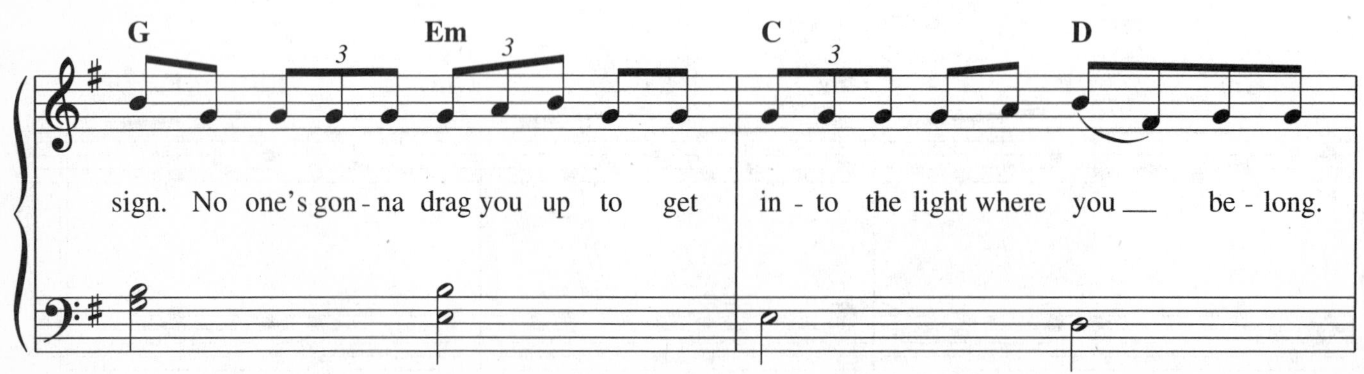
G
3
Em
3
C
3
D
sign. No one's gon - na drag you up to get in - to the light where you be - long.

G
Em
C
D
3
I saw the sign I saw the sign. I saw the sign.

G
Em
C
D
I saw the sign. I saw the sign.

G
Em
C
D
(I saw the sign. I saw the sign.) I saw the

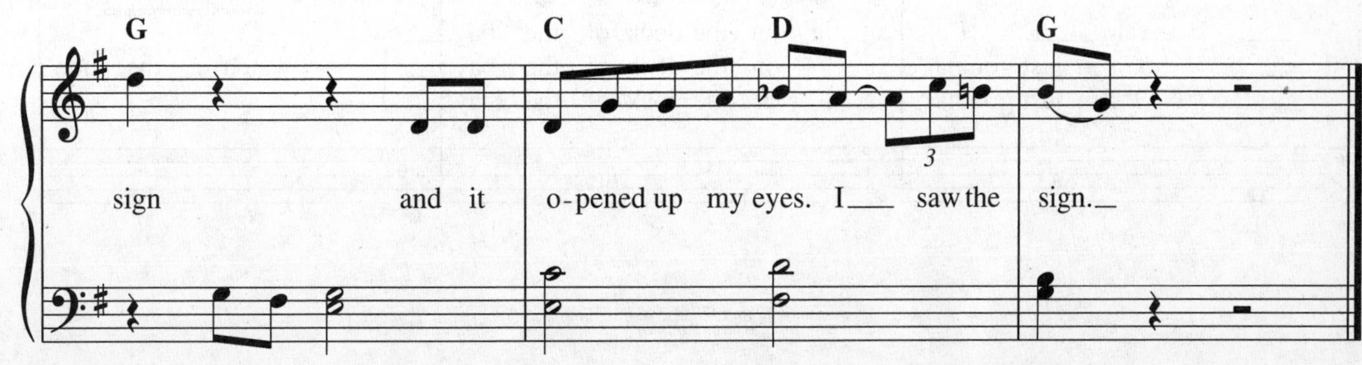
G
C
D
G
3
sign and it o-pened up my eyes. I saw the sign.

(Sittin' On)
THE DOCK OF THE BAY

Words and Music by STEVE CROPPER
and OTIS REDDING

G
E11
E
G
roll a - way.
Ooh, I'm just
sit - tin' on the dock of the bay,

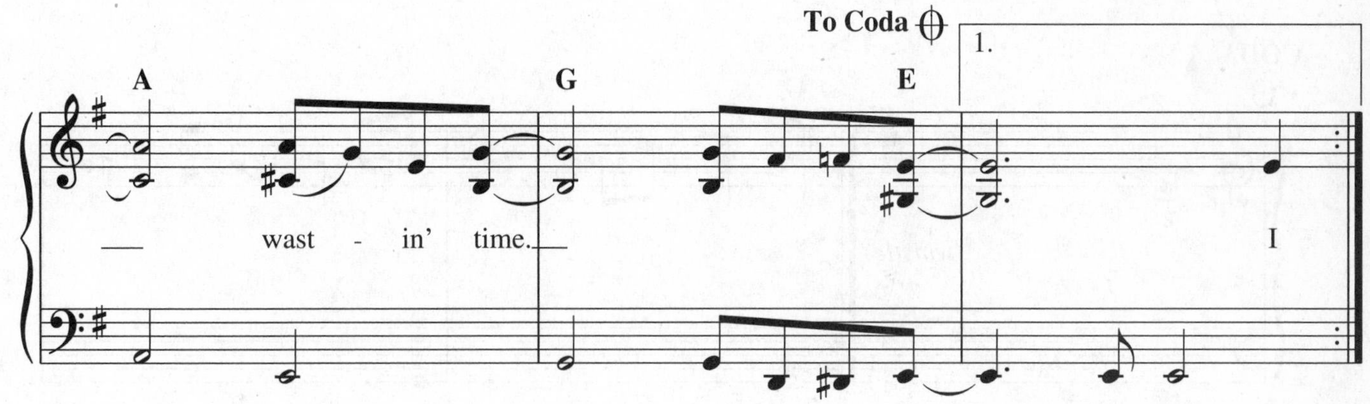
To Coda
1.
A
G
E
wast - in' time.
I

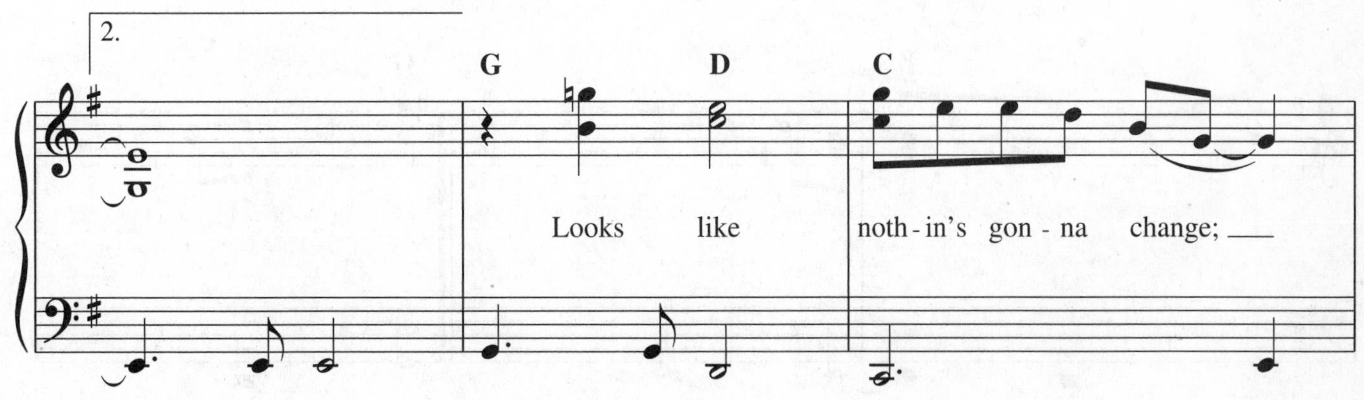
2.
G
D
C
Looks like
noth - in's gon - na change;

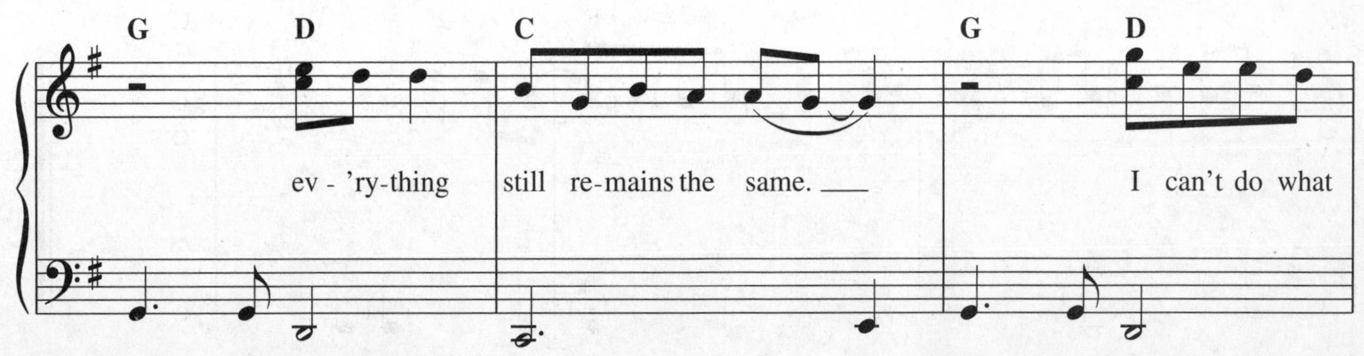
G
D
C
G
D
ev - 'ry-thing still re-mains the same.
I can't do what

D.S. al Coda
C
F
D
ten peo - ple tell me to do,
so I guess I'll re - main _ the same. _

CODA
G
(whistle)

E
G

E
G

STOP! IN THE NAME OF LOVE

Words and Music by LAMONT DOZIER,
BRIAN HOLLAND and EDWARD HOLLAND

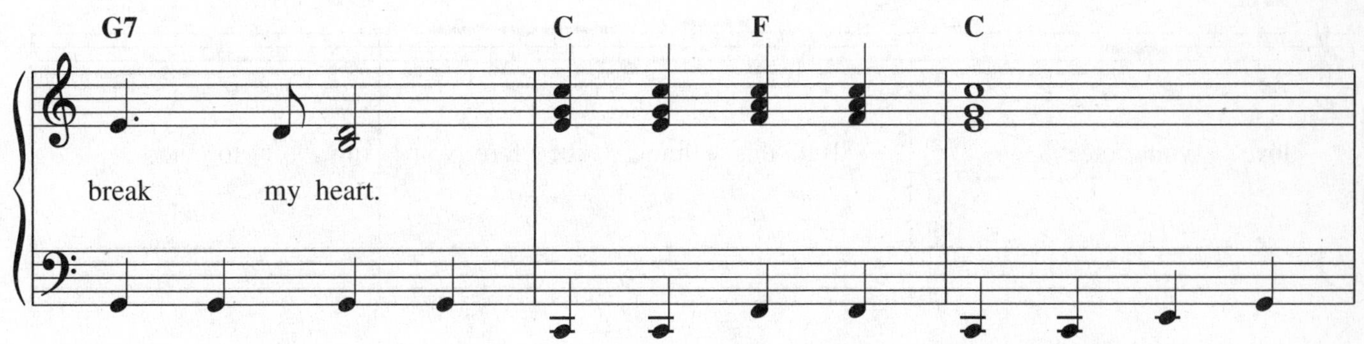

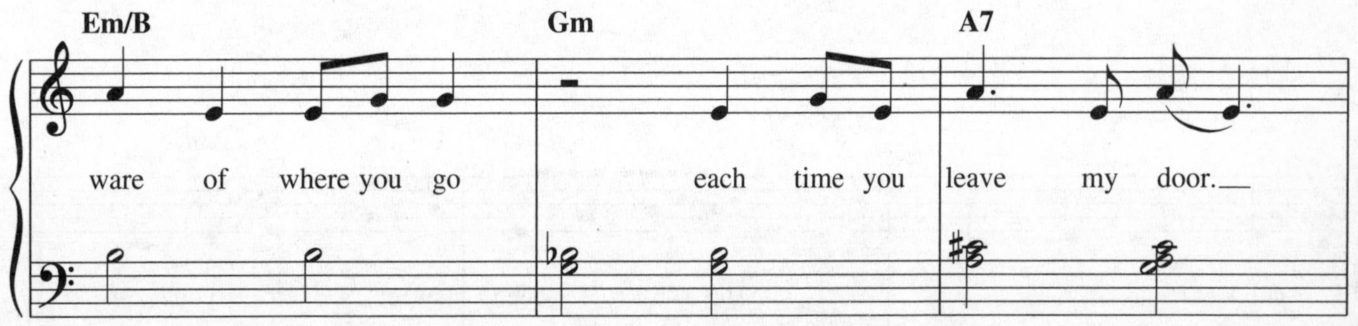

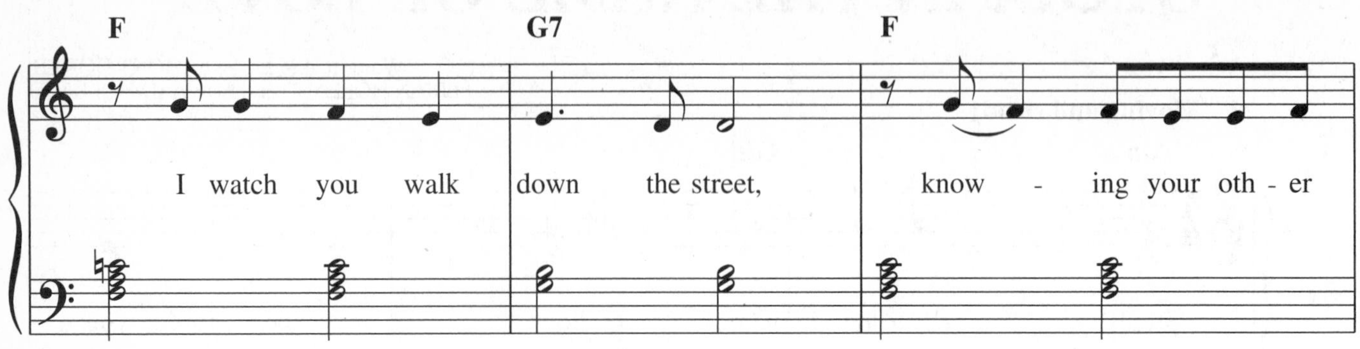
F
G7
F
I watch you walk down the street, know - ing your oth - er

G7
C
G/B
love you meet. _ But this time _ be - fore you run to her,

F
C
F
leav - ing me a - lone _ to cry... Have - n't I been
2
4

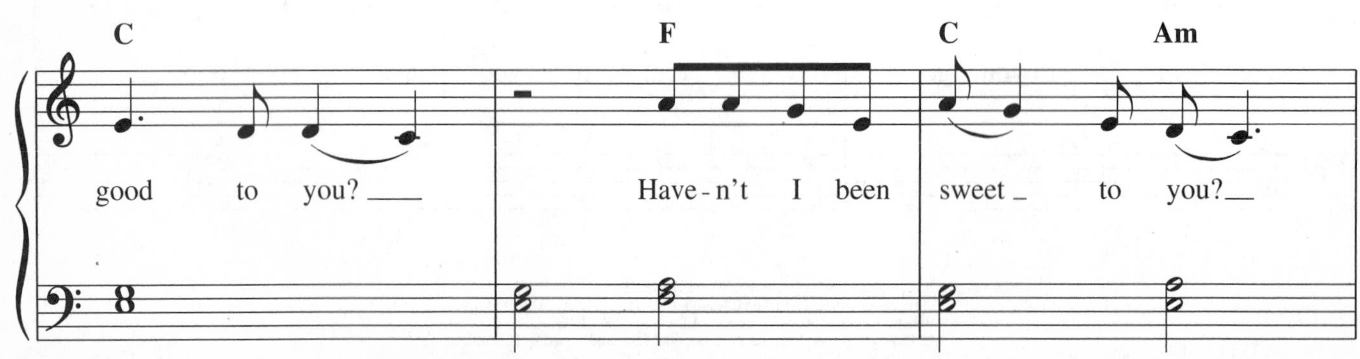
C
F
C
Am
good to you? ___ Have - n't I been sweet _ to you? __
8

Am
G/B
F
Stop! In the name of love be - fore you

G7
Am
G/B
break my heart. Stop! In the name of love

F
G7
C
F
be - fore you break my heart. Think it o - ver.

C
F
C
Think it o - ver.

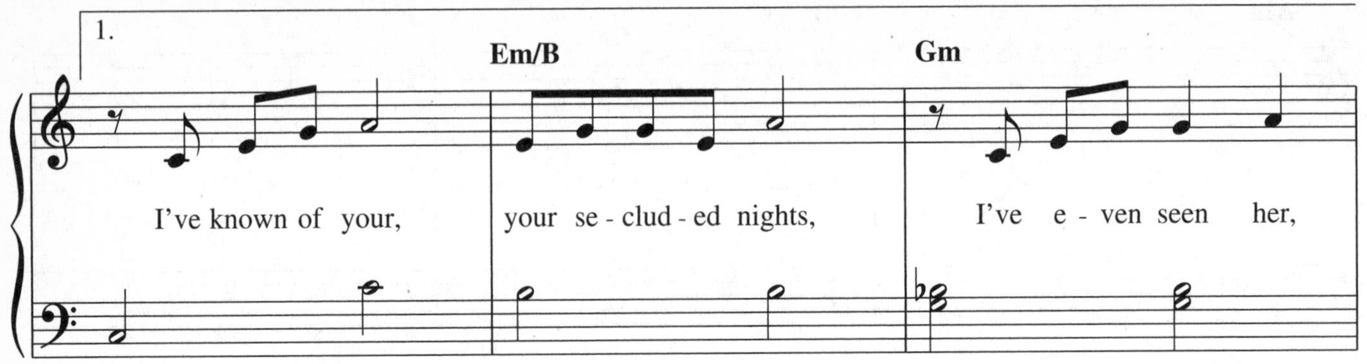
1.
Em/B
Gm
I've known of your,
your se - clud - ed nights,
I've e - ven seen her,

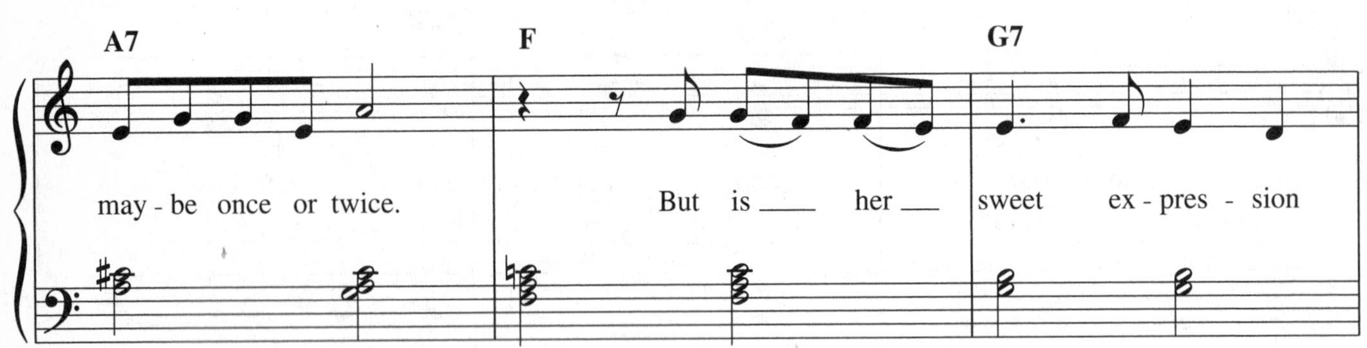
A7
F
G7
may - be once or twice.
But is ___ her ___
sweet ex - pres - sion

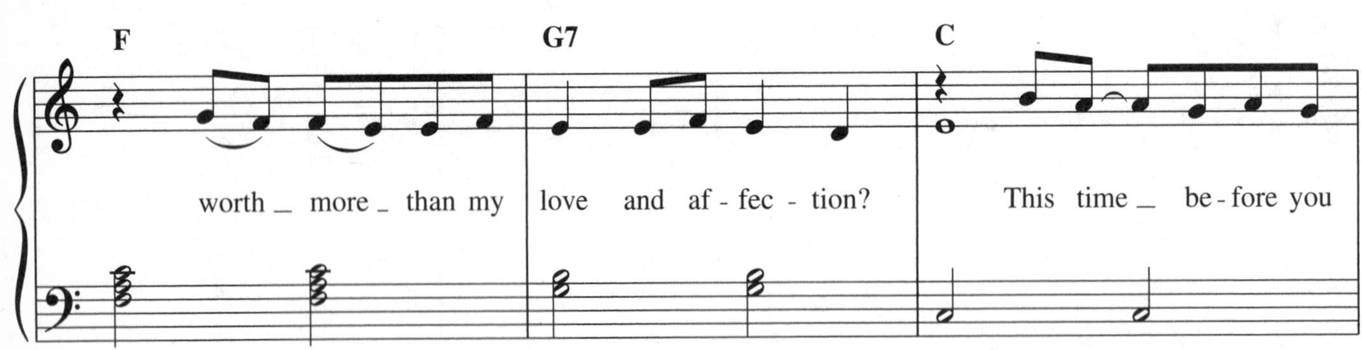
F
G7
C
worth _ more _ than my
love and af - fec - tion?
This time _ be - fore you

G/B
F
leave my arms ___
and rush off
to ___ her charms...

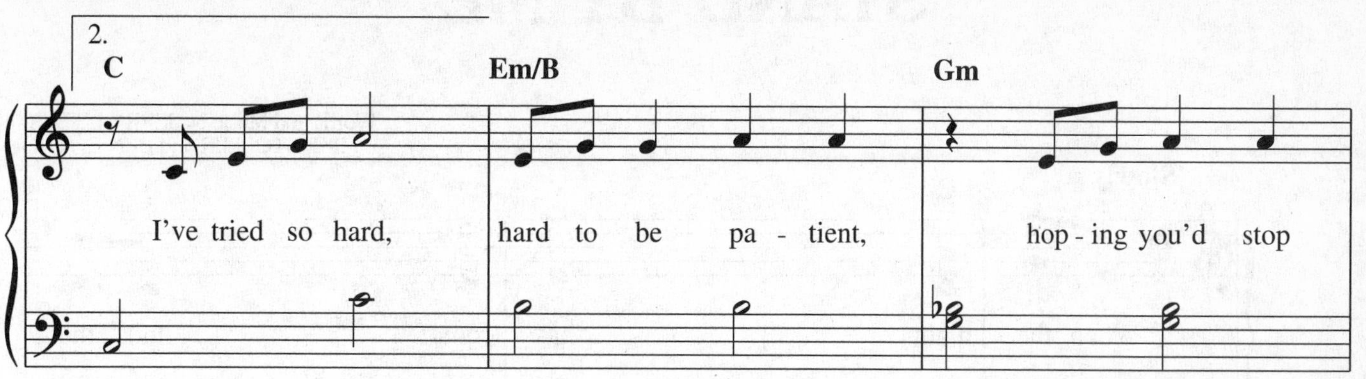
2.
C
Em/B
Gm
I've tried so hard, hard to be pa - tient, hop - ing you'd stop

A7
F
G7
this in - fat - u - a - tion. But each time you are to - geth - er

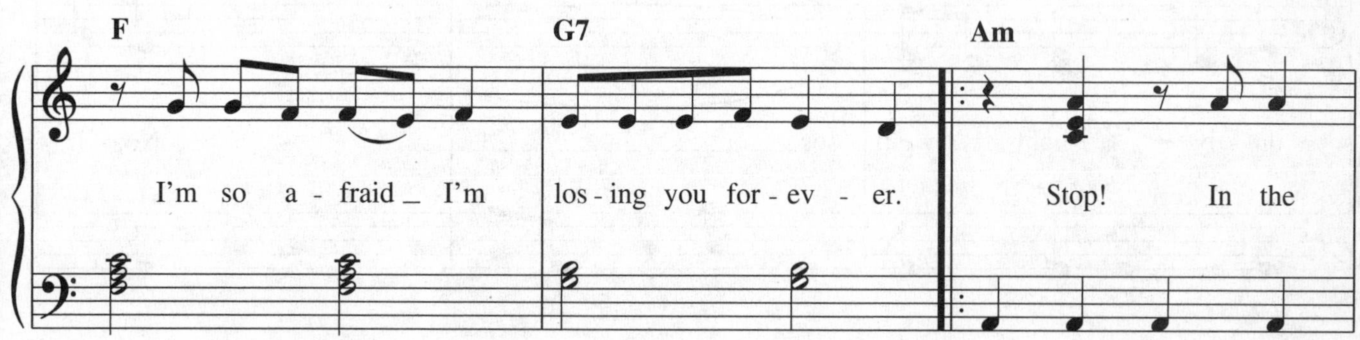
F
G7
Am
I'm so a - fraid I'm los - ing you for - ev - er. Stop! In the

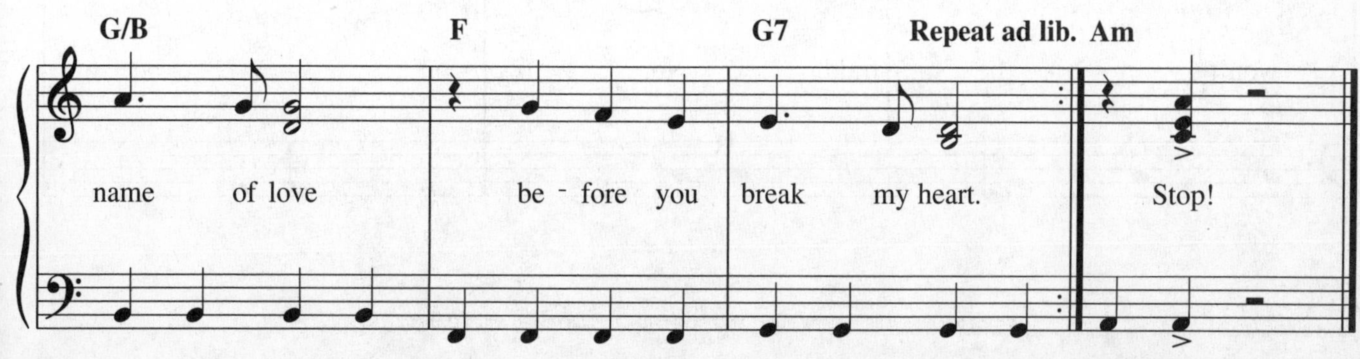
G/B
F
G7
Repeat ad lib. Am
name of love be - fore you break my heart. Stop!

STAND BY ME

Words and Music by JERRY LEIBER,
MIKE STOLLER and BEN E. KING

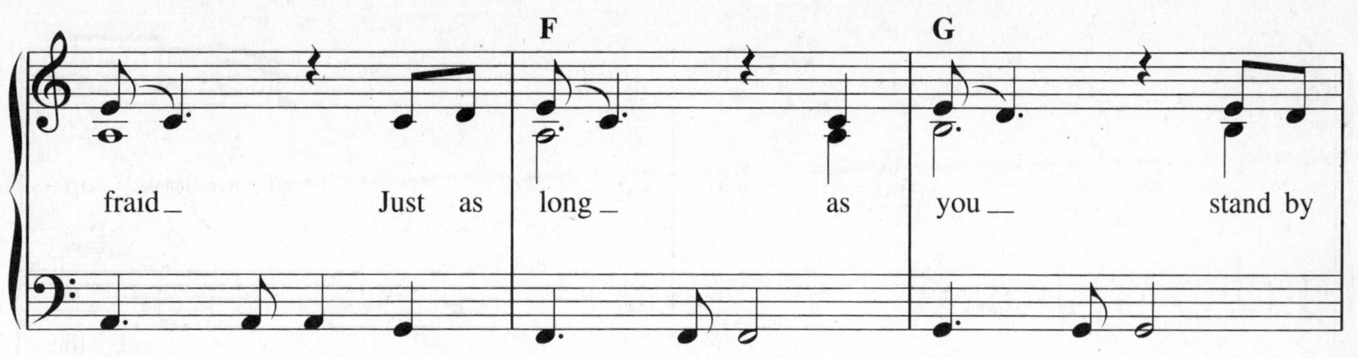
F
G
fraid_ Just as long_ as you_ stand by

C
me. Dar - ling, stand by

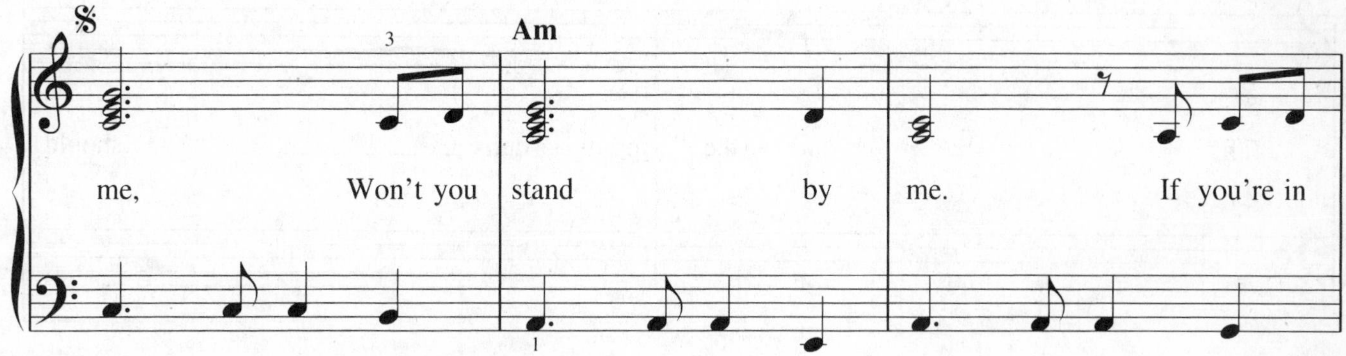
Am
me, Won't you stand by me. If you're in

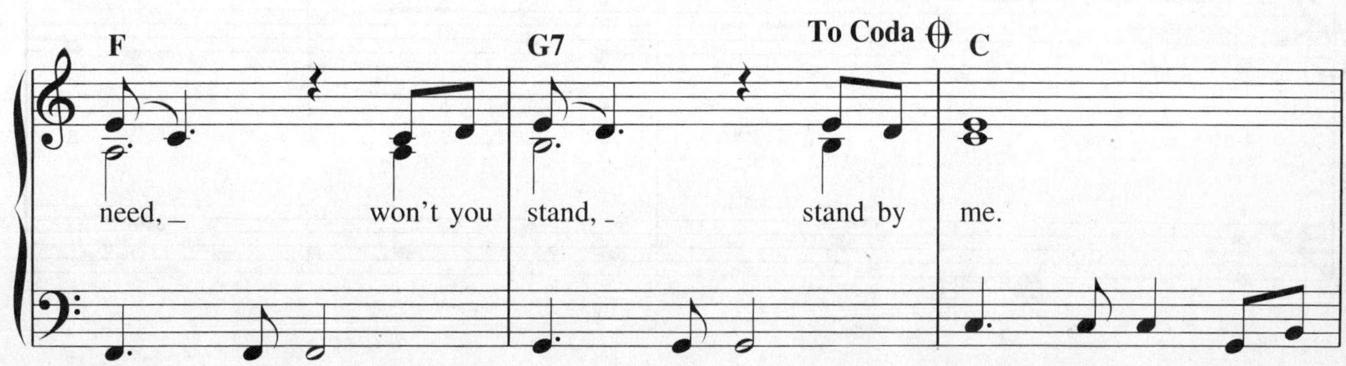
F
G7
To Coda
C
need,_ won't you stand,_ stand by me.

And if the sky that we look up -

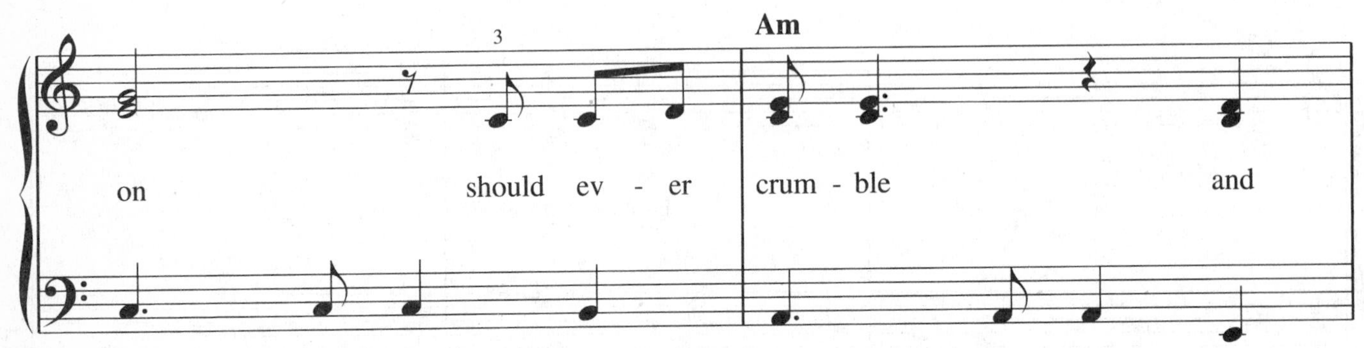
Am
3
on should ev - er crum - ble and

F
fall, and the moun - tains should
1
4
5
2

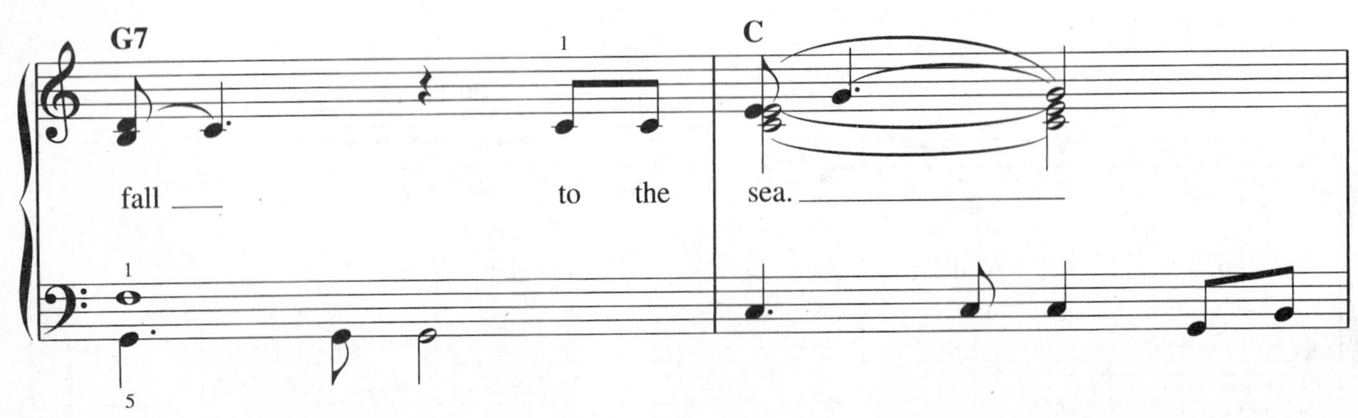
G7
1
C
fall to the sea.
1
5

No, I won't be a - fraid, No, I

Am
F
won't shed a tear, just as long as you

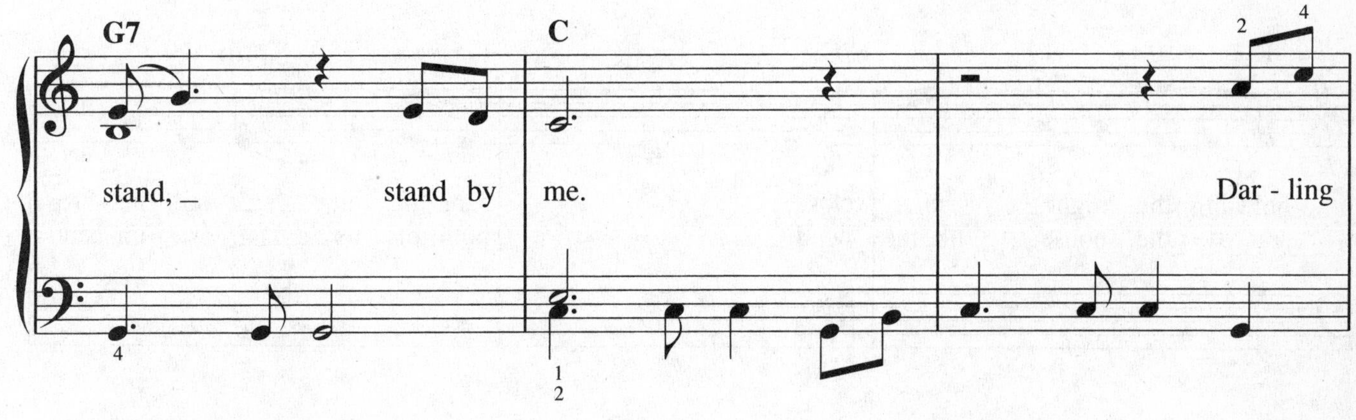
G7
C
stand, stand by me. Dar - ling

D.S. al Coda
stand by

CODA
C
me.

THE SWEETEST DAYS

Words and Music by JON LIND,
WENDY WALDMAN and PHIL GALDSTON

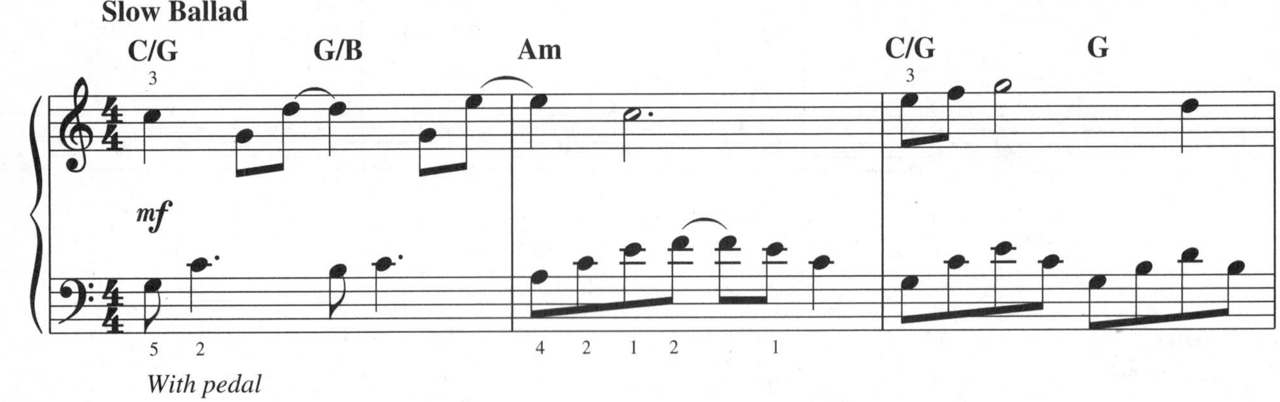

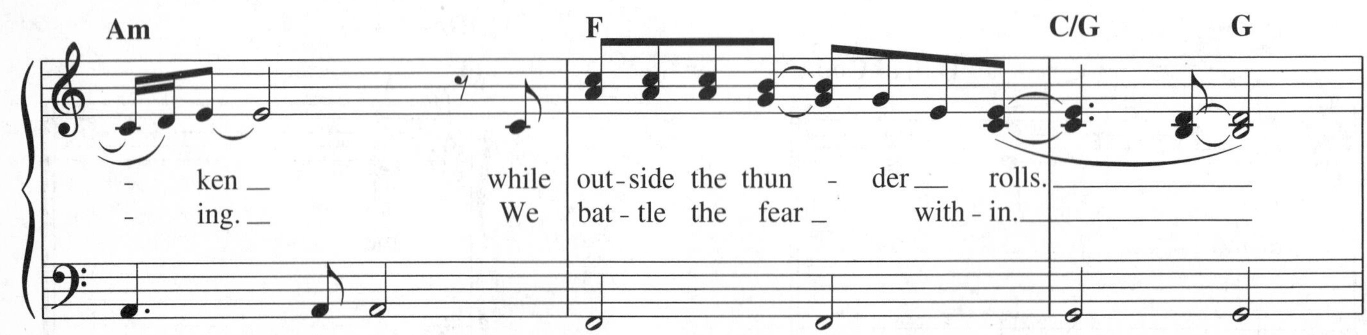

F
C/E
E/G♯
List-ten now,
All the while
you can hear my heart-beat
life is rush-ing by us.
warm a-gainst life's_ bit - ter
Hold it now and don't let

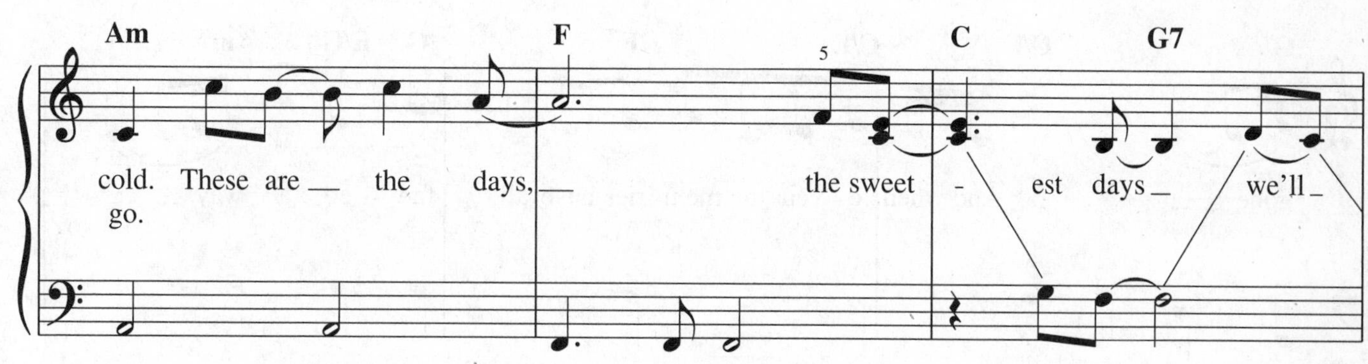
Am
F
C
G7
cold. These are — the days, —
go.
the sweet - est days — we'll —

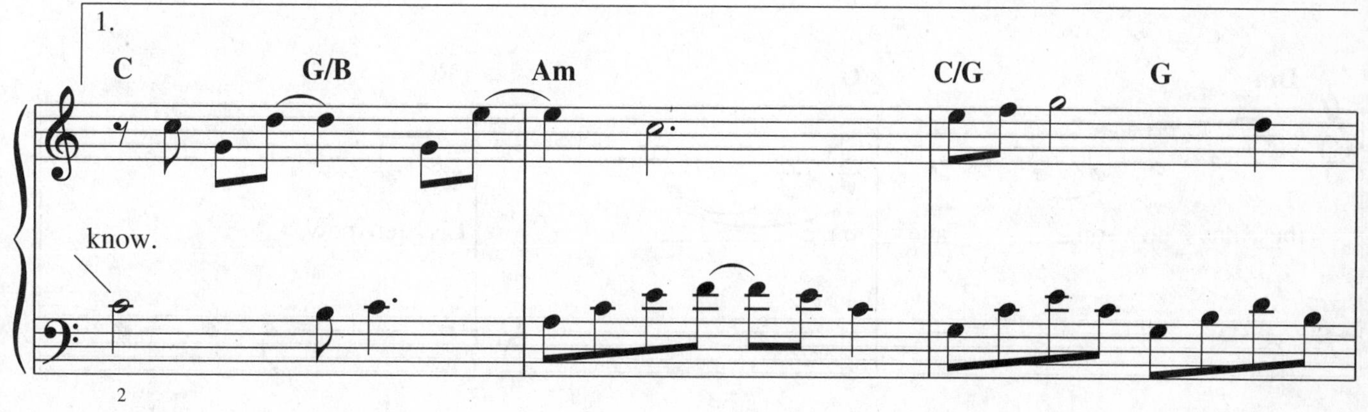
1.
C
G/B
Am
C/G
G
know.

F
2.
Csus
C
Csus
C
know.
So, we'll

C/E
F
Am
G
C/E
F
whis-per a dream
here in the dark - ness,
watch-ing the stars
till they're

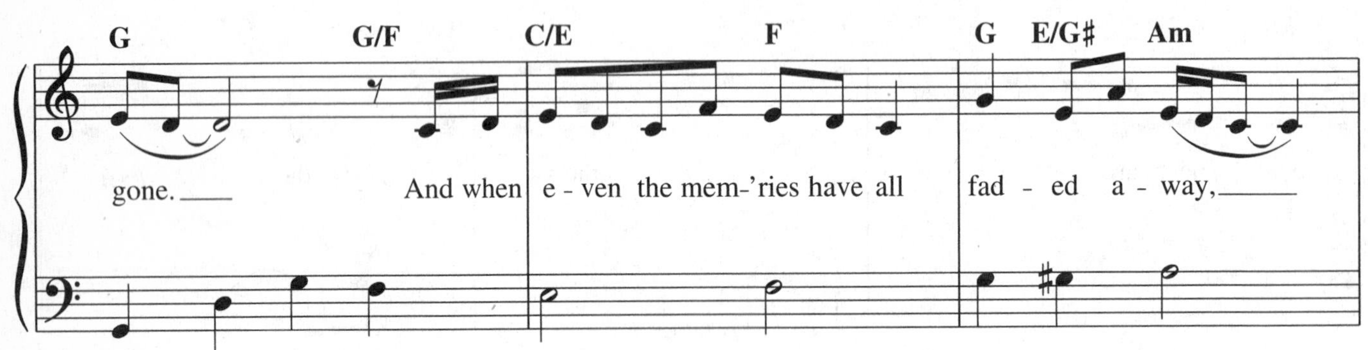
G
G/F
C/E
F
G
E/G#
Am
gone.
And when
e - ven the mem-'ries have all
fad - ed a - way,

Dm
G
F
these days go on
and
on.
Lis - ten now,

C/E
E/G#
Am
you can hear my heart-beat.
Hold me now and don't let
go.
(These are
the days,

F
Dm
G
ev' - ry day is the sweet - est day we'll

Am
F
8
know. The sweet -

Dm
G7
C
G/B
- est days we'll know.

Am
C
G
F(add9)
rit.

TEQUILA

By CHUCK RIO

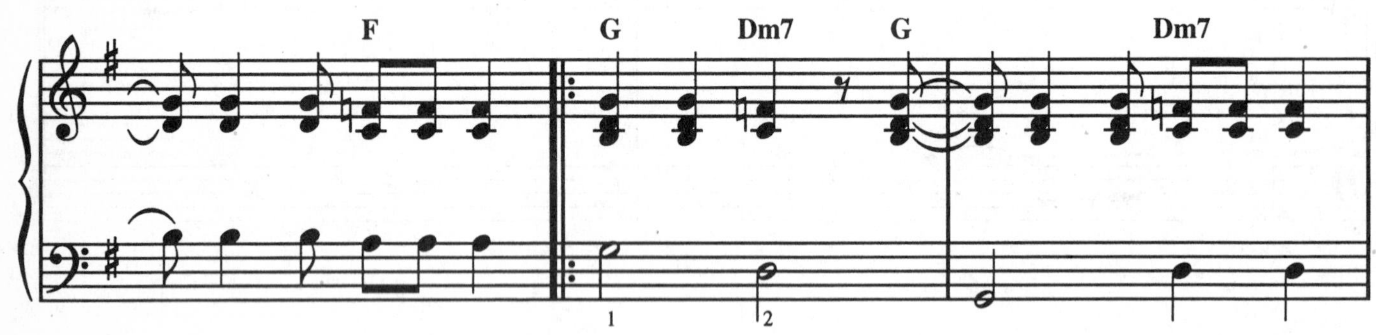

Dm7
G
Dm7
G
Dm7
G
Dm7
G
G
Dm7
G
Dm7
G

Gdim
G6

Gdim
G6
Gdim

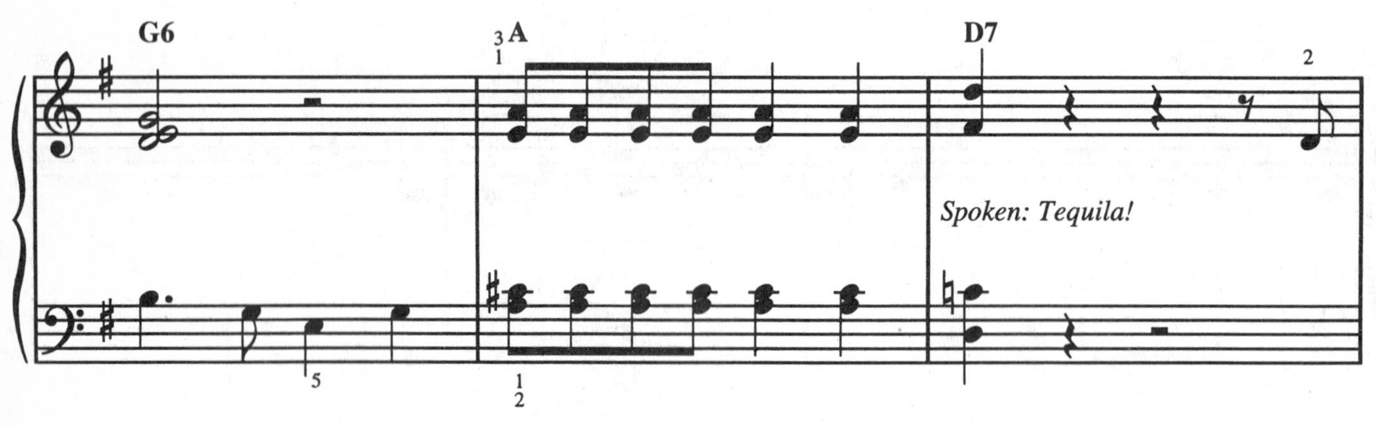
G6
A
D7
Spoken: Tequila!

G
Dm7
G
Dm7
G

Dm7
G

Dm7
G
Dm7
G

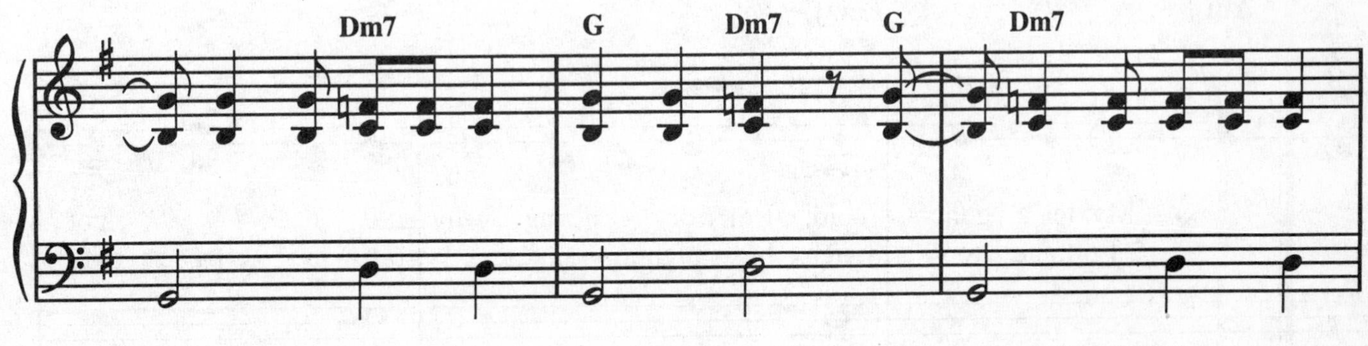
Dm7
G
Dm7
G
Dm7

G
F
G
F
G
F
G
f
Spoken: Tequila!

THANK YOU

Words and Music by PAUL HERMAN
and DIDO ARMSTRONG

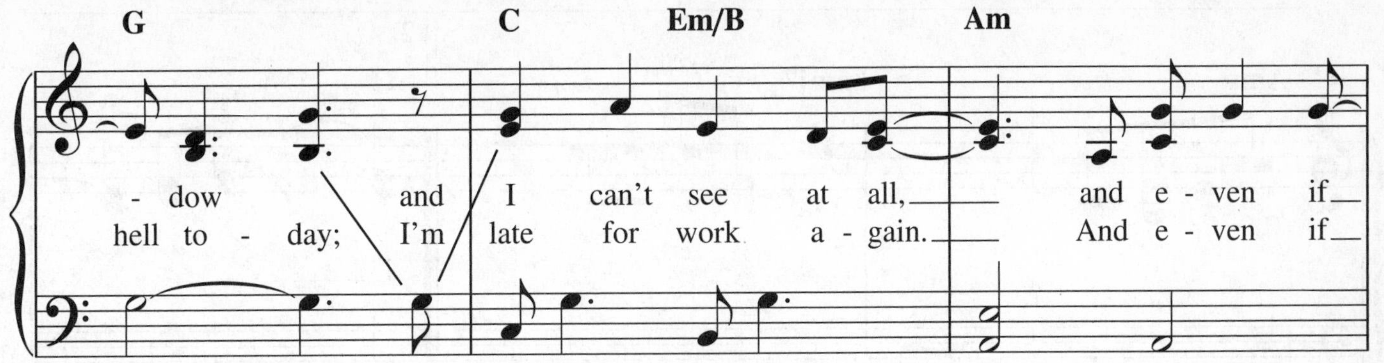
G
C
Em/B
Am
- dow and I can't see at all, and e - ven if
hell to - day; I'm late for work a - gain. And e - ven if

Fmaj7
G
C
Em/B
I could it-'d all be grey, but your pic - ture on my wall,
I'm there they'll all im - ply that I might not last the day,

Am
Fmaj7
Am
it re - minds me that it's not so bad, it's
and then you call me and it's not so bad, it's

Fmaj7
1.
Am
Fmaj7
not so bad.
not so bad. And

2.
Am
Fmaj7
C
I
C/E
Fmaj7
F/G
want to
thank you
for giv-ing me the
C
C7
C7/E
Fmaj7
F/G
best day
of
my
life.
And,
C
C/E
Fmaj7
oh,
just to
be with you
is hav-ing the

Em7
Dm7
1 2 3
best day of my life.

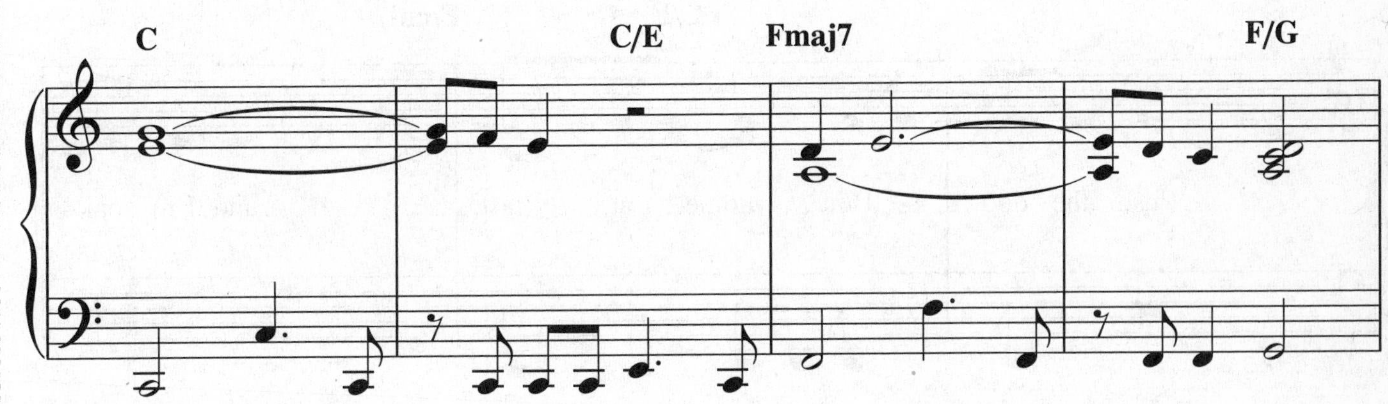
C
C/E
Fmaj7
F/G

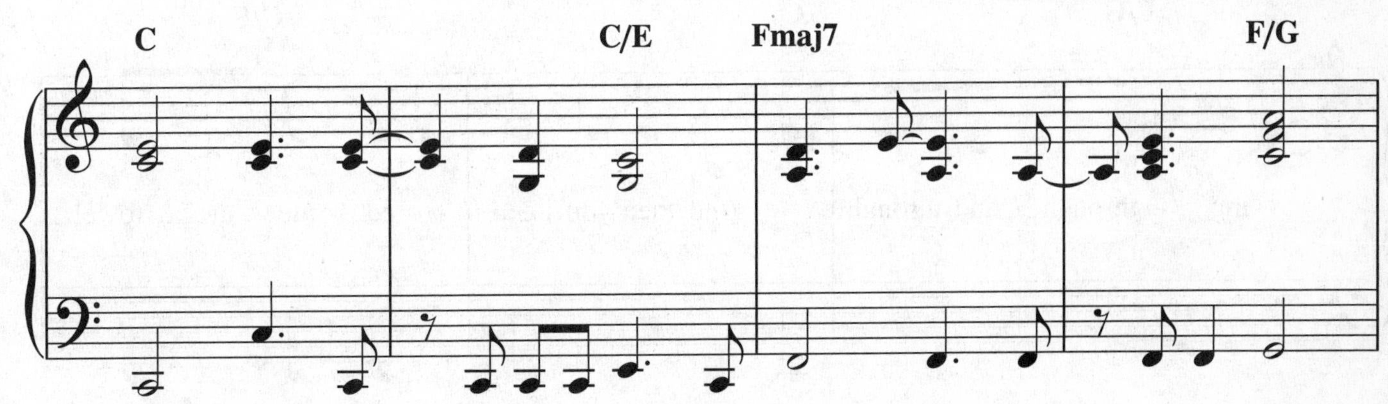
C
C/E
Fmaj7
F/G

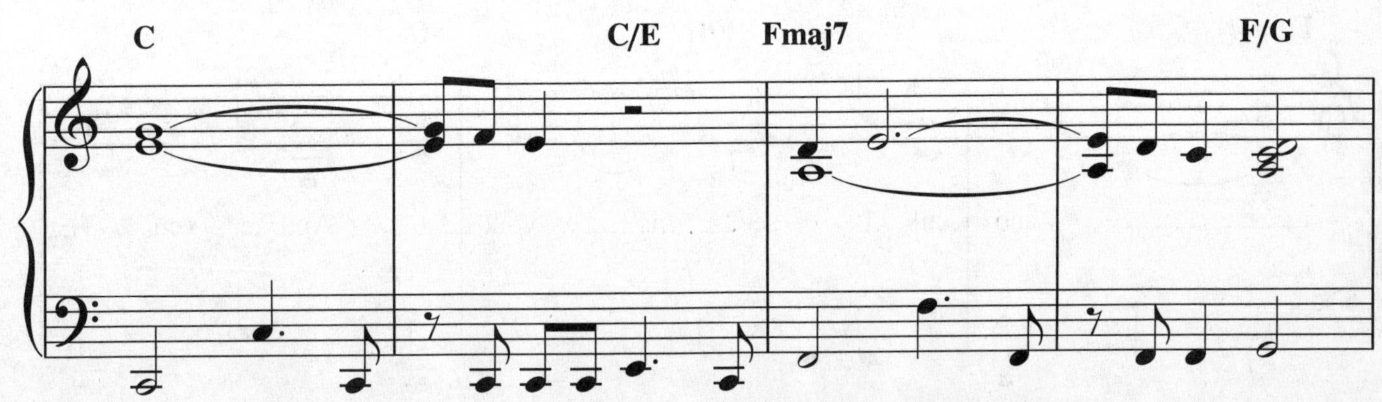
C
C/E
Fmaj7
F/G

Em7
Dm7

C
C/E
Fmaj7
3
1
Push the door; I'm home at last, and I'm soak -

F/G
C
C/E
4
1
4
2
1
- ing through and through. And then you hand - ed me a towel,

Fmaj7
F/G
C
and all I see is you. And e - ven if

C/E
F7
F/G
4 5 2
4
my house falls down now, I would - n't have a clue,

Em7
Dm7
be - cause you're near me.

C
C/E
4 3 2
2 1 1
1 3
And I want to

Fmaj7
F/G
C
thank you for giv - ing me the best day

C7/E
Fmaj7
F/G
of
my
life.
And
C
C/E
Fmaj7
F/G
oh,
just to
be with you
is hav-ing the
1.
Em7
Dm7
best
day
of
my
life.
And
2.
Dm7
life.

TOP OF THE WORLD

Words and Music by JOHN BETTIS
and RICHARD CARPENTER

D
G
3
see, not a cloud in the
same, in the leaves on the
2
3

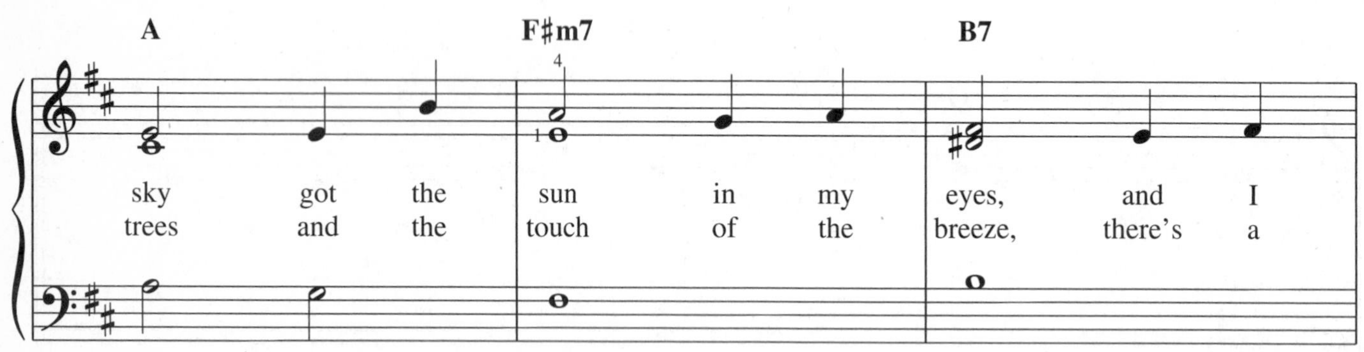
A
F♯m7
B7
4
1
sky got the sun in my eyes, and I
trees and the touch of the breeze, there's a

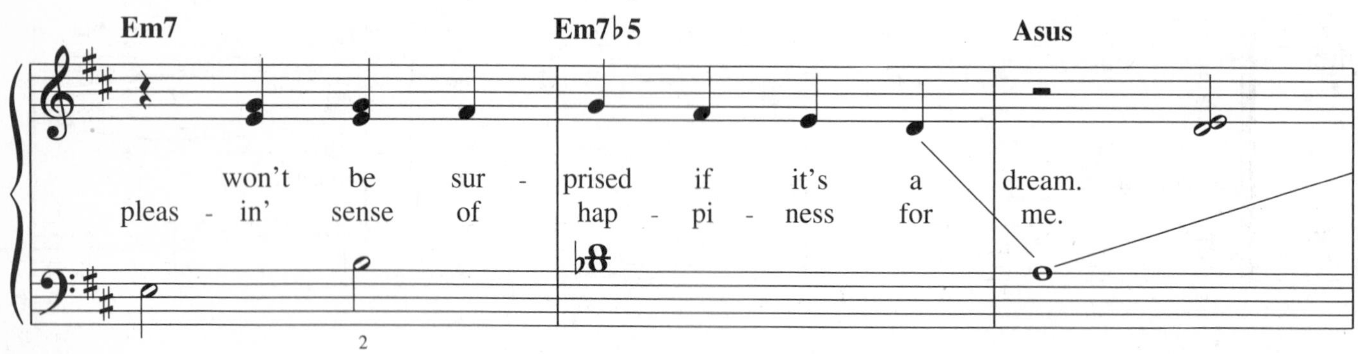
Em7
Em7♭5
Asus
won't be sur - prised if it's a dream.
pleas - in' sense of hap - pi - ness for me.
2

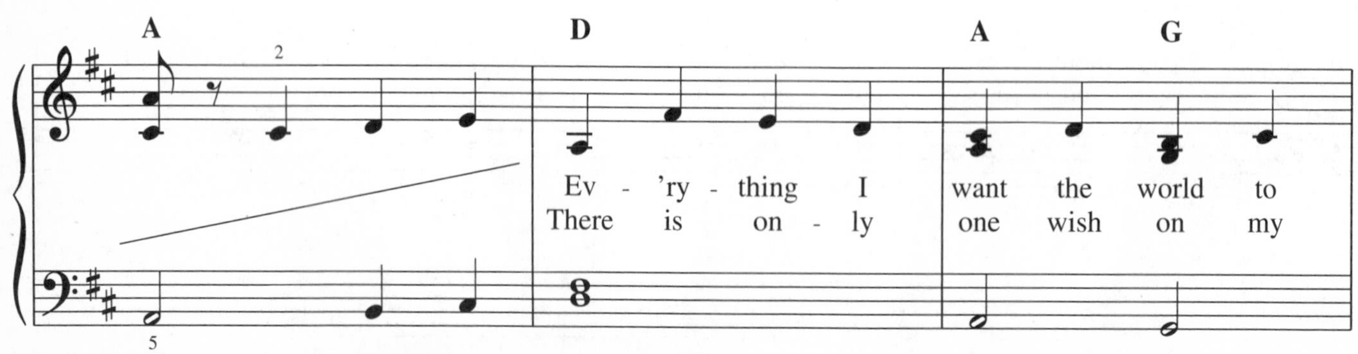
A
D
A
G
2
Ev - 'ry - thing I want the world to
There is on - ly one wish on my
5

D
F#m
be, is now com - ing true es -
mind, when this day is through I

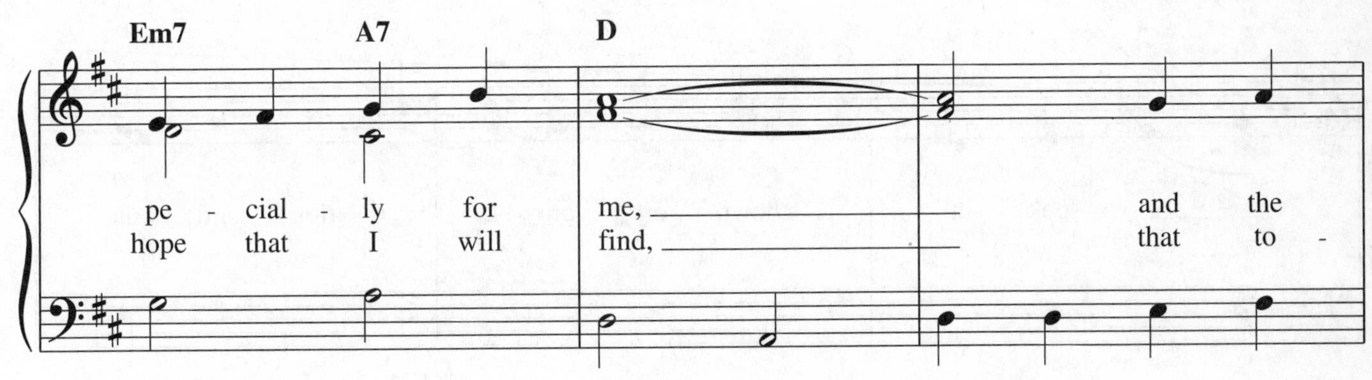
Em7
A7
D
pe - cial - ly for me, and the
hope that I will find, that to -

G
A
F#m7
rea - son is clear, it's be - cause you are
mor - row will be just the same for you and

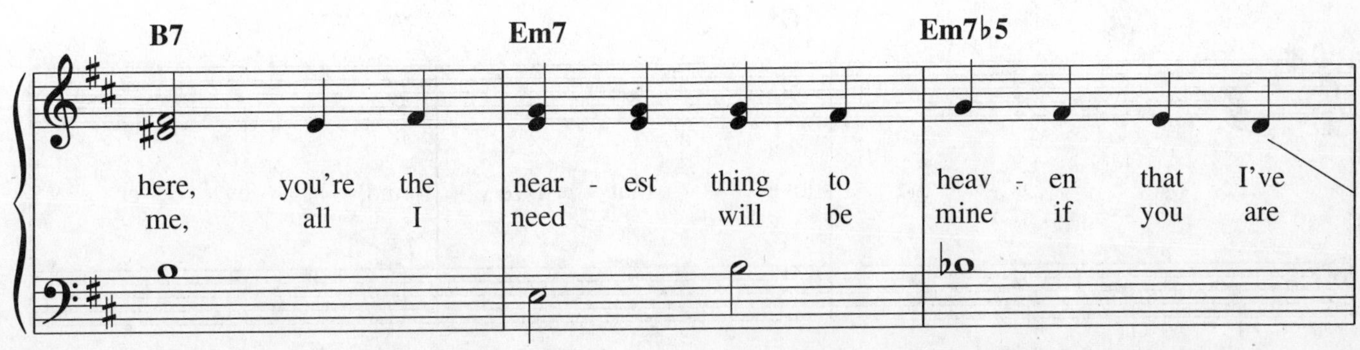
B7
Em7
Em7♭5
here, you're the near - est thing to heav - en that I've
me, all I need will be mine if you are

Asus
A
D
seen.
here.
I'm on the top of the world

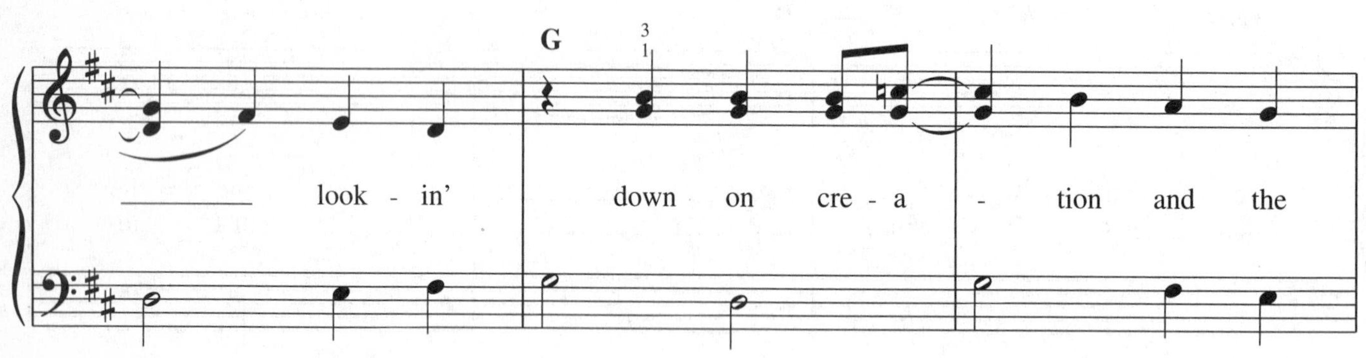
G
look - in' down on cre - a - tion and the

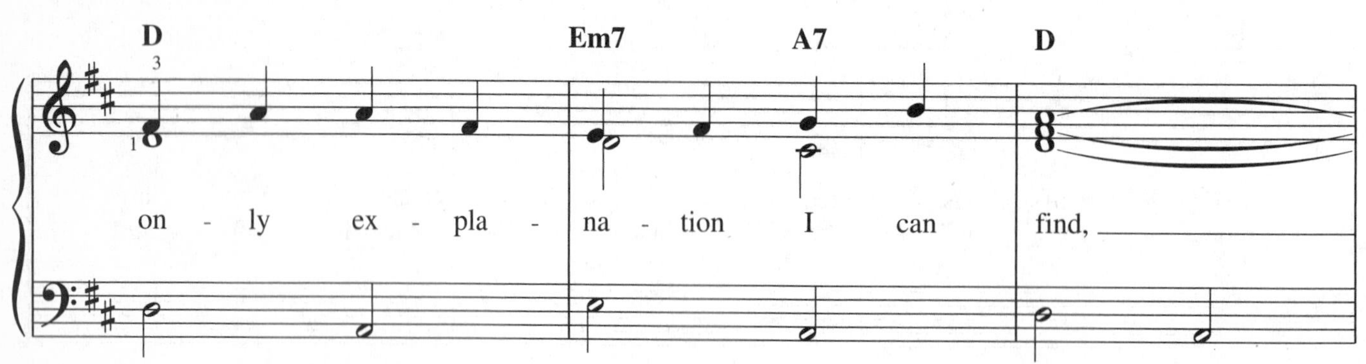
D
Em7
A7
D
on - ly ex - pla - na - tion I can find,

G
A
is the love that I've found, ev - er

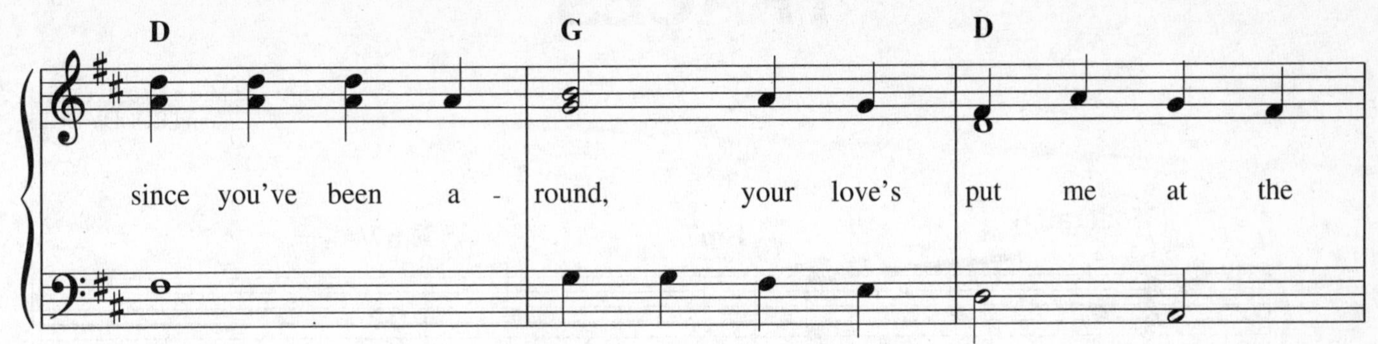
D
G
D
since you've been a - round, your love's put me at the

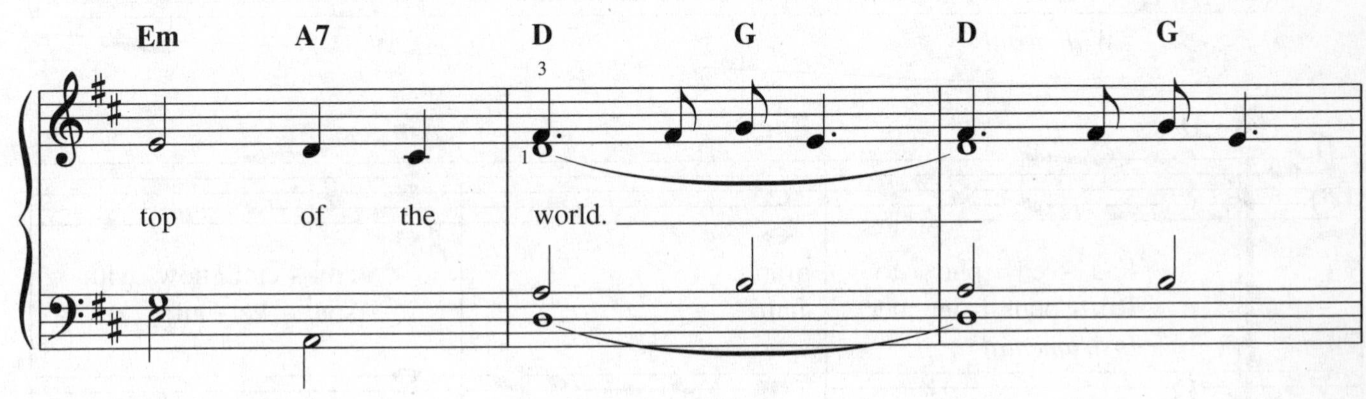
Em
A7
D
G
D
G
3
1
top of the world.

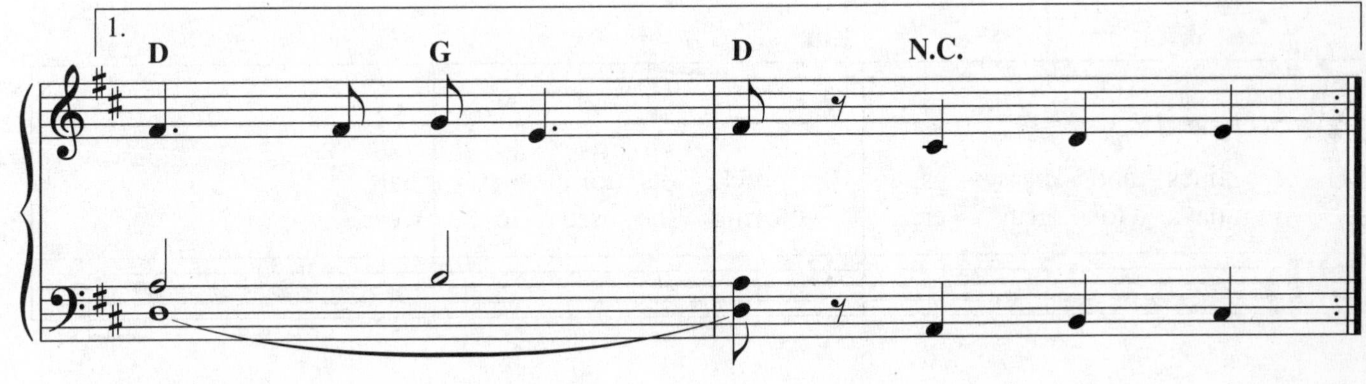
1.
D
G
D
N.C.

2.
D
G
D

TRACES

Words and Music by J.R. COBB
and BUDDY BUIE

Bm/A
G♯m7♭5
G
love long a - go that did - n't work out
love long a - go that did - n't work out
hope in the night that she'll come back and

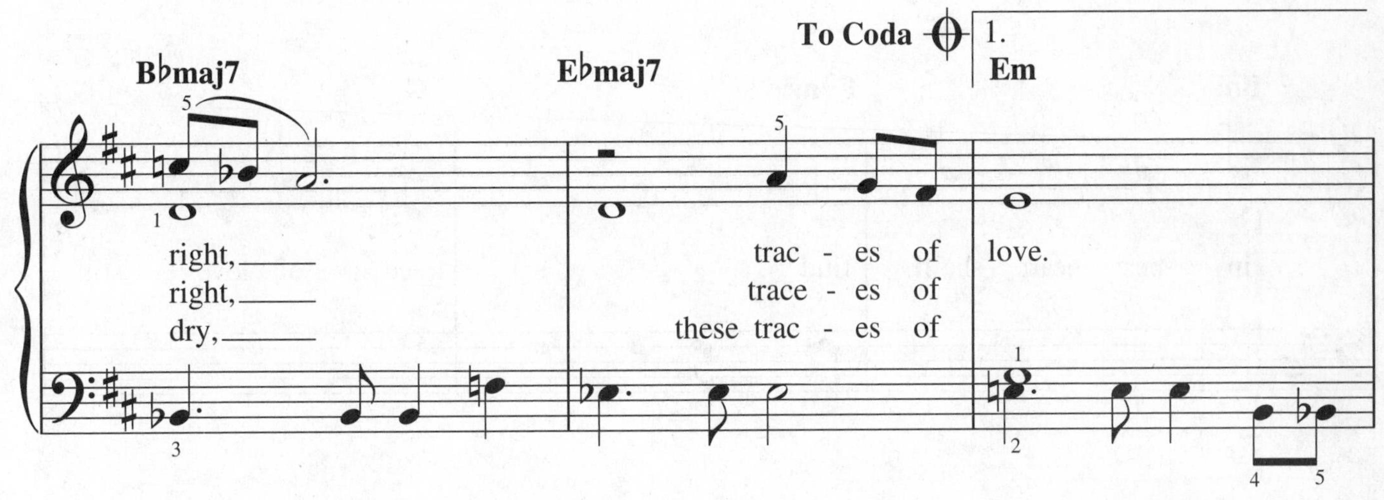
To Coda
1.
B♭maj7
E♭maj7
Em
right, trac - es of love.
right, trace - es of
dry, these trac - es of

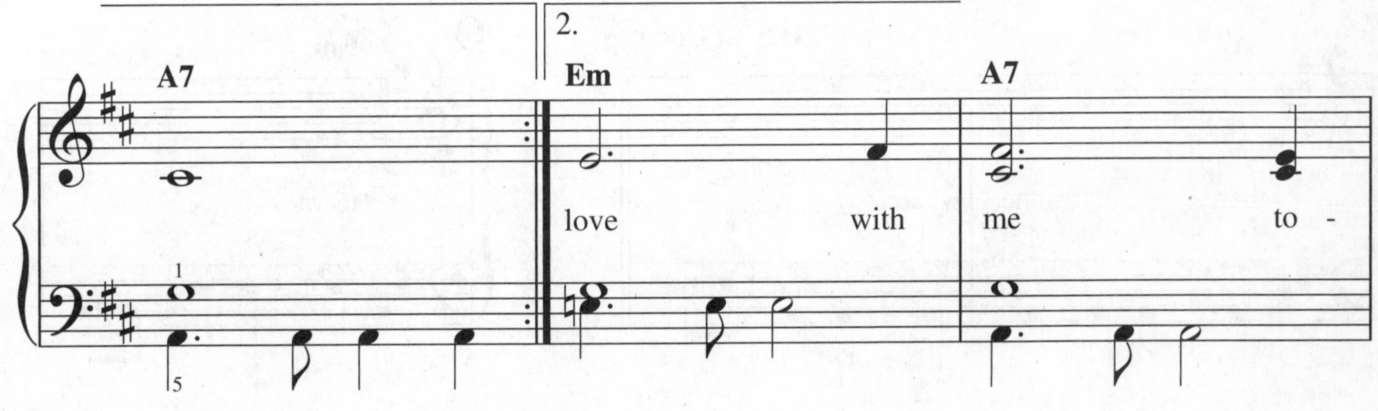
2.
A7
Em
A7
love with me to -

D
Bm
night. I close my

F♯m
Bm
F♯m
eyes
and say a
prayer
that

Bm
F♯m
G
in her heart she'll
find a
trace of love still

A7
D.S. al Coda
CODA
Em
there some - where.
tears

Em7/A
A7
D
from my
eyes.

THE TRACKS OF MY TEARS

Words and Music by WILLIAM "SMOKEY" ROBINSON,
WARREN MOORE and MARVIN TARPLIN

Moderately

C
D
G
C
good look at my face you'll see my smile looks out of

D
G
C
D
To Coda
place. If you look clos - er, it's eas - y to trace the tracks of my

G
C
G
C
G
tears. Hey, _

C
G
C
G
C
G
hey, yeah. _ (Out - side) I'm mas - que - rad - ing. _

C G C G C G
(In - side) My hope is fad - ing (Just a clown) a since you

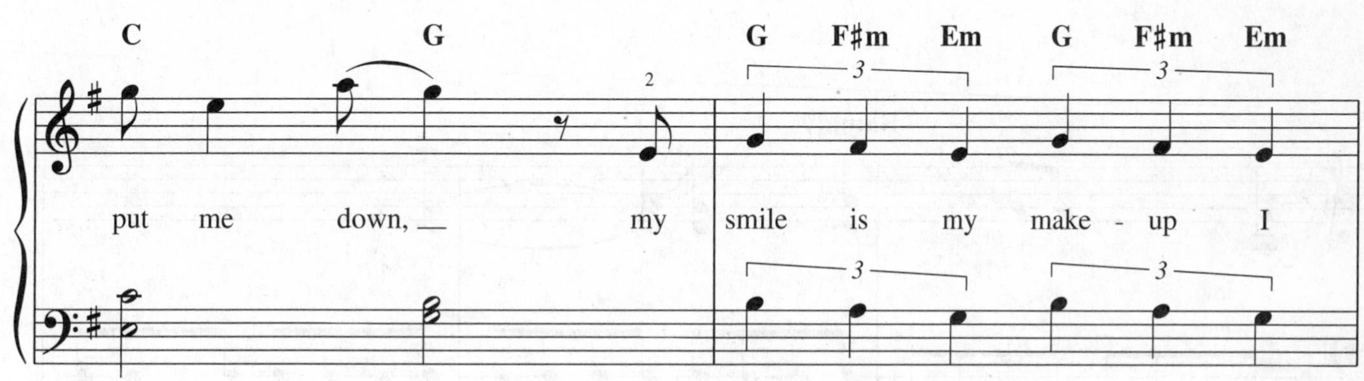
C G G F#m Em G F#m Em
put me down, my smile is my make - up I

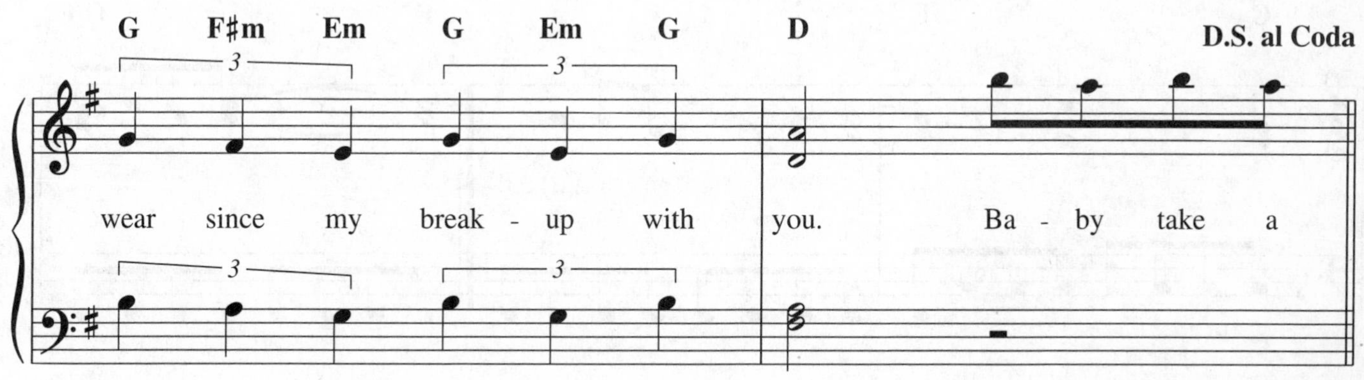
G F#m Em G Em G D
D.S. al Coda
wear since my break - up with you. Ba - by take a

CODA
G C G
tears. rit.

TWO HEARTS

Words and Music by PHIL COLLINS
and LAMONT DOZIER

F
G/F
F
G7/F

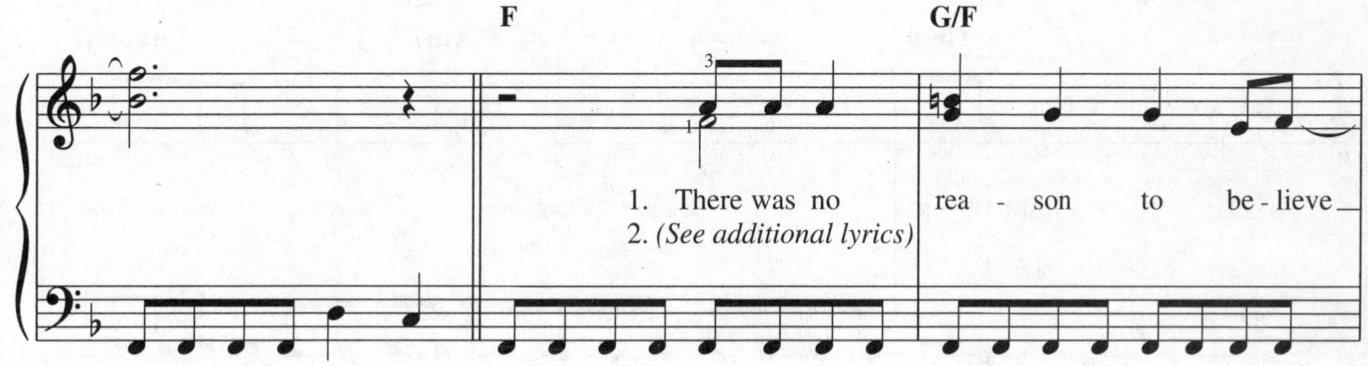
F
G/F
1. There was no rea - son to be - lieve
2. (See additional lyrics)

F
G/F
F
she'll al - ways be there.
But if you don't put

G/F
F
G/F
faith in what you be - lieve in, it's get-ting no - where.

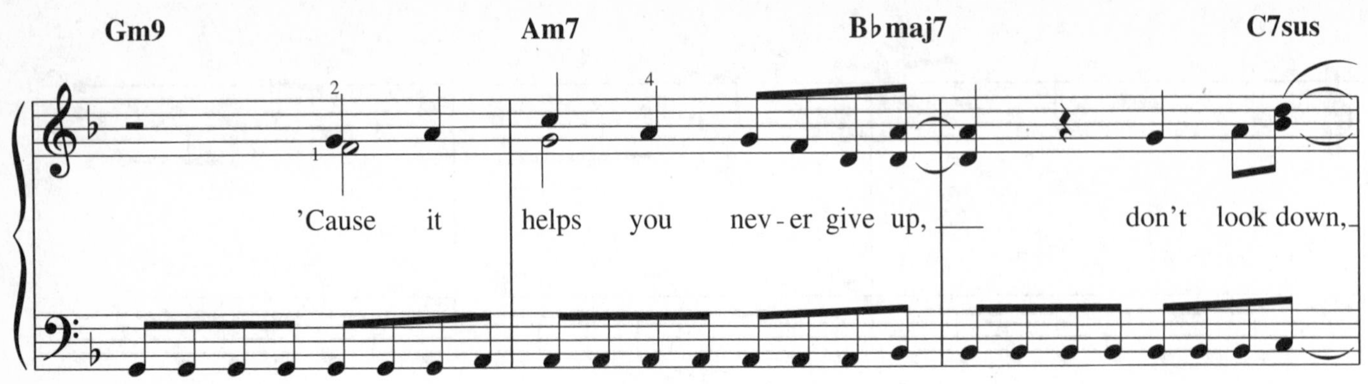
Gm9
Am7
B♭maj7
C7sus
'Cause it helps you nev-er give up, don't look down,

Gm9
Am7
B♭maj7
just look up. 'Cause she's al - ways there be-hind

Chorus
C7sus
B♭maj7
B♭6
you, just to re - mind you.
Two hearts
Two hearts

C
F
liv-ing in just one mind. You know we're
liv-ing in just one mind. Beat - ing to -

B♭maj7
B♭6
C
F
2
two hearts_
liv-ing in just one mind._
geth - er ___
'til the end of time._

1.
2.
B♭maj7
B♭6
3
You know we're two hearts _

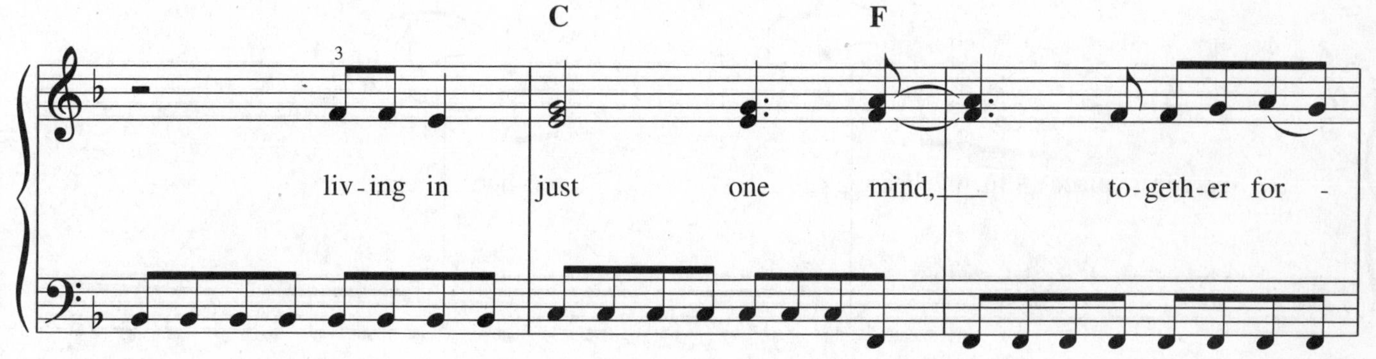
C
F
3
liv-ing in just one mind,___ to-geth-er for -

B♭maj7
C
2
1
2
1
ev - er ______
'til the end of time._

F
D♭/F
G♭
E♭/G
A♭
G♭/B♭
Amaj7
F♯m7
G♯m7
She knows there'll al - ways be a
C♯7sus
F♯m7
spe-cial place in my heart for her,
G♯m7
F♯/G♯
Amaj7
she knows, she knows, she knows.
Yeah, she knows

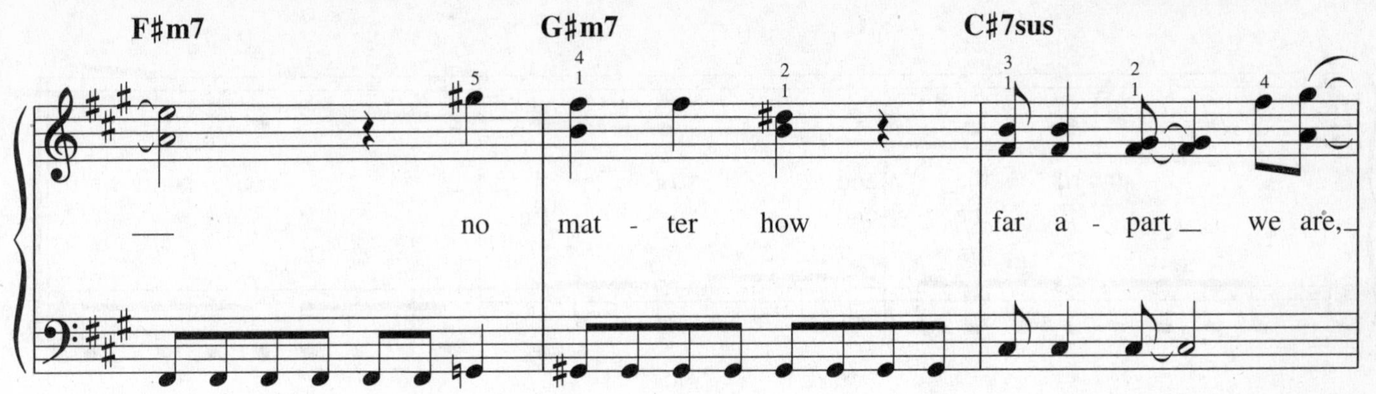
F♯m7
G♯m7
C♯7sus
no mat - ter how
far a - part we are,

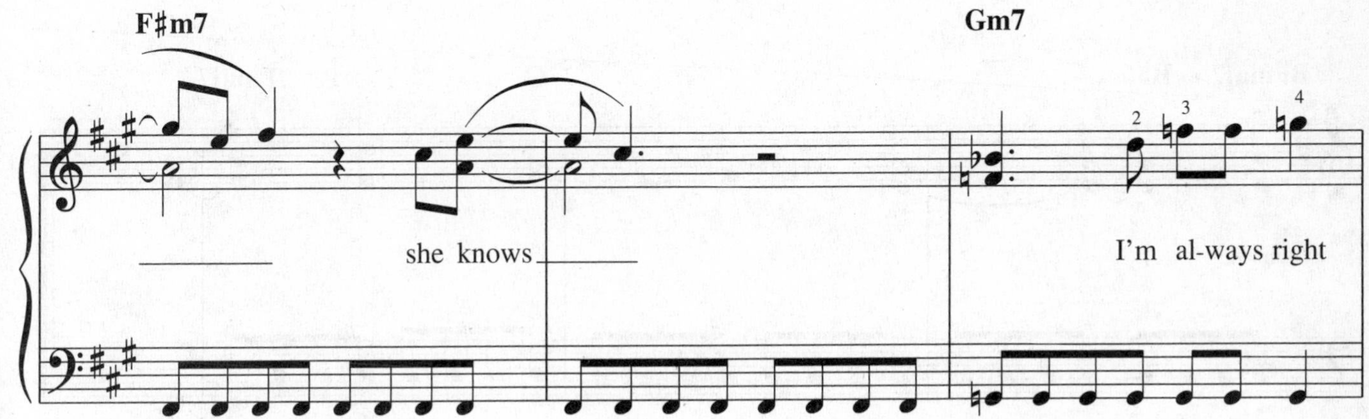
F♯m7
Gm7
she knows
I'm al-ways right

Gm7/C
B♭maj7
B♭6
there be - side her.
Two hearts
liv-ing in
two hearts
liv-ing in

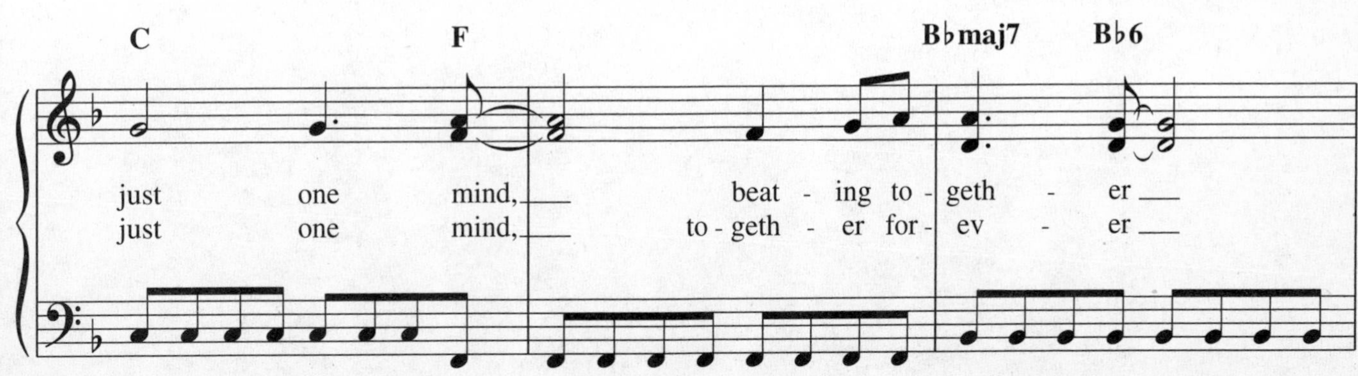
C
F
B♭maj7
B♭6
just one mind,
beat - ing to - geth - er
just one mind,
to - geth - er for - ev - er

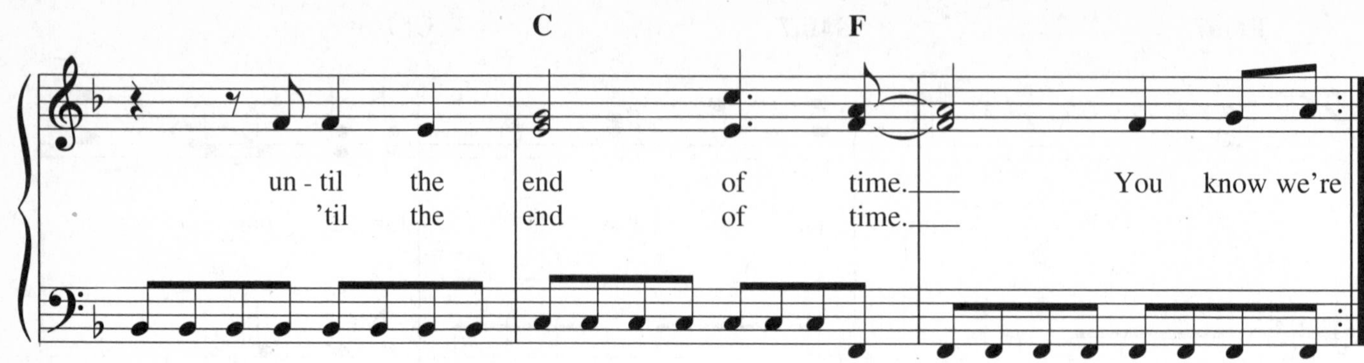

Additional Lyrics

2. Well, there's no easy way to, to understand it.
There's so much of my life in her
And it's like I planned it.
And it teaches you to never let go,
There's so much love you'll never know.
She can reach you no matter how far,
Wherever you are.
Chorus

VISION OF LOVE

Words and Music by MARIAH CAREY
and BEN MARGULIES

F
lieved
lieved
some - how the one that I need - ed
and now I know I've suc - ceed - ed

E+
E7
would find me e - ven - tu - al - ly.
in find - ing the place I con - ceived.

E♭6
D7
1.
F
I had a vi - sion of love and it was

F/G
C
C+
all that you've giv - en to me.

2.
C
B♭
F
Prayed through the
and it was
3 4
1
5
F/G
E♭6
all that you've giv - en to me. I had a
D7
F
F/G N.C.
vi - sion of love
and it was
all that you've giv - en me.
B♭
C
I've re - al - ized a dream,

Am
B♭
and I vi - su - al - ized the

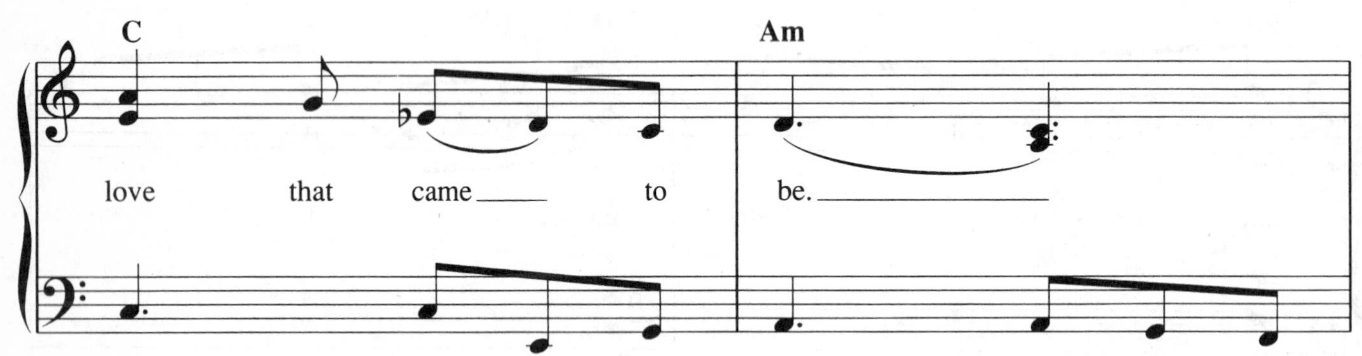
C
Am
love that came to be.

B♭
F/G
C
Feel so a - live. I'm so thank - ful that I've re -

Am
Dm
ceived the an - swer that hea - ven has

F/G
N.C.
C
sent down to me. You treat - ed me kind,
Gm6/B♭
s - weet des - ti - ny,
F
E+
and I'll be e - ter - nal - ly grate - ful hold - ing you
E7
C
so close to me. Prayed through the nights.

Gm6/B♭
F
So faith - ful - ly
know - ing the

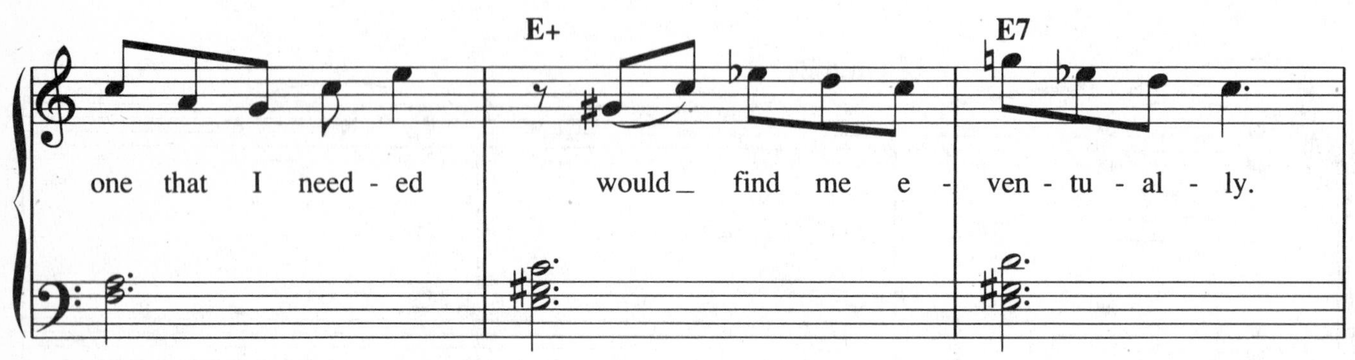
E+
E7
one that I need - ed
would_ find me e - ven - tu - al - ly.

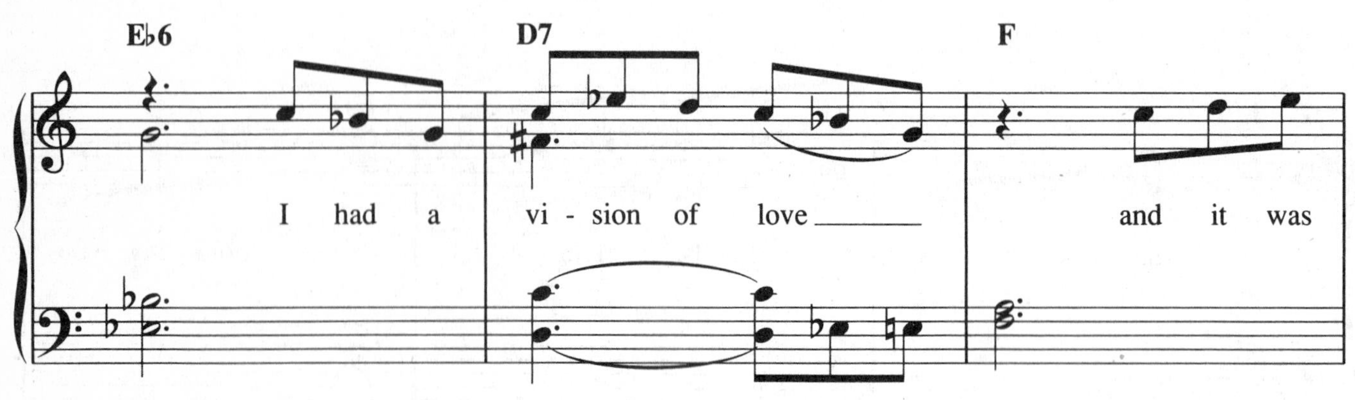
E♭6
D7
F
I had a vi - sion of love
and it was

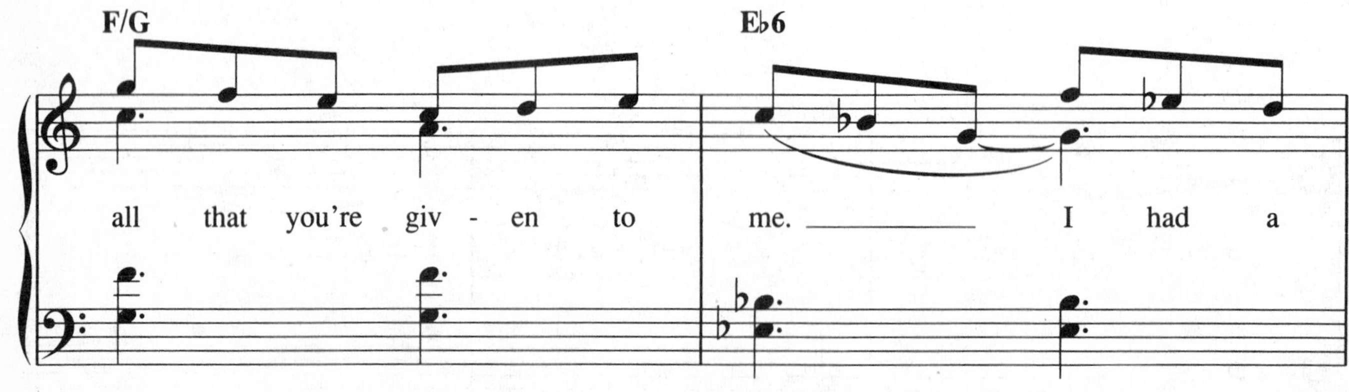
F/G
E♭6
all that you're giv - en to me.
I had a

D7
F
F/G
vi - sion of love
and it was all
E♭6
D7
F N.C.
that you
C
C+
turned out to
be.
C
B♭7
C
rit.

WALK RIGHT IN

Words and Music by GUS CANNON
and H. WOODS

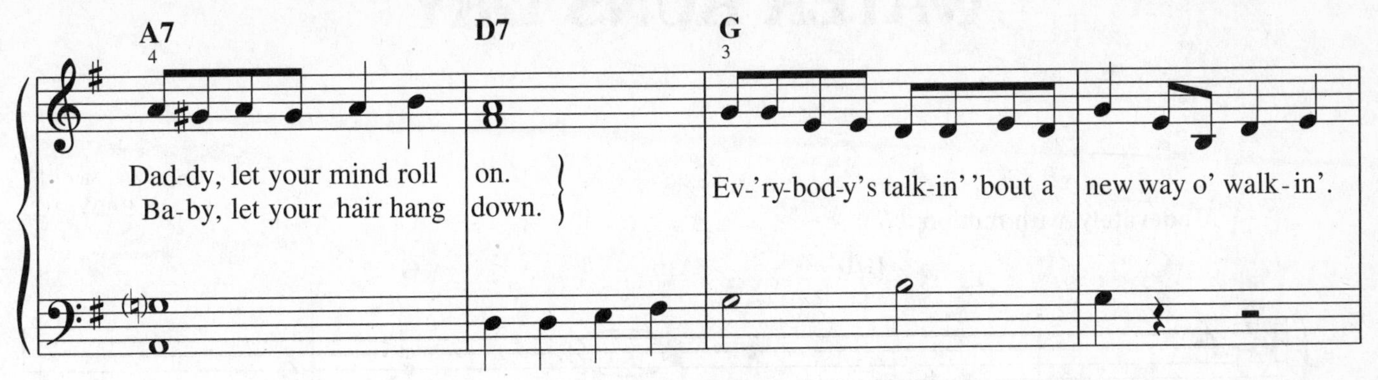
A7
D7
G
Dad-dy, let your mind roll on.
Ba-by, let your hair hang down.
Ev-'ry-bod-y's talk-in' 'bout a new way o' walk-in'.

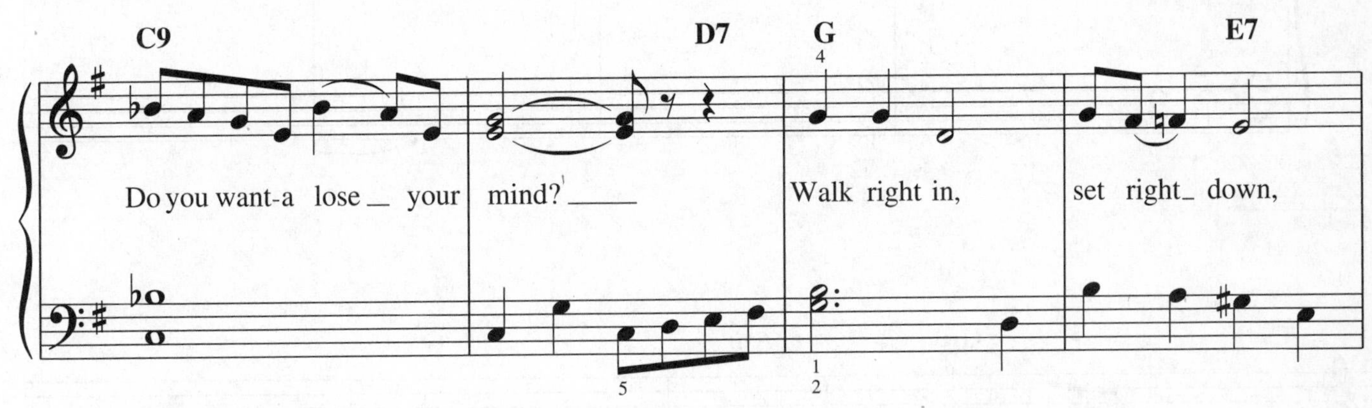
C9
D7
G
E7
Do you want-a lose your mind?
Walk right in, set right down,

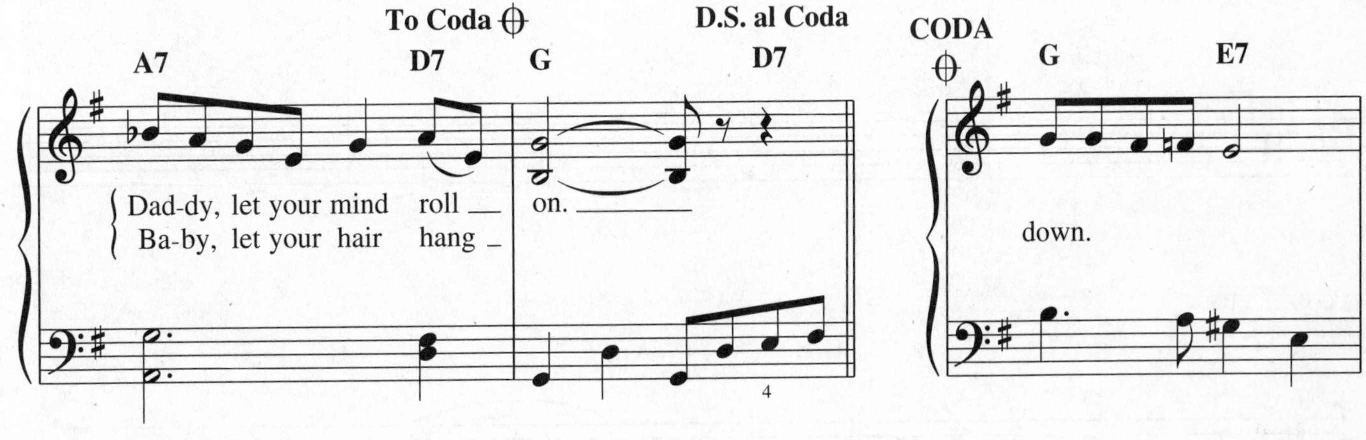
To Coda
D.S. al Coda
CODA
A7
D7
G
D7
G
E7
Dad-dy, let your mind roll on.
Ba-by, let your hair hang
down.

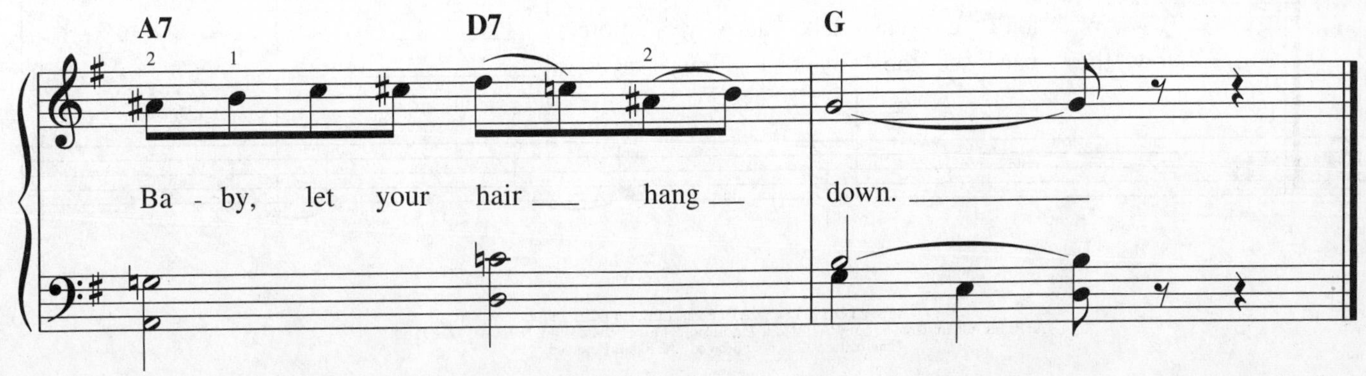
A7
D7
G
Ba - by, let your hair hang down.

WATER RUNS DRY

Words and Music by
BABYFACE

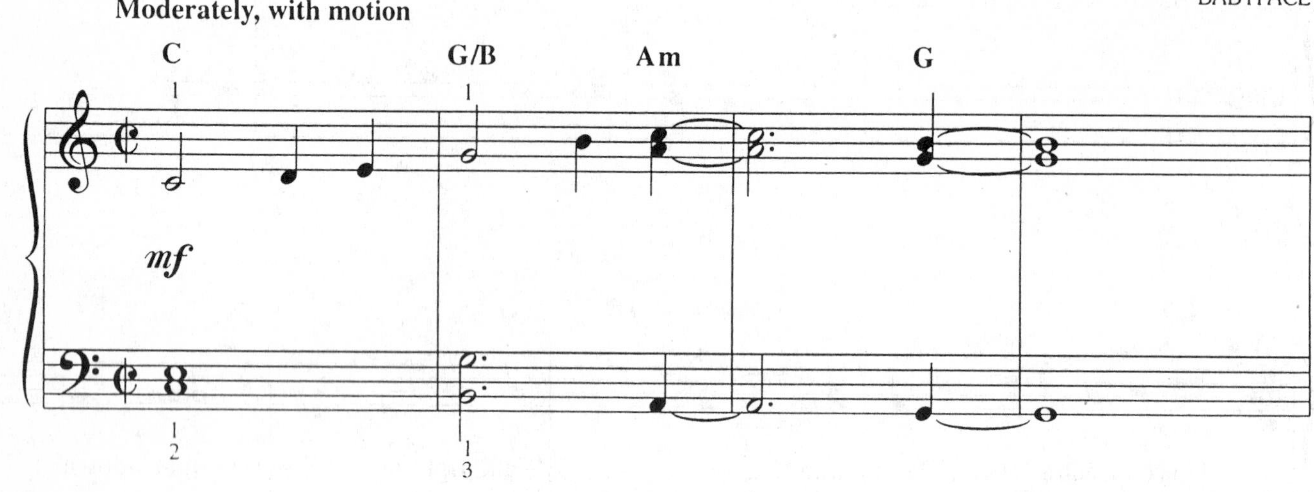

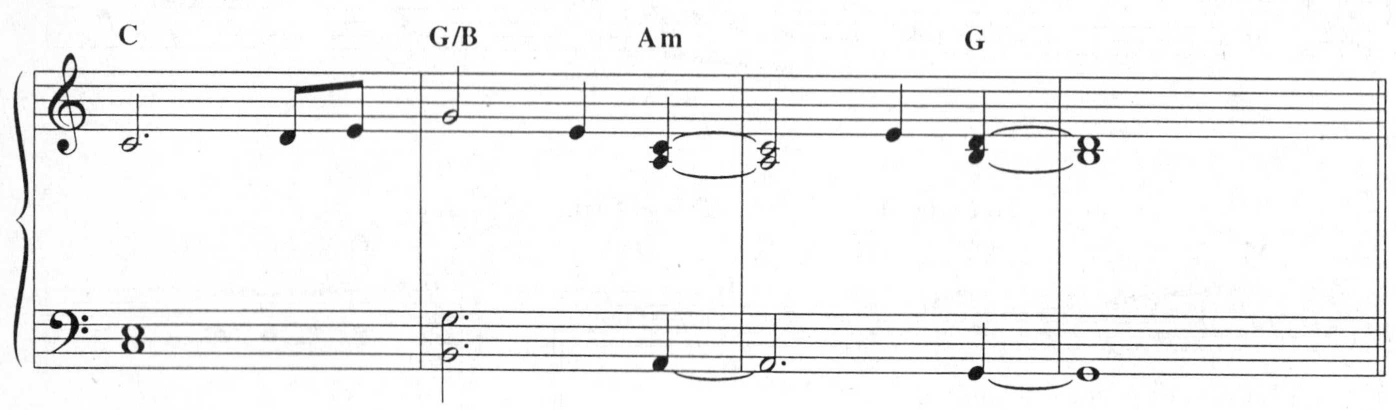

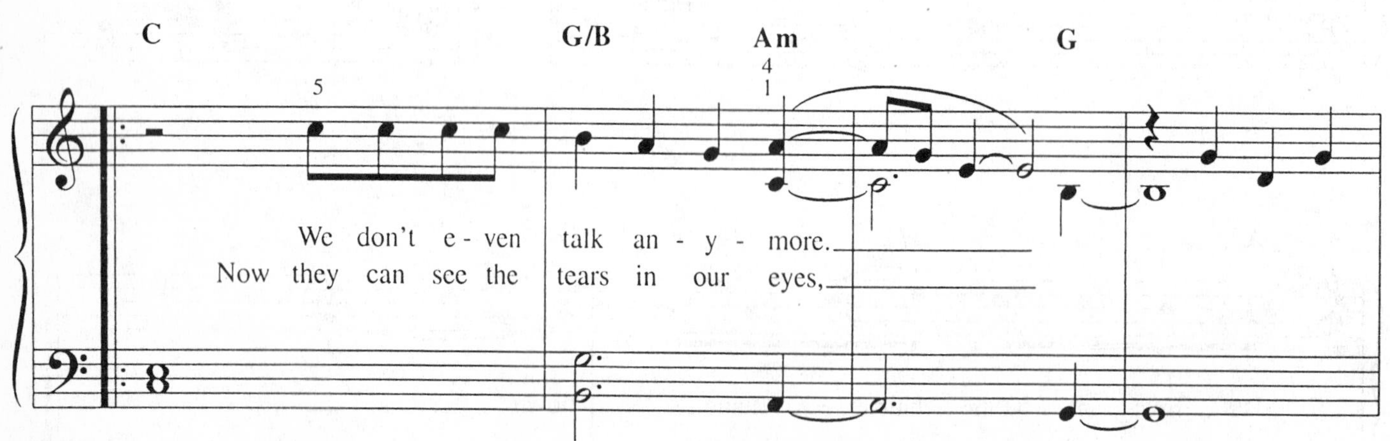

C G/B Am G
And we don't e - ven know what we ar - gue a - bout.
but we de - ny the pain that lies deep in our hearts.
C G/B Am G
Don't e - ven say, "I love you," no more,
Well, may - be that's a pain we can't hide,
C G/B Am G
'cause say - in' how we feel is no long - er al - lowed.
'cause ev - 'ry - bod - y knows that we're both torn a - part.
F E7
Some peo - ple will work things out and some
Why do we hurt each oth - er? Why
Some peo - ple will work things out and some

Am
Am/G
F♯m7♭5
3
just don't know how to change.
do we push love a - way?
just don't know how to change.
Let's don't
Fmaj7
Em7
Dm7
wait till the wa - ter runs dry.
We might
1
3
Fmaj7
Em7
Dm7
watch our whole lives pass us by.
Let's don't
Fmaj7
Em7
Am
D7
wait till the wa - ter runs dry.
We'll make the

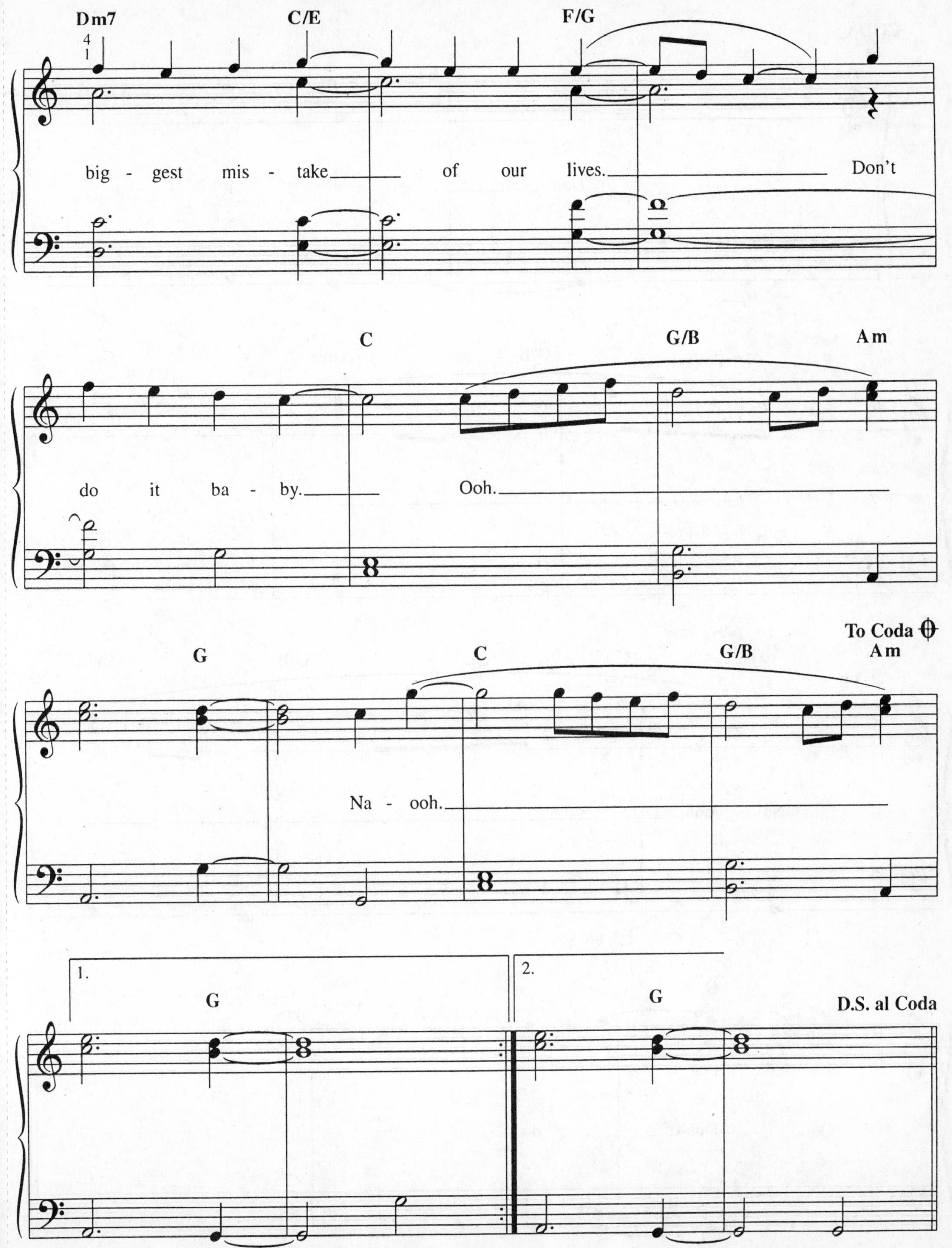
Dm7
C/E
F/G
big - gest mis - take of our lives. Don't
C
G/B
Am
do it ba - by. Ooh.
To Coda
G
C
G/B
Am
Na - ooh.
1.
G
2.
G
D.S. al Coda

CODA
G
Don't do it ba -
C
G/B
Am
G
by. Ooh,
C
G/B
Am
Na - ooh.
G
C
Don't do it ba - by.

WHAT'S GOING ON

Words and Music by MARVIN GAYE,
AL CLEVELAND and RENALDO BENSON

Cmaj7
Broth - er, broth - er, broth - er, there's far too man - y
war is not the an - swer, for on - ly love can
who are they to judge us sim - ply 'cause our
Am7
of you dy - ing. You know we've
con - quer hate. You know we've
hair is long. Ah, you know we've
Dm7
got to find a way to bring some
got to find a way to bring some
got to find a way to bring some un - der -
1.
Dm7/G
G7
lov - in' here to - day, yeah.

2.,3.
Dm7/G
G7
lov - in' here to - day, oh.
stand - ing here to - day, oh.

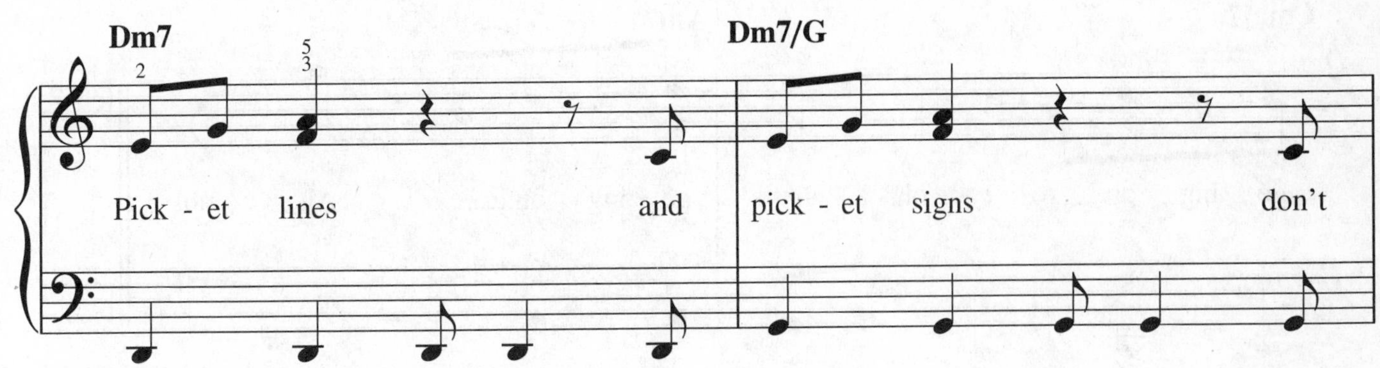
Dm7
Dm7/G
Pick - et lines and pick - et signs don't

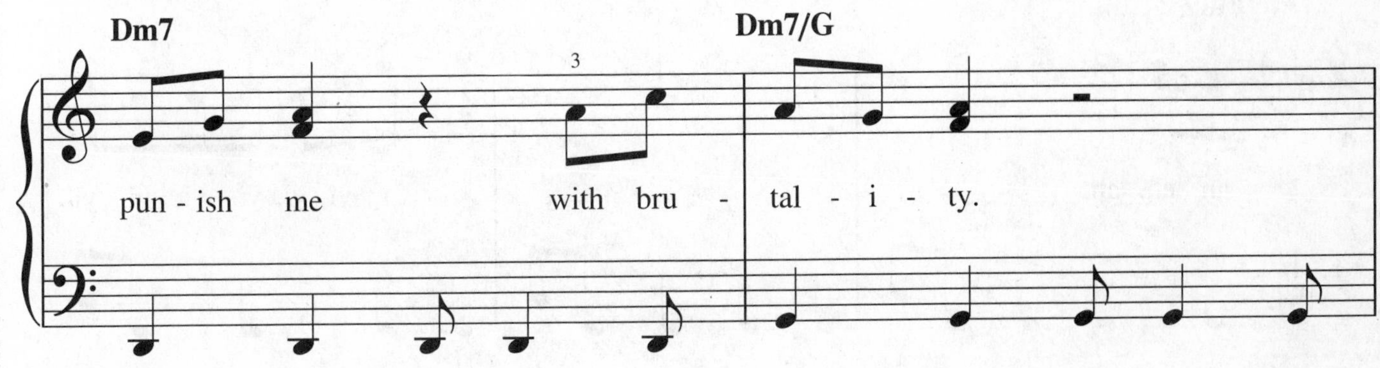
Dm7
Dm7/G
pun - ish me with bru - tal - i - ty.

Dm7
Dm7/G
Talk to me so you can see, oh, what's

Cmaj7
Am7
go - ing on, what's go - ing on, yeah, what's

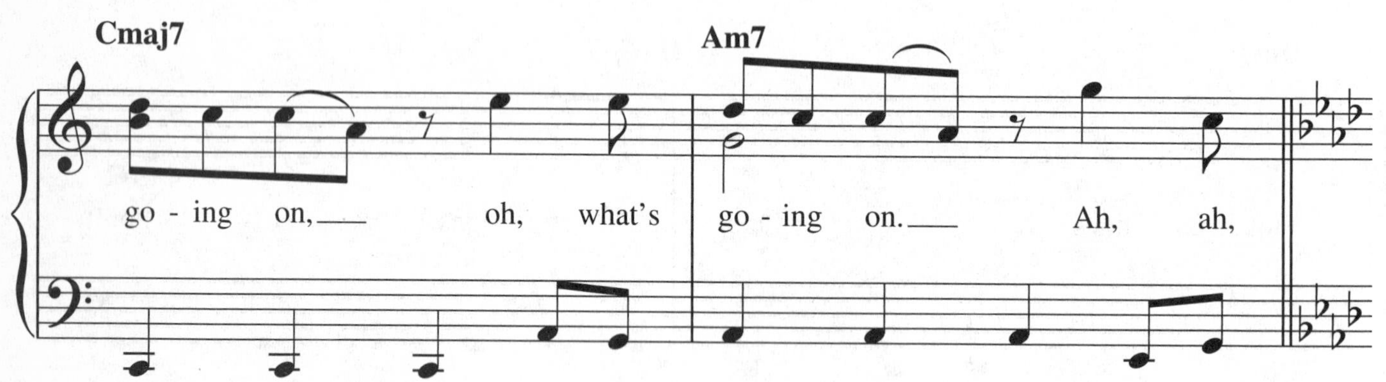
Cmaj7
Am7
go - ing on, oh, what's go - ing on. Ah, ah,

Fm9
ah, ah, ah. I, yi, yi, yi, yi, yi, yi,

ya, ya, ya, ya.

I, yi, yi, yi, yi, yi, ya, ya, ya, ya, ya.

F/G
Be, doot, de doot; Be, be, be, doot; Be be, be, doot;

To Coda
D.S. al Coda
(take 2nd ending)
Bu, doot, be, be, be, doot; Be be, be, be, be, doot.

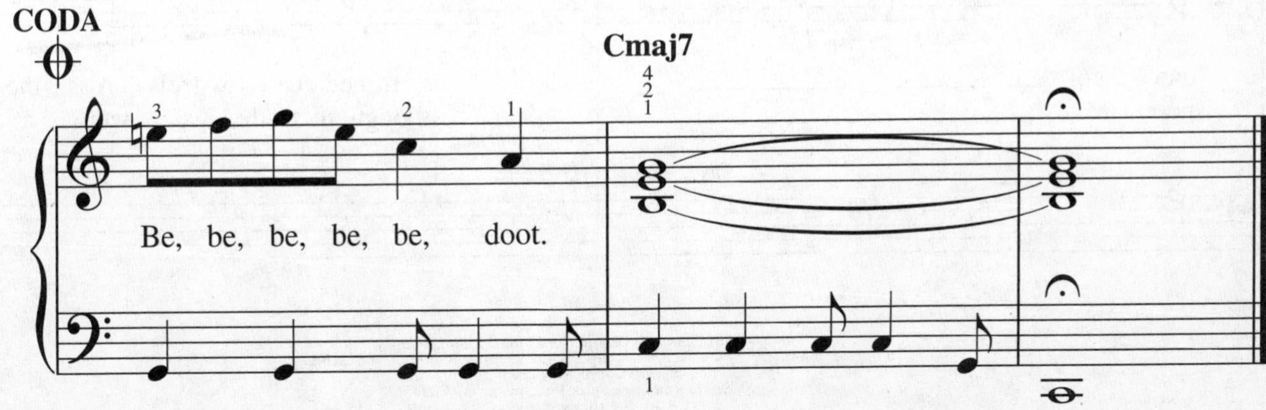
CODA
Cmaj7
Be, be, be, be, be, doot.

A WHITER SHADE OF PALE

Words and Music by KEITH REID
and GARY BROOKER

Dm7
G
G/F
floor;
sea;
I was feel - ing kind of
So I took her by the

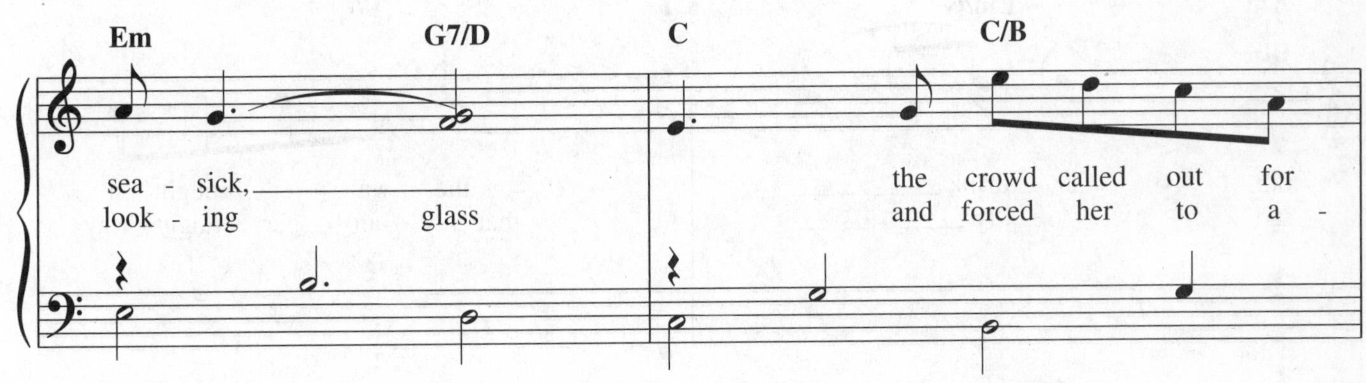
Em
G7/D
C
C/B
sea - sick,
look - ing glass
the crowd called out for
and forced her to a -

Am
Em/G
F
F/E
more.
gree.
The room was hum - ming
Say-ing "You must be the

Dm7
G
G/F
hard - er
mer - maid
as the ceil - ing flew a -
who took Nep - tune for a

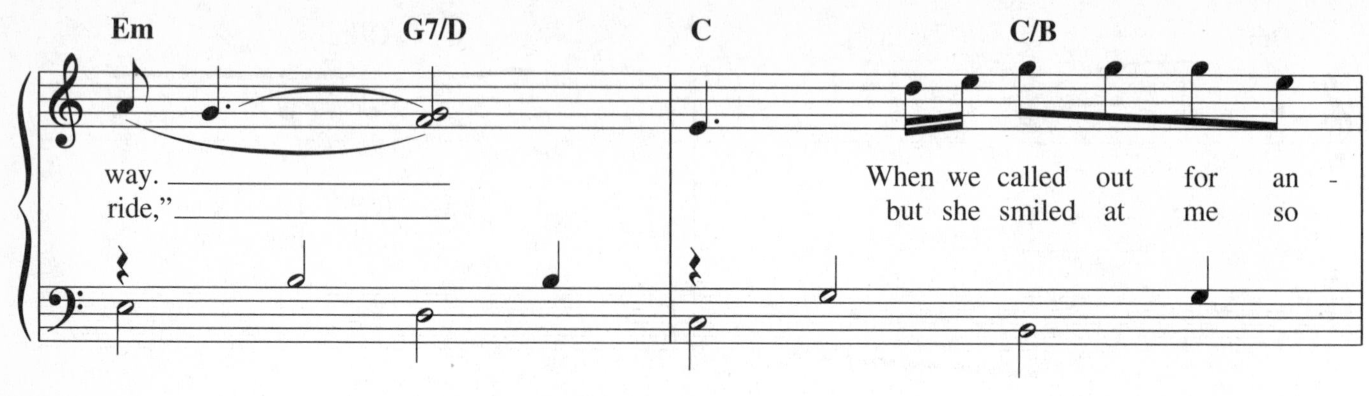
Em
G7/D
C
C/B
way.
ride,"
When we called out for an -
but she smiled at me so

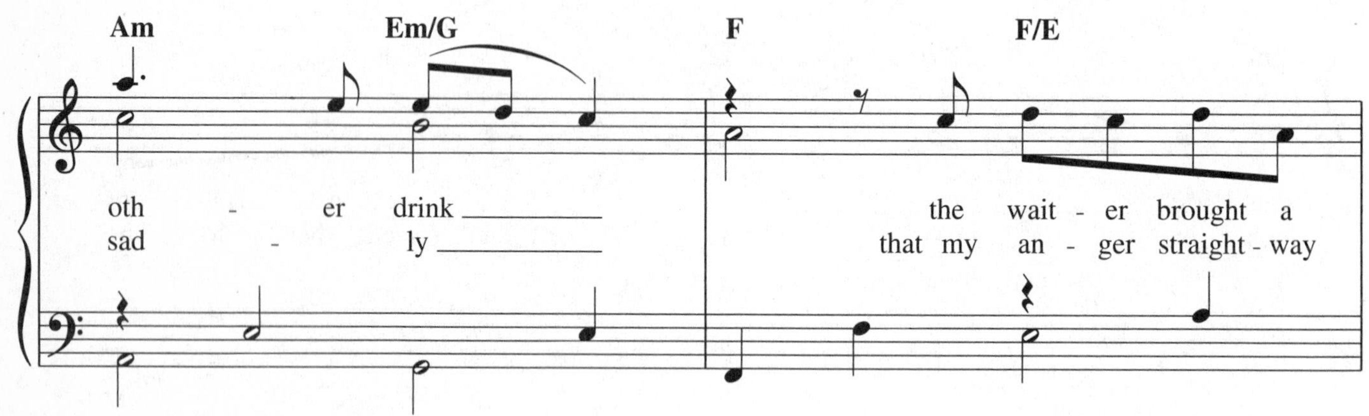
Am
Em/G
F
F/E
oth - er drink
sad - ly
the wait - er brought a
that my an - ger straight - way

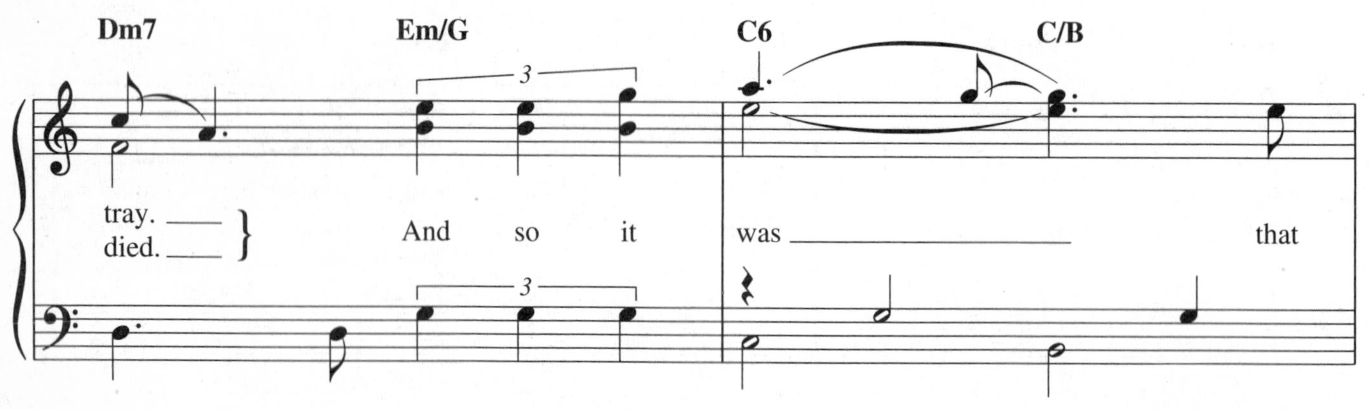
Dm7
Em/G
C6
C/B
3
tray.
died.
And so it
was
that

Am
C/G
F
F/E
Dm7
la - ter
as the mil - ler told his
tale,

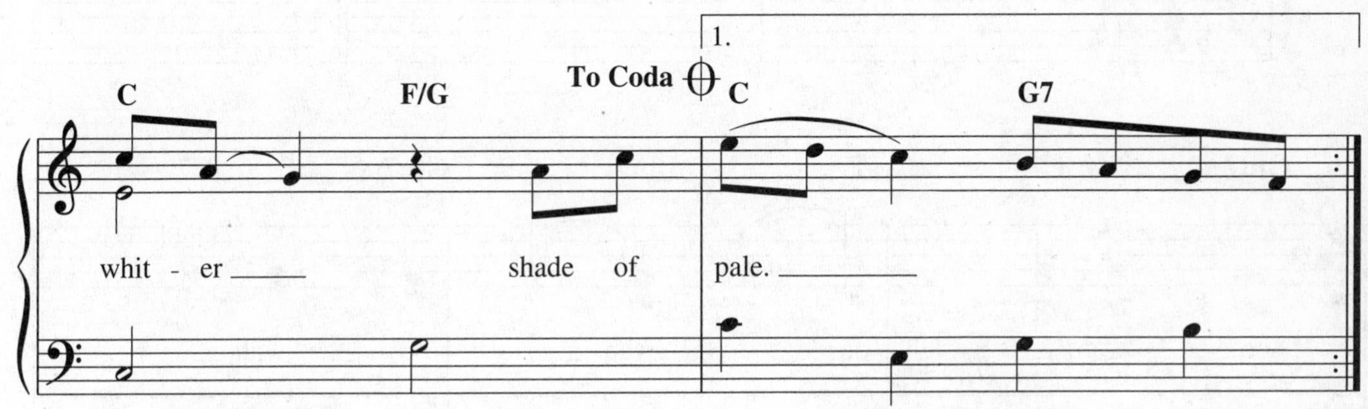

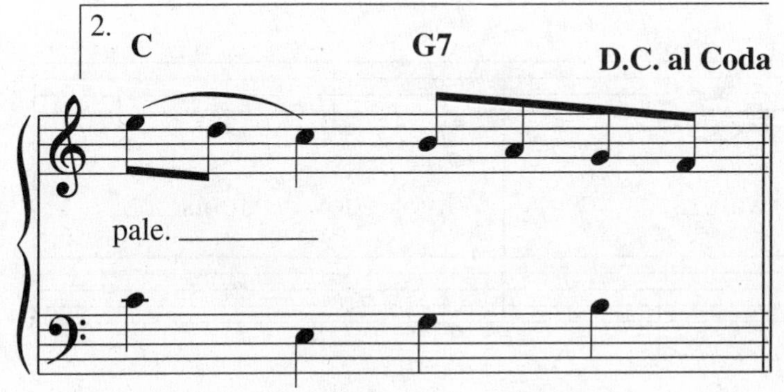

Additional Lyrics

She said, "There is no reason,
and the truth is plain to see,"
But I wandered through my playing cards
and would not let her be
one of the sixteen vestal virgins
who were leaving for the coast.
And although my eyes were open
they might just as well been closed.

WHY DO FOOLS FALL IN LOVE

Words and Music by MORRIS LEVY
and FRANKIE LYMON

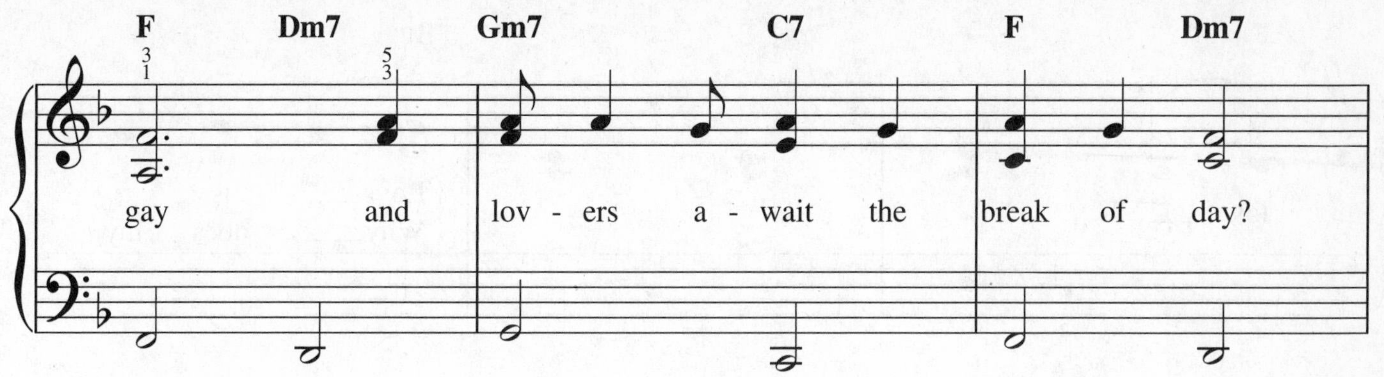
F
Dm7
Gm7
C7
F
Dm7
gay and lov - ers a - wait the break of day?

Gm7
C7
F
Dm7
Gm7
C7
Why do they fall in love?

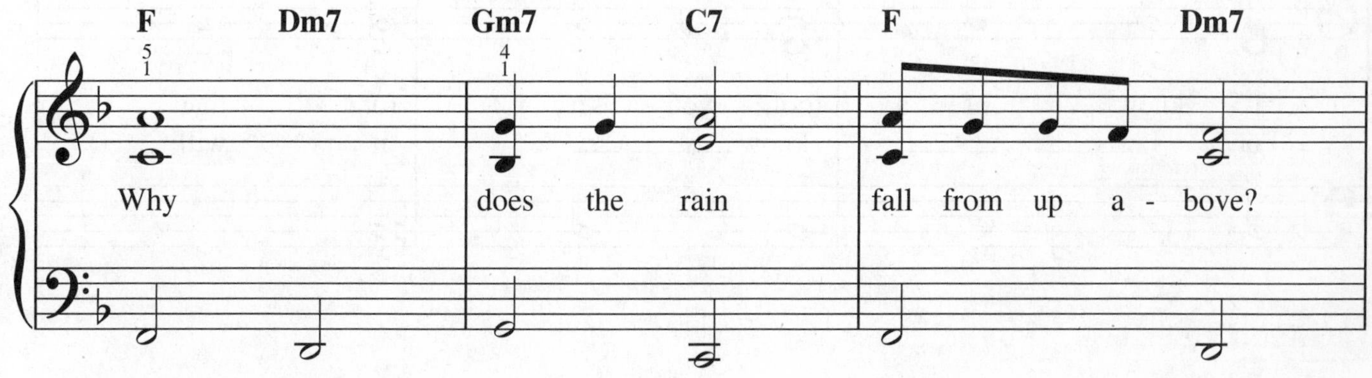
F
Dm7
Gm7
C7
F
Dm7
Why does the rain fall from up a - bove?

Gm7
C7
F
Dm7
Gm7
C7
Why do fools fall in love? Why do they fall in

F
Bb
love?
Love is a
Why does my

Bbm
F
F7
los - ing game.
heart
Love can
skip a cra - zy
be a shame:
beat?

Bb
Bbm
G7
I know of a
For I
fool, you see,
know
for that
it will

C7
F
Dm7
Gm7
C7
fool is me!
reach de - feat!
Tell me
why!

F
Dm7
Gm7
C7
F
Dm7
Gm7
C7
Tell me
F
1.
Gm7
C7
2.
F7
why!
B♭
C7
Why
do
fools
fall
in
F
Dm7
Gm7
C7
F
love?

WINCHESTER CATHEDRAL

Words and Music by
GEOFF STEPHENS

C
as
my ba - by left town.

You could have done some - thing,

G7
but you did - n't try.

C
You did - n't do noth - ing.
You let her walk

C7
by. Now ev - 'ry - one knows just how much

F
I need-ed that girl. She would-n't have gone

D7
G7
far a - way if on - ly you'd start - ed ring - ing your bell.

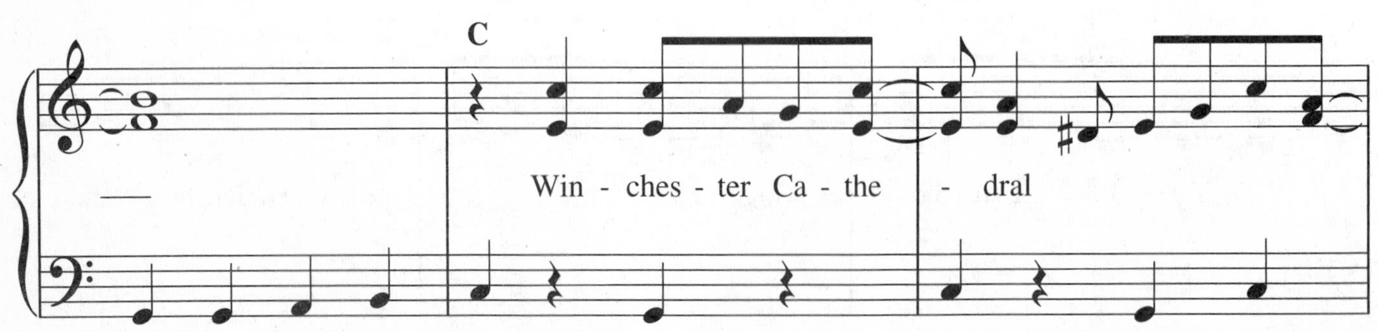
C
Win - ches - ter Ca - the - dral

G7
5
1
3
1
you're bring - ing me down.

C
You stood and you watched as my ba - by left

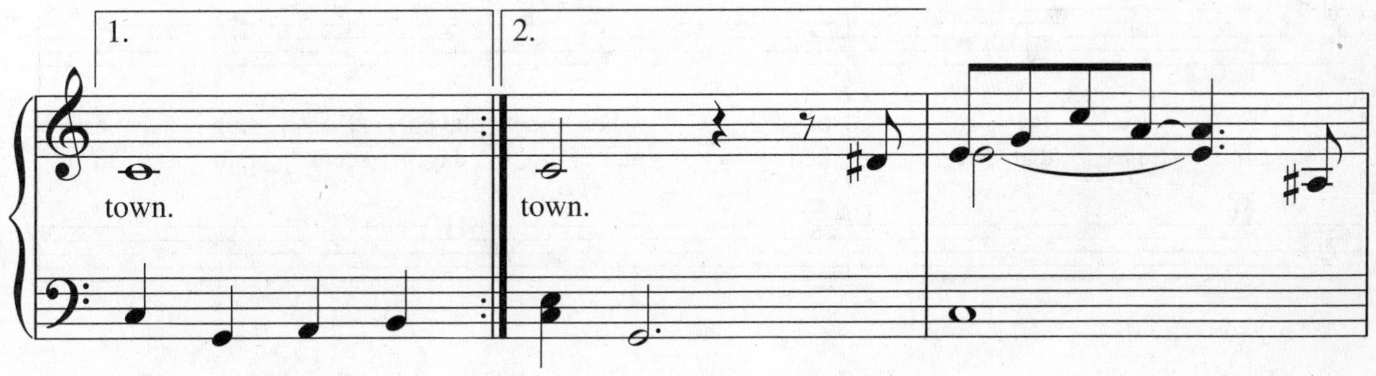
1.
2.
town.
town.

G7
C
4

YESTERDAY ONCE MORE

Words and Music by JOHN BETTIS
and RICHARD CARPENTER

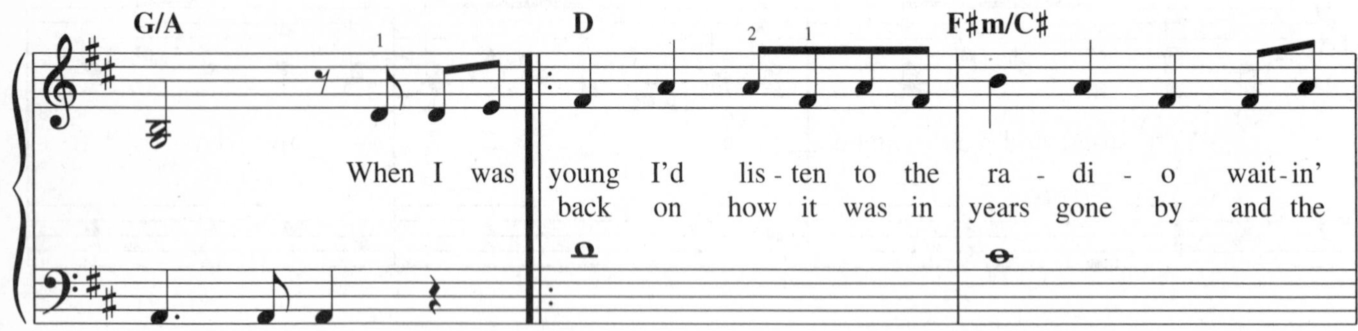

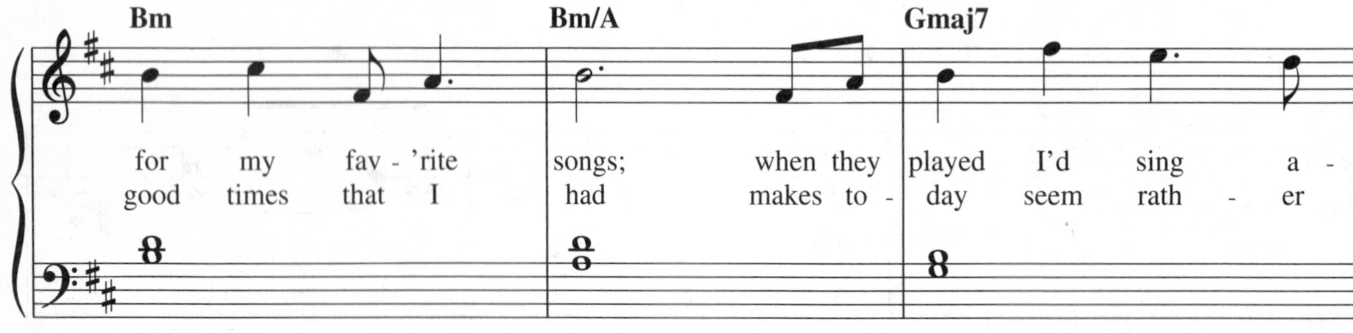

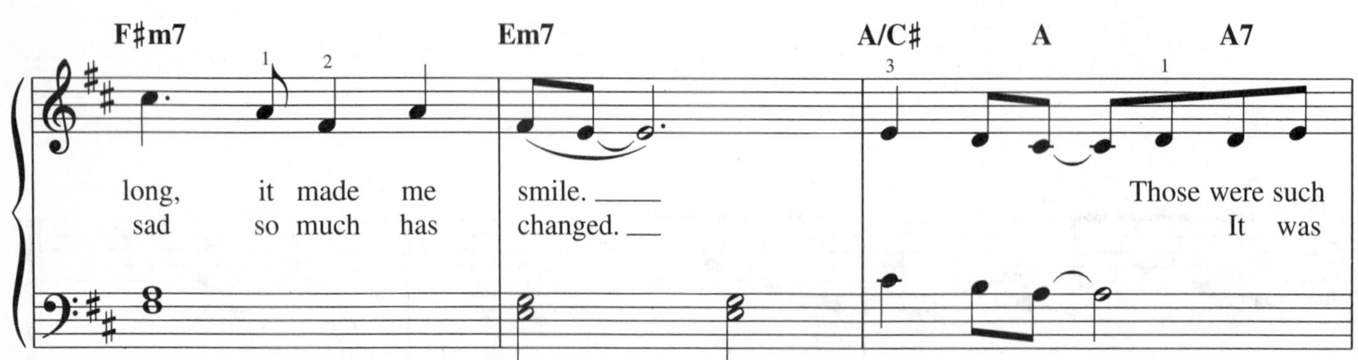

D
F#m/C#
hap - py times and not so long a - go how I
songs of love that I would sing to then and I'd

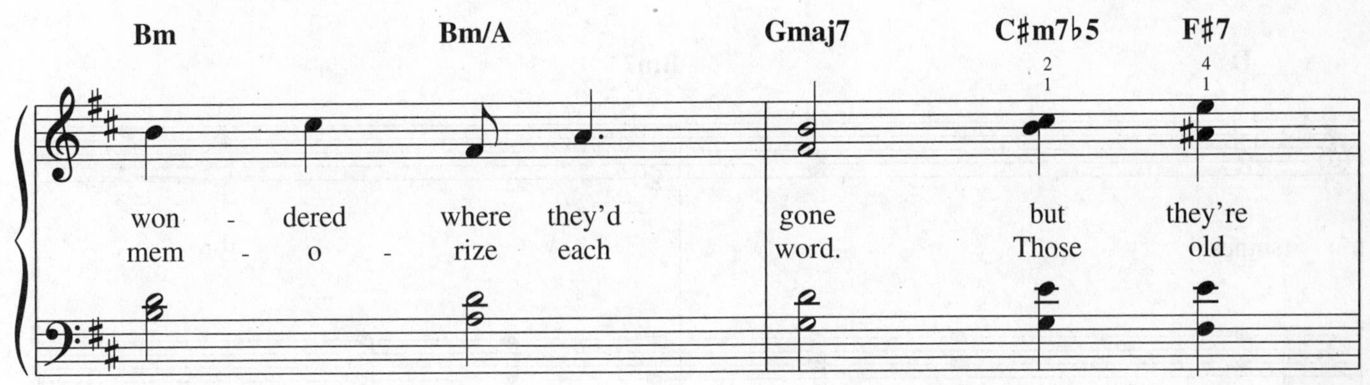
Bm
Bm/A
Gmaj7
C#m7♭5
F#7
won - dered where they'd gone but they're
mem - o - rize each word. Those old

Bm
Bm/A
back a - gain just like a long lost friend all the
mel - o - dies still sound so good to me as they

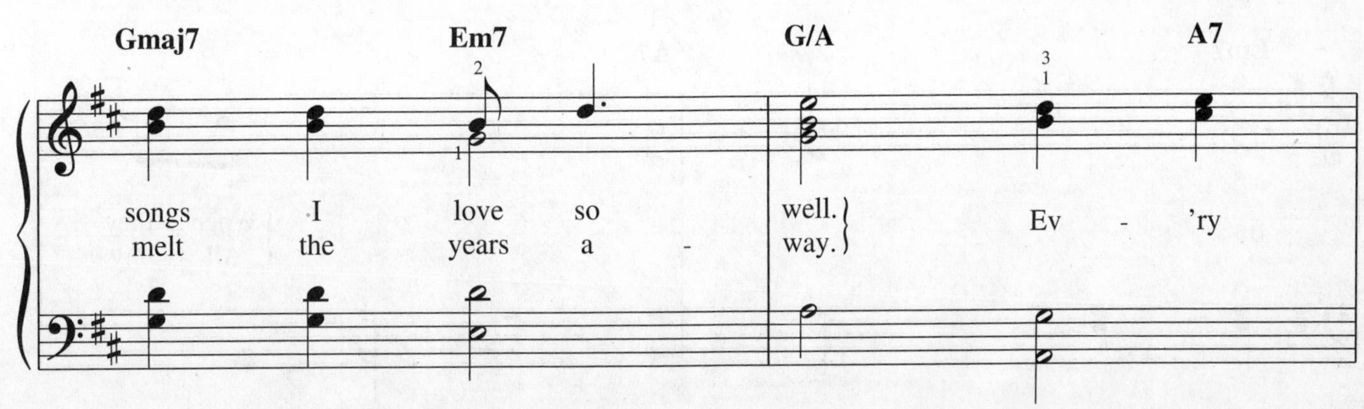
Gmaj7
Em7
G/A
A7
songs I love so well.
melt the years a - way.
Ev - 'ry

D
Bm
sha - la - la - la ev - 'ry wo wo still
D
Bm7
shines. Ev - 'ry
D
Bm
shing - a - ling - a - ling that they're start - in' to sing so
Em7
A7
fine.
When they
All my

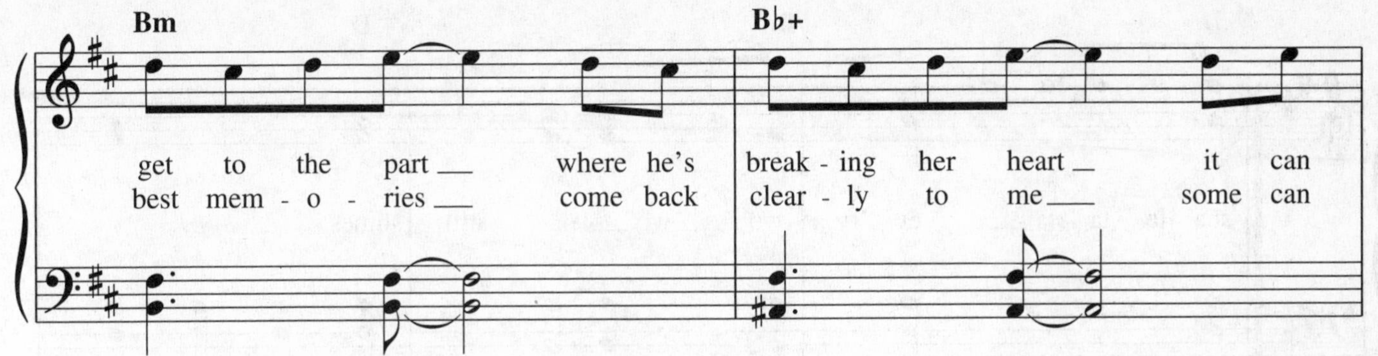
Bm
B♭+
get to the part where he's breaking her heart it can
best mem - o - ries come back clear - ly to me some can

D/A
G#m7♭5
D/A
real - ly make me cry just like be - fore.
e - ven make me cry just like be - fore.

G/A
Dmaj7
1.
G/A
It's yes - ter - day once more.

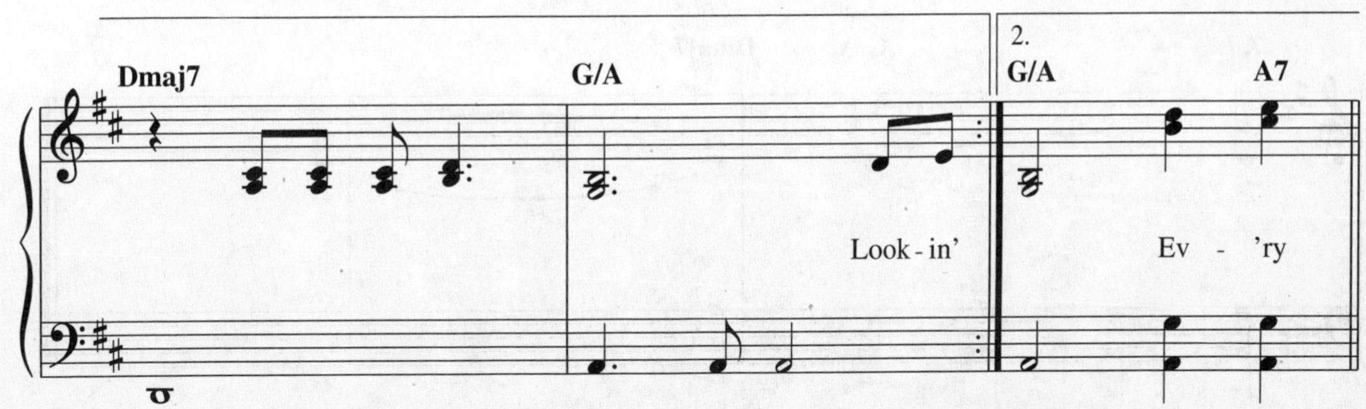
Dmaj7
G/A
2.
G/A
A7
Look - in'
Ev - 'ry

D
Bm
D
sha - la - la - la ___ ev - 'ry wo _ wo _____ still shines.
Bm7
D
Ev - 'ry shing - a - ling - a - ling that they're
Bm7
Em7
1.
A7
G/A
A7
start - in' to sing _ so fine. Ev - 'ry
2.
A7
G/A
Dmaj7

YOU LIGHT UP MY LIFE

Words and Music by
JOSEPH BROOKS

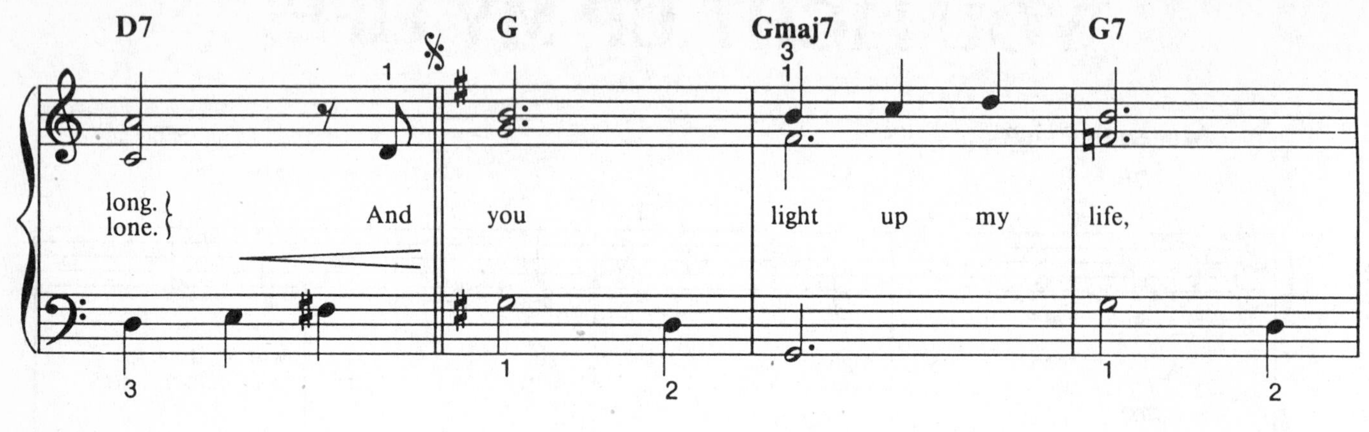
D7
G
Gmaj7
G7
long.
lone.
And
you
light
up
my
life,

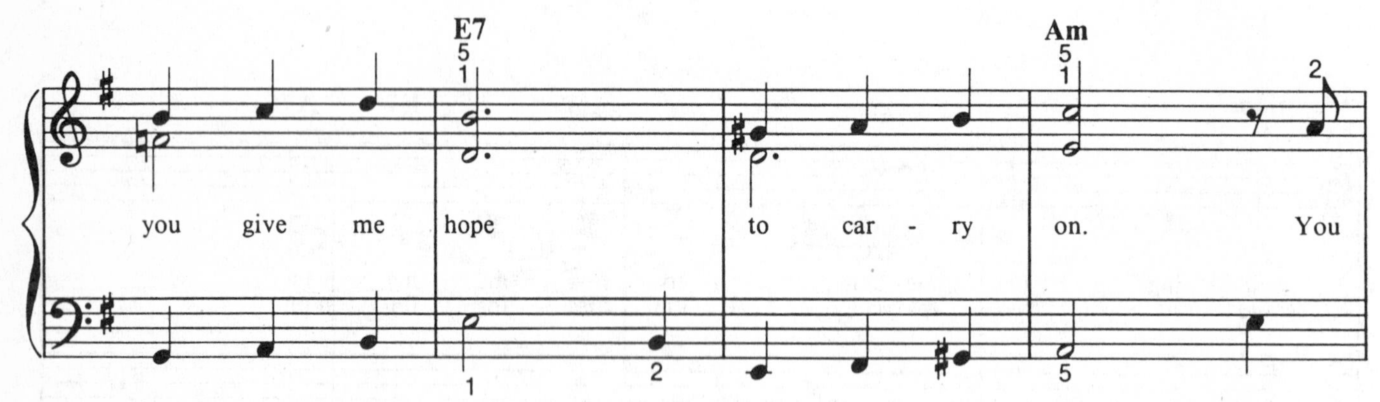
E7
Am
you
give
me
hope
to
car
-
ry
on.
You

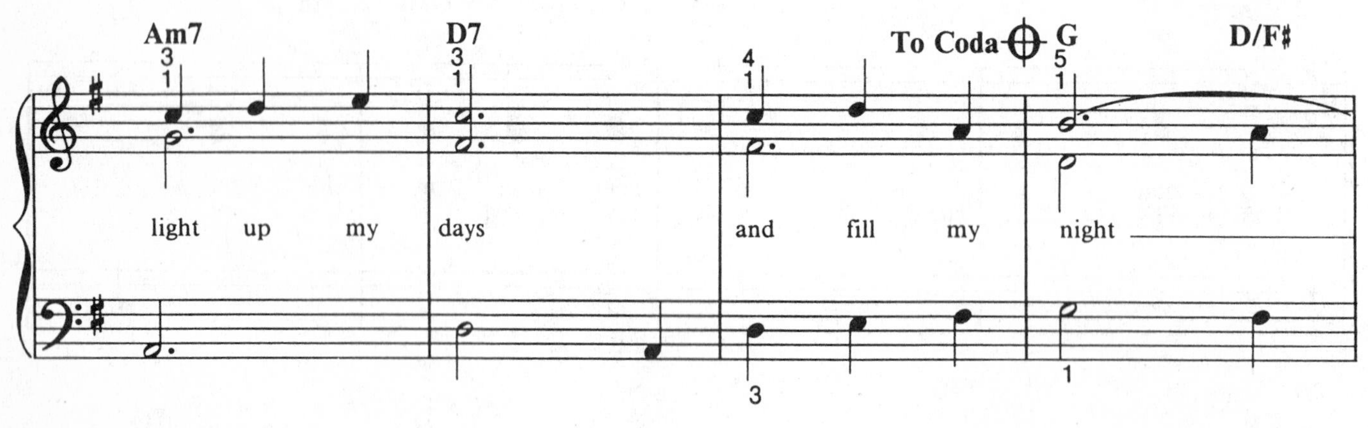
Am7
D7
To Coda
G
D/F♯
light
up
my
days
and
fill
my
night

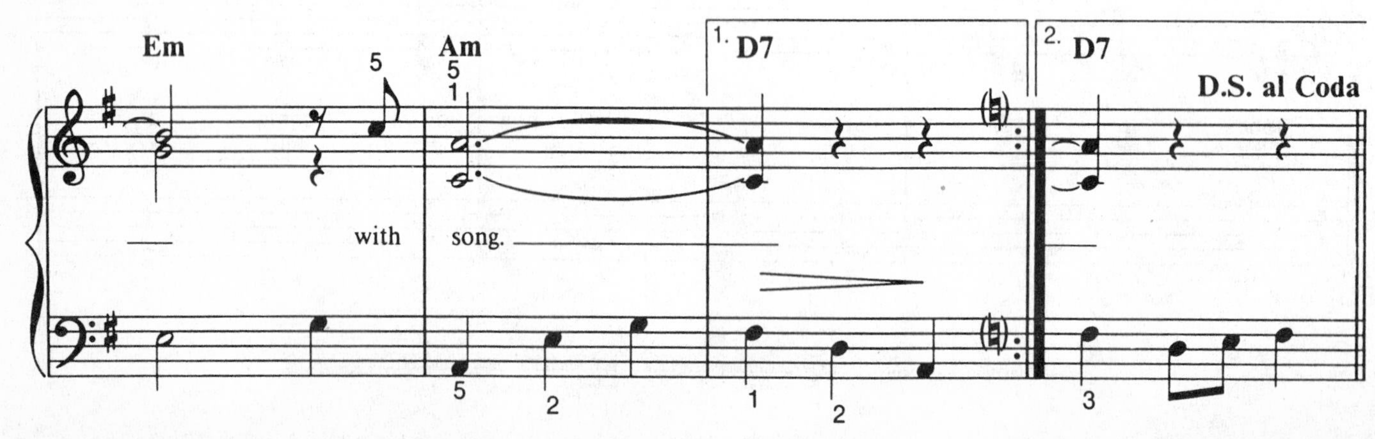
Em
Am
1. D7
2. D7
D.S. al Coda
with
song.

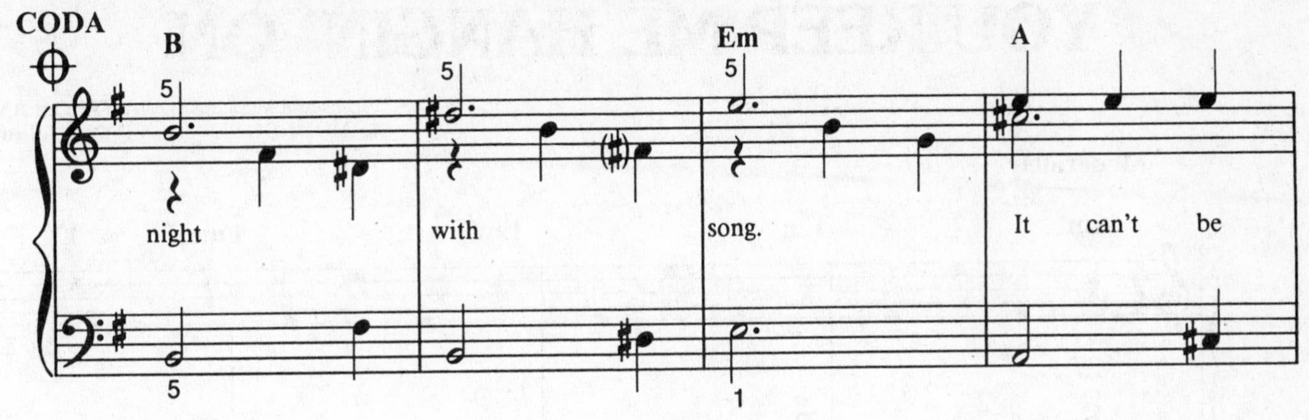
CODA
B
Em
A
night
with
song.
It can't be

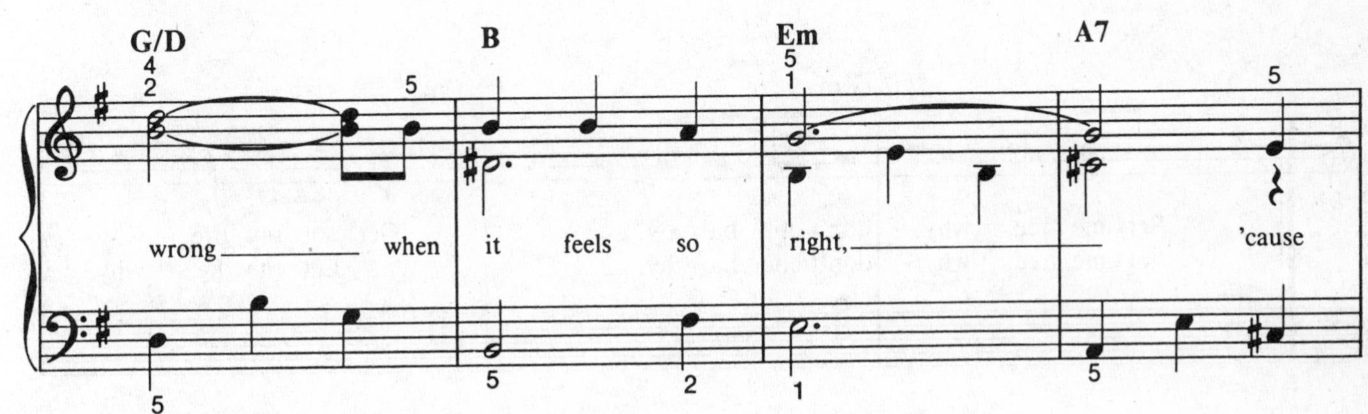
G/D
B
Em
A7
wrong when it feels so right,
'cause

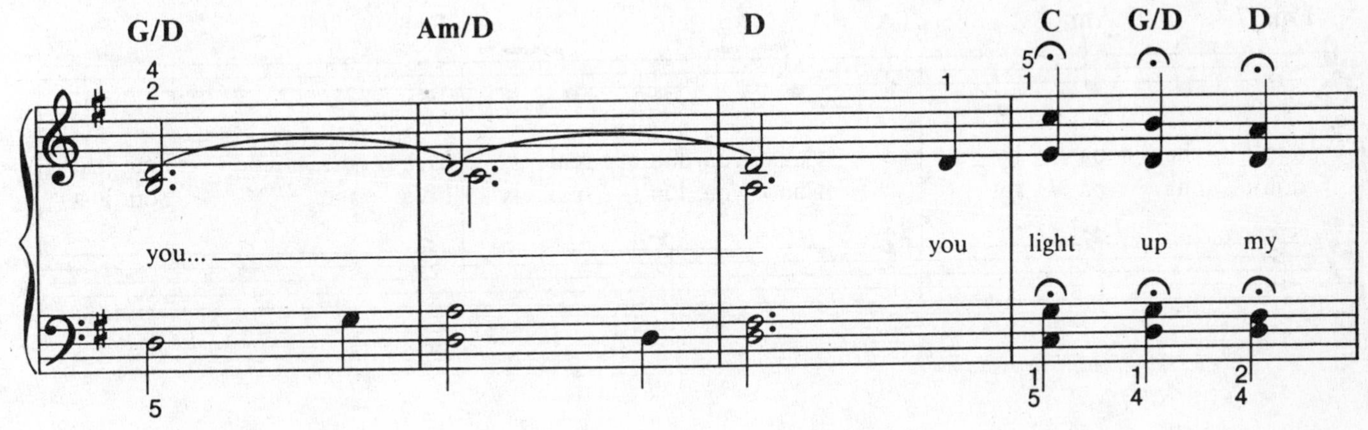
G/D
Am/D
D
C
G/D
D
you...
you light up my

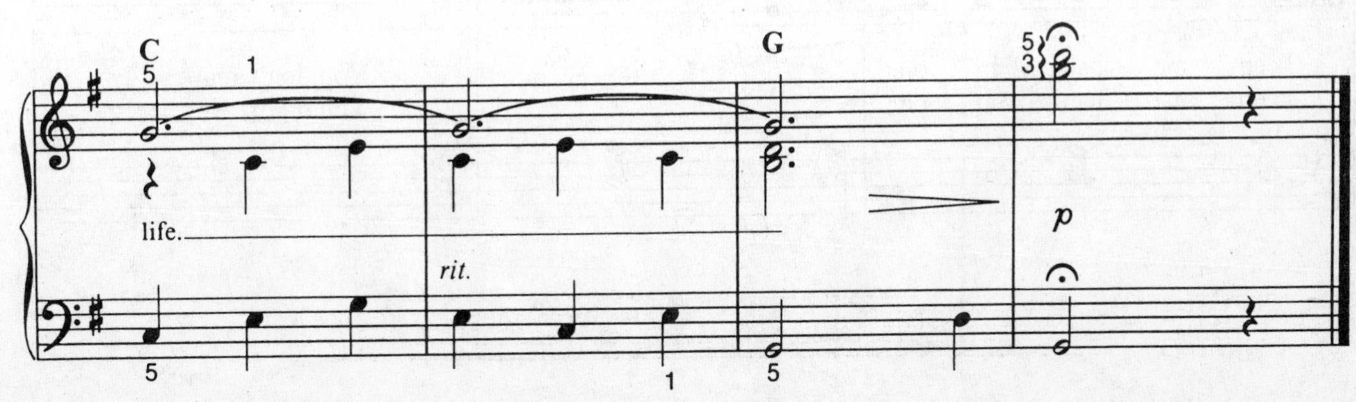
C
G
life.
rit.
p

YOU KEEP ME HANGIN' ON

Words and Music by EDWARD HOLLAND,
LAMONT DOZIER and BRIAN HOLLAND

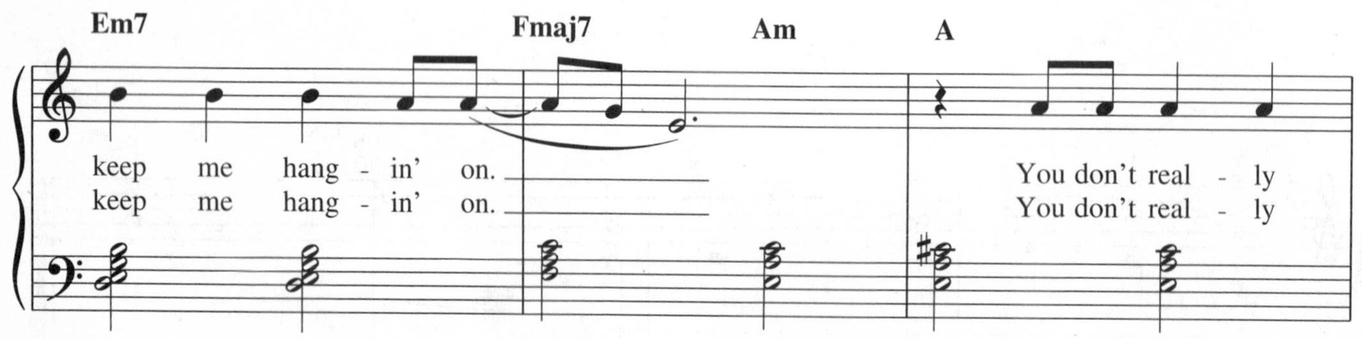

Em
Em7
Fmaj7
Am
need me, but you keep me hang - in' on.
want me, you just keep me hang - in' on.

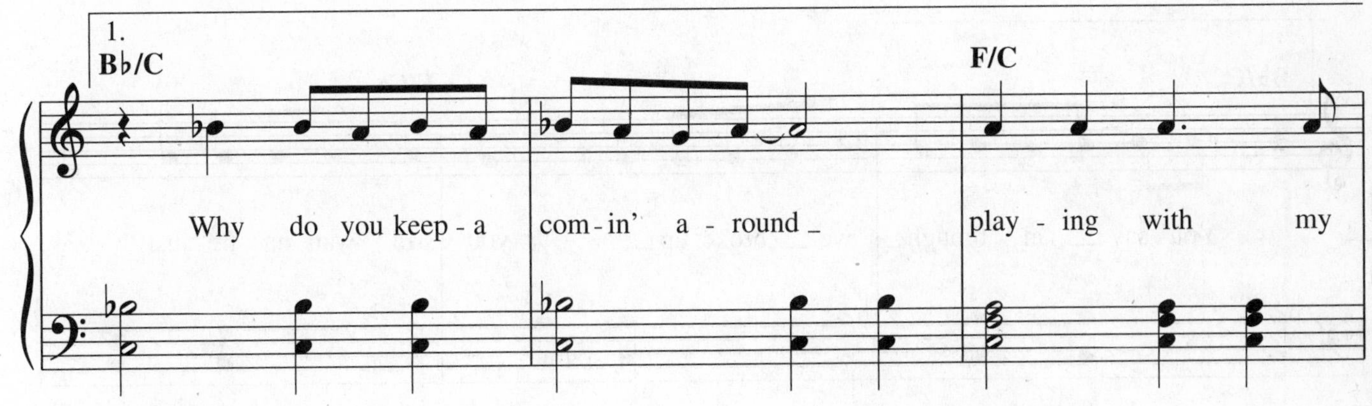
1.
B♭/C
F/C
Why do you keep - a com - in' a - round
play - ing with my

C
B♭/C
heart?
Why don't cha get out of my life

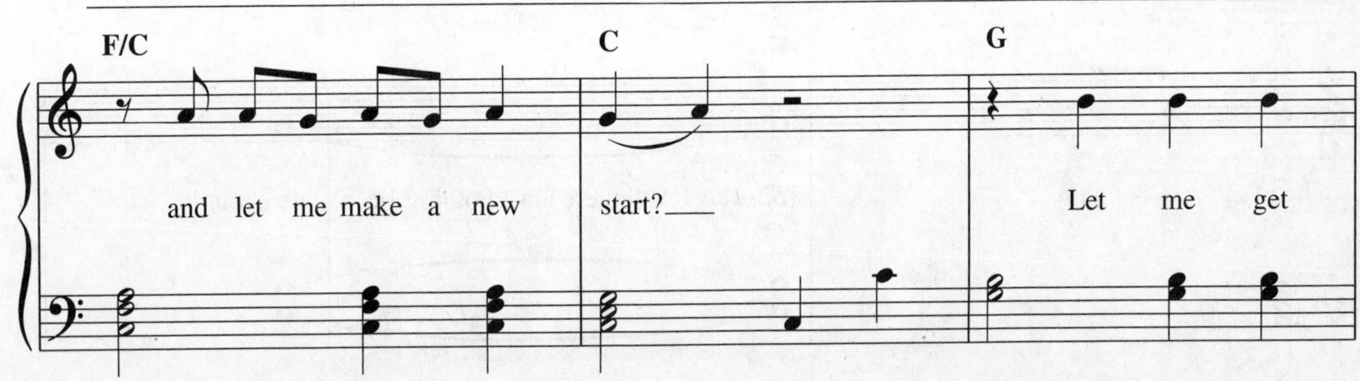
F/C
C
G
and let me make a new start?
Let me get

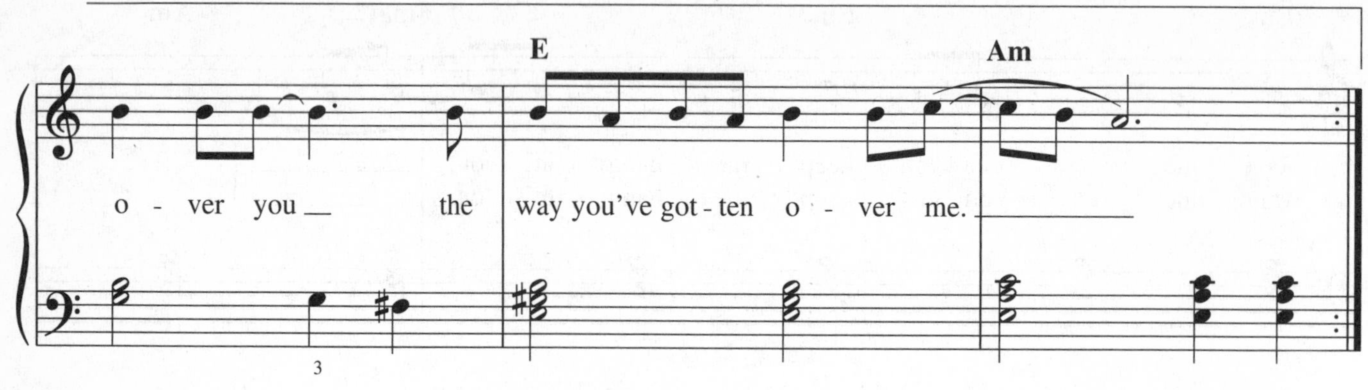
E
Am
o - ver you the way you've got - ten o - ver me.
3

2.
B♭/C
F/C
You say al - though we broke up you still wan - na be just

C
B♭/C
F/C
friends. But how can we still be friends when see - ing you on - ly breaks my

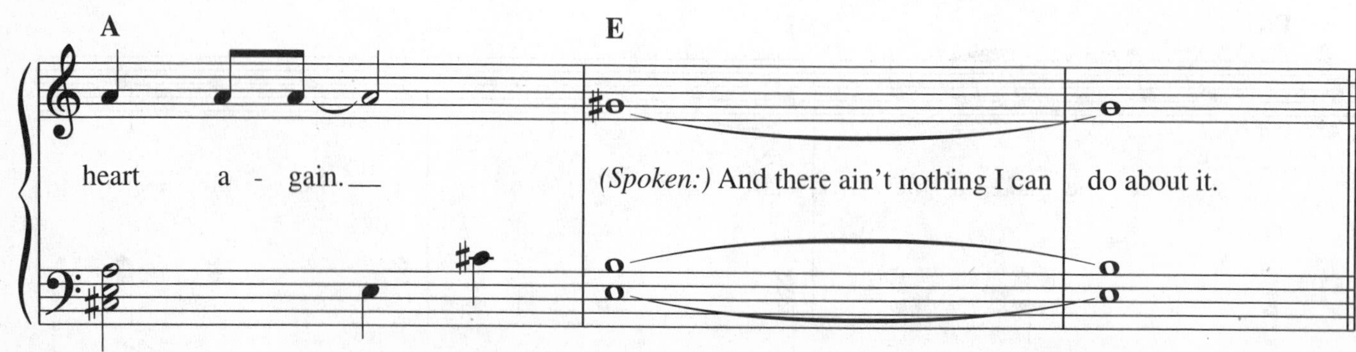
A
E
heart a - gain.
(Spoken:) And there ain't nothing I can do about it.

A
Em
Em7
Set me free why don't cha ba - by, __ get out my life __ why

F
Am
B♭/C
don't ya ba - by. __ You claim you still care a - bout me __ but your

F/C
C
B♭/C
heart and soul needs to be free. ______ Now that you've got __

F/C
C
______ your free - dom you wan - na still hold on to me. ____

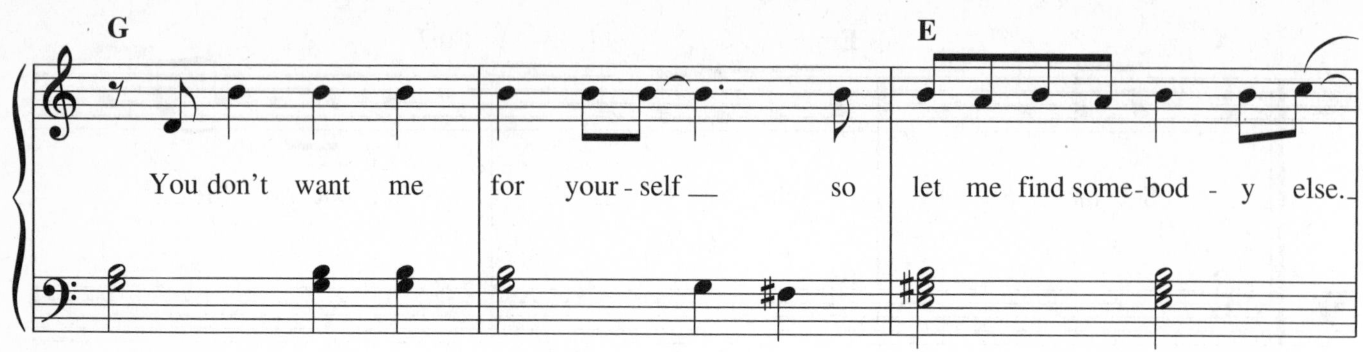
G
E
You don't want me for your-self so let me find some-bod - y else.

Am
A
Em
Why don't cha be a man a - bout it

Em7
F
Am
A
and set me free. Now you don't care a

Em
Em7
F
Am
thing a - bout me. You're just us - ing me. Boy,

A
Em
Em7
get out, __ get out - ta my life __
and let me sleep at night. _

Fmaj7
Am
A
Em
'Cause you don't _ real - ly love me, you just

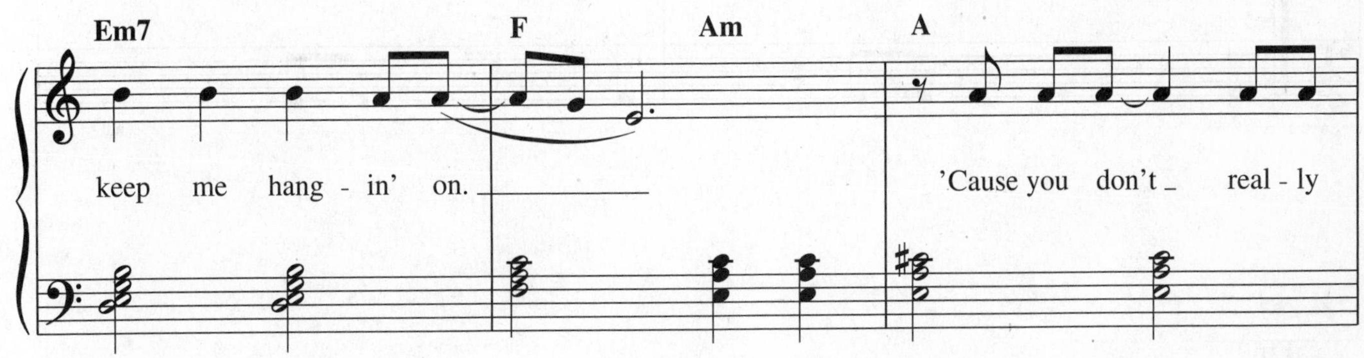
Em7
F
Am
A
keep me hang - in' on. ___
'Cause you don't _ real - ly

Am
Em
F
Am
need me, so let me be, set me free. ___

YOU SANG TO ME

Words and Music by CORY ROONEY
and MARC ANTHONY

Rock Ballad

G D

mf

Oh. I just

With pedal

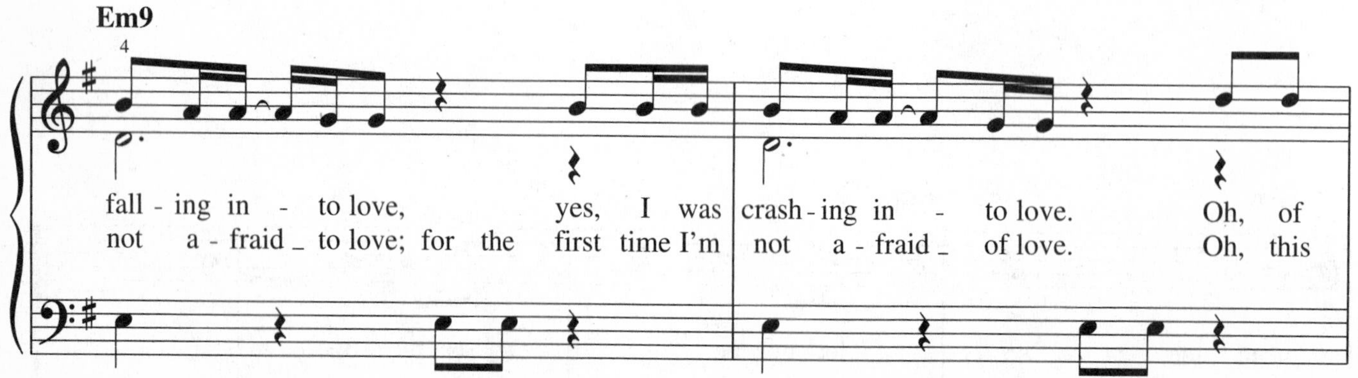

C
D
all the words you said to me — a - bout life, the truth, and be - ing free, yeah, you
day seems made for you and me — and you showed me what life needs to be, yeah, you

G
1.
D
sang to me, — oh, — how you sang to me. — Girl, I
sang to me. — Oh, — you

2.
D
G
sang to me. — All the while you were in front of me I nev - er
long to hear you sing be - neath — the —

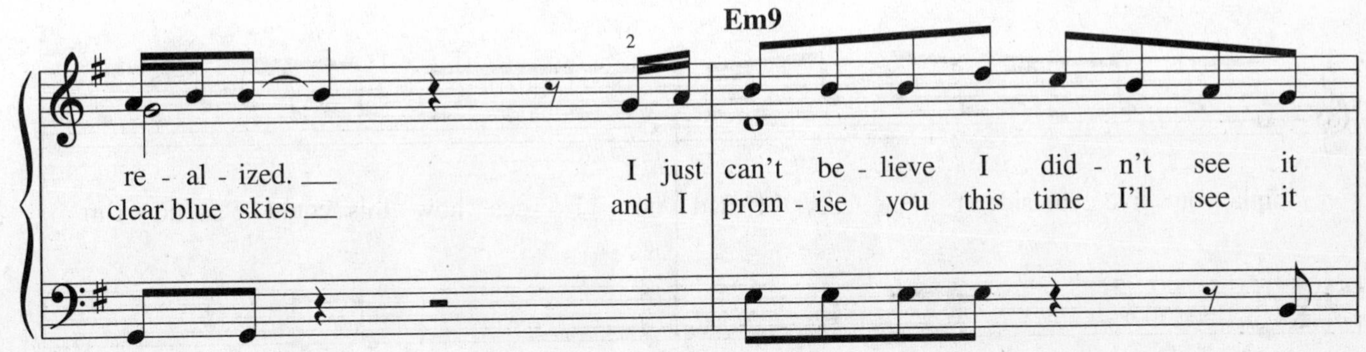
Em9
re - al - ized. — I just can't be - lieve I did - n't see it
clear blue skies — and I prom - ise you this time I'll see it

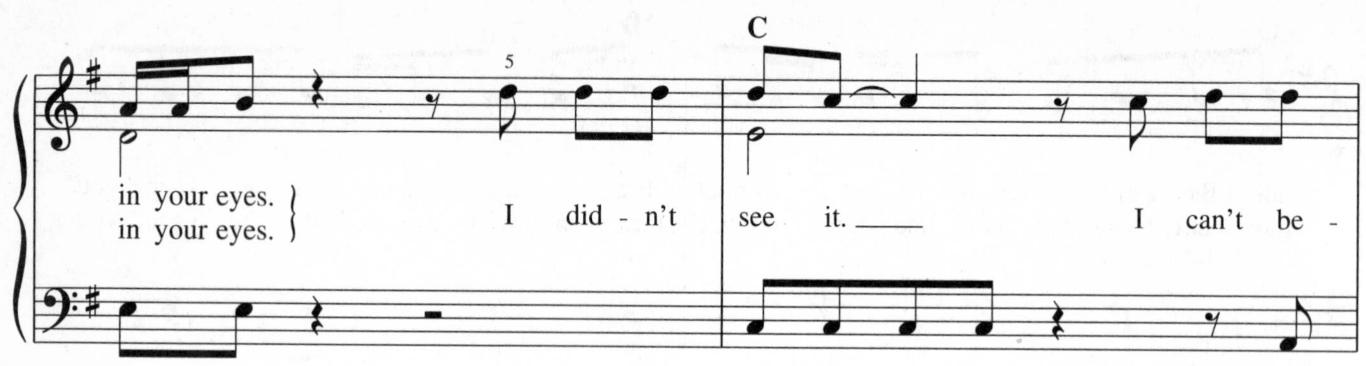
C
5
in your eyes.
in your eyes.
I did - n't see it. I can't be -

D
5
G
To Coda
lieve it, oh, but I feel it when you

1.
D
2.
D
sing to me. How I sing to me. Just to

G
4
think you live in-side of me. I had no i - dea how this could be now I'm

Em9
cra - zy for your love. Can't be-lieve I'm cra - zy for your love. The

C
D
words you said just sang to me ___ and you showed me where I wan-na be. ___ You

G
D
D.S. al Coda
(with repeat)
sang to me, oh, ___ you sang to me. All the

CODA
D
G
3
4
sing to me.

Em7
C
D
1.
2.
All the

G
while you were in front of me I nev-er re - al - ized. I just
long to hear you sing be-neath the clear blue skies and I

Em9
can't be - lieve I did - n't see it in your eyes. I did - n't
prom - ise you this time I'll see it in your eyes. I did - n't

C
D
see it. I can't be - lieve it, oh, but I
see it. I can't be - lieve it, oh, but I

1.
G
D
2.
G
Gmaj9
feel it when you sing to me. How I feel it.

YOU'RE THE INSPIRATION

Words and Music by PETER CETERA
and DAVID FOSTER

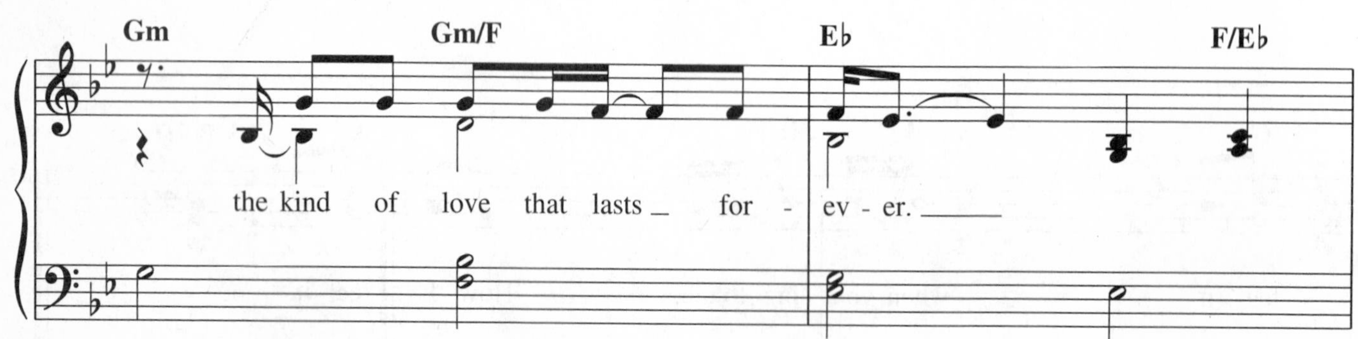

B♭
Dm7
And I want you here with me

Gm
Gm/F
E♭
from to - night _ un - til the end of time.

F/A
B♭
E♭/G
A♭
You should know __ ev - 'ry - where I go; __

D/F♯
Gm
C/E
D/F♯
G
A/C♯
al - ways on my mind, _ in my heart, __ in my soul, _ ba - by.
cresc.

D
D/F♯
G
D/F♯
A
You're the mean - ing of my life, _
you're the in - spi - ra - tion.
f

D
D/F♯
G
D/A
A
You bring feel - ing to my life, _
you're the in - spi - ra - tion.

F
C/F
B♭/F
B♭m/F
Wan-na have you near me, I
wan-na have you hear me say - ing ___

1.
F/C
B♭/C
C
no one needs you more _ than I need

F/E♭
F
B♭
you.
mp
f
F/E♭
F
2.
F/C
B♭/C
no one needs you more than
A
D
D/F♯
I need
you.
G
D/A
A
D
D/F♯

G
D/A
A
F
C/F
Wan-na have you near me, I

B♭/F
B♭m/F
F/C
B♭/C
wan-na have you hear me say yeah,
no one needs you more than

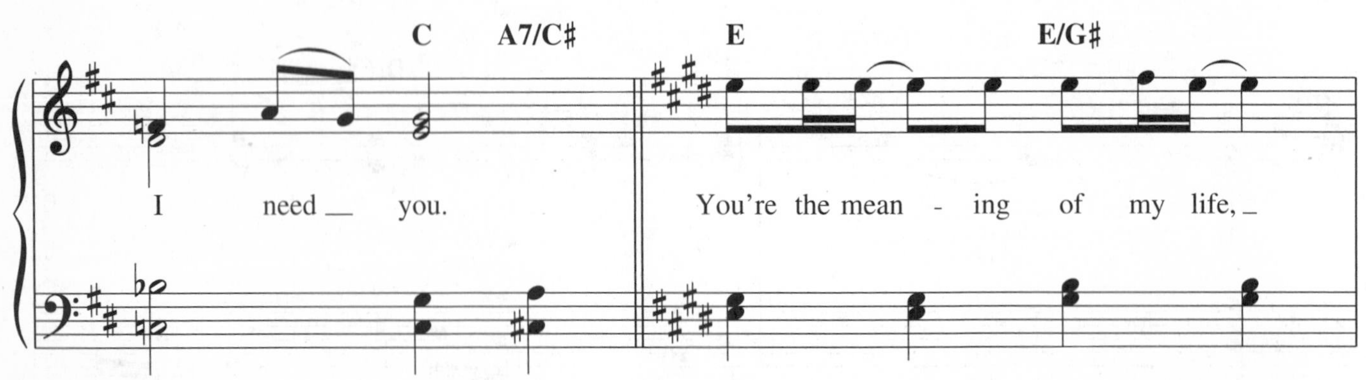
C
A7/C♯
E
E/G♯
I need you.
You're the mean - ing of my life,

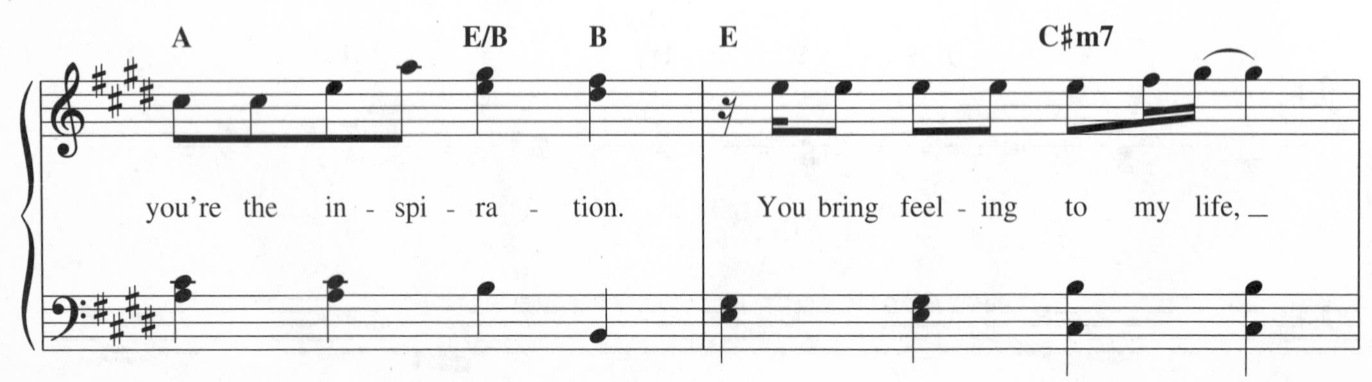
A
E/B
B
E
C♯m7
you're the in - spi - ra - tion.
You bring feel - ing to my life,

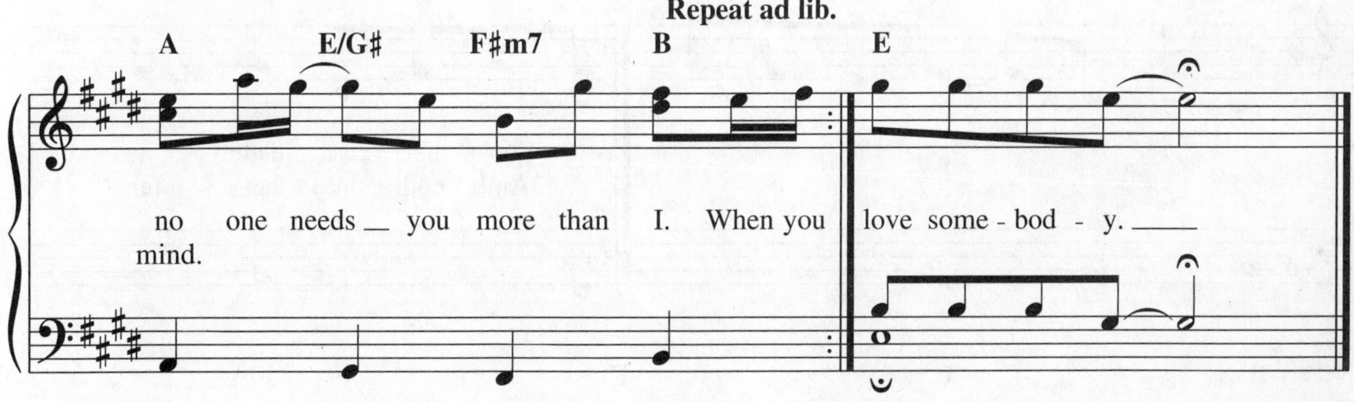

Additional Lyrics

2. And I know (yes, I know)
That it's plain to see
We're so in love when we're together.
Now I know (now I know)
That I need you here with me
From tonight until the end of time.
You should know everywhere I go;
Always on my mind, you're in my heart, in my soul.
(To Chorus:)

YOU'RE STILL THE ONE

Words and Music by SHANIA TWAIN
and R.J. LANGE

B♭
C
F
F/A
We knew we'd get there some - day.
Look at what we would be miss - in'.
They said, "I bet

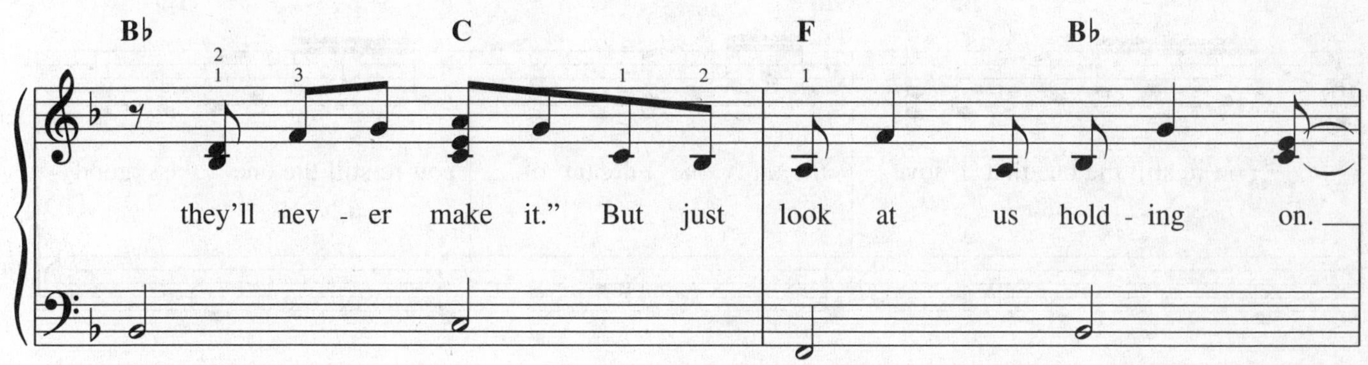
B♭
C
F
B♭
they'll nev - er make it." But just look at us hold - ing on.

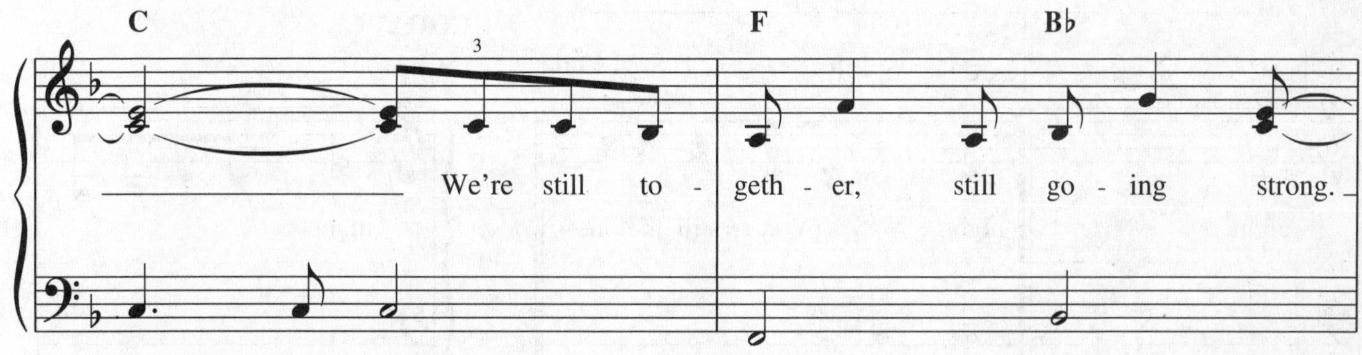
C
F
B♭
We're still to - geth - er, still go - ing strong.

C
B♭
F
B♭
(You're still the one.) You're still the one I run to,

Gm C F B♭ C B♭
the one that I be-long to. You're still the one I want for life. (You're still the one.)

To Coda
F B♭ Gm C F B♭
You're still the one that I love, the on-ly one I dream of. You're still the one I kiss good -

1. 2. D.S. al Coda CODA
C C B♭ C
night. night. (You're still the one.) night.

F F/A B♭ C
I'm so glad we made it. Look how far we've come, my ba - by.